Population, Ethnicity, and Nation-Building

Published in cooperation with
the Population Studies and Training Center
and
the Watson Institute for International Studies
Brown University

Brown University Studies
in Population and Development

Population, Ethnicity, and Nation-Building, edited by Calvin Goldscheider

Population and Social Change in Israel, edited by Calvin Goldscheider

Migration, Population Structure, and Redistribution Policies, edited by Calvin Goldscheider

Fertility Transitions, Family Structure, and Population Policy, edited by Calvin Goldscheider

In honor of
Harold W. Pfautz
and
Martin U. Martel

In memory of
Edward T. Pryor

Population, Ethnicity, and Nation-Building

EDITED BY

Calvin Goldscheider

Westview Press

BOULDER • SAN FRANCISCO • OXFORD

Brown University Studies in Population and Development

Copyright © 1995 by Westview Press, Inc.

Published in 1995 in the United States of America by Westview Press, Inc., 5500 Central Avenue, Boulder, Colorado 80301-2877, and in the United Kingdom by Westview Press, 12 Hid's Copse Road, Cumnor Hill, Oxford OX2 9JJ

Library of Congress Cataloging-in-Publication Data
Population, ethnicity, and nation-building / edited by Calvin
   Goldscheider.
      p.   cm.
   Includes bibliographical references.
   ISBN 0-8133-8953-4
   1. National state.   2. Ethnic groups—Political activity.
3. Ethnic relations.   4. Demographic transition.   5. Population
geography.   I. Goldscheider, Calvin.
JC311.P665   1995
321'.05—dc20   95-14820
                                                                                CIP

Printed and bound in the United States of America

The paper used in this publication meets the requirements
of the American National Standard for Permanence of Paper
for Printed Library Materials Z39.48-1984.

10   9   8   7   6   5   4   3   2   1

Contents

Preface

Hardly a day passes that issues of ethnic conflict do not appear on the front pages of our newspapers, on the evening news, or in special magazine articles and television programs. Ethnic-based issues have become conspicuous in the revolutions in Eastern Europe and in the collapse of the Soviet Union. They are central to the emerging societies, economies, and politics of Asia, Africa, and the Middle East. They are continuing features of the politics of race and immigration in Western pluralistic nations decades after assimilation, economic development, political mobilization, and legislation were expected to eliminate discrimination, ethnic identification, and the salience of ethnic communities. Foreign workers and former colonial subjects have re-defined the meaning of ethnic group in "homogeneous" Western countries. Ethnicity, linked to discrimination and racism, remains the source of intergenerational disadvantage and inequality in countries around the world—East, West, North, and South.

The research reported in this volume focuses on the linkages between ethnicity and population processes in the context of nation-building. Using historical and contemporary illustrations in a variety of countries, parts of the complex puzzle are scrutinized through the prisms of history, political science, anthropology, sociology, and demography. Themes of ethnic group formation and transformation, persistence and assimilation, demographic transitions and convergences, and the processes of political mobilization and economic development are described, compared, and analyzed. The examples were carefully selected to illustrate both the diversity of contexts and the shared processes that link population dynamics, nation-building, and ethnicity. In nine research chapters, preceded by an introductory overview of themes and guidelines, a rich array of findings, insights, and new questions about ethnicity, population processes, and nation-building is presented.

Each chapter focuses on a particular country or set of countries. The introductory chapter offers some general guidelines, definitions, and interpretations of ethnic differentiation. The research studies begin with several Third World areas. Chapter 2 by Charles Hirschman examines the historic and contemporary bases of ethnic changes in ten Southeast Asian countries. Rong Ma follows in Chapter 3 with the documentation of ethnic changes in the Tibet Autonomous Region of China, clarifying changes in the economic basis of their relationship to the Han majority. In Chapter 4, Philip Leis reviews some of the issues of ethnic conflict in Africa by contrasting Nigeria and Somalia and comparing the Ijo of Nigeria and the Galim of Cameroun. History and ideology are central to Thomas Skidmore's analysis of the "racial" problem in Brazil in Chapter 5. The complexities of Jewish-Arab ethnic differences and ethnic stratification among Jews in Israel are spelled out in Chapter 6, with an emphasis on the changing importance of demographic factors. Moving toward more economically developed countries, Barbara Anderson and Brian Silver examine in Chapter 7 the relationship among ethnicity, political conflict, and population change in the former Soviet Union. In Chapter 8, Edward Pryor uses demographic data to bring ethnic issues and national political integration together by examining the cultural partitioning of Canada. This is followed in Chapter 9 by Alan Zuckerman's analysis of Vienna and Warsaw in the 1920s, comparing the relative importance of social class and ethnicity as bases of political cohesion. Our case studies conclude in Chapter 10 with an analysis of the changing meanings of United States census data on ethnic categories. Michael White and Sharon Sassler examine data from the 1910 and 1980 censuses to study the residential and employment bases of group competition and assimilation. Taken together, the results of these comparative studies challenge past research and should generate new studies of these linkages.

These chapters originated in two workshop conferences that were held at Brown University under the auspices of the Thomas J. Watson Jr. Institute for International Studies. The workshops were organized around the global theme "North-South/East-West: Establishing a Common Agenda in an Interdependent World." The first, in 1990, was a preliminary get-together to see whether scholars from different disciplines could begin to clarify the conjunction of nation-building, population, and ethnic processes. We drew primarily from the rich resources of scholars at Brown University and we invited critical expertise from elsewhere to enhance our intellectual scope. To cover the range of disciplines we included a historian (Skidmore), anthropologist (Leis), political scientists (Zuckerman and Silver), along with sociologists and demographers (Pryor, Hirschman, Goldscheider, Ma, and White). We were joined by several graduate students in Sociology and Political Science who were participating in my graduate seminar on ethnicity.

Our goal was to unite the major disciplines that have struggled with ethnic issues in comparative contexts and to focus attention on cross-national illustrations of ethnic processes. My own biases make demographic issues a central element in the study of ethnic processes. Experts in demographic transitions in many parts of the world were included, as were others who tended to integrate population factors in their research, even if they were not experts in the field. We wanted some insights into the past and contemporary patterns of ethnicity within Europe and America (North and South), so that we could compare them to studies of Asia and Africa. We considered it a bonus to have a Latin American expert, and particularly to have scholars with special research expertise in the minorities of China and the Soviet Union. We were fortunate to have so many areas of the world covered, even as we knew that we could not cover all places and include all illustrations.

The goal of the first working group session was to examine the variety of linkages among three complex processes demographic change, ethnic group conflict, and nationalism. In the process, these themes were clarified, sharpened, and expanded to include a wide range of family and residential patterns among the demographic processes, to focus on nation-building, not nationalism, and to consider ethnicity in its broadest sense, including, where appropriate, race and religious groups. We did not limit our analysis to ethnic conflict. In two days of intense conversations, we addressed broad and abstract questions of how ethnic groups emerge in the context of nationalism (nation-building); how demographic changes (including immigration, internal migration, fertility, population growth and distribution) influence, shape, and erode ethnic distinctiveness culturally and structurally; and how these changes might be linked to ethnic assimilation and the re-definition of ethnic power and inter-ethnic conflict. We discussed how these themes are connected to global interdependence and linkages between nations; how these patterns vary between economically more and less developed states; and how changes in political contexts shape emerging patterns of ethnicity in modern nation states.

We selected illustrations of these processes from a variety of countries and observed their growing interdependence toward the end of the twentieth century. We hoped to find common examples of complex processes, and to broaden our individual areas of expertise in both the disciplinary and regional senses.

We began with the premise that the interrelationships among demographic, ethnic, and political processes of nation-building are crucial for understanding international relations and the emergence of ethnic and national groups around the world. We wanted to identify the major factors of demographic change in the various countries; to assess how changes in ethnic differentiation were linked to these factors; and to identify how ethnic variations are linked to national political developments. Therefore, we had to address central issues of political science and history, social development and modernization, as well as the cultural and structural dimensions of ethnicity, of the intersections of changes in ethnicity, political community, and demographic processes. These goals led inexorably to the interdisciplinary issues of history and culture, anthropology and comparative development, political science, sociology, and demography.

We hoped that scholars from different disciplines discussing common issues would generate interesting ideas and new research foci to better understand commonalities and differences cross-nationally and over time, and in conjunction with East-West and North-South relationships.

We held several formal and informal sessions with rich and lively discussions. We examined ethnicity and race; theoretical issues and theories; nationalism and ethnic change; conflict and communities. We reviewed the differential demographic transitions of ethnic groups, investigated links between nationalism and demography, and outlined the main themes of nation-building, population, and ethnic conflict that we thought should be investigated, reviewed, and highlighted in our own research. Most important, we attempted to develop a shared vocabulary of communication. We did not all agree and the papers that follow do not all share a common emphasis. Nevertheless, we learned much from each other; forced our analysis to be clearer and more consistent; and questioned some of the basic assumptions underlying our research efforts.

On the strengths of these exchanges, we planned research papers in our special areas of expertise for another workshop a year later (1991) to review what we had each learned and how our research reflected some of the issues and linkages that emerged. The foundations of the papers that appear in this volume were prepared and presented at the second workshop. Again, working together over two days, sharing our re-search results, and listening to our colleagues' responses added to the quality of our studies. We discovered interesting and unexpected commonalities and parallels in these studies, important comparative points, even as each of the papers was valuable in and of itself. In the light of our further discussions, these drafts were revised again, some extensively, and make up the chapters in this volume. Brian Silver was able to attend only the first session but his research with Barbara Anderson addressed directly the issues of population and ethnicity in the political economic development of the Soviet Union. We thank them for allowing us to include a version of their paper that appeared in *Population and Development Review.*

My special thanks go to the authors of these papers for the time they took to share their ideas and prepare these materials. I think that we learned much from one another, even as we each sharpened our own analysis. I want to thank the late Howard Swearer, president of Brown University and director of the Watson Institute, who encouraged me to organize the workshops and was always supportive of my research and the work of the Population Studies and Training Center at Brown. My gratitude is also extended to Tom Weiss, the associate director of the Watson Institute and to Julia Emlen, who was an editorial associate with the Institute. Both were supportive in every way of our role in the workshops. Julia and her staff made organizing a conference a pleasure.

The book was first edited and formatted by Daryl Twitchel, an undergraduate student concentrating in international relations and history at Brown University. Subsequently, I relied on Joan Picard, Sheila Harris, and Mary Lhowe to prepare the final manuscript for publication. They carried out their tasks efficiently and expertly, under very difficult circumstances. I thank them for making my tasks easier.

I am grateful to the Population Studies and Training Center at Brown, the co-sponsor of this volume, and Frances K. Goldscheider, its director at that time, for supporting our research. Fran's insightful comments on my chapter on ethnicity and nation-building in Israel helped focus the analysis. I am thankful every day that she shares my life.

This volume is dedicated first to Harold Pfautz and Martin Martel, my teachers and colleagues in the Department of Sociology at Brown. They taught generations of students at Brown University about race and ethnicity. May we be worthy of carrying on and expanding their tradition. During the final preparation of this volume, Ed Pryor died. He had been my friend since we were graduate students at Brown. We remained friends and colleagues as each of us moved to new countries and new challenges. He was a very special person, recognized by all of us who participated in the conference. He struggled through his pain to complete his chapter for this book. We have been enriched by his life and his scholarship and are saddened by his departure. He sparked our discussions and contributed practical insights and humor that brought many of us down to earth. The workshop participants re-dedicate this book to his memory.

Calvin Goldscheider
Brown University

1

Population, Ethnicity, and Nation-Building: Themes, Issues, and Guidelines[1]

Calvin Goldscheider

Ethnic conflicts have been among the most-reported international events in the early 1990s. While some observers may have expected the decline or demise of ethnicity in industrialized and in post-industrialized nations and the weakening of ethnic ties in Third World countries undergoing nation-building, ethnic conflicts continue to underlie social cleavages in many countries. In the economic, social, political, and cultural upheavals around the globe, ethnicity remains important; ethnic conflict is continuous; and ethnic loyalties are a major axis of social definition. Ethnicity is a powerful source of intergenerational stratification and a key factor in the control of resources.

Why did social scientists, among others, expect ethnicity to wither away? Why did some scientists expect social class to replace ethnic identification as the primary basis of social stratification? What has redirected our thinking back toward ethnic issues? Did our theories of universalistic social change distort our expectations about the importance of ethnic particularism? Have ethnic and tribal loyalties experienced a revival of past patterns, or have they been transformed, linked to but different from the past? These are complex questions that require systematic, comparative, and historical analysis. However we resolve these issues, it is clear that we have tended too often to view changes in ethnicity as ethnic decline.

1

At times we have observed transformation, and have interpolated linear patterns of continuous reduction from this. We have identified ethnic differences and defined them as ethnic "revival." Our viewpoint often has treated ethnicity as "primordial" in origin, and individualistic in terms of self identity. As a result, we have missed the social networks, economic enclaves, and political interests that shape ethnic communities. We have concentrated on ethnic identity and the "assimilation" of ethnic groups, rather than on the processes that lead ethnic groups to form and the settings that enhance ethnic continuity and change.

The studies in this volume examine ethnic processes in the contexts of nation-building and demographic change. The comparative and historical study of ethnic group formation, ethnic identity, and ethnic conflict first requires the detailed accumulation of case studies to identify the many factors in ethnicity, and to specify the settings that shape ethnic expressions. As part of these analyses, we focus on demographic transformations in industrialized nations and Third World countries. Our collective goal was to enrich our comparative studies of ethnicity, and to gain insight into the dimensions of ethnicity in the processes of nation-building and demographic change.

We examine the social structural and the cultural bases of ethnicity in political and ideological settings. Our orientation considers the dichotomy between ethnicity as structure or as culture to be false and misleading. Within each context and for each variable we can identify both structural and cultural dimensions, so it is not valuable to debate the primacy of one over the other. We separate the structural features of ethnicity from their associated values and do not infer one set from the other. We also argue (and this is our bias) that culture derives from context; that values are variables, not constants; and that changes in the context are more likely than not to alter values. Whether values are determinants or consequences of structure, we assume that values are always anchored in a social context and are not suspended in abstraction.

General Guidelines in Studying Ethnicity

Several theoretical and methodological guidelines inform our understanding of ethnic differences. We treat ethnic differences as variable over time, as the distinctiveness of groups changes and as differences among them in some areas of social life narrow or widen. The importance of ethnic differentiation compared to the importance of other characteristics such as education, region, or occupation may be more pronounced among some social-economic groups. Convergence of ethnic differences in some areas of social life do not necessarily imply convergence in all areas. Therefore, ethnic differentiation may end in time and vary from one social dimension to another. It follows that the changing contexts of ethnic differences need to be considered explicitly for a period of time among groups, and for various spheres of social life.

There are many ways to identify ethnic groups in comparative and historical contexts. Ethnic groups have been identified by the birth place of the individual, regional area of parental birth or origins, and generation in the country of destination. Other, more subjective measures include language usage, religious affiliation, ethnic self-identification, and ancestry. Ethnicity is almost always some combination of self-identification and a label imposed by others. As distance from immigrant origins increases, or as ethnic groups are integrated politically, mixed ethnic parentage may become more common. As a side effect of political mobilization, economic development, social integration, and cultural changes, the boundaries defining some ethnic origins have become fuzzy. Who is in and who is out of the group tends to become more variable as time passes, depending on how one defines affiliation and group identification. The increasing fluidity of boundaries among ethnic groups and the varying definitions of ethnicity makes it more difficult to compare the same group historically and among communities.

A wide range of groups-race, religion, and national origin-are included within the rubric "ethnic," especially in cross-national and historical contexts. Within the United States, for example, we include diverse populations: African Americans (and other black Americans such as West Indian immigrants), Hispanics (including Cuban, Mexican, Puerto Rican, and recent immigrants from other Spanish-speaking countries), Asians (Chinese, Japanese, Filipinos, and others), and Native Americans. When Europeans of ethnic origins such as German, Irish, Italian, Portuguese, French Canadian, Russian, Polish, and Jewish are included (the data are collected less often on ethnic white non-Hispanics), the range widens considerably. Some have argued that racial variation should be distinguished from ethnic groupings, and that both should be distinguished from differences of religion, but the lines dividing these constructed categories are often blurred. Comparisons among a wide range of groups allow us to isolate the unique and culturally specific, and to generalize about what is shared among ethnic groups. We know that it is problematic to generalize from the findings about one group to other groups, as it is from one time period to another. Our focus is on processes and connections that may characterize ethnic and racial groups in general, even as we recognize the unique culture of individual groups, their special histories, and their particular features in different contexts.

It is unlikely that one grand theory will provide a systematic explanation for the complex linkages between ethnic groups, on the one hand, and social life, on the other. The diversity of ethnic groups in contemporary societies; the dimensions that comprise social life; and the changes over time in the meaning of ethnic differentiation weigh against overarching theories of ethnic assimilation or pluralism.

We do not intend to construct such a grand theory to cover the case studies in this volume. Rather we identify general guidelines for studying ethnicity. These include the following:

1. Macro, socio-historical, political, and economic contextual features are critical in examining ethnic differences. These include the historical bases of ethnic ideologies, policies, and practices, along with changes in the labor market and in socioeconomic opportunities. Among the factors that shape ethnic patterns are demographic processes that affect the size and distribution of populations, their reproductive patterns, and their migration. These processes interact with socio-historical and economic dynamics.

2. The state has an eminent role in reinforcing ethnic differentiation. It has a direct influence in enforcing policies that are ethnically specific, and an indirect influence through its policies about school patterns, real estate and housing, business practices, jobs, public welfare, and health systems. Changes in the entitlement system of welfare states and their link to ethnic factors often are critical in understanding ethnic continuities and change. The nature of political regimes and political change, including colonialism and nation-building, are particularly important in historical context.

3. Formal and informal discrimination in jobs, housing, schools, and government allocations reinforce ethnic distinctiveness. In particular, we need to consider different economic and social opportunities, along with different access to them. However, the perception that discrimination occurs (independent of whether it can be documented objectively) may have implications for ethnic distinctiveness.

4. The changing overlap of socioeconomic factors with ethnic differentiation needs to be addressed directly. The concentration of ethnic groups in particular jobs, neighborhoods, industries, and schools can imply socioeconomic disadvantage and inequalities. Usually, the ethnic-social class overlap indicates more intensive interaction within the ethnic community than outside it. This overlap combines with

broad family-economic networks to forge bonds of community and generational continuities.

5. Part of the meaning of ethnic group attachment is in the ways that power is distributed and the extent to which political institutions are affected by and affect ethnic groups. Ethnic loyalties are enhanced when it is in the political and economic interests of persons and institutions to express them. When the allocation of resources favors some ethnic groups; when the entitlement system is unequal and the basis of inequality is ethnic; when power and position are linked to one's own group; ethnicity becomes entrenched within the political system. An ethnic group's sharing of common values and culture may matter less than their shared political power and access to economic resources. Political interests and economic commonality are the cornerstones of ethnicity, even when the cultural symbols are more conspicuous.

6. Changes in the generational reproduction of groups and their general demographic contours are important in understanding ethnic group change. Population size, structure, and cohort succession are features that bring marriage markets, childbearing, schooling, and the socialization of the next generation into the ethnic community. Internal migration (and for some groups, immigration), residential concentration, and intra-ethnic marriage patterns are significant in the generational continuity of ethnic groups at both the national and community levels. The demographic connection operates as part of the societal context and at the level of family, gender roles, and community.

7. Ethnic institutions are also important in sustaining group continuity. These include family, political, social, cultural, and community-based institutions that reinforce ethnic distinctiveness or weaken ethnic attachments by emphasizing national loyalties. In the absence of discrimination or ethnic markers that distinguish groups, and in the presence of ethnic convergences in social characteristics and socioeconomic opportunities, ethnic institutions are among the major constraints on the assimilation of ethnic populations.

Using these guidelines, we should be able to identify the political, economic, and historical sources of ethnic group formation; to disentangle cultural from social class factors of ethnic groups; to separate issues of perception from issues of access; to distinguish technological factors from those embedded in the social, demographic, political, and economic structure; and to analyze settings that reflect intergenerational continuities and those that are cohort-specific. We should separate individual factors from those that relate to the family and household, the community, the state, and the broader society. We also should be able to link institutional and community contexts to individual ethnic identification over the life course in order to identify which contexts reinforce or weaken ethnicity.

When we study ethnic distinctiveness in the context of nation-building and also emphasize demographic factors, we introduce the connection between the life course and ethnicity. Emphasis on the relationship between ethnic categories and the life course appears odd at first glance, since ethnic categories are often viewed as fixed at birth and constant throughout the life course. However, such a view may be distorted. The classification of persons into ethnic categories is a social construction that varies with who categorizes, who is categorized, and when these categories are applied within the life course. For example, young adults living alone may be less likely to identify themselves ethnically, while families with young children may be linked to ethnic communities through family networks, jobs, schools, friends, and neighborhoods. Since the boundaries dividing some ethnic groups tend to be flexible, people can shift between groups, and often these shifts occur at particular points during the life course.

Multiple social identities have emerged in modern pluralistic societies. The prominence of any one identity varies with the particular context, so life course transitions are of special importance because of the link between the life course and family networks. As persons marry and form new families, become ill or seek medical treatment, have children or die, issues of community and family support and of local institutions and networks that are based on ethnic origins become more highlighted. In contrast, at points in the life course where there is an emphasis on independence, individual goals, and autonomy, ethnic networks are likely to be less prominent.

Life course transitions occur in a cohort context. Consider, for example, ethnic variation in terms of the composition of generations (who has relatives and family for support in times of health care needs, reflecting in part the fertility and family history of the group); the history of migration (who lives where and near whom, revealing degrees of generational family access); the pattern of family structure and work (the extent of divorce and remarriage; and the changing proportion of women working). Cohort contexts reveal exposure to integration policies, economic opportunities, distance from origins, and connections to cultures. Combined with effects of time, the cohort perspective is of particular importance in the study of ethnic differentiation over the life course.

A related consideration in the study of ethnic groups is the examination of the intensity of ethnic affiliation. Research should focus on the intensity of ethnic commitments and the variety of attachments within ethnic communities, not only on the categories of ethnic affiliation. Generation status and language usage are obvious bases for greater ethnic intensity among some groups. The ethnic composition of neighborhoods or the participation in an ethnic economic enclave or in ethnic political institutions are other bases of ethnicity. The composition of neighborhoods or the presence of other ethnic groups competing for services is also important. There also may be specific family values or norms that are generationally transmitted or institutional structures that facilitate their continuity within ethnic communities.

Ethnic intensity is likely to be greater when the ethnic origins (and hence the intergenerational bonds) of a married couple are the same. When ethnic family members live close to each other; attend the same schools; have similar jobs and leisure activities; marry within their own ethnic groups; and are involved in ethnic social and political institutions, ethnic attachments within groups are more intense. Examining the intensities of ethnic attachments reinforces the belief that ethnic classifications should be treated not only with movable boundaries in time, but also with varying involvements in the ethnic community over the life course.

The complexities of ethnic pluralism and the extent of formal and informal discrimination against particular groups are important contexts for exploring the macro links between ethnicity and social life. In this regard, the state as a socio-political institution shapes the extent of ethnic pluralism; in designing and enforcing policies the state may reduce or increase ethnic differentiation. Entitlement systems that encourage ethnic political mobilization often become the basis of new forms of institutional expressions of ethnic interests. The state has an influence on ethnic communities through local policies about socioeconomic opportunities, housing, education, and residence. In these ways, the focus on nation-building and state are of major significance in unraveling changes in ethnicity over time.

Operating between the life course changes of the individual and the influence of the state is the level of families and households, with their extensive patterns of exchanges that we call community. Community and family factors seem to be the social basis of ethnic continuity, shaping the ways individuals identify themselves. The conjunction between ethnicity and social life may be most conspicuous at the community level. The shift away from an emphasis on populations and groups toward the self-identification of individuals has often resulted in an overemphasis on questions of "identity" and individual based constructs, rather than social contexts.

Ethnicity has often been assumed to diminish with passage of time and longer exposure to the place of destination. As the number of generations exposed to a place of destination increases, the impact of the place of origin recedes in memory and diminishes in effect on the life of the group. As the third and fourth generations are socialized in places of destination; are integrated into the economy; are dispersed residentially and geographically; and are exposed to educational institutions and mass media, they get homogenized into the larger culture and become undifferentiated through inter-group marriages and national identification. This view assumes the importance of the past to the continuity of groups in the present, and emphasizes too much the individual to the exclusion of family and community. In the past, an awareness of the cultures of communities of origin was needed to retain connections to ethnic origins, as was language and foreignness. As a result, ethnicity was viewed as part of the past and our question was: how much of the past could be retained in the face of pressures toward integration and cultural homogenization? How long would it take before ethnicity becomes "nostalgia" and more difficult to transmit to new generations?

This is a limited perspective, misguided by the assumptions that underlie it and distort the questions we need to ask. Ethnicity is often constructed (or reconstructed) out of the present circumstances and reinforced by selected elements from the past. Ethnicity is shaped not simply by what was, but by what is, incorporating selected pieces from the past into the present. Ethnicity revolves around institutions created to sustain ethnic communities, either by the groups themselves or by the state. In the process, new ethnic cultural forms emerge, as different institutions develop to sustain them. Both the emergent culture and the adapting institutions are constructed from the past, but are shaped by the present. Even when cultural differences weaken, institutions can retain and reshape communities. These institutions include family and kin, social, economic, cultural, and political organizations.

Interpreting Ethnic Differentiation: General Orientations

Three types of basic interpretations have been used to analyze ethnic variation.[2] The first is an emphasis on cultural aspects of ethnic groups that posits that ethnic variation reflects the culture or values of the group. Within this cultural perspective, ethnic differences are reduced over time through the acculturation of groups into the mainstream of society. Becoming culturally similar to the dominant group proceeds through increased educational attainment; contacts with others in schools, neighborhoods, and on the job; through changes in the use of a foreign language and adoption of local cultural values. The prominence of ethnic distinctiveness recedes as groups of many cultural origins adopt similar values. Residual ethnic differences reflect the legacy of the past that is temporary, or maintained by the state through multi-cultural policies.

To the extent that cultural factors are the primary sources of ethnic distinctiveness, they are more likely to characterize the foreign-born and their immediate family members, and those that speak a language other than that used by the majority, and who have received most of their socialization elsewhere. Those who are second- and third-generation, and who have, along with their parents, received their socialization in places of destination, are more distant from their cultural roots and more likely to have patterns similar to the native-born. Ethnic groups that are culturally closer to the native population also are more likely to lose their cultural distinctiveness than others whose cultural roots are less similar. Ethnic groups that are more concentrated within particular regions or are residentially segregated within urban places also are more likely to maintain their cultural distinctiveness.

An emphasis on cultural themes and values focuses our measurement attention on indicators of values, foreignness, and closeness to ethnic and cultural origins. Our questions about acculturation address themes of becoming similar to the majority population, or the attempt to salvage the cultures of the past. Distinctiveness revolves around the cultural transmission among groups and its weakening as generational exposure to new cultures increases.

A second set of explanations treats ethnic distinctiveness as a reflection of the social class and economic composition of ethnic groups. The association of ethnic differences with socioeconomic disadvantage reflects the argument that ethnic differences reflect the disadvantaged socioeconomic status of the group as a whole and the inequalities represented in the overlap of social class and ethnic origins. Differences among ethnic groups that are observed are social class differences.

In its more extreme form, this social class argument views ethnic and racial differences as derivative, and distorting of the underlying socioeconomic disadvantage of disenfranchised groups. This perspective directs the study of ethnic differences to the analysis of poverty and inequality, social class discrimination and competition, and their attendant consequences. Reducing economic discrimination and changing the overlap of social class and ethnic origins through educational mobility, job opportunities, residential mobility, and generational discontinuities in socioeconomic characteristics should reduce the basis of ethnic and racial distinctiveness.

The cultural and social class perspectives both tap important dimensions of the differences among ethnic groups in society. Taken together, they argue that ethnic differences are the combined consequence of cultural and social class factors. When social class factors are neutralized and discrimination minimized, the remaining ethnic differences are "only" cultural; the unmeasured residual "cultural" factors are minor and tend to weaken generationally. Cultural factors are reinforced by the disadvantaged socioeconomic position of ethnic groups that arise from economic origins (including skills of the first generation acquired elsewhere), discrimination, and blocked opportunities. In more complex interaction, cultural forms of ethnicity are considered more intense among the less-educated, poorer social classes since social mobility and the attainment of middle class and higher statuses reduces ethnic distinctiveness.

Each perspective projects the demise or diminishing of ethnic differences when cultural integration occurs, usually with greater length of generational and linguistic exposure, and when job discrimination and residential segregation are reduced, i.e., when social class factors are equalized. Both perspectives come from a theoretical framework that assumes that ethnic particularism and discrimination are likely to decline with time as a result of modernization and the integration of groups into a political and economic system based on merit, achievement, and universalism. With modernization, one argues (often implicitly) that the social class basis of ethnic differentiation declines and cultural differences are homogenized. In short, the importance of group differences diminishes. When discrimination blocks the integration of groups and their access to economic opportunities, and when political conditions do not allow for full social integration, continued inequality and ethnic distinctiveness are reinforced. Residential segregation and family patterns are reinforced by state policies and, in turn, are linked to the generational continuity of ethnic differentiation.

An alternative and complementary view to the cultural and social class arguments, and the third framework, emphasizes the structural networks and the power of community and its institutions that reinforce ethnic distinctiveness and identity. The networks of ethnic communities may be extensive: they often are tied to places of residence and family connections; are linked to economic activities and enclaves; and are expressed in political ties, cultural expressions, and lifestyles. The networks are reinforced by institutions and organizations that are ethnically based. When we ask what are the conditions in which ethnic communities become stronger and weaker, we move beyond the question of whether culture and/or social class is at the core of ethnic differentiation. The key argument in this perspective is that the cohesion of ethnic communities is based on institutions and networks; therefore the greater the social networks and the more intense the institutions, the greater the cohesion of the ethnic community. Both interaction patterns and cultural expressions reflect cohesion. The larger the number of spheres where interaction occurs within the ethnic community, the more cohesive the group; the greater the arenas of cultural activities, the higher the number of ethnic attachments.

According to this perspective, the basis of the ethnic community is the extent of ethnic ties to the labor market over the life course, not simply the overlap of ethnicity and social class. Changing economic networks forge interactions within ethnic and racial communities, and develop bonds of family and economic activities for family members at different points during the life course. The support of kin and family and the geographic concentration of ethnic groups become important bases of ethnic cohesion. Whatever the values, common background, history and unique culture that may bind ethnic members in a "primordial" sense, the key factors in this framework are structural-residence, jobs, schooling, and family. The cultural bases of ethnic groups, which are variable themselves, reinforce and justify the cohesion of the community, but do not determine its continuity. Cultural distinctiveness and values occur in structural contexts and change over time as contexts change. Even the standard indicators of culture for immigrant groups, such as language, are linked to structural cohesion because ethnic languages are bases for communication among ethnically and racially affiliated communities and for family and economic networks.

When the networks and the communication within ethnic groups are strong, then ethnic group attachments are more prominent. Viewed in this way, ethnic distinctiveness is not limited to un-acculturated immigrant groups or to religious-political groups that have experienced discrimination and are economically disadvantaged. Although these groups are likely to be distinctive, ethnic differentiation is unlikely to be limited to them. Ethnic communities are sustained by informal institutions and networks, often reinforced by politics and policy, and enhanced by family connections. In this perspective, modernization does not necessarily imply the reduction of ethnic group distinctiveness, even when discrimination diminishes and social mobility occurs. Under some conditions, modernization processes reinforce distinctiveness, particularly when the social processes imply increased socioeconomic competition among groups, intensified forms of economic concentration, and residential segregation. Often processes of modernization redefine the nature of communities in ways that go beyond issues of cultural values. The redefinition may occur precisely when acculturation takes place; when the values among groups become more similar; and when competition among groups sharpens. So even with social mobility and generational improvements in education and income, there may be increased job and economic concentration at the upper levels of socioeconomic status, just as there was concentration in the past at lower socioeconomic levels. In these ways, there is an overlap of social class and ethnic groups but that overlap is not confined to disadvantaged social classes. The concentration of ethnic groups in particular jobs and industries helps shape the emerging definitions of ethnic communities. Under some conditions, modernization results in the total assimilation of ethnic groups through the erosion of community and family-based institutions, residential integration, intergroup marriages, open market forces, universal schooling, and state policies that open opportunities and enforce non-discrimination. This is not always valid for all groups; it is not an inevitable by-product of nation-building, urbanization, economic growth, and social mobility.

This view of ethnicity argues explicitly against the notion that ethnicity is prominent only when it is consistent with or derived from ideology. The focus is on the structural underpinnings of ethnicity at the community level. Ethnicity is treated as a variable, not a constant, that varies with time and the life course of people. We can best understand the processes associated with ethnicity when the broader political and economic contexts are integrated in the analysis of families and communities. Hence, our focus in the studies that follow is on political and economic changes associated with nation-building and demographic processes of population size, migration, and reproduction.

Case Studies

The studies included in this volume take up these themes. They include case studies covering East and West, North and South with the perspectives of historical, anthropological, sociological, demographic, and political analyses of ethnicity and nation-building. They build in a wide range of demographic factors as part of their analysis.

When examining nation-building, particularly in Third World countries, the colonial setting is considered explicitly. The challenging comparative question is how colonialism and industrialization differentially affect the formation and continuities of ethnic groups. The way that post-colonial and post-industrial societies transform ethnic patterns also is relevant. In investigating demographic factors that are linked to ethnicity on the one hand, and to nation-building on the other, we have taken into account the many demographic processes involved. These include the size, distribution, and composition of populations, and the processes underlying their dynamics. The processes are fertility and mortality and their relative balance; they include population movements within countries as well as movements between countries. We have noted aspects of family demography and in particular the role of family structure. Since we are examining units smaller than total societies or countries, we have considered the boundaries of groups and their changing definitions over time. This is important to assure that our comparisons measure the same periods over time.

The studies start with several Third World areas-Southeast Asia, Tibet in China, examples from Africa, Israel in the Middle East, and Brazil in Latin America. These are followed by studies in the former Soviet Union, Europe, and the United States. We do not assume that the ethnic experiences, the historic formation of ethnic populations, expressions of ethnicity, ethnic conflict, and ethnic competition are directly transferable from one society to another. Yet some general processes and connections emerge only when comparisons are made and contrasts studied. We present these studies as part of an analytic strategy that builds up a repertoire of examples that should be the basis of theoretical, methodological, and substantive syntheses.

Chapter 2, subtitled "Ethnic Diversity and Change in Southeast Asia," combines history and social science to address questions of ethnic group developments in Southeast Asia. Charles Hirschman provides an overview of ten countries; shows their commonalities and differences; and attempts to identify basic patterns to understand ethnic changes. His review examines ethnic issues in pre- and post-colonial contexts as well as contrasting immigrant and indigenous ethnic groups. He touches on issues of racial ideologies, languages, and discrimination that have shaped how ethnicity emerged in contemporary Southeast Asia, and he identifies the role of institutionalized economic competition as a strong basis for ethnic continuity. Hirschman argues against an inevitable trend in ethnicity among countries in the process of economic-political development. He postulates that the perception of an ethnic group as a distinctive class of people and the subjective use of ethnicity as a tool to reach political and economic goals are important bases of informal attachments and perceived common interests.

Economic and political systems mobilize ethnic groups as efficient ways to pursue their interests.

The changing ethnic minority populations in the People's Republic of China and their political implications are carefully presented by Rong Ma in Chapter 3, titled "Dependent Economy, Migration, and Ethnic Relationships: The Tibet Autonomous Region of China." Focusing on the Tibet Autonomous Region, he shows that there is a clear overlap of region and minority population concentration. He clearly spells out the link between political changes and the economic characteristics of the region. Rong Ma analyzes their connections to the continuing economic and communal basis of ethnic minorities in China. This "dependent development" links ethnic origin to issues of inequality and differential access to opportunity, and is conditioned largely by geographic concentration. It is likely that these constraints exacerbate and are exacerbated by cultural differences and political discrimination.

Ethnicity in Africa appears in many forms. In Chapter 4, "Ethnic Conflict, History, and State Formation in Africa," Philip Leis reviews some of the issues of ethnic conflict by contrasting Nigeria and Somalia and comparing the Ijo of Nigeria and the Galim of Cameroun. He shows how the colonial status in these areas accentuated social divisions within each area, and he offers an evolutionary view of national integration in terms of cultural adaptation. Arguing that there were significant differences in political systems of Africa before colonial control, he cautiously suggests that centralized political systems may develop because of ethnic diversity, and that some kinship systems (particularly segmentary lineage systems) are more amenable to modern bureaucratic regimes. He argues further that the old and new colonial regimes were more supportive of some types of groups than others, and these need to be considered in understanding the emergence of ethnic tensions in Africa.

History and ideology are most closely intertwined in Thomas Skidmore's analysis of the "racial" problem in Brazil. He shows its multi-racial-not bi-racial-character, although in the half century to 1940, official data collection did not include any "racial" categories. He disentangles the historical reasons for the denial of the importance of race in Brazil; returns to the colonial period and shows the ideological foundation that distinguishes white superiority from white supremacy and the anticipation of assimilation to the white majority. He compares the ideological basis with the social reality, and contrasts the ideological denial of ethnicity with the omnipresence of race in everyday life. Using empirical data, he connects skin color with social stratification in Brazil and identifies the clear overlap of race and social class. With data from the National Household Survey of 1976, which was the first time the government published data on employment and income by race, Skidmore documents that race has an impact on income independent of social class factors. These findings reappeared in later research studies. Empirical evidence does not automatically reverse an embedded ideology. He ends Chapter 5, "Fact and Myth: Discovering a Racial Problem in Brazil," with a modest research agenda to enhance our understanding of race in Brazil.

With its own ideology of ethnic denial, Israeli society reflects a complex set of ethnic factors. The pluralism of Israeli society encompasses the broad divisions between Jews and Arabs, and also the major differentiation among Jews by ethnic origin, and among Arabs largely by religion. As in Brazil, these divisions have been denied ideologically and politically, although their contours do not fully reflect ideology or policy.

In Chapter 6, "Ethnicity and Nation-Building in Israel: The Importance of Demographic Factors," the origins of ethnic group formation in Israel are reviewed and the links to ethnic conflict are outlined. The focus is on the changing importance of demographic factors in the ethnic pluralism of Israeli society as it has traversed the politics of national integration. Research documents the convergence among ethnic groups in some demographic processes (mortality and fertility) and the powerful role of residential concentration in the perpetuation of ethnic differences between Jews and Arabs and among Jews.

No case study more vividly links the three processes of ethnicity, political conflict, and population change than that on the Soviet Union. In their important synthesis of demographic data, Barbara Anderson and Brian Silver document in Chapter 7, "Demographic Sources of the Changing Ethnic Composition of the Soviet Union," key changes since 1959 in the ethnic character of the Soviet Union. The changing role of language, the lack of political and economic control, and the implications of these processes for the autonomy of non-Russian ethnic groups are conspicuous. Moreover, they show convincingly how these ethnic-political connections are grounded in demographic processes. The changing residential-regional concentrations of ethnic groups and their differential population growth rates, particularly fertility and migration, led to changes in the ethnic composition of the country. Sensitive to the limitations and the value of official data, they cut through the detail to identify ethnic categories over time and to analyze changes in the ethnic composition in the former Soviet Union as a whole, along with changes in the Union republics. They argue that the decline of ethnic Russians to demographic minority status has symbolic and political significance. Recent political events in the former Soviet Union dramatically remind us about the centrality of ethnic conflict, even as we recognize the historical and demographic sources of these political changes.

In "The Cultural Partitioning of Canada: Demographic Roots of Multinationalism," Edward Pryor brings ethnic issues and national political integration together by examining the cultural fissures of Canada. Focusing on its demographic roots, his analysis shows the multi-cultural bases of Canadian ethnicity. Pryor uses demographic evidence to challenge the construction of "two founding peoples" of Canada by showing that almost one-third of all Canadians and an increasing proportion of Quebec's population had origins other than British or French. Demographic aspects of bilingualism and the regional population shares are displayed effectively and creatively with official data sources. Consequently, Pryor's review of fertility, internal migration, and immigration documents the declining population of Quebec, and emphasizes how the issues of Quebec nationalism are embedded in demographic analysis. Pryor presents evidence that demonstrates how Canada exemplifies the profound prominence of ethnicity, language, and culture for the political agenda of the 1990s.

The United States and Canada are viewed as ethnically rich and diverse nations because of voluntary and forced immigration, and the political reassertion of indigenous populations. In contrast, contemporary European societies are treated too often as ethnically homogeneous. Alan Zuckerman's detailed analysis of Vienna and Warsaw in the 1920s challenges this view of Europe. Studying cities rather than national aggregates, and juxtaposing social class and ethnic bases of cohesion, he focuses on electoral politics in "On the Structure of Ethnic Groups: Crisscrossing Ties of Social Class, Ethnicity, and Politics in Europe." His context is both historical and political, and he draws on the broader theories of social science to understand the role of ethnic factors in politics. As in the chapters on the regional analysis of Canada, the micro analysis of Africa, the concentration of ethnic groups in Israel, the former Soviet Union, and minorities in China, Zuckerman views the issues of occupation, education, and ethnicity in the setting of residential neighborhoods. Analyzing electoral cohesion and party politics, he shows not only the power of ethnic communities and networks but also their importance, relative to social class, for electoral cohesion. The key role of residential concentration and community cohesion in sustaining ethnic politics emerges clearly. The comparisons of Warsaw and Vienna show the importance of neutralizing social class in order to demonstrate the net effects of the ethnic factor on politics, and to document the interaction of ethnicity and social class.   He stresses the political-economic structure of ethnic communities and not their different values, a finding that parallels the conclusions about the ethnic factor in Southeast Asian countries. The effects of ethnic ties on electoral cohesion, while based on case studies in the 1920s in Warsaw and Vienna, have broader significance for cross-national contemporary politics.

We conclude our case studies with a thorough review of the changing meanings of official ethnic and racial categorization as reflected in the decennial censuses of the United States.   In "Ethnic Definitions, Social Mobility, and Residential Segregation in the United States," Michael White and Sharon Sassler describe ethnic historical change through the lens of the developing census concepts.   They document the changing meanings of ethnicity over time and then examine data from the 1910 and 1980 censuses to study ethnic group competition and assimilation. They focus on residence and employment, and confirm the very strong patterns of assimilation for some ethnic groups and the powerful role of residential concentration on socioeconomic status for other groups. As they poignantly note, their results are "prisoners to the measurement scheme," as is the case with previous studies and the studies presented in this volume.

Indeed, we are all prisoners of the measurement and theories that inform our analysis.   Similarities among case studies and the documentation of differences do not constitute a theory or a comparative or historical explanation of ethnicity. They are the basis for such an emergent theory. Only careful and detailed cross-national and historical research sensitizes us to the limitations of our own research and allows us to build on the wisdom and insight of related research.

Notes

1. This chapter introduces some theoretical and methodological guidelines that were shaped by the two workshops I described in the preface to this volume. While they emerged through intensive discussions with my colleagues, we did not always agree.   I am deeply indebted to all the participants for their contribution to this essay, although they are not responsible for its specific formulation and presentation.

2.   As in all generalizations, this is oversimplified, although useful for a broad orientation.

2

Ethnic Diversity and Change
in Southeast Asia

Charles Hirschman

Lying on the maritime crossroads between the great historical civilizations of India and China, the populations of Southeast Asia have been exposed continuously to influences from people, commodities, and ideas from inside and outside the region. These external influences have been layered over the many indigenous variations in cultures, languages, and settlement patterns (coastal entrepots, densely settled lowland areas, and sparsely settled highlands). These geographical and historical forces have created a rich and complex mosaic of peoples across the countries and regions of Southeast Asia.

The aim of this essay is to present an overview of ethnic diversity and change in Southeast Asia. First, I sketch the basic features of the region, including a brief account of the ethnic dimension in each country. Then I offer a broad historical account of ethnic dynamics in the region over the last few centuries, organized into the crude categories of the pre-colonial, colonial, and post-colonial eras. This is an attempt to outline the broad features and dynamics of Southeast Asian ethnic relations—and to provide a preliminary interpretation of these patterns and their implications for a theory of ethnicity. I acknowledge that many of the ideas and interpretations offered here will require considerably more empirical research before anyone, including myself, finds them entirely convincing.

The Geography and Demography of Southeast Asia

There are 10 countries in Southeast Asia. The map of the region (Figure 2.1) and some basic statistics from the World Bank's *World Development Report* (Table 2.1) provide a basic orientation (also see Hirschman, 1992).

FIGURE 2.1 Countries of Southeast Asia

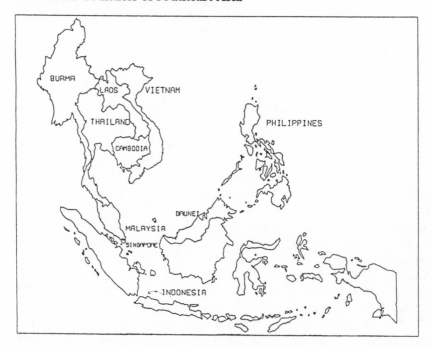

The standard geographical division of Southeast Asia is between the mainland (Myanmar, which was formerly Burma, Thailand, Laos, Cambodia, and Vietnam) and insular Southeast Asia (Malaysia, Indonesia, the Philippines, Singapore and Brunei). The common religious thread of the mainland societies is Thervada Buddhism, while Islam is the primary religion of Indonesia and Malaysia, and Christianity, largely Catholicism, is dominant in the Philippines. Even though Malaysia is on the mainland, the dominance of Islam and its common language with Indonesia place Malaysia in the sociocultural matrix of insular Southeast Asia.

Southeast Asian societies have certainly experienced significant cultural, political, and economic influences from the great civilizations of India and China, but scholars of Southeast Asia note the presence of authentic indigenous social and cultural roots in the region (Osborne, 1985; Wolters, 1982). Although the evidence is not conclusive, rice cultivation may have originated in the region (Bray, 1986:9).

But perhaps the most important signs of the uniqueness of Southeast Asia are the regional patterns of bilateral family structure and the relatively positive status of women (Reid, 1988). Both of these features are in stark contrast to East Asian and South Asian cultural traditions. These shared cultural patterns provide some sense of unity to Southeast Asia in spite of the tremendous diversity of the region—in terms of religion, language, and colonial histories.

TABLE 2.1 Population Size and Selected Socioeconomic Indicators of Ten Countries of Southeast Asia: 1987

Country	POP (millions)	GDP ($US) per capita	Life Expectancy at birth
Brunei	0.2	$15,390	74
Singapore	2.6	$7,940	73
Malaysia	16.5	$1,810	70
Thailand	53.6	$850	64
Philippines	58.4	$590	63
Indonesia	171.4	$450	60
Vietnam	65.0	NA	66
Laos	3.8	$170	48
Cambodia	NA	NA	NA
Burma	39.3	NA	60

Source: World Bank, 1989: 164-165, 230.

The contemporary arrangement of the region into ten states is an arbitrary division of geography and peoples. Over the last 2,000 years, a number of great civilizations rose and fell. At the center of these states there was typically a politically dominant group with a common cultural tradition. But as power grew and influence spread over a wider geographical area, empires became more culturally and linguistically diverse. Europeans arrived in the region early in the sixteenth century. While European powers meddled in local politics for the first few centuries after their arrival, most of Southeast Asian life remained within the orbit of regional powers. This changed dramatically in the nineteenth century when European imperialism divided the region into formal colonies and spheres of influence. Modern nationalism emerged in the twentieth century and led after World War II to the formation of independent states that largely conformed to the boundaries of the colonial territories.

Although it is very unlikely for a nation-state to arise with only one cultural group, the colonial origins of modern Southeast Asian states have contributed to multiethnic societies in two ways: 1) the incorporation of regionally concentrated cultural groups within the same state; and 2) the sponsorship of long-distance labor migration across different regions of Asia in the late nineteenth and early twentieth centuries. Based on this distinction, scholars have emphasized two types of ethnic diversity in the region: 1) indigenous ethnic relations arising from regional variations of cultural and linguistic groups; and 2) immigrant minorities, primarily the Chinese (Esman, 1975; Hirschman, 1984). While many assumptions of this distinction break down under close examination, it does highlight some differences among ethnic groups.

Regional minority groups are usually identified as those peripheral to the center of power. They range from hunting and gathering populations that live in the uplands to large lowland populations that are the majority in other states. While there are significant political and economic differences between the majority ethnic population and other indigenous groups, all are considered full and legitimate members of the political community.

The Chinese minorities are distinctive for their over-representation in small-scale commerce and their marginal political status. Even though there has not been any migration of magnitude from China to Southeast Asia for more than 50 years, and almost all Southeast Asian Chinese are locally born, they are still considered immigrant minorities (Somers-Heidhues, 1974; Lim and Gosling, 1983; Cushman and Wang, 1988). The Indian minority in Malaysia (and formerly in Burma) is in a similar structural position as are the Chinese.

An Overview of Ethnic Divisions in Individual Countries

Myanmar, formerly known as Burma and with a current population size comparable to Spain's, gained its independence from Great Britain in 1948. During the colonial period, there was a substantial Indian minority of traders and money lenders (middleman minority); they were forced to return to India after independence. The other major ethnic division was between the dominant Burman group (Burmese is the term for a citizen of the country) and the regional minorities. Demands for regional autonomy have broken down into civil war for most of the last 30 years (Silverstein, 1977). The national philosophy of "Unity through Diversity" has yet to be realized.

Thailand, with a population comparable in demographic terms to the United Kingdom, France, or Italy, is the only Southeast Asian country that was not colonized. The Thais of Thailand are one of a number of regional populations that speak variant dialects of Thai (Osborne, 1985:7), including the Shan minority populations in Burma and the Lao population of Laos. The Lao-speaking population of northeast Thailand is larger than the number of Lao speakers in Laos. There is also a very substantial Malay-speaking Muslim minority in southern Thailand. In the late nineteenth and early twentieth centuries, a very substantial Chinese immigrant population came to Bangkok and other urban areas. Most Chinese seem to have been absorbed into the Thai population through intermarriage within three generations (Skinner, 1957). What remains at present is a Sino-Thai population that speaks Thai and has Thai surnames, but with an identity rooted in Chinese ancestry. In spite of Thailand's ethnic diversity, there have been rather peaceful ethnic relations in recent decades.

Laos is a very small country with a population about the size of Ireland's. After independence from France was granted after the 1954 Geneva Conference, a domestic civil war erupted as local proxies fought on behalf of Cold War protagonists. The policy of the United States was to play upon traditional enmities between upland and lowland peoples to create what became known as the CIA's "secret war" (secret only to the U.S. population) in the 1960s and early 1970s. Perhaps not too surprisingly, many of the Laotians who were on the American side fled the country after the opposition won in 1975. More than 50,000 Hmong, an upland minority population, came to the United States as refugees.

The recent political history of Cambodia is equally tragic. The majority ethnic population speaks Khmer and follows Thervada Buddhism (the same religion as in Burma and Thailand). The great Khmer empire of the twelfth century built Angkor, one of the great architectural monuments of the pre-modern world. Cambodia was part of French colonial Indochina, which was dissolved after the 1954 Geneva Conference. Cambodia was home to many minorities, including both urban and rural Chinese populations, Vietnamese, and a Muslim community of Chams (descendants of a population that ruled a major Southeast Asian state from the third to fifteenth centuries). There were fairly peaceful ethnic relations in the 1950s and 1960s.

This relative peace, however, came to an end in 1970 with the military coup that ousted the neutral regime of Prince Norodom Sihanouk and installed the right-wing Lon Nol government. The ensuing nightmare included government-sponsored anti-Vietnamese violence and a U.S. bombing campaign that turned almost the entire country into a virtual free-fire zone (Shawcross, 1979). Following the defeat of the American-sponsored Lon Nol government in 1975, the Khmer Rouge (a Cambodian communist movement) came to power. In less than four years, the Khmer Rouge are believed to have caused more than one million "excess" deaths through starvation, neglect and murder (Ea Meng-Try, 1981). Chinese and Vietnamese suffered dispro-portionately (Kiernan, 1986), and there is some evidence that the Muslim Cham population was targeted for elimination (Kiernan, 1988).

Vietnam has a population of about 65 million. The historic center of the Vietnamese population is the Red River delta area near the modern city of Hanoi. Although they were conquered and ruled for almost 1,000 years by the Chinese, the Vietnamese maintained a distinct national identity and language. From the seventeenth to eighteenth centuries, the Vietnamese cultural and political world moved south and absorbed the Champa and Khmer populations that formerly had dominated the middle and southern regions of modern Vietnam.

Vietnam was incorporated into the French colonial empire in the late nineteenth century. When the French tried to re-impose colonial rule following the defeat of the Japanese in 1945, the Vietnamese declared independence. After Vietnam fought a long and costly war of independence against the French, the Geneva Conference of 1954 planned a temporary division, with elections for reunification planned for 1956. This was prevented, however, when the United States installed a separate regime in the South. The second Indochina war then began in the early 1960s and led to the eventual unification of Vietnam in 1975.

Minorities comprise about 12 percent of the population of Vietnam. They include a significant Chinese population and many upland minorities in the North and in the Central Highlands. There is a very mixed record of ethnic relations in Vietnam. For the indigenous minorities, socialist Vietnam follows the Soviet model of local autonomy in education and language, and offers affirmative action programs with special schools for national minorities. The relocation of Vietnamese populations to "New Economic Zones" in the Central Highlands has been resented by the local communities. When the limited war with China broke out in 1979, there were reports of more than 250,000 Chinese in Vietnam who fled to China (Benoit, 1981:140). It was once assumed that the Chinese population in northern Vietnam was highly integrated, but the limitations on private enterprise in the south in the late 1970s hit the Chinese rather hard, leading to a disproportionate number of Chinese "boat people" refugees.

Malaya (peninsular Malaysia) was composed of small Malay sultanates located along rivers (similar to Sumatra) when the British took direct control in the nineteenth century. The Malayan colony was built as a tin mining and natural rubber plantation export economy. The need for cheap labor led to massive immigration from China and India. By the early twentieth century, the size of the immigrant populations rivaled the size of the Malay population. As a result of urban residence and exposure to the modern sector, Chinese and Indians became more economically advanced than the Malay population (Sundaram, 1986; Snodgrass, 1980: Chapter 2).

Malaya (peninsular Malaysia) gained independence in 1957 with a multi-ethnic coalition government, but real power was in the hands of the dominant Malay party. There were moderate affirmative action programs in 1960s, but gains for Malays were probably less than those for the Chinese. Severe ethnic riots took place in 1969 in the capital city of Kuala Lumpur following a national election in which non-Malay parties gained ground. Since then, the government's affirmative action program (New Economic Policy) has been greatly intensified, with formal quotas in education and employment. While the program has been successful in creating a larger number of middle-class Malays, there has been growing alienation among many middle-class Chinese and Indian Malaysians.

Singapore is a city-state of 2.5 million people. More than two-thirds are Chinese, while the balance is of the smaller Malay and Indian minorities. Historically, Singapore was the commercial hub of British Malaya. Singapore was briefly a part of Malaysia, from 1963 to 1965, but ethnic frictions were too intense, and the country (city) became an independent state in 1965. In economic terms, Singapore has been very successful, but its people enjoy very little political freedom. There are ethnic strains below the surface, but everyday inter-ethnic relations are relatively peaceful.

Indonesia is the largest country in the region, with a population of over 170 million spread over a 3,000-mile-long archipelago. There are hundreds of ethnic groups and languages in Indonesia, but only a moderate number with any demographic significance. The Chinese community has a strong representation in small-scale commerce and also in the towering heights of the economy. In sharp contrast to Malaysia, most Indonesian Chinese are not recognizable in everyday interaction because few are able to speak Chinese and most have had to adopt Indonesian names. Except for their identity and economic roles, it is difficult to specify their "Chineseness." There is a recent history of anti-Chinese violence, but the pattern is one of sporadic acts rather than a cumulative trend (Coppel, 1983; Mackie, 1976).

Indonesia is also divided into several major ethno-linguistic groups. The Javanese are the largest community and are concentrated in central and east Java. There is considerable intermarriage across linguistic groups in Indonesia. Malay, the historical trade language throughout the archipelago, was selected as the language of the nationalist movement in the 1920s. While Indonesian (Malay) is a second language for most Indonesians, it has become the language of education and a major source of national integration over the last 40 years. The tempo of Indonesian civil life has been stable, although it has been punctuated with several major upheavals, the most spectacular being the revolution of the late 1940s and the massacres following the alleged coup of 1965.

Brunei is more of a microstate (population of only 200,000) in the Middle Eastern style than a Southeast Asian society. Oil revenues have created a very wealthy welfare state ruled by an autocratic sultan. Historically, Brunei was a remnant of a significant Malay sultanate whose territory on the island of Borneo was lost in the expansion of colonial territories. The population is primarily Malay and other indigenous minorities.

The Philippines, another Southeast Asian archipelago, has a population of about 58 million. The collection of islands was a Spanish colony for 300 years, before it shifted into the American imperial orbit for another half-century. There is some ethnic diversity, measured in terms of linguistic-cultural groups. But overall the differences among the different Filipino populations are fairly minor. The most important exception is the Muslim minority in southern Mindanao that has been waging a war of liberation for the last 20 years. There are also some upland tribal peoples who are not integrated into overall Philippine culture. While earlier waves of Chinese immigrants have been absorbed into the Filipino population (similar to the Thai case) a twentieth century Chinese immigrant population faces some discrimination. There is no barrier to intermarriage and the trend seems to be toward assimilation (Tan, 1988).

Precolonial Era

The ecological setting of Southeast Asia was favorable to the development of ethnic diversity. Most of the land was originally covered by dense rain forest or mangrove swamps. Mountain ranges and rivers are common geographic divides. The sea surrounds the region and is a barrier to easy travel, although the sea was the major highway for inter-regional contact and exchange. Over the centuries, these natural barriers meant that local populations could develop with little contact from other societies. In many areas, political units were probably small, and different languages and cultures were preserved in local areas.

Over the past 2,000 years, two types of larger political units had important integrating consequences in specific historical periods (Wertheim, 1968). The first was the land-based polities (usually kingdoms) based on wet rice cultivation. These civilizations were found in northern Vietnam, central Thailand, Cambodia, northern Burma, central Java, and a few other places. High population densities led to the construction of irrigation systems, which led to centralized political units (or the reverse causal order). The second type was the maritime empires founded on the coasts (or upriver from the coast) in port cities. Some of these cities grew very rich from the control of navigation and regional trade throughout Southeast Asia and beyond to China, India, and even Africa. Both of these political systems led to ethnic change in Southeast Asia.

The land-based empires, if they were successful in maintaining political stability, generated enough food and manpower to expand their power over neighboring areas. Over the centuries, the area that was Khmer at one point later became part of the Thai kingdom and cultural region. What is now Vietnam was once three civilizations: Vietnamese in the north, Champa in the middle, and Khmer in the south. Over the centuries, the Vietnamese language and culture became dominant throughout the region. Were the other peoples driven out, or did they change their ethnic identity to assimilate with the dominant group? The cultural and social absorption of the peoples of conquered areas into the dominant population is not inevitable. The Vietnamese (or at least many of them) did not become Chinese after 1,000 years of Chinese rule. I suspect that political factors (force, compulsion, access to opportunities) and cultural variables (differences in cultural expression and ideology) were important determinants of variations in the assimilation of conquered peoples in different times and places.

The economies of the port cities were based on the fragile links of long-distance trade across linguistic and cultural boundaries. Visitors to early Southeast Asian cities have described the diverse populations and vibrant markets of these cities (Reid, 1980). There was rarely an adjacent agricultural hinterland and rice was often brought long distances in exchange for other products (spices, cloth, metals, etc.). The threat to these cities was attacks from other trading empires and getting outmaneuvered in commercial networks. It seems likely that trust, institutionalized through alliances, was the most valuable commodity for the economic success of these cities. Openness to new ideas and opportunities; respect or at least tolerance of cultural differences; and willingness to arrange inter-ethnic marriages to cement alliances are some of the traits reported in these cities.

The emergence of Malay as the *lingua franca* of maritime Southeast Asia probably was due to the development of a shared cultural tradition among the trade networks of the region. Later, in the fourteenth and fifteenth centuries, Islam traveled throughout Southeast Asia along these networks, and was strongest in the port cities of Sumatra, Malaya, Borneo, Sulawesi, and the Sulu Islands. I conclude that trade was a powerful motivation to bridge the enormous cultural divisions across the Southeast Asian world. I do not claim that the port cities were a multi-cultural paradise or even that ethnocentrism was absent, but rather that there were powerful economic incentives to link diverse peoples for common objectives. The openness to a blending of different cultural traditions and the emergence of a "Malay World" (language and Islam) across insular Southeast Asia are some of the outcomes.

Ethnic Dynamics During the Colonial Era

Except for a few early travelers such as Marco Polo, the first Europeans arrived in Southeast Asia in the opening years of the sixteenth century. The Portuguese came first, followed by the Spanish and then the Dutch in the early seventeenth century. The British and French arrived in the following centuries. The record of European powers before the nineteenth century is not easy to summarize. In some areas, such as Java and parts of the Philippines, the European powers played a decisive role from the beginning. In other areas, Europeans were important economic actors, but local polities continued to rule much as before. Indigenous economic and political expansion by Southeast Asian port cities was halted with the Dutch control of the seas in the seventeenth century. For insular Southeast Asia, the consequence was a succession of weak states in later centuries.

The major impetus to direct colonization of all of Southeast Asia occurred in the nineteenth century. Pushed by the need for raw materials for the industrial-commercial revolutions in Europe, and armed with superior military power, the British, Dutch, and French carved the region into separate spheres of influence. Tempted by the weakness of the Spanish empire and a desire to join the great imperialist adventure, the United States grabbed the Philippines in the last few years of the nineteenth century. The imperialist dream was for the colonies to yield immense wealth through the extraction of raw materials and tropical plantation crops. Some colonies were indeed successful, but others were only marginally profitable.

The colonial experience shaped ethnic relations in Southeast Asia in many ways, but two factors were important above all others: 1) the importation of European racist beliefs; and 2) the processes of Chinese immigration and accommodation. Ethnicity, or race, as it was called by the British, became the central principle of social relations during the last century of colonial societies (Harris, 1968). In the pre-colonial world, ethnic differences were real and societies often were structured by ethnic divisions, but there were also important political and economic incentives to bridge and minimize these differences. It also was possible for individuals to transcend ethnic lines in the pre-colonial world. Acculturation was the mechanism. The acculturated children of mixed marriages were free to pass as natives. After the colonial world was put in place in the late nineteenth century, however, the barrier between Europeans and Asians was deemed to be permanent, with no possibility of crossing the line.

The widening technological gap between Europe and Southeast Asia in the nineteenth century allowed for direct political dominance of the colonies, often after military intervention. Once control was established, a local class of intermediary elites was established, usually based upon the local aristocracy or traditional leaders. But ultimate power, in every dimension that mattered, was held by the colonial power. As these political changes were occurring in the nineteenth century, there were related changes in European social thought about the natural order of races throughout the world.

The ideas of the Darwinian theory of evolution were applied in a rather simple-minded fashion to account for the different technological status of peoples around the globe. This set of ideas, known as Social Darwinism or just white racism, posited that European political and economic superiority were due to innate abilities that were inherited, like skin color and other aspects of physical appearance. This ideology, backed by all the leading scientific knowledge of the time, was accepted by almost everyone. Social Darwinism provided a strong ideological base for the expansion of direct colonial rule and the construction of "color bars" in almost every aspect of colonial societies. While there was variation in practice and some ambivalence among individuals, the construction of "race relations" was one of the most lasting legacies of colonial rule (Hirschman, 1986, 1987).

The Chinese are typically seen as a case apart from the other ethnic groups in Southeast Asia. While there have been Chinese settlements in the region for 1,000 years or more, the major Chinese migration to the region began in the eighteenth century and increased throughout the nineteenth century and the early decades of the twentieth century. While some Chinese came as merchants to manage long-distance trade, most came as laborers to work in mines and as the urban proletariat in the growing economies of the region. The construction of the export economies of the region, especially tin mining and plantation agriculture, was pioneered by Chinese capital and labor. Only later did European capital assume dominance. As a consequence of the large-scale Chinese presence, there were opportunities for the emergence of small-scale Chinese traders and shopkeepers to service the domestic economy of almost every country in the region.

The Chinese minorities were thought to be especially resistant to assimilation and acculturation because of the unique character of Chinese identity and culture. For example, the Chinese in Malaysia have retained their culture, identity, cuisine, and even are identified as key supporters of several political parties. As noted earlier, there are significant variations in the assimilation of Chinese minorities across countries in the region. In Thailand, the Chinese have intermarried easily after a generation or two, while in Indonesia and Malaysia there has been less intermarriage in modern times. The conventional explanation is that the Buddhism of Thailand provides a more welcome environment for Chinese, while Islam in Indonesia and Malaysia creates few common cultural similarities for the Chinese and erects serious barriers to shared experiences and assimilation.

William Skinner (1960) has suggested an alternative sociological interpretation that is more convincing. He argues that the difference between the Chinese in Java and the Chinese in Thailand arises from the presence of a colonial regime. In Thailand, the Chinese learned the Thai language; adapted to Thai culture; and, within a few generations, intermarried with Thai women (almost all Chinese immigrants were men). This does not mean that there was an absence of Thai-Chinese frictions or hostility, only that ethnic problems were subordinated to other social and economic processes. The structural incentives for social mobility in the Thai case, Skinner argues, encouraged Chinese to adapt to local customs. Political power and high social status were in the hands of the Thai elite. Ambitious Chinese entrepreneurs had to adapt to Thai culture to succeed. In Java, the elite were not Indonesians, but Dutch. Indonesians did not hold the keys to power or high social status. In fact, the popular stereotype was that Indonesians were "backward," both economically and culturally. These stereotypes were reinforced by European values and prejudices. In this environment, it is not surprising that the Chinese community, at least the upwardly mobile portion of it, was more interested in acculturation to the Dutch language and culture than the Indonesian culture (Hoadley, 1988).

In Malaysia, the pattern was similar to Indonesia, with the British setting the terms for social and economic mobility. Colonialism inhibited the assimilation of the Chinese (and other minorities) into Southeast Asian cultures. The combination of structural disincentives and the racial ideology fostered by colonial rule had a lasting legacy for post-colonial societies that is still around, though quite attenuated.

Ethnicity in the Post-Independence Era

Colonialism ended in 1948 in Burma and the Philippines. Wars of liberation were necessary to attain independence for Indonesia in 1950, and for the French territories of Indochina in 1954 (not really until 1975). Malaya received her independence in 1957, and the creation of Malaysia in 1963 led to Singapore's exit from British control. After 30 to 40 years, we might expect ethnic relations to have improved. The racial ideology of the colonial era has been discredited and most governments have worked actively at policies of national integration. Moreover, common national cultures have been fostered by standardized educational systems and the ubiquitous mass media, radio, and television. However the record is mixed, with progress in some areas and heightened ethnic tensions in other areas.

One major area of progress is the acceptance and increasing use of national languages. Indonesian, a language learned only in school for more than 80 percent of the population, is fully accepted as the means to the modern world—schools, the mass media, literature—throughout the country. Filipino is supposed to be an integration of several regional languages, but is basically Tagalog, the mother tongue of peoples in central Luzon. Even though English is widely spoken by the middle class around the country, Tagalog seems to have been accepted as the national language without a great deal of fuss. And even in the deeply divided country of Malaysia, the national language of Malay seems to be increasingly accepted for all official purposes, including secondary and tertiary schooling. During the early post-colonial era, efforts to encourage the use of Malay had a small impact on the middle-class Chinese and Indian minorities, who went to English-language schools and barely disguised their contempt for the Malay language, viewing it as useful only for the marketplace. But government actions eliminated the English language schools, and young Chinese and Indian students have developed complete fluency in the national language.

There are also many signs of continued and even growing ethnic consciousness and tension. Official discrimination against Chinese is common almost everywhere in the region. There have been occasional attacks in Chinese neighborhoods in Indonesia and Malaysia. Demands for regional autonomy have led to civil wars in Burma and in southern Philippines. Discouragement caused by unequal treatment has led to significant emigration of Chinese from Malaysia to Singapore, Australia, and Canada. As mentioned earlier, Chinese fled Vietnam in the late 1970s and 1980s. In every country, including the ones with highly assimilated Chinese minorities, such as Thailand and the Philippines, there is popular resentment against Chinese economic success. What are the possible reasons for the maintenance and even heightened ethnic awareness and antagonism in post-colonial Southeast Asia?

Basically, independence has meant a new area of institutionalized competition in politics. In every country, politics is not far removed from economics. Access to power means opportunities to secure contacts, licenses, and other avenues to avoid or circumvent the market. In some countries, ethnic groups are identified as blocs of voters. In Malaysia, the Chinese are a large enough minority to sponsor or to be the primary base of several political parties (none are able to dominate, but they are serious actors). In other countries, the Chinese are too small in relative demographic terms to be a significant electoral base, but they can use their economic base to support political groups that can then compete for power. Ethnic divisions are reinforced with the perception that politics is a zero-sum game where one group gains at another's expense.

The other dimension that reinforces ethnic antagonism is the continued over-representation of Chinese in small- and large-scale business activities (Bonacich, 1973). There has been a substantial growth of large-scale business, including international linkages around the region, extending to Hong Kong and Australia. Familial ties among

Chinese and pseudo-kinship ties based on Chinese identity may engender trust in highly competitive environments that allows for business cooperation and success.   The very impersonality of the modern sector may give rise to ethnic connections and sponsorship as a means of dealing with the uncertainty of market forces and bureaucratic relationships.

There is, of course, an official and popular backlash that reinforces Chinese persistence in business, especially family enterprises. Chinese, and other groups, probably do work harder, risk more, and do whatever is necessary to succeed in the commercial world. This has less to do with Chinese cultural traditions than with the well-founded belief that economic survival is dependent on getting ahead at all costs. The barely hidden public hostility and official governmental policies restricting Chinese economic activities reinforce the admonitions of parents and kinsmen that they have to stick together and work harder.

Conclusions

Sociological theories of race and ethnicity are heavily influenced by the American experience, especially the historical circumstances that faced African-Americans and European immigrant ethnics. The major theme in the literature has been the debate between the theories of the assimilation (or at least the Anglo-conformity model, in Gordon's (1964) terms) and white racism. The natural history model of the race relations cycle (contact, conflict, accommodation, and assimilation) of Robert Park has been discredited, but there is no new and revised assimilation theory to take its place. Industrialization and modernization have not led to the disappearance of ethnic divisions and conflict, but the situation nonetheless has changed. There is a great need for a more complex and subtle theory of ethnic change to accommodate the wide range of historical experiences in the United States and other societies.

On the basis of the empirical materials from this historical review of Southeast Asia, I offer some tentative suggestions toward an alternative sociological perspective on race and ethnicity in the modern world. The basic insight is that there is no inherent or inevitable trend of ethnic relations in a single direction. But there is a finite number of recurrent patterns that can be used to create a topology of ethnic relations.

The dynamics of ethnicity are linked to the broader social forces of society, and there are certain fundamental constraints on the ways in which ethnic groups can be manipulated or mobilized. Two features of central importance are the perception of an ethnic group as a distinctive class of people, and the subjective basis of ethnicity as a resource for the economic or political mobilization of a group. These two characteristics give ethnicity central importance in certain types of societies.

Ethnicity can be used to transform class relations into "race relations" in certain types of societies. The most striking example is a structural setting where there is a great demand for cheap labor, and a very exploitative labor system with the bulk of the workers of a certain ethnic origin. While the slave societies of the New World are clear examples of this type, so are the colonial societies of Southeast Asia of the early twentieth century. White racism or Social Darwinism provide legitimation of exploitation and subordination even in modern settings. Once racism is institutionalized, it can be perpetuated even after the conditions that created it have changed. Racism, however, requires a powerful (and costly) repressive system to maintain it. Major political changes, including the independence of former colonies and the political empowerment of minorities (e.g., the results of the civil rights movement), seriously erode racist belief systems.

Racism is also a common response in circumstances of split labor markets (Bonacich, 1972; Bonacich and Modell, 1980) where the standard of living of higher-priced labor is threatened by the immigration of lower-priced labor from different cultural areas. While there are some instances of this pattern in Southeast Asia, this has been less common since immigrant workers rarely competed in the same labor markets as indigenous workers.

The other role for ethnicity is a means for interest group mobilization. Just as kinship often provides a basis for trust in economic, social, and political activities, common or imagined ethnic ties can provide the means to organize businesses, political movements (from parties to mobs), and informal networks (to trade information or favors). In modern societies, interpersonal contacts often take place in bureaucratic settings where relationships can be formal and impersonal. Shared ethnicity is often the bridge that creates familiarity and mutual assistance. Ethnicity is not the only channel for the creation of pseudo-familial relationships; shared class origins, common geographical background, and other ascriptive ties that offer the basis of common culture or shared interest can also do the job. But in many settings, ethnic ties form the bases of informal attachments and perceived common interests in modern societies.

The big question is, in what circumstances do these factors emerge to shape the role of ethnicity in different societies? Ethnicity is a variable, not a constant. In some societies, ethnicity is a more or less trivial distinction. In other societies, ethnic differences do matter, but other factors loom larger. And in still other societies, ethnicity is the central organizing principle of political, economic, and social relations. Only through comparative research is it possible to clarify the theoretical issues and to attempt to explain these variations.

References

Benoit, Charles. 1981. "Vietnam's Boat People." Pp. 139-162 in *The Third Indochina Conflict*, edited by David W.P. Elliot. Boulder: Westview Press.

Bonacich, Edna. 1972. "A Theory of Class Antagonism: The Split Labor Market." *American Sociological Review* 37: 547-559.

Bonacich, Edna. 1973. "A Theory of Middleman Minorities." *American Sociological Review* 38: 583-594.

Bray, Francesca. 1986. *The Rice Economies: Technology and Development in Asian Societies*. New York: Basil Blackwell.

Coppel, Charles A. 1983. *Indonesian Chinese in Crisis*. Kuala Lumpur: Oxford University Press.

Cushman, Jennifer and Wang Gungwu (eds.). 1988. *Changing Identities of the Southeast Asian Chinese Since World War II*. Hong Kong: Hong Kong University Press.

Ea Meng-Try. 1981. "Kampuchea: A Country Adrift." *Population and Development Review* 7 (June): 209-228.

Esman, Milton. 1975. "Communal Conflict in Southeast Asia." Pp. 391-491 in *Ethncity: Theory and Experience*, edited by Nathan Glazer and Daniel P. Moynihan. Cambridge University Press.

Gordon, Milton. 1964. *Assimilation in American Life*. New York: Oxford University Press.

Harris, Marvin. 1968. "Race." Pp. 263-268 in *International Encyclopedia of the Social Sciences*, Volume 13, edited by David L. Sills. New York: The MacMillan Company and the Free Press.

Hirschman, Charles. 1984. "Ethnic Diversity and Social Change in Southeast Asia." Pp. 106-122 in *Southeast Asian Studies: Options for the Future*, edited by Ronald A. Morse. Lanham: University Press of America.

_____. 1986. "The Making of Role in Colonial Malaya: Political Economy and Racial Ideology." *Sociological Forum* 1(2): 330-361.

_____. 1987. "The Meaning and Measurement of Ethnicity in Malaysia: An Analysis of Census Classifications." *Journal of Asian Studies* 46: 555-582.

_____. 1992. "Southeast Asian Studies." In *Encyclopedia of Sociology*, edited by Edgar and Marie Borgatta.

Hoadley, Mason C. 1988. "Javanese, Peranakan, and Chinese Elites in Cirebon: Changing Ethnic Boundaries." *Journal of Asian Studies* 47: 503-518.

Kiernan, Ben. 1986. "Kampuchea's Ethnic Chinese Under Pol Pot." *Journal of Contemporary Asia*. 16 (1): 18-39.

_____. 1988. "Orphans of Genocide: The Cham Muslims of Kampuchea Under Pol Pot." *Bulletin of Concerned Asian Scholars* 20 (October-December): 2-33.

Lim, Linda Y.C. and L.A. Peter Gosling (eds). 1983. *The Chinese in Southeast Asia*. Singapore: Maruzen Asia.

Mackie, J.A. C. (ed.) 1976. *The Chinese in Indonesia*. Honolulu: University of Hawaii Press.

Osborne, Milton. 1985. *Southeast Asia: An Illustrated Introductory History*. Sydney: Allen and Unwin.

Reid, Anthony. 1980. "The Structure of Cities in Southeast Asia: Fifteenth to Seventeenth Centuries." *Journal of Southeast Asian Studies* 11 (September): 235-250.

_____. 1988. *Southeast Asia in the Age of Commerce, 1450-1680: Volume One, The Lands Below the Winds*. New Haven: Yale University Press.

Shawcross, William. 1979. *Sideshow: Kissinger, Nixon and the Destruction of Cambodia*. New York: Washington Square Press.

Silverstein, Josef. 1977. *Burma: Military Rule and the Politics of Stagnation*. Ithaca: Cornell University Press.

Skinner, G. William. 1957. *Chinese Society in Thailand: An Analytical History*. Ithaca: Cornell University Press.

_____. 1960. "Change and Persistence in Chinese Culture Overseas: A Comparison of Thailand and Java." *Journal of the South Seas Society* 16 (1/2): 86-100.

Somers-Heidhues, Mary F. 1974. *Southeast Asia's Chinese Minorities*. Hawthorn, Victoria: Longman Australia Pty. Limited.

Snodgress, Donald R. 1980. *Inequality and Economic Development in Malaysia*. Kuala Lumpur: Oxford University Press.

Sundaram, Jomo Kwame. 1986. *A Question of Class: Capital, the State, and Uneven Development in Malay*. Kuala Lumpur: Oxford University Press.

Tan, Antonio S. 1988. "The Changing Identity of the Philippine Chinese, 1946-1984." Pp. 177-203 in *Changing Identities of the Southeast Asian Chinese Since World War II*, edited by Jennifer Cushman and Wang Gungwu. Hong Kong: Hong Kong University Press.

Wertheim, W.F. 1968. "Southeast Asia." In *International Encyclopedia of the Social Sciences* 1: 423-434, edited by David Sills. New York: The MacMillan Company and the Free Press.

Wolters, O.W. 1982. *History, Culture, and Region in Southeast Asian Perspectives*. Singapore: Institute of Southeast Asian Studies.

3

Economic Patterns, Migration, and Ethnic Relationships in the Tibet Autonomous Region, China

Rong Ma

Studies on Tibet have concentrated on the issues of history, religion, traditional culture, ethnic relations, Han immigration, and human rights (Pye, 1975; Dreyer, 1976; Grunfeld, 1987; Goldstein, 1989). The pattern of Tibet's economy has received less attention than other issues. Ethnic conflict often arise from economic interests (Glazer and Moynihan, 1975:8), and religious groups might have their own economic interests and participate differently in economic affairs (Weber, 1963:223). Migration between regions where different ethnic groups are concentrated is also affected by the economic relationship between the regions (De Jong and Fawcett, 1981). To understand the impact of social and economic structures on ethnic relations, we examine the Tibet Autonomous Region's economy, past and present, and place ethnic migration issues and the Han-Tibetan relationship in this economic context. We focus on three sets of questions:

1. What are the major characteristics of the modern Tibetan economy? What were the economic relations between Tibet and the Han regions in the past? How did these economic relations affect migration and ethnic relationships in Tibet?

2. What changes have occurred in Tibet's economy during the past three decades? What are the major characteristics of todays economy in the Tibet Autonomous Region (TAR)? What is the impact of these changes on migration and Han-Tibetan relations?

3. What role have the central government and the Han played in Tibet's economy since 1959?

Most Tibetans reside outside of the TAR[1] and have been under the administration of the respective provinces for a long time. They have been integrated into the local economies in these provinces for the most part, and we therefore focus only on the TAR.

The data and information were derived from several sources: (1) official statistics and census results released by the Chinese government; (2) books and other materials on Tibet published in Chinese before 1949; (3) articles published in *Xizhang Yanjiou (Tibet Studies)*, a journal edited by The Tibet Academy of Social Sciences in Lhasa; and (4) books on Tibet published in English. Materials in the Tibetan language were not covered.[2]   The quality of census and government statistics is questionable, but they are the only systematic economic data available. This study may be seen as a first step in an examination of the Tibetan economy, suggesting some propositions for further research.

The Theoretical Framework

Based on the literature of migration and regional economic development (Goldlust and Richmond, 1974; Shaw, 1975; Todaro, 1985; and Hansen et al., 1990), an outline of a theoretical framework was designed to examine the factors affecting ethnic relationships in Tibet (Figure 3.1).

FIGURE 3.1 Model for Examining the Factors Affecting Economic Exchanges and Migration Between Ethnic Groups in Two Regions

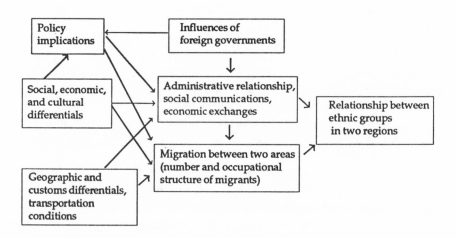

In this model, differences in social and economic systems (e.g., land ownership and administration) and cultural aspects (e.g., religion and language) between two regions (Tibet's and other areas in China) are assumed to affect the content and extent of administrative and social communications, economic exchanges (aid and trade), and migration (official exchanges, circular or settled merchants, labor migration) between these the regions. Large differences in economic patterns may set limitations on trade and migration (Findley, 1977). People are less likely to migrate into a region where the social system, ownership system, and language are different from what they had been accustomed to in their own locale. Social, economic, and cultural differentials between two regions also might have an indirect impact on trade and migration through their influence on the attitudes and policies of regional authorities toward these activities. When geographic features (elevation, humidity, natural resources and life customs (diet, living conditions) are very different in the two regions, and transportation conditions are also poor, trade and migration between these two regions will be affected (cf. Ma, 1987 for a similar migration scheme of Inner Mongolia).

Economic opportunities, related to the availability of natural resources in rural areas (cultivated land, grassland, forest, mineral resources, etc.), and jobs in urban areas directly affect people's motivation to migrate. Policies of foreign governments, viewed as an intervening variable, sometimes may influence attitudes and policies of one region's local authorities toward the other regions with regard to trade and migration. Foreign countries, through their trade activities with one or another region, may affect economic exchanges between regions.

Administrative relationship, social communications, and economic exchanges between the two regions also may be linked to inter-regional migration. The general relationship between two ethnic groups in different regions depends on administrative, social, and economic relations, as well as migration between the regions. We shall examine the range of factors in this model and their interrelationship to see how this model fits the Tibetan case.

Hechter (1975:6-8) proposes two models of national development to assess the relationship between the majority (core) region and the minority (periphery) region within a country: the diffusion model and the internal colonial model. The first assumes that under conditions of equal rights for all groups, the social structure and economic patterns in the core region gradually will diffuse, or spread, into the peripheral region. In contrast, the internal colonial model assumes that the core region dominates the periphery politically and exploits the population economically. As two models of long-term national development, they will be used to evaluate the socioeconomic relationships between the TAR and other regions in China.

Economy in Tibet Before 1952

The Tibet Autonomous Region covers of 1.23 million square kilometers and is located on a high plateau averaging 3,600 meters above sea level in southwestern China. According to the national census, the total population in the TAR was 2.2 million in 1990 (CPIRC, 1991). It has a strong religious tradition (Tibetan Buddhism), and its special religion-related culture has lasted for centuries. In order to understand the basic economic patterns in the TAR, it is necessary to examine its main economic activities, its economic organization and productivity, its economic relations with other regions, the distribution of income and the use of its resources for economic activities.

Agricultural and Pastoral Production

For centuries, agriculture and animal husbandry have been the major economic activities in Tibet. They provide food, clothing,[3] raw materials for handicrafts, and goods for trade. The Tsangpo River valley (around 3,500 meters above sea level with an annual average temperature of 4 to 10 degrees centigrade) is its main agricultural area. Most of the cultivated land in Tibet is located in river valleys. Northern and western Tibet are pastoral areas with very low population densities. In the north, some areas as the highest elevation (above 4,600 meters) are largely "uninhabited areas" (Figure 3.2). Generally, Tibet's geographic and climatic conditions set certain limitations on the development of agricultural production and on population distribution.

In 1952, there were 2.45 million *mu* of cultivated land in the TAR (*mu* = 0.165 acre) and grain production totaled 155,335 tons (Statistical Bureau of Tibet (SBT), 1989:211-218).[4] Major types of grain produced in Tibet are: barley, peas, buckwheat, etc. In the 1940s, it was estimated that barley comprised 70 percent of the total grain production, peas 20 percent, and the rest 10 percent (Wu, 1953:113). Total population (including Chamdo District, which became a part of the TAR in 1961) was 1.15 million in 1953.[5] Therefore, grain production was approximately 135 kg. per capita in 1952 (SBT, 1989:133).

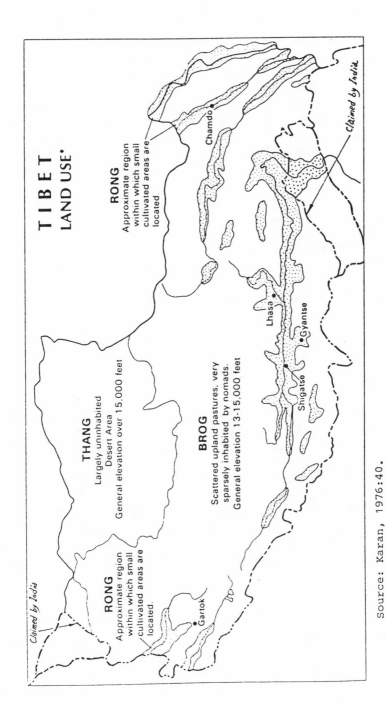

Source: Karan, 1976:40.

FIGURE 3.2 Location of Agricultural Areas in Tibet

Before 1952, grain production in Tibet was generally at a self-sufficient level. Rice and wheat imports were very small and mainly consumed by aristocrats and wealthy Tibetans, as well as by merchants who had come from the Han regions and were not accustomed to the Tibetan diet (parched barley mixed with butter).

Of the 9.7 million animals in the TAR in 1952, 2.25 million were yaks, 4.7 million sheep, and 2.5 million goats (SBT, 1989:233). Most of these animals were located in the pastoral areas of northern and western Tibet. It is difficult to estimate the production of animal husbandry before 1952, but trade records reveal that animal husbandry provided most export products.

Transportation and Communication

In 1950, there was no other place in the world "where no wheeled vehicles were used," and "principal rivers were unbridged." "For centuries, all transportation in Tibet was by porters and pact animals" (Karan, 1975:46). The first 600-kilowatt hydroelectric power plant in the TAR was established in Lhasa in 1956 (Karan, 1976:50).[6] Telephone and postal services became available to the public only since the late 1950s (SBT, 1989:27).

Handicrafts

By modern standards, industrial production did not exist in Tibet before 1952. While the economy and finance in Tibet relied heavily on agriculture and animal husbandry, handicrafts were the main non-agricultural production; only 6 percent of the total population was engaged in non-agricultural activities in 1952 (SBT, 1989:133).[7] The major handicraft products in Tibet were Pulu (a woolen fabric), Kadian (rugs), tents, wooden bowls, boots, knives, and jewelry (Labapingcuo, 1984: 478). Except for local products such as wool, leather, and wood, handicraft production relied on the import of other raw materials (cotton cloth, silk, and metal) from either nearby Han regions or India and Nepal.

Trade

Other than some raw materials for handicraft production, daily consumer goods (tea, cotton cloth, china, and industrial products) were available only as imports. For centuries, "tea-horse trade" was the main form of trade between Tibet and other regions in China (especially

Sichuan, Yunnan, and Gansu). Sichuan provided Tibet with tea, cotton cloth, silver, sugar, and silk. Yunnan was the main area from which Tibetans bought tea and copper. Tibet provided the Han regions with wool, leather, and must. An estimate made by a British consul general in Chengdu in the early twentieth century suggested that trade between Tibet and the Han regions was four times the trade between Tibet and India (Huang, 1982:50).[8] "Retingsang" (a company owned by regent Reting Rempoche)[9] and a Han company "Heng-Sheng-Gong" (from Yunnan province) controlled the tea trade between Sichuan and Tibet for decades. There were over two thousand Han trading companies and stores in Lhasa in the late Qing dynasty (Chen Fanzhou, et al, 1988:53).

Trade between Tibet, India, and Nepal was also important. The Yatung customs records[10] indicate that annual export of wool to India reached 544 tons during 1895-1898, (Huang, 1982:49) over 150 stores in Lhasa were owned by Nepalese in the 1940s (Wu, 1953:112). In tandem with the increasing influence of British India on Tibet around the beginning of this century, Yatung customs records also show a significant growth of trade between India and Tibet. The value of exports from Tibet to India increased from 131,548 rupees in 1889 to 805,338 rupees in 1902, while imports increased from 561,395 rupees in 1896 to 962,637 rupees in 1899.[11] The value of imports was generally higher than that of exports (e.g., 962,637 rupees import compared to 822,760 rupees exports in 1899. See Huang, 1982:48).

Pastoral products comprised the major parts of the total value (822,760 rupees) of exports to India in 1899: they included wool (581,944 rupees), yak tails (42,628 rupees), horses and mules (31,823 rupees), and sheep leather (14,183 rupees). The above items comprised 81.5 percent of the total value of export goods. Musk, and 14 percent of the total (Huang, 1982:49), was another major export good (116,024 rupees in 1899). After the 1911 revolution, with the encouragement of some foreign governments, the Dalai Lama government sought independence. The relationship between Tibet and China's central government deteriorated. Trade between Tibet and other regions in China decreased rapidly. One report estimated that in the 1930s wool exports from Tibet to India were about 1,500 tons, but wool exports to the Han provinces totalled only 500 tons (Chen Fanzhou, 1988:55).

It is clear that a very primitive agricultural production system in Tibet (e.g., use of wooden plows, threshing by yak tramping) supported a population of over one million. Over 10 percent were monks (114,103 monks in 1958, Liu Ruei, 1989:298).[12] The army consisted of about 60,000 soldiers (Chen, 1937:134);[13] and the government had several hundred officials.[14] The monasteries and government took most of the peasants' and herdsmen's products to support monks, nobles, officials, and soldiers, and to maintain religious activities and the governmental administration.

The serf system dominated in Tibet for centuries (Goldstein, 1989:3-6). Three groups (government officials, nobles, and monasteries) owned almost all cultivated land, most animals, and the serfs. Table 3.1 shows the structure of land ownership in Tibet in 1959. Self-employed peasants, who owned 0.3 percent of cultivated land, lived in areas bordering the Han regions; and most peasants were serfs without land.

TABLE 3.1 Ownership of Cultivated Land in Tibet (1959)

Land owner	Land (acre)	Percentage
Government	160,976	38.9
Monasteries	152,286	36.8
Noble	99,317	24.0
Self-employed	1,241	0.3
Total	413,820	100.0

Source: Labapiengcuo, 1984: p. 253.

TABLE 3.2 "Class" Structure in Shan-nan Prefecture, Tibet (1961)

"Class"	Household	%	Population	%
Serf owner	152	0.4	606	0.4
Manager of serf owner	1,460	4.0	8,611	5.5
Rich serf	1,195	3.3	8,574	5.5
Middle serf	5,413	14.8	34,567	22.1
Poor serf	18,413	50.4	74,271	47.4
Slave*	7,245	19.8	18,251	11.7
Herdsman**	2,327	6.4	10,064	6.4
Handicraftsman	130	0.4	555	0.4
Merchants	113	0.3	438	0.3
Vagrant	104	0.3	510	0.3
Total	36,557	100.0	156,447	100.0

Source: Labapiengcuo, 1984: 251 * Many were single ** They were not classified

Shan-nan prefecture is one of the major agricultural areas in Tibet (Figure 3.2). The population structure by "class" before the "democratic reform" in 1961 is shown in Table 3.2. A group of "rich serfs" (*tsampa*) who worked on "Cha-gang" land provided a certain amount of labor service, products, and money to estate owners each year. They might own their tools and some animals, but they were not allowed to leave the land. Most serfs in this group worked land directly owned by the government. Serfs who worked for nobles and monasteries were usually poorer. Poor serfs and slaves comprised about 60 percent of the total population in this prefecture.

Serf owners and managers working for serf owners comprised 6 percent of the population, while self-employed handicraftsmen and merchants comprised 1 percent. Thus, only 7 percent of the total population was free. There were 195 noble families throughout Tibet in 1959, and some were rich and powerful (Labapingcuo, 1984:242-245). "On large estates owned by monasteries and noblemen, agriculture had slumped through centuries of neglect and the failure to make permanent improvements of the cropland by the theocratic feudal owners" (Karan, 1976:81).

The regime in Tibet before 1952 was a combination of religious institutions and civil administration. "One of the most unusual aspects of the Tibetan polity was the dual systems where every lay official had a clerical counterpart" (Grunfeld, 1987:9). Religious organizations controlled the whole society. Not only had the Dalai Lama become the ultimate ruler of Tibet, but the position of both Lonchen (prime minister) and the chief official at the prefecture level were also restricted to monk officials. During the spring religious ceremony, the administration in Lhasa was directly under the control of the Drepung monastery. Large monasteries had their own military forces and had often been involved in power struggles (Labapingcuo, 1984:309). Tibetan civilization, including its philosophy, art medicine, astronomy, and literature, has been based on Tibetan Buddhism. Education had mainly been carried out within monasteries.[15] Visitors to Lhasa obtained the strongest impression from its religious atmosphere (Chapman, 1940). In 1952, of an urban population of 37,000 in Lhasa, 16,000 were monks (*People's Daily*, April 17, 1991).

In 1959, three famous "seat" monasteries (Drepung, Sera, and Ganden) owned 18,435 acres of cultivated land, 110,000 animals, and 40,000 serfs (Labapingcuo, 1984:243-244).[16] Usually, the serfs of monasteries were required to transfer 70 percent of their harvest to the monasteries (Huang, 1984:12). Monasteries controlled estates, serfs, and handicraft workshops, and also engaged in trade and loan business. All large monasteries had their own organizations (Lab-rang) which engaged in trade affairs (Bell, 1928:125). The extent that monasteries were involved in trade activities can be deduced by their storage of goods. For example, it was found that the amount of tea stored in Xiege monastery (in Digre county) was the equivalent of 90 years of consumption by its monks (Zhou, 1985:44).

According to an incomplete record, the Dalai Lama's loan office loaned 254,488 pounds.t. of silver in 1950 and collected interests of 27,961 pounds.t. of silver. The total amount of grain loaned by Drepung monastery was over 80,000 tons in 1952 (Ya, 1988). A general interests rate for loans from monasteries was about 25 percent and for loans from nobles about 20 to 25 percent.[17] The interest earned comprised 25 to 30 percent of the total income of the three "seat" monasteries and about 11.5 percent of the total income of the local government (Labapingcuo, 1984:284-285).

Although monasteries were very rich, they provided only limited supplies to ordinary monks (Goldstein, 1989:34-35). Monasteries and monks received a large amount of money and items from pilgrims, and many monks actually lived on these items. Most of these pilgrims were serfs and herdsmen. In the 1950s, the Drepung monastery's annual income from pilgrims included 25,963 pounds.t. of silver,[18] 13.75 tons of barley, and 106.25 tons of butter (Huang, 1983:12). After making their contributions to serf owners, government, and monasteries, the serfs and herdsmen had to live at subsistence levels.

Several records exist about income of the Tibetan government and its use. A document sent to the Qing emperor in 1795 reported that "the Tibetan government at Potala Palace has, besides the income in terms of items (barley, animals, butter, etc.), an annual cash income around 127,000 Liang silver (10,637 pounds.t.). But their expenses of 143,600 Liang exceeded this income: 79,000 Liang was for the main religious ceremony in January and February, 39,200 Liang for monthly religious rituals, and 24,400 Liang to buy grain, medicine and other items for monks. The shortage was subsidized by the Qing government" (Wu, 1953:85). The income and expenses of the Tashilhunpo monastery under the Panchen Lama had a similar ratio: 66,900 Liang silver income compared to 74,600 Liang expenses (Zhang, 1983:35).

Sir Charles Bell cited the financial records of the Tibetan government in 1917. The Lhasa civil government received 720,000 British pounds (in British currency) in that year while the church (Potala Palace) received 800,000 pounds. The government gave the church an additional of 274,000 pounds from its own funds (Bell, 1946:165-166).[19] Another study reported that local governments at Zhong (county) levels also gave 50 to 60 percent of their annual income to the monasteries each year (Zhou, 1985:43). Therefore, the Potala and the monasteries were the main wealth collectors through direct taxes from estates and contributions from government and pilgrims. Most of the wealth in Tibet was used for religious activities.

The characteristics of Tibet's economy before 1952 can be summarized as follows:

1. Tibet had a primitive agricultural economy using manpower, animal power, and primitive tools, Generally, there was no modern industry, transportation or electricity and no application of modern science and technology in production and consumption. Handicrafts and trade were at a very primitive level (small workshops, street peddlers, and transportation by porters and yaks) and there was a very low level of urbanization.[20]

2. Both agricultural and pastoral production in valley areas with a relatively high population density were controlled by monasteries, the government, and nobles under a serf system, with some variations (some serfs were allowed to keep a higher proportion of their products than others, while there were some slaves). There was a looser control on herdsmen who lived in remote pastoral areas, and some of them even lived within a tribe society.[21]

3. Tibet had a self-supporting agricultural production; it exported mainly wool and other pastoral products in order to import tea, cotton cloth, metal, and other necessities for daily consumption and handicraft production.

4. Religious groups (or more precisely, senior monks on behalf of monasteries) were very powerful. Monks comprised over 10 percent of the total population of Tibet and over one-half of the urban population in the 1950s.[22] Monasteries controlled the government and economy, owned over one-third of cultivated land, many pastures, and a large number of serfs and slaves.

Examining the use of societal wealth in Tibet helps place into context the nature of Tibet's economy and production. A small part of Tibet's products was used to keep serfs and herdsmen alive. Most wealth, which was collected through different channels, was used for very costly annual religious rituals. The expenses for the January and February rituals in Lhasa were about 62 percent of the total annual income of the Dalai Lama's government in the eighteenth century (Wu, 1953:85).[23] Millions of butter lamps burn day and night in about three thousand monasteries.[24] Other funds were used to support the monks and their activities. In the 1950s, on average, two households were needed to support one monk (Liu Ruei, 1989:198).[25] More than half the income of the Tibetan government also went to monasteries. Finally, a large amount of gold and silver collected by monasteries was melted down and made into Buddha statues or to decorate towers containing the corpses of senior incarnated monks. Following this tradition, the central government recently provided over 600 kg. of gold and over 500 kg. of silver to decorate the tower of the tenth Penchen Lama, and another 64 million yuan to build a 33-meter-high temple for this tower (*Chinese Tibet*, Spring, 1990). A huge amount of money was also used to build and maintain thousands of monasteries. Some of them were very large, e.g., Drepung monastery had 10,000 monks in 1951 (Goldstein, 1989:25).

The Tibetan government and its army also needed support. Because more than half of the government officials were monks, and lay officials obtained their reward mainly from the estate appointed to them, the administrative budget in Tibet was relatively small before 1952. While half of the government's income went to monasteries, the other half was used to support its army. In large part, the economy in Tibet before 1952, therefore, can be called a "monastery economy."

Generally, Tibetan society before 1952 can be compared with the European Middle Ages. In both, "the great religions prospered and overwhelmed the masses. Hierarchies in both the organized Christian Church in Europe and Lamaist monasteries in Tibet played a major role in society and in the government of the two areas. The Middle Ages in Europe were followed by the Renaissance. In Tibet no comparable renaissance occurred. The hierarchies of the Gelugpa sect, the Dalai Lamas, continued to maintain a monastic monarchical state from 1578 until ... 1951" (Karan, 1976:12).

Administrative, social, and economic relationships between the Han regions and Tibet, therefore, were established under these historical conditions. The geographic features and poor transportation conditions made social, economic, and cultural exchanges between Tibet and other areas very difficult. the landlord-tenant system in the Han regions was very different from serfdom, and Han farmers could not obtain or rent land from estate owners in Tibet. In contrast to Tibet, there was a multi-religion system in other regions of China; Taoism, Mahayana Buddhism,[26] and Christian religious groups had limited influence on the administration of other areas of China.

The relation between Tibet and the Han regions before 1952 seems to fit the first stage of the "diffusion model" quite well. "The core and periphery regions exist in virtual isolation from one another. Events in the core have but slight influence in the periphery,...and there are many significant differences in their economic, cultural, and political institutions" (Hechter, 1975:7).

Because social, economic and cultural systems in Tibet were very different from those in the Han regions, and communication and transportation conditions were so poor, the policy goal of the Qing dynasty was limited to maintaining the subordination of Tibet. This was the main function of its two commissioners (*ambans*) and troops[27] in Lhasa. "There can be no question regarding the subordination of Tibet to Manchu-ruled China following the chaotic era of the sixth and seventh Dalai Lamas in the first decades of the eighteenth century" (Goldstein, 1989:44). According to the documents and materials released by the Chinese government, Tibet has been a part of China since the thirteenth century (Labapingcuo, 1984:111).

The main official economic relationship between the emperors in central China and the Dalai Lama's government was described as "tribute and reward." (Huang, 1988) Besides a large amount of tea, the trade taxes collected in western Sichuan had also been rewarded to the Dalai Lama each year during the Qing dynasty (Zhang, 1983:32). A document signed by the Qing emperor (Qian-Long) announced that the empire will "exempt Tibetans from imperial taxes" and "all the taxes and fines collected by the local government in Tibet should be used for religious rituals and local administration" (Ibid., 32).

The commissioners in Lhasa were also responsible for arranging trade between Tibet and other regions. This trade often had been regulated by an administrative system. For example, three times during the period of the Qian-Long emperor (A.D. 1736-1795), the Tibetan government bought copper from Yunnan through the Chinese commissioners in Lhasa. When the Yunnan governor (Li Sirao) refused to provide copper to Tibet in 1779, the Dalai Lama complained through the commissioners, and Qian-Long formally rebuked this governor (Chen Fanzhou, 1988:54).

The Han regions in China have been major partners of Tibet in the exchange of goods (Bell, 1928:12).[28] Even though relations between Tibet and the central government worsened after the 1911 revolution, trade between Tibet and the Han provinces continued. The records show that during 1929 to 1938, the tea sold and transported into Tibet from a single county (Fohai) in Yunnan was about 634 tons each year (Tan Fangzi, 1940).

During 1911 to 1950, the Tibetans who lived outside the percent TAR (Qinghai, Gansu, and Sichuan claimed about one-half the total Tibetan population in China) were still under the total Tibetan population in China) were still under the administration of these respective provinces, even as the Dalai Lama severed the relationship with the central government. These Tibetans' economic activities were integrated into the local economy and their relations with the Dalai Lama were mainly religious.

Trade was the major economic link between Tibet and other regions in China. Special economic systems (estate, serfdom) made it impossible for Han immigrants to engage in agriculture and animal husbandry in Tibet. The geographic features of the plateau (high elevation, rarefied air, mountains, etc.) limited the volume of trade and migration between Tibet and other regions.

The Han and members of other ethnic groups in Tibet (e.g., Manchu, Hui)[29] included officials and troops sent by the central government (about 1,000 before 1911, and a few officials remained in Lhasa after 1911); merchants in cities and towns, and handicraftsmen and gardeners.[30] Although their total number was several thousand and comprised only a very small percentage of the population in Tibet, they maintained administrative, social, economic, and cultural relations between Tibet and other parts of China. After the Kuomintang government's failure in the civil war, the Dalai Lama government expelled most Han officials and merchants from Lhasa in 1949.

Major Changes in Tibet's Economy Since 1959

The Communist Party won the civil war in 1949. After a battle in Chamdo, the "Agreement on Measures for the Peaceful Liberation of Tibet" (17-point) was signed by the central government and the Dalai Lama's government in 1951. The Dalai Lama agreed to carry out social reform and to help the People's Liberation Army (PLA) troops enter Tibet, while the central government agreed not to change the social and economic systems (serfdom and estate systems) by force (Karan, 1976:90). The Chinese central government became a key factor in Tibet once again. During 1952 to 1959, the basic situation in Tibet did not change very much. However, "democratic reform" brought some social and economic changes to the Chamdo District (the former Xikang province that became part of the TAR in 1961), which was under the direct control of the central government. The industrial productive value which was mainly produced by the factories located in Chamdo, reached 1.7 million yuan in 1956 and 53.3 million yuan in 1959 (SBT, 1989:84). The main social and economic changes in the TAR occurred after 1959.

In 1959, serfdom was abolished and monasteries lost their administrative power. In the "democratic reform" of 1959 to 1960, all serfs and slaves were liberated, and land and animals were distributed to serfs, herdsmen, and slaves. During 1965 to 1975, the commune system was gradually established in most rural areas in the TAR (Labapingcuo, 1984:455-459). In the 1980s, the household responsibility system was introduced and land and animals were redistributed among peasants and herdsmen. An administrative network (government, social organization, party organizations, and urban and neighborhood committees) as well as other systems (education, health care, welfare, and resident registration) were established in the TAR, based on models in other Han regions. Therefore, the social and economic systems in the TAR were becoming the same as those in other regions of China, influenced by all the policy changes of the central government. Tibetans suffered as other ethnic groups did during the "Cultural Revolution," and they also are benefitting from new policies of the recent "system reform" (Goldstein and Beall, 1990). This reform period is similar to the second stage of the "diffusion model:" through equal rights and development programs (education, health care, and most important, industrial production), the social and economic structures of the core gradually diffused into the peripheral region.

In 1959, many monks went in exile to India with the Dalai Lama[31]. The number of monks and monasteries in Tibet then decreased significantly: there were 114,103 monks and 2,711 monasteries in 1958, but only 18,104 monks and 370 monasteries in 1960. In 1976, after the "Cultural Revolution," only 800 monks and 8 monasteries were left (Liu Ruei, 1989:298).

The situation began to change after 1980. The government has reemphasized religious freedom and tried to recover the damage done during the "Cultural Revolution." Many monasteries were rebuilt and the number of monks increased rapidly, to 6,466 monks and 234 monasteries by 1986. The newest report indicates that there were 34,680 monks in the TAR in 1990, a five-fold increase within four years (*People's Daily*, January 17, 1991). Religion again has wide influence, even among Tibetan cadres and intellectuals (MacInnis, 1989:187). Since 1959, monasteries had lost their traditional power in both the economy and administration; they lost most of their estates, serfs, slaves and high positions in government. However, along with the increased number of monks has become a request from these monasteries for more power.

Because the income of peasants and herdsmen increased significantly in the past decade,[32] they have increased their support of monasteries and monks. A study in 1988 reported that the average annual income from donations was 1,000 to 1,300 yuan per monk in Lhasa's monasteries, three times the peasants' and herdsmen's incomes. The TAR government also gives a "salary" to monks and provides subsidies to monasteries as its payment to government employees and monks in other Han regions.[33]

Also, an effective road network has been established since 1959 (totalling 13,567 miles in 1990). There were 20,000 cars and trucks and 6,565 tractors in the TAR in 1988 (SBT, 1989:340). The power of agricultural machinery in the TAR is now close to the national level of China (Ibid., 190). It reached 450 million watts in 1988, about 212 watts per capita. Chemical fertilizer and other techniques for improving production are used in rural areas in the TAR (11 kg. chemical fertilizer per capita in 1988). With improved transportation, the introduction of machinery and new technology, the value of agricultural production in the TAR increased four-fold in the past three decades.

The increases in the main items in both agricultural and industrial production are shown in Table 3.3. Cultivated land increased from 2.45 million *mu* in 1952 to 3.45 million *mu* in 1988; grain production increased from 80 kg./*mu* in 1952 to 181 kg./*mu* in 1988, or 135 kg. per capita in 1952 compared to 242 kg. per capita in 1988 (SBT, 1989:211-230). The number of animals increased from 9.74 million in 1952 to 23.51 million in 1980, about 12.6 animals per capita (22.3 per capita in pastoral areas, 5.6 per capita in agricultural areas) (Labapingcuo, 1984:463). Agricultural and industrial production has increased faster than population growth. Many factories also have been established in Tibet since 1959, but the development of industry in the TAR has a tortuous history. It tried to follow the industrial structure and development plans of other regions, ignoring the actual situation in the TAR (scarcity of fuel, high expenses of transportation, and inexperienced local laborers). Many factories established in the TAR rapidly acquired a financial deficit and became a burden on the government. So, the value of industrial production of state-owned enterprises first increased to 141.7 million yuan in 1960, then decreased to 11.2 million yuan in 1968. The adjusted value of industrial production increased to 120.8 million yuan in 1988, still lower than that in 1960 (SBT, 1989:270).

TABLE 3.3 Major Indexes of Economy in Tibet

Index	1952	1959	1965	1970	1975	1980	1985	1988
Population (10,000)	115	122	135	151	169	185	199	212
Agricultural product								
(million yuan)	183.2	184.5	338.2	358.8	435.6	579.5	716.5	731.1
Grain (1,000 ton)	155.3	182.9	290.7	294.9	445.8	505.0	530.7	508.7
Livestock (10,000)	974	956	1,701	1,919	2,117	2,348	2,179	2,319
Industrial product								
(million yuan)	--	53.3	28.8	45.8	123.0	166.9	173.6	201.8

Index	1952	1959	1965	1970	1975	1980	1985	1988
Cr ore (1,000 ton)	--	--	--	0.3	0.2	50.3	14.1	72.1
Coal (1,000 ton)	--	45.8	19.7	9.4	61.9	29.8	29.8	6.0
Lumber	--	6	8	7	17	21	21	25
Knitting wool (ton)	--	--	--	--	353	371	146	211
Cement (1,000 ton)	--	--	10.6	3.6	34.0	52.2	46.7	94.8
Borax (1,000 ton)	--	--	--	0.3	0.2	50.3	14.1	72.1

Source: Labapingcuo, 1984: 63, 84, 218, and 233.

In contrast to the situation before 1952, the conditions for economic development in the TAR (systems and organizations, channels of funds, technology, and supplies,) are now similar to those in other regions. By national standards, the TAR is still the least-developed area in China.

Since the social and economic reform in the 1980s, people's income in the TAR increased significantly. For employees of state-owned enterprises (which comprises 82 percent of the total urban laborers, SBT, 1989:164), the average annual salary income per capita increased from 852 yuan in 1978 to 2,739 yuan in 1988, and average annual welfare per capita (including health care, pension, and labor protection) increased from 161 yuan in 1983 to 583 yuan in 1988 (SBT, 1989:499). In the same year, average annual salary income per capita for state-owned enterprise employees was 1,810 yuan, and welfare was 537 yuan in China (Statistical Bureau of China (SBC), 1990:101-151). Meanwhile, average annual income per capita was 1,211 yuan for urban residents in Tibet (SBT, 1989:521) and 1,192 yuan in China as a whole (SBC, 1989:726). The income level in urban areas in the TAR is higher than the national level of China.[34]

Since Han comprise 36.8 percent of the total Lhasa population, 59 percent of the urban population lived in Lhasa in 1982 (Liu Ruei, 1989:184), and the income data are not available for specific ethnic groups, the extent to which the income level of urban residents in the TAR represents the income of urban Tibetans remains unknown. Since most adult Han living in cities or towns in the TAR work in government institutions and earn salaries, the average income level of the Han can be assumed to be higher than urban Tibetans.

In 1988, the average annual "pure income" per capita was 374 yuan for rural residents in the TAR (SBT, 1989:517).[35] Average annual pure income per capita was 545 yuan for rural residents in China (SBC, 1990:719). But considering free health care, free education and other welfare programs in Tibet, which cover a very large proportion of the rural population, rural income differences between the TAR and the Han regions are not significant. The rural-urban income difference is greater in the TAR than in the Han regions.

Generally, Tibet seems to have reached, or closely approached the last stage of the "diffusion model."

Data in Table 3.4 show the growth of retail sales within the TAR during 1978-1988. Four trends are noteworthy:

1. Sales of consumer goods increased much faster than that of productive materials (4.3 times compared to 1.3 times). As a region, the TAR is becoming a consumptive unit rather than a productive unit.

TABLE 3.4 Total Retail Sales of Social Goods (in million yuan)

	1978	1980	1983	1985	1988
By object:					
Agricultural					
production	62.9	73.9	48.0	150.3	80.6
Consumer goods	244.8	286.9	393.9	949.8	1062.4
To residents	210.0	249.4	338.5	751.1	617.3
To units	34.8	37.0	55.4	198.7	445.1
By rural/urban:					
In rural areas	142.5	165.1	229.2	501.9	397.4
In urban areas	165.1	195.6	212.7	598.2	665.0
Total retail	307.6	360.7	441.9	1100.2	1143.0

Source: Statistical Bureau of Tibet, 1989: 422

2. Sales in urban areas increased faster than that in rural areas (4 times compared to 2.8 times). The urban sector expanded rapidly in the TAR but actually produced very little. All economic activities that have taken place in the urban sector (industrial production, construction, and trade, etc.) have had huge deficits.

3. The percentage of consumer goods sold to units (work units related to the government, distinguished from individual customers) increased very quickly (12.8 times compared to 3 times for individual customers). These work units bought 42 percent of consumer goods, even though employees of these units only comprise 7 percent of the total population.

4. Accompanying the new economic policies which began in 1980 was the development of collective and private business. Data in Table 3.5 document that the value of goods imported from other regions increased very rapidly (e.g., from 7.1 million yuan in 1955 to 390.9 million yuan in 1988). The value of goods exported to other regions also increased, from 0.8 million yuan in 1959 (the first year of export) to 58.4 million in 1988. The difference in import and export of the TAR to other regions in China reached 332.5 million yuan in 1988; export was only 13 percent of the total import-export value.

The structure of goods imported and exported in the TAR is shown in Table 3.6. Transportation records indicate that grain and oil are the two major food and fuel imports. Consumer goods (industrial products, cloth, and sugar,) and "distributive goods," which were bought by the government and distributed directly to government units outside trade channels, include construction materials and equipment are other major categories. Pastoral products and traditional medicine are still the main goods for export along with chromium ore and timber.

During 1955 to 1983, the value of goods imported from other regions comprised 82 percent of total goods sold in the TAR. This rose to 94 percent in 1983. The trade between the TAR and other Han regions has a strong bias and is sometimes called "one-way supply," "blood transfusion," or "using the central government's money for buying goods from the central government to maintain Tibet's economy and consumption"(Wang and Bai, 1986:109). After three decades, Tibet still depends on other parts of China for consumer goods.

TABLE 3.5 Purchase, Sale of State-Owned Trade Organizations (10,000 yuan)

Period	Bought from indiv.	Imported from other regions	Imported from other countries	Sold within TAR	Exported to other regions	Exported to other countries
1951-54	--	--	1,313	2,327	--	--
1955-59	1,127	9,445	2,065	13,128	79	73
1960-64	4,740	34,588	842	43,944	4,538	335
1965-69	4,971	41,158	764	59,209	6,279	312
1970-74	10,368	61,232	647	81,149	8,497	443
1975-79	25,970	100,101	1,535	152,648	13,864	705
1980-84	29,297	169,262	3,876	225,859	10,959	1,858
1985	11,712	39,090	--	63,466	5,843	--

Source: Statistical Bureau of Tibet, 1989: 426

TABLE 3.6 In- and Out-Transportation of Goods (ton)

In-transportation	1960	1965	1970	1975	1980	1985	1988
Consumer goods	16,300	17,569	13,000	27,940	44,700	42,100	44,039
Grain	9,053	16,259	3,510	13,056	34,700	39,400	98,051
Oil	19,451	22,547	18,068	59,407	79,200	92,300	97,051
Distrib. goods	3,452	10,760	6,600	26,898	41,500	77,700	50,301
Others	14,244	9,465	940	23,398	34,300	231,900	55,197
Total	62,500	76,600	42,118	150,699	234,400	483,400	344,639

Out-transportation	1971	1975	1980	1985	1988
Pastoral products	1,768	5,631	4,200	3,300	2,607
Cr ore	924	--	22,500	43,800	57,873
Lumber	--	1,566	900	--	34,832
Other	1,602	19,541	14,900	19,500	62,092
Total	4,292	27,630	42,500	66,600	157,404

Out-transported	1960	1965	1970	1975	1980	1985	1987
Pastoral goods (10,000 yuan)	158	1,259	--	1,499	1,648	294	381
Traditional medicine (10,000 yuan)	95	273	--	333	707	602	544

Source: Statistical Bureau of Tibet, 1989: 343, 344, 441, 442.

There has been very limited foreign influence on the economy of the TAR since 1959. International trade comprises only a small proportion of total trade in the TAR with other regions. The total value of international trade in the TAR was 152 million yuan in 1988 (22.7 million yuan imports, 59.5 million exports, and 70 million border trade)

(SBT, 1989:458); while trade between the TAR and other regions in China was 1025.6 million yuan in 1985 (Table 3.5). Although income from tourism increased from 1.8 million yuan in 1984 to 26.6 million yuan in 1988, it comprised only 2.6 percent of the total annual income of the TAR government.

In sharp contrast to the slow growth of production, there has been a rapid growth in the financial deficits of the TAR government. From the data in Table 3.7 it is clear that industry, trade and grain management (buying grain and other consumer goods from other regions and selling them to the residents in the TAR) in Tibet were major sources of deficit for the government. Until 1988, the deficit of enterprises had been higher than the sum of tax and other local income. The deficit of local enterprises and local income (mainly tax) became balanced in 1988.

Meanwhile, expenses of the TAR government have increased rapidly. In 1988, the local income of the TAR government was only 2.3 million yuan; the expenses were 1,047.7 million yuan. So, the subsidy of 1,030.8 million yuan from the central government (99.8 percent of the income of the TAR in 1988) was essential in maintaining the TAR government and its economy. Of the TAR government's total income during 1952 to 1959, 89 percent was financial aid from the central government. In the 1960s, financial aid as a portion of the TAR income was 84.3 percent; it increased to 106.7 percent in the 1970s and to 105.7 percent during 1980 to 1988 (it was over 100 percent because sometimes it also covered the deficit of local production) (SBT, 1989:470).

In order to understand the new characteristics of the TAR's economy, it will be helpful to examine the sources of the deficit of the TAR government. The structure of annual expenses of the TAR are shown in Table 3.8. During 1960 to 1988, administration expenses increased ten times; expenses of "cultural units" (including education, health care, scientific research, and sports) increased 45 times;[36] and funds for improving agriculture increased 40 times.

One of the major sources of financial deficits in the TAR is administration. The number of government employees increased rapidly, from 40,487 in 1959 to 161,000 in 1989. Bank records in the TAR show that, in 1988, cash withdrawals for the "salary of the employees of state-owned institutions" was 316.9 million yuan.

TABLE 3.7 Income of Tibet Autonomous Region (10,000 yuan)

Year	1952	1960	1965	1970	1975	1980	1985	1988
Income within the region:								
A. Enterprise								
Industry	--	3,222	124	-230	122	-537	-2,647	1,945
Construction	--	69	-24	-69	-27	74	184	-36
Agriculture*	--	43	6	-1,084	476	-1,432	-47	3
Post, transport	--	2,773	-146	-1,844	-2,421	-3,029	-1,816	-640
Grain, trade	--	--	-221	-268	-3,098	-1,904	-6,406	4,041
Other	4	35	-83	-390	-174	-1,596	-816	2,051
Subtotal	4	6,143	-343	-3,885	-5,122	-8,254	-11,548	8,711
B. Tax	137	1,316	1,208	1,187	1,953	2,030	4,544	6,989
C. Other	118	2,360	881	556	184	251	967	1,950
D. Depreciation	--	342	493	--	--	--	--	--
Total	258	10,167	2,239	-2,142	-2,985	-5,973	-6,037	226
Financial aid from gov't	1,047	2,725	11,805	18,345	29,179	60,104	105,772	103,077

Source: Statistical Bureau of Tibet, 1989: 470-471 * includes forestry & irrigation

TABLE 3.8 Expense of Tibet Autonomous Region (10,000 yuan)

Year	1952	1960	1965	1970	1975	1980	1985	1988
Admin	712	1,843	2,899	2,494	3,873	7,599	13,249	19,236
Cultural	206	595	1,268	1,062	3,430	7,692	17,099	26,668
Industrial	--	1,362	1,452	1,190	1,785	1,446	6,077	5,572
Agriculture	22	262	531	524	2,805	6,130	10,903	10,573
Urban	3	24	39	100	50	273	1,933	1,221
Indust subsidy	--	1,361	1,452	1,190	2,012	2,245	7,148	6,634
Construction	28	7,510	3,648	4,619	8,146	15,716	34,241	12,901
Prospecting	--	172	114	192	1,865	189	698	680
Welfare	2	26	192	104	249	1,532	1,391	2,192
Price subsidy	--	--	--	--	--	--	2,239	2,901
Circulating	--	2,984	583	166	1,220	221	190	30
Militia	--	--	--	--	94	171	115	136
Other	--	402	587	163	285	4,834	13,725	21,595
Total	973	15,450	11,313	10,613	24,026	46,602	102,941	104,766

Source: Statistical Bureau of Tibet, 1989: 473-475
"Cultural" pertain to culture, education, scientific research, health care, etc.
"Industrial" pertain to industry, transportation, and trade. "Welfare" includes
those related to employment arrangements for urban youth.

Cash withdrawal for "bonus to the employees of state-owned institutions" was 19.58 million yuan (Table 3.9). The sum of these two items, 336.5 million yuan, was about 32 percent of the total expenses of the TAR government in 1988. Considering the additional expenses for their housing, transportation (including Hans' return to place of origin for vacation), these employees actually consumed a very large proportion of the government's money.

TABLE 3.9 Structure of Cash Payment, Withdrawal from Banks (in 10,000 yuan)

	1960	1965	1970	1975	1980	1985	1988
State employees' sal.	1,365	3,692	4,567	6635	15175	27552	31690
State employees' bonus	--	--	--	--	66	2,061	1,958
Others to individuals	--	295	318	695	1,889	9,200	10,878
Withdrawn by military	1,084	3,129	3,888	3,857	3789	7,558	11,516
Salary, bonus of urban collectives	31	65	62	34	866	1,656	1,525
Expenses of town Xiang enterprises	--	--	--	--	--	681	205
Withdrawal of private enterprises	--	--	--	--	--	207	807
Payment for farm prod.	1,258	2,059	1,697	1,527	1,226	3,178	9,094
To rural credit coop.	--	146	208	1,546	4,612	6,210	10,246
Expenses of admin.	199	1,034	908	2,110	3,564	4,512	5,755
Pay for indust. products	--	--	--	16	79	197	345
Withdrawal of indiv. deposit	360	1,116	1,512	1,671	3,629	13,438	23,846
Remittance	16	64	15	122	296	1,086	1,552
Others	402	672	650	1,652	2,006	7,199	14,225
Total	4,715	12,272	13,825	19,865	37,131	84,735	123,642

Source: Statistical Bureau of Tibet, 1989: 482-483

The second major source of deficits is enterprises in industry, construction, transportation, trade, grain-buying and selling. Due to a scarcity of many kinds of raw materials for industrial production (metal, cloth, paper, wood, etc.), local fuel, and power supply (oil, coal), and a low level of education and technical training of local laborers, the cost of developing industrial production has been much higher than enterprises can afford.

As in other Chinese cities and towns, the TAR government has supplied urban residents with grain, oil, and other necessities at low prices similar to those in the Han provinces. But the cost of these goods is actually much higher in Tibet because they have been transported for thousands of miles from other regions.

Buying agricultural products (especially grain) at a high price and selling at a low price is the government policy to promote agricultural production while keeping the urban residents (who have enjoyed low-priced supplies for decades) satisfied. The problem is even worse in Tibet. Since 1980, no agricultural tax has been collected in the TAR, in line with the policy of the central government. Therefore, the TAR government is able to buy only a small amount of grain from local sources, but must import grain from Han provinces, which is more expensive. The TAR government bought 30,162 tons of grain within Tibet in 1987 (only 6.5 percent of the total grain production), while it imported 65,725 tons to supply urban residents (SBT, 1989:427 and 440).

One noteworthy phenomenon is the increase in "other" expenses since 1978: from 3.64 million yuan in 1977, to 15.56 million yuan in 1978, to 215.95 million yuan in 1988 (Table 3.8). This increase was due largely to "reimbursement" for damages and losses to monasteries and individuals during the "Cultural Revolution." The "other" item does not appear in statistical yearbooks in other autonomous regions (e.g., Inner Mongolia). It consists of 20.6 percent of the total the TAR government expenses in 1988, or 96 times the local income of the TAR government that year. Bank records show that cash paid to "individuals besides salary and bonus" was 108.78 million yuan in 1988, the amount under this classification has increased 15 times since 1977 (Table 3.9).

As the main consumers in Tibet before 1952, monasteries have lost their power in society and administration since 1959. The number of monks also has decreased. However, administration has expanded and the number of "cadres" has increased. They have become the main consumers of wealth in Tibet. There were 161,000 employees working in government institutions or other units under government management in the TAR in 1989. They received salaries, bonuses, and all kinds of subsidies (about 470 million yuan in 1989) (Statistical Bureau of China (SBC), 1990:121-135). Actually, they were paid by the central government because the TAR government's income was close to zero, if not a deficit.

The picture develops as follows: the central government paid money to maintain the local government (administration); fed 161,000 government employees (63 percent of them were Tibetans, SBC, 1990); maintained systems of free education, health care, welfare, public services, and urban construction and created jobs for urban youth; provided subsidies and materials to improve agricultural and pastoral production; supported local industrial productions, which have continuously maintained deficits; and provided funds to rebuild monasteries and subsidies to monks to implement the policy of "religious freedom" and maintain social stability.

At the same time, the social and economic structures of the Han regions merged into the TAR, and the urban Tibetans and Han actually earn more than the average level for the nation. It is assumed that, at the last stage of the "diffusion model," "cultural differences should cease to be socially meaningful; ... the core and peripheral regions will tend to become culturally homogeneous because the economic, cultural, and political foundations for separate ethnic identification disappear" (Hechter, 1975:8).

But it seems that the situation in the TAR is more complex than this. Cultural differences, especially religious differences, still exist. Efforts to develop modern industry in the TAR to a certain extent have failed. The "diffusion" of the administrative and economic systems of the Han regions into Tibet has had some unintended consequences.

In 1989, financial aid given by the central government was 486 yuan per capita in the TAR, while the net income of the rural population in China, as a whole, was 630 yuan in 1990 (*People's Daily*, January 17, 1991). Maintenance of administration, economy, society, and all other affairs in the TAR has relied entirely on the central government's money. The economy in the TAR should be called a "dependent economy," rather than one characterized by "dependent development" (Evans, 1979:32). No accumulation of capital and industrialization occurred in the TAR, though the central government plays a key role in Tibet's economy by its "alliance" with the local government. The post-1959 Han-Tibetan relationship has acquired some new characteristics with the new social and economic relations between the TAR and the Han regions.

The Han in the Tibet Autonomous Region

In 1951, some Han officials and merchants returned to Tibet accompanying People's Liberation Army troops after the "17-Point Agreement" was signed.[37] When construction of Qinghai-Tibet Road and Sichuan-Tibet Road was completed in 1954, transportation between Tibet and other parts of China was greatly improved. The Preparatory Committee of the TAR was established in 1956, and many Han officials were transferred into Tibet to work for this Committee and its institutions. The Han cadres and workers in Tibet reached 17,631 in that year.[38]

Because the central government decided to avoid conflict with the Dalai Lama's government, "democratic reform" was not carried out in Tibet during 1956 to 1960. Many Han left and their number decreased to 2,200 in 1957 (1,500 to 1,600 cadres and 600 workers) (Liu Ruei, 1989:141).

After the Dalai Lama fled to India in 1959, the local government and its institutions patterned after those in other Han regions (bureaus, social organizations) were established. New factories, hospitals, schools, stores, and post offices were established throughout Tibet, and the number of Han increased again. In 1980, the number of Han in the TAR reached 122,356 (about 6.6 percent of the total population), the highest number in history.

In the same year (1980), the central government decided to have Tibetans as the "main body" of cadres and workers in the TAR after Hu Yaobang's visit to the TAR. This new policy resulted in Han emigration in the following years (Table 3.10). According to the 1990 Census, there were 81,217 Han in the TAR, about 3.7 percent of the total population (CPIRC, 1991).

TABLE 3.10 Han Population in the Tibet Autonomous Region

Year	Han	Total (%)	Year	Han	Total (%)
1956	17,631	--	1983	79,650	4.12
1957	2,100-2,200	--	1984	76,322	3.88
1964	36,700	2.93	1985	70,932	3.56
1978	112,569	6.46	1986	72,340	3.57
1980	122,356	6.60	1987	78,804	3.79
1981	99,873	5.37	1988	79,871	3.76
1982	91,720	4.85	1990	81,217	3.70

Source: Liu, 1989: 140-141; Statistical Bureau of Tibet, 1989: 140-141.

Major differentials in social and economic systems between the Tibetan and Han regions decreased in the 1950s and 1960s, and disappeared in the 1970s along with the establishment of the commune system in the TAR. The impact of the religious differential also decreased. These tremendous changes in the TAR increased the possibility of Han immigration, especially in urban areas where the traditional culture was not as strong as in the rural areas. Controls on immigration to the TAR were generally slack, especially during the "Cultural Revolution."

However, it seems that few Han wanted to migrate into the TAR. The question is why Han immigration did not occur in Tibet as it occurred in other autonomous regions such as Xinjiang and Inner Mongolia. In these other two large frontier autonomous regions, the Han population increased from 0.3 million in 1949 to 5.7 million in 1990 in the Xinjiang Uygur Autonomous Region, and from 5.2 million in 1949 to 17.3 million in 1990 in Inner Mongolia (CPIRC, 1991). Referring back to the model in Figure 3.1, what variables have had negative impact on Han migration into Tibet?

I raised this question with both Han and Tibetan cadres and intellectuals during my survey in the TAR (June-September, 1988). I asked why people did not want to migrate into Tibet and why those who were already working in the TAR wanted to leave. It seems that there are different migration patterns in urban and rural areas in the TAR. The reasons given by cadres and intellectuals for urban areas are summarized below.

1. The importance of geographic factors was confirmed by all Han respondents. High elevation and scarcity of oxygen make many Han physically ill. I was told that, after some incidents, in which either a mother or baby died, no Han women wanted to give birth in the TAR. They returned to the Han regions for childbirth and left their babies there with relatives. Some Han believed that after a long period of work on the plateau they could not survive heart attacks or other diseases they might suffer upon their return to the Han areas after retirement. Concern for their and their children's health made many Han hesitant to work in the TAR.

2. Because transportation in the TAR still is not as convenient as in other regions, and entertainment is so limited, well-educated young Han cadres and intellectuals cannot visit their families often and complain that life in the TAR is very boring (Bass, 1990).

3. The educational level and development of science and technology is generally lower in the TAR than in other regions. Therefore, young Han teachers, doctors, and engineers complain that the TAR is not a good environment to develop their professional careers. They feel they are disadvantaged when they return to the Han regions after several years of service in the TAR. Because of these personal concerns, only a very few Han university graduates are willing to work in the TAR, and those who already have been sent to the TAR want to leave.

Although the number of volunteer migrants has been small, the central government successfully arranged for thousands of Han to work in the TAR. Every year, many institutions of the central or provincial governments are requested to send a certain number of employees (with required professional training) to work in the TAR for a designated period of time.[39] The government raises the salary of these employees one or two ranks; allows them to keep their place of origin resident registration, and provides many subsidies and benefits to them.[40] They have an all-expense paid six-month vacation after the first year of service, and self-postponement of return to their jobs in the TAR has not been an unusual occurrence. Both the TAR government and their work units also try to make them comfortable in Tibet. The Han usually live in separate residential zones with better housing, water and electricity supplies (Ma, 1990:60).

A large proportion of Han migrants in Inner Mongolia and Xinjiang were spontaneous rural-rural migrants and these migrations mainly occurred during the 1950s and 1960s (Ma, 1987; Ji Ping, 1990). Why did this kind of immigration not occur in the TAR during the "Cultural Revolution," when the administrative control on migration was also loose?

First, arable land is very limited in the TAR. During 1952 to 1988, the area of cultivated land increased from 2.45 to 3.45 million *mu*, but because of natural population growth, cultivated land per capita decreased from 2.1 to 1.6 *mu*. Of cultivated land, only 48.6 percent has irrigation facilities. Because of the conditions of temperature, rainfall, irrigation, and fertility of land, area grain production (181 kg. per *mu* in 1988) in the TAR is less than half that in nearby Sichuan. An investigation by the Chinese Academy of Sciences reports that arable land not in use is only 0.2 million *mu* in the TAR (Shang, 1989). Cultivated land in the TAR (both quality and quantity) cannot provide opportunities for farmer immigrants. Besides, the grain (barley) able to be grown in a plateau climate is different from those in Han regions (wheat and rice), and this difference also has a negative impact on immigration of Han farmers into the TAR.

Second, several Tibetan autonomous prefectures are located between the TAR and Han areas (in Qinghai, Sichuan, and Gansu). The elevation in these prefectures is lower than that in the TAR and the climate is closer to that of Han areas. When Han farmers moved to Inner Mongolia and Xinjiang in the 1950s and 1960s, some also moved into these prefectures. During 1953 to 1982, the Han population in these Tibetan autonomous prefectures increased from 0.43 million to 1.54 million (Ma and Pan, 1988). But, this migration was restricted by the central government and local authorities after the "Cultural Revolution."

During 1981 to 1988, the total number of registered immigrants (for both urban and rural areas) was 44,068, while the total number of emigrants was 104,585 (SBT, 1989:135). There has been a trend of emigration among the Han population who were officially registered in the TAR.

The recent economic reform and its policies allow people to manage a private business and travel with fewer restrictions. In the past several years, spontaneous temporary immigration occurred in urban areas of the TAR. Many Han peddlers, craftsmen, construction workers, and businessmen arrived in Lhasa and other cities to make money. Their numbers were very large in Lhasa, at about 45,000 to 50,000 in the summer of 1988, or 30 percent of permanent residents in Lhasa (Ma, 1990:62). But they stay in the TAR for only a short period of time.

In Tibet, policies and government regulations, therefore, are crucial to understanding migration issues, in both urban and rural areas, in the case of government arranged migration for a long period or of spontaneous temporary and circular migration.

In order to understand the role the Han population has played in Tibet, we examine the age and occupational structure of the Han, and their geographic distribution in the TAR.

The age structures of both the Han and Tibetan populations in the TAR shown in Figure 3.3 are based on the data from the 1982 census. The pattern of Tibetan age structure was a normal population pyramid. Among the Han, the 25 to 29-year-old group was the largest, and there was a relatively much smaller group under age 14.

This pattern is clearly because a large proportion of Han in the TAR were cadres, professionals, and workers aged 20 to 34. Their migration was arranged by the government, and they worked in the TAR for a designated period of time, leaving elders and children in their place of origin.

The occupational structure of the Han is also very different from that of Tibetans. Of a total of 91,720 Han in the TAR in 1982, the "worker" group comprised 40 percent. Other groups were "professional" (25.4 percent), "cadre and clerical" (22 percent), "service worker" (7.6 percent), "trade worker" (2.4 percent) and "worker in agriculture" (2.3 percent). In contrast, "peasant and herdsman" comprised 87.1 percent of the Tibetan population. Other groups were "worker" (6.3 percent), "professional" (2.9 percent), "cadre and clerical" (2.4 percent), "service worker" (0.9 percent) and "trade worker" (0.4 percent) (Liu Ruei, 1989:294).

FIGURE 3.3 Age Structure of Han and Tibetan Population in the Tibet Autonomous Region (1982)

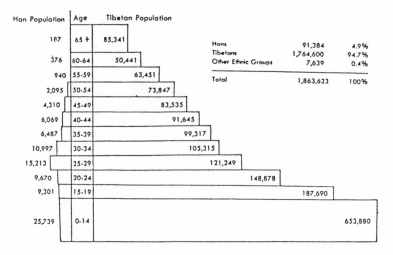

Hans				91,384		4.9%
Tibetans				1,764,600		94.7%
Other Ethnic Groups				7,639		0.4%
Total				1,863,623		100%

The geographic distribution of the Han population in the TAR shows that in 1982 the percentage of Han in the total population was less than 5 percent in most counties and less than 1 percent in more than half the total counties in the TAR (Ma, 1990:59). In 1986, 52.5 percent of the Han in the TAR lived in Lhasa City, where the government and its institutions are located.

Because most Han intend to stay in Tibet for only a short period of time, they maintain their life customs and assimilate less with the native Tibetans compared with the Han in other minority nationality areas. On the other hand, accompanying the increasing influence of the central government in the TAR, many urban Tibetans learn the Mandarin (Han) language and have been influenced by the Han culture (Ma, 1990). Ethnic integration is obviously Han-biased in the TAR.

In sum, the Han in the TAR have been mainly cadres, professionals, and workers, working in government, schools, hospitals, and factories. Their immigration was arranged by the government and they work in the TAR only for a period of several years. The Tibet Autonomous Region relies not only on the central government for consumer goods and financial aid, but also relies on the Han regions for professional laborers.

A Comparison of the Situation in Tibet and Inner Mongolia

Is the situation in the TAR unique in China? To what extent does Tibet share its experiences with other autonomous regions of ethnic minority groups? Inner Mongolia is another large autonomous region in China, with an area of 1.18 million square kilometers and a population of 21.5 million in 1990. A brief comparison between the TAR and Inner Mongolia helps us understand the factors affecting social, economic, and demographic changes in the TAR.

Like Tibetans, Mongolians have their own language and a glorious history. They ruled all of China during the Yuan dynasty (A.D.1271 to 1368), and were expelled from central China by the Ming emperors. Therefore, their relationship with the Han group was looser than that between Tibetans and Han during the Ming dynasty (A.D.1368 to 1644). Mongolians have a close relationship with Tibetans because they have accepted Tibetan Buddhism since the Yuan dynasty. When the Manchu ruled China, both Tibet and Inner Mongolia (also Outer Mongolia) came under the direct administration of the Qing dynasty (A.D.1644 to 1911). In order to separate different ethnic groups for easier domination, the Qing emperors forbade the Han from emigrating either to Tibet or to Inner Mongolia.

The situation began to change in the late nineteenth century, when the British won the Opium War and Russians expanded their territory into Siberia. The Qing Court released restrictions on, and even encouraged, Han migration into Inner Mongolia, Manchuria, and Xinjiang (the northwestern frontier) to protect border areas. Mongolian princes obtained a large amount of money by selling grasslands to Han farmers. In 1912, the Han population in Inner Mongolia reached one million, exceeding the number of native Mongolians (0.8 million). Meanwhile, due to several reasons (the negative attitude of the Tibetan authority towards Han immigration, the large differences in social and economic systems, and the geographic factors), few Han farmers moved into Tibet.

When the Manchu Qing dynasty was overthrown in 1911, the civil war started. With military support from the Russian Red Army, Outer Mongolia claimed independence (although its legitimacy in international forums was not confirmed until 1945 after the Yalta Meeting). The Dalai Lama's government also tried to become independent at this time. Because of Inner Mongolia's geographic closeness to central China and the strong influence of the large Han population, the central government established several provinces in the area of today's Inner Mongolia and placed them under its direct control.

During 1912 to 1949, the Han population in Inner Mongolia increased from 1 million to 5.3 million, while the number of Han in Tibet decreased. It could be argued that the main reason for such a large difference in immigration in Inner Mongolia and Tibet was due to administrative and political factors.

In 1959, the central government controlled Tibet. Social reform abolished serfdom, and monasteries lost their traditional power. Administrative systems and other organizations similar to those in other regions were established in the TAR. Other than the poor transportation conditions (no railway connects the TAR with other regions), other situations in the TAR are quite similar to those in Inner Mongolia. There were few spontaneous Han immigrants to the TAR but the Han population increased from 5.2 million in 1949 to 17.3 million in 1990 (a large proportion of the growth was due to natural increase).

One could argue that the distance from central China is an important factor in Han immigration to the TAR and Inner Mongolia. For comparison, let us examine another autonomous region—Xinjiang. Xinjiang is located in the northwestern frontier area, as distant from central China as is Tibet. The Han population in Xinjiang increased from 0.3 million in 1949 to 5.7 million in 1990 (CPIRC, 1991). Transportation conditions in Xinjiang are better than those in the TAR (a railway connects the capital city of Xinjiang to central China), although the distance is about the same. Geographic distance is certainly a negative factor affecting immigration in Xinjiang compared with Inner Mongolia.

But Han population growth in Xinjiang is still significant. With social, economic, and administrative systems similar to those in Inner Mongolia and Xinjiang; with a similar geographic distance from central China as Xinjiang; with the same religion as that in Inner Mongolia (although its influence has weakened in Inner Mongolia since 1949); with similar religious differences from the Han regions as in Xinjiang (Moslems in Xinjiang supposedly have a more negative attitude towards Han immigrants because they eat pork) geographic conditions (mainly the high elevation) in Tibet may be the only important factor left to explain the low volume of Han immigration to the TAR.

Central government financial subsidies are also very important in Inner Mongolia. In 1988, the local income of the Inner Mongolia Autonomous Region was 2.4 billion yuan while expenses were 5.1 billion. The 2.7 billion yuan difference was covered by the central government.

But differences in production and population size between Inner Mongolia and Tibet are significant. An industrial productive system (steel and coal productions, electricity production, manufacture, light industry) has been established in Inner Mongolia since 1949. In 1988, the value of industrial and agricultural production per capita was 986 yuan in Inner Mongolia compared to 440 yuan in the TAR. On the side of consumption, the average salary of state-owned enterprise employees was 1,641 yuan (plus 213 yuan for social welfare) in Inner Mongolia in 1988 compared to 2,739 yuan (plus 582 yuan for social welfare) in the TAR. Compared with Inner Mongolia, the TAR produces very little while consuming much. Results show that the central government subsidy was 128 yuan per capita in Inner Mongolia compared to 493 yuan in the TAR (Statistical Bureau of Inner Mongolia, 1990:351). Local income of the TAR government has always been zero, or a deficit, so it has relied entirely on money from the central government.

The percentages of the central government's aid in local expenses to five autonomous regions in China were 44.7 (Guangxi), 52.7 (Inner Mongolia), 60.4 (Xinjiang), 63.3 (Ningxia) and 99.8 (Tibet) in 1988 (Pan, 1989:143; Ji Xiade, 1989:286; Wei, 1989:271). The degree of financial dependence of the TAR is much higher than other autonomous regions.

Concluding Observations

Before the twentieth century, the administrative, social and economic relations between Tibet and the Han regions were limited due to significant differences in social, economic and religious systems in Tibet. The official function of the relationship was to keep Tibet subordinate to China. Trade with the Han regions was important for Tibet's economy and consumption. During 1911 to 1950, the influence of foreign governments in Tibet increased and had a negative impact on the administrative relationship and trade between Tibet and the Han regions. Geographic features of Tibet (mountains and high elevation) have been important factors affecting trade, transportation and migration.

Monasteries were the dominant group in Tibet before 1959. Monks comprised a large proportion of the population. They were very powerful in the economy and they controlled the administration. Religious activities had consumed the majority of Tibet's wealth in the past. After 1959, monasteries lost their power. Under the new "freedom of religion" policy of the government, their influence has increased again since 1980.

Since 1959, social and economic systems of other Han regions were introduced into the TAR.   Although agricultural and pastoral production increased, productivity has been very low in state-owned enterprises. Accompanying the expansion of the TAR government and institutions, and with other disadvantages in Tibet due to the generally low level of educational and economic development, the deficit in the TAR increased rapidly. Gradually, the finances of the TAR government have become entirely dependent on aid from the central government. The "dependent economy" of the TAR becomes a new factor in the relationship between Tibet and the Han regions.

The Han comprise a very small proportion of the total population in the TAR. They mainly are cadres and professionals. Their migration is arranged by the government and they usually work in the TAR for a designated period of time.   The main reason why so few Han immigrated to the TAR was because of its high elevation. Spontaneous Han migration occurred only recently and they are temporary migrants, working in services, trade, construction, and handicrafts.

Referring to two development models proposed by Hechter, as Tibetans have obtained equal legal rights compared to the Han and other groups after 1959, the political and economic systems of the Han regions have indeed diffused into Tibet. But these systems did not work well and resulted in a complete "dependent economy." People's income and welfare in the TAR now are even higher than the national level, but both urban residents' income and all people's welfare programs rely entirely on the financial aid of the central government. It cannot be called a successful example of the "diffusion model."

The Tibet case suggests that if social and economic systems and cultural traditions had been so different between the core and peripheral region in the past, "diffusing the core's socioeconomic systems into periphery," at least as a short transition alternative, might be an oversimplified strategy. Besides the system reform, other aspects such as cultural and economic traditions, religion, and the knowledge of modern education and production need to be considered and play an important role in policy planning.

Notes

1. According to the 1990 Census, the total population of ethnic Tibetans in China was 4.59 million. Of that number, 2.49 million lived outside the TAR (CPIRC, 1991).

2. This study was carried out at Harvard University. The materials and data were obtained from several libraries at Harvard, but Tibetan materials

there were limited. Further research should include local economic records and other materials available in the Tibetan language in the TAR and at western university libraries.

3. They were made of wool and leather. Cotton cloth has relied on imports.

4. The total annual grain production was around 176,000 tons during the 1940s (Wu, 1953:85).

5. In the first National Census (1953), the Tibet Government under the Dalai Lama reported one million Tibetans living in the Tibet Region. The Chamdo District under the control of the central government was reported to have a population of 0.15 million (Ma and Naigu, 1988:4).

6. There was a small hydroelectric plant in Lhasa before 1950; it was used to make Tibetan currency.

7. But it is not clear how monks were classified into its categories.

8. The value of goods transported from the Han regions to Tibet was 96,771 pounds.t. of silver each year at the beginning of twentieth century, and the value of goods from Tibet to the Han regions was 85,887 pounds.t. of silver (Huang, 1982:51).

9. "Nearly half of Tibet's trade with India was carried on Siliguri-Kalimpong road (through Yatung)"(Karan, 1976:43).

10. It was one of three largest trading companies in Tibet (Goldstein, 1989:331).

11. The value of Rupee increased in 1900: One (British India) Rupee equalled 0.196 U.S. gold dollar in 1897. (One Rupee equalled 0.207 U.S. gold dollar in both 1898 and 1899, and it equalled 0.324 U.S. gold dollar in 1900 and in 1903). (*The World Almanac and Encyclopedia 1898* and volumes of the following years, see "money foreign".) The increasing value of the Rupee shows a more significant growth of Tibet-India trade during the period.

12. In history, the number of monks was 316,231 in 1737, about 35 percent of the total population (Liu Ruei, 1989:35). Another study reported that this number of monks included only those under the Gelugpa sect, and the total number of monks was about one half of the total population (Wang Sen, 1984:193). The Dalai Lama claimed to have 250,000 monks in Tibet in the 1950s (*Le Figaro*, Oct. 5, 1982).

13. A much smaller number (6,500 soldiers) was reported to the central government in 1940 (Wu, 1953:75). Other reports based on Tibetan sources indicate that Tibetan army recruited 15,000 new troops in 1920 (Goldstein, 1989:84). The military budget was about 50 percent of the total government income during 1947 to 1950 (Labapingcuo, 1987:344).

14. In the 1930s and 1940s, there were 200 lay officials and 230 monk officials in the government (Grunfeld, 1987:9). It should be noted that the numbers of monks, solders, and officials mentioned above are from different sources, so these numbers can be used only as references.

15. Until 1050 "there were no schools for the populace. The only schooling available to a young man was in the monasteries"(Karan, 1976:13). There were also several private schools in Lhasa, mainly for nobles' children (Goldstein, 1989:7). For detailed information on education in Tibet in the 1940s, see Wu, 1953:90 to 94 and Liu Ruei, 1989:301.

16. Drepung monastery alone had 185 estates, 20,000 serfs, 300 pastures, and 16,000 herdsmen (Goldstein, 1989:34).

17. The annual interest rate of the usury arranged by three famous monasteries was somewhere between 30 to 50 percent. For small amounts, interest sometimes reached 100 or 150 percent (Zhou, 1984:44).

18. 1 pound (pounds.t.) = 11.94 Liang = 0.3732 kg..

19. In the 1940s, the annual income of the Tibet government included barley (750 tons), butter (363 tons), tea (183 tons), cash (7 million Liang silver) (Wu, 1953:86).

20. Urban population comprised 7 percent of the total in 1958, and most urban population lived in Lhasa (Liu Ruei, 1989:184).

21. The Xiang administration was first established in 1985 in these areas (*People's Daily*, July 9, 1990).

22. Among the total 50,000 to 60,000 urban population in Lhasa in the 1950s, there were 30,000 to 40,000 monks and 20,000 other residents (Liu Ruei, 1989:69).

23. In the 1950s, the January ritual cost about 0.62 million yuan each year (Kuang, 1990:146).

24. There were 2,711 monasteries in 1958 (Liu Ruei, 1989:298). A report to the Qing emperor in 1737 mentioned that there were 3,477 monasteries in Tibet at that time (Zhang Yuxin, 1983:34).

25. In the eighteenth century, each household had to support 2.5 monks (Zhang Yuxin, 1983:34).

26. Mahayana Buddhism is different from Tibetan Lamaism (see Karan, 1976:65-67).

27. There were 1,000 Han and Mongolian soldiers in Lhasa in 1792 (Chen Jiafu, 1937:12).

28. "Tibetan civilization and culture of the present day are largely due both to China and India; to the latter for the religious side, to the former in the main for the material side" (Bell, 1928:12).

29. There were several hundred Hui in Lhasa before 1952, living in a neighborhood (He-Ba-Lin) near the Jokang. A study reported that about 1,000 Hui went into exile in 1959 (Fang Jianchang, 1988:109-112).

30. There were also some Han handicraftsmen and gardeners (planting vegetables) in Tibet (Bell, 1928:31), but no data on their numbers are available.

31. It was estimated that total Tibetan refugees who went to India in exile in 1959 were about 50,000 to 55,000, including 5,000 to 6,000 monks (Grunfeld, 1987:187).

32. The net income per capita was 397 yuan in 1990 for the rural population in the TAR, about 2.3 times their income in 1978 (*People's Daily*, Nov. 14, 1990).

33. All monks officially registered in monasteries and temples in China have a salary system, with ranks parallel to cadres in administration; their salaries are paid by the government. It is not a joke, therefore, to ask how many "bureau-director rank" monks and "section-director rank" monks there are in a monastery.

34. Because of long-distance transportation, the prices of many consumer goods in the TAR are little higher than those in other regions although the government pays large subsidies in controlling market prices.

35. According to the definition of SBC: "pure income" of rural residents = total annual income minus productive expenses minus tax minus depreciation on fixed productive assets minus contract contribution minus survey subsidy. (SBC, 1989:759)

36. The funds for education alone were 145 million yuan in the TAR in 1990 (*People's Daily*, Jan. 30, 1991).

37. "Agreement on Measures for the Peaceful Liberation of Tibet" was signed by the representatives of the Dalai Lama's government and the central government on May 23, 1951 (for its content, see Karan, 1976:89-91).

38. The Han population discussed in this article excludes military forces because no data are available.

39. During the 1950s to 1970s, they worked in the TAR for a undetermined period of time. In the 1980s, people were sent to the TAR to work for a three- or five-year period. The total accumulated number of people who were sent to the TAR since the 1950s was about 200,000 (*People's Daily*, April 8, 1991).

40. A Han cadre in Gyantse county calculated his monthly income for me: 82 (salary) + 5 (bonus) + 23 (food price subsidy) + 2.5 (haircut) + 2.5 (subsidy of service length) + 7 (one rank extra salary) + 80 (plateau subsidy) + 35 (oxygen subsidy) + 11 (temporary subsidy) = 248 yuan. He would earn only 115 yuan (the first 5 items) if he worked in a Han region.

References

Bass, C. *Inside the Treasure House*. London: Victor Gollancz,1990.

Bell, C. *Tibet Past and Present*. London: Oxford University Press, 1927.

Bell, C. *The People of Tibet*. Oxford: Clarendon Press, 1928

Bell, C. *Portrait of the Dalai Lama*. London: Collins, 1946.

Chapman, F.S. *Lhasa: the Holy City*. London: R & R Clark, 1940.

Chen Fanzhou et al. "Studies on Yunnan-Tibet Trade," *Xizang Yanjiou (Tibet Studies)* 4 (1988): 51-58. (in Chinese)

Chen Jianfu. *Xizang Wenti (Issues on Tibet)*. Shanghai: Shangwu Press, 1937. (in Chinese)

CPIRC (China Population Information and Research Center). *China's 4th Census Data Sheet*. Beijing: CPIRC, 1991.

De Jong, G.F. and J.T. Fawcett. "Motivations for Migration: An Assessment and a Value-Expectancy Research Model." In *Migration Decision Making*, edited by G.F. De Jong and R.W. Garder. New York: Pergamon Press, 1981.

Dreyer, J.T. *China's Forty Millions*. Cambridge: Harvard University Press, 1976.

Evans, P. *Dependent Development*. Princeton: Princeton University Press, 1979.

Fang Jianchang, "Hui in Tibet and Their Temples: Spread of Islam in Tibet and its Impact." *Xizang Yanjiou (Tibet Studies)* 4 (1988): 102-114. (in Chinese)

Findley, S. *Planning for Internal Migration*. ISP-RD-4. Washington: U.S. Government Printing Office, 1977.

Glazer, N. and Moynihan, D.P. eds. *Ethnicity.* Cambridge: Harvard University Press, 1975.

Goldlust, J. and Richmond, A. "A Multivariate Model of migrant Adaptation." *International Migration Review* 8 (Summer 1974): 193-226.

Goldstein, M. *A History of Modern Tibet.* Berkeley: University of California Press, 1990.

Goldstein, M. and Beall, C.M. *Nomads of Western Tibet.* Berkeley: University of California Press, 1990.

Grunfeld, A.T. *The Making of Modern Tibet.* New York: M.E. Sharpe, 1987.

Hansen, N. et al. *Regional Policy in a Changing World.* New York: Plenum Press, 1990.

Hechter, M. *Internal Colonialism.* Berkeley: University of California Press, 1975.

Huang Wanluen. "Economic Relationship Between Tibet and the Central Government During Yuan, Ming, and Qing Dynasties," Xizang Yanjiou (Tibet Studies) 3 (1988): 8-17. (in Chinese)

Huang Wanluen. "Historical Studies on British and Russian Economic Invasions in Tibet," Xizang Yanjiou (Tibet Studies) 2 (1982): 40-52. (in Chinese)

Huang Wanluen. "Several Essays in Democratic Reform in Tibet," *Xizang Yanjiou (Tibet Studies)* 4 (1984): 5-20. (in Chinese)

Ji Ping. Frontier Migration and Ethnic Assimilation: A Case of Xinjiang Uygur Autonomous Region of China. Ph.D. diss., Brown University, 1990.

Ji Xiade. *The Advancing 40 Years (Xinjiang Volume).* Beijing: Statistical Press of China, 1989. (in Chinese)

Karan, P.P. *The Changing Face of Tibet.* Lexington: University Press of Kentucky, 1976.

Kuang Haolin, "Monastery's Economy in Modern Tibet," *Zhonggo Shehui Kexue (Social Sciences in China)* 3 (1990): 133-153. (in Chinese)

Labapingcuo, ed. Xizang Zizhiqu Gaikuang (General Situation of the Tibet Autonomous Region). Lhasa: People's Press of Tibet, 1984. (in Chinese)

Liu Ruei. China's Population (Tibet). Beijing: China's Finance and Economy Press, 1989. (in Chinese)

Ma, Rong. Migrant and Ethnic Integration in Rural Chifeng, Inner Mongolia, China. (Ph.D. diss., Brown University), 1987.

Ma, Rong. "Residential Patterns of Han and Tibetans in Lhasa, the Tibet Autonomous Region," *Shehuixue Yanjiou* (Sociological Studies) 3 (1990): 57-65. (in Chinese)

Ma, Rong and Pan Naigu. "Demographic Changes in Tibetan- Inhabited Areas," *Beijing Review* (April 4-10, 1988): 21-24.

MacInnis, D.E. *Religion in China Today.* New York: Orbis Books, 1989.

Pan Jimin. *Forty Years of Ningxia (1949 to 1989).* Beijing: Statistical Press of China, 1989. (in Chinese)

Pye, L.W. "China: Ethnic Minorities and National Security," In *Ethnicity,* edited by N. Glazer and D.P. Moynihan. Cambridge: Harvard University Press, 1975: 489-512.

Shang Jiali. "Study on Bearing Capacity of Land in Tibet," *Xizang Yanjiou (Tibetan Studies)* 2 (1989): 5-15. (in Chinese)

Shaw, R.P. *Migration: Theory and Fact. Bibliography series No. 5*. Philadelphia: Regional Science Research Institute, 1975.

Statistical Bureau of China (SBC). *Statistical Yearbook of China (1990)*. Beijing: Statistical Press of China, 1990. (in Chinese)

Statistical Bureau of Inner Mongolia. *Statistical Yearbook of Inner Mongolia (1990)*. Beijing: Statistical Press of China, 1990. (in Chinese)

Statistical Bureau of Tibet (SBT), *Statistical Yearbook of Tibet (1989)*. Beijing: Statistical Press of China, 1989. (in Chinese)

Tan Fangzi. "Yunnan's Tea Trade to Tibet," *Bianzheng Gonglun (Discussions on the Affairs of Frontier Regions)* 3, no. 11 (1940). (in Chinese)

Todaro, M.P. *Economic Development in the Third World*. (3rd edition). London: Longman, 1985.

Wang Seng. *Xizang Fojia Fazhan Shilue (History of Buddhist Development in Tibet)*. Beijing: Press of Chinese Social Sciences, 1984. (in Chinese)

Wang Xiaoqiang and Bai Nanfeng, *Furao de Pinkuen (Poverty of the Rich)*. Chengdu: People's Press of Sichuan. 1986. (in Chinese)

Weber, M. *The Sociology of Religion*. Boston: Beacon Press, 1963.

Wei Zonghui. *Statistical Yearbook of Guangxi (1989)*. Beijing: Statistical Press of China, 1989. (in Chinese)

World Almanac and Encyclopedia. New York: The Press Publishing Co. the New York World, 1898 to 1904.

Wu Zhongxin. *Xizang Jiyao (Summary of Mission to Tibet)*. Taipei: Central Antique Press, 1953. (in Chinese)

Ya Hanzhang, "On Feudal Serfdom in Tibet," *Xizang Yanjiou (Tibet Studies)* 1(1988): 2-15. (in Chinese)

Zhang Yuxin. "Main Reasons for the Long-Term Underdeveloped Economy in Tibet During the Early Qing Dynasty," *Xizang Yanjiou (Tibet Studies)* 2(1983): 32-36. (in Chinese)

Zhou Benjia. "Monastery Economy Before Democratic Reform in Tibet," *Xizang Yanjiou (Tibet Studies)* 2(1985): 39-50. (in Chinese)

4

Ethnic Conflict, History, and State Formation in Africa[1]

Philip E. Leis

A famous phrase that heralded the spurt of independence for African countries during the 1960s was that a "wind of change was sweeping the continent." From those optimistic times, when development seemed inevitable, to the present we see that there has been change, but not in the direction that was expected. The new popular phrase used to characterize Africa is "crisis."[2]

As Parpart and Staudt point out, "Only in Africa has per capita food production declined in the last two decades. Gains have been made in health care, housing, and education, but crisis threatens them all" (1989:2). Sub-Saharan Africa, Ravenhill states, is "suffering an economic crisis of a magnitude unprecedented in its recent history" (quoted in Parpart and Staudt 1989:2). The UN recently announced that six countries face the immediate possibility of mass starvation, and seventeen others are in danger.

The crisis is manifold in its dimensions. A major dimension is a continually high fertility rate combined with a lower mortality rate because of improving health care. Lesthaeghe observes that "sub-Saharan demographic growth is currently breaking all records with rates of 2.5 to 4.0 percent in most areas" (Lesthaeghe 1989:8).

These catastrophes identify the crises; the causes are less clear. The fragile nature of African states and their multi-ethnic complexions appear to be part of the root problem. Notwithstanding the element of drama that makes us more aware of the repeated coups, assassinations, and civil wars in places like Mali, Sudan, Liberia, Ethiopia, and

77

Mozambique, than of the peaceful relations elsewhere, the political histories of most African states have, indeed, been chaotic.[3]

I begin this paper with these bleak references to the present condition of Africa as a kind of *mea culpa*. Crises of the order of magnitude that I have alluded to seem too complex to confront, especially considering the difficulty of generalizing about Africa because of the diversity there in almost every dimension of social analysis. Also, crises call for public policy responses rather than analysis, although we might argue that response in place of analysis may be a part of the problem.

I propose to examine the relationship of ethnic diversity, and to some extent population, to the crisis of statehood. Bernstein and Campbell have argued that "the concrete analysis of concrete situations" might contribute to a "knowledge of Africa that is adequate to its profoundly contradictory realities" (1985:7-8, quoted in Graf 1988:xi). In other words, we need more concrete studies before we offer any general theory. Yet, we are aware that such studies are problematic in their degree of objectivity, no matter how concrete they may be. Exposing our assumptions is one of the ameliorating conditions we can bring to our study.

I begin by briefly describing certain propositions, which less grandly should probably be called "assumptions" that inform the basis for my study. Second, I offer two pairings of concrete situations; one at the macro level of the state, comparing Nigeria and Somalia; and one at the micro level of small communities in Nigeria and Cameroon. Finally, I assess how well the propositions I put forth have held up in the light of comparative-evolutionary studies.

Propositions

My first proposition refers to a generally held, almost commonsensical view, of the inverse relationship between ethnicity and state stability. In this view, inter-ethnic relations are seen to contradict the kind of social interaction that would support and respond to an ideology of nationhood, or at least a sense of the state that goes beyond "tribal" boundaries. Generally speaking, ethnic conflict is the independent variable in this equation; civil wars, military coups, and the overall chaotic condition found in African states are the dependent variables.

My second proposition pertains to the relationship of the past to the present. Here I am referring to the significance of culture—conceptually speaking—for interpreting the ethnic versus state conundrum. The culture concept, on the one hand, refers to the way individuals cognitively construct or translate events in terms of the past. Essentially, this refers to a filtering of experience through a sieve of accepted meanings, rather than comprehension based on "objective facts." On the other hand, the culture concept refers to the historical process of people reformulating, restructuring, and inventing or reinventing both past and present. How the latter is to be understood (which, of course, is also a product of the experiential filtering I just mentioned) depends on theory, whether you place an emphasis on biological, material, ecological, economic, ideological or other factors. The interpretation I shall explore here will be an evolutionary one.

Nigeria and Somalia

Nigeria and Somalia both became independent in the same year, 1960. Hardly another similarity can be found, except that both have undergone civil or near-civil wars and bloody military coups. Nigeria, with a population estimated to be over 100 million,[4] is by far the largest country in Africa; Somalia may have 4 million to 8 million people; Nigeria is the world's sixth-largest producer of oil and one of the wealthiest countries; Somalia is one of the poorest and one of the six countries referred to earlier as being on the verge of a massive famine. Somalia was of strategic interest during the Cold War; it has now lost even that advantage.

I chose to compare these two countries because of another major difference between the two. Nigeria is the quintessential heterogeneous state, including anywhere from 250 to 340 different linguistic-cultural divisions; major religious divisions among Christian, Moslem, and indigenous religions; major differences in forms of social organization and pre-colonial types of political systems; urban and rural; highly educated and non-literate segments of the population; and so on. Somalia is the only African country that contains a homogeneous population (Lewis 1988:196; Cassanelli 1982:3). Ethnically and linguistically the people are Somalian; the predominate religion is Islam; the pervasive occupation is herding; and the clan structure represents a nation in the throes of defining its state boundaries (Laitin and Samatar 1987; Selassie 1980:97).

It would appear that the conflicts affecting Somalia should not properly be called "inter-ethnic" if the people are all of one ethnic group. I shall return to this contradiction below. The story of British colonial control in Nigeria is especially well known because the colonial administrative structure is frequently cited as one of contributing causes to the ethnic conflicts that followed independence. According to this interpretation, the British achieved and maintained their administrative control by dividing the country into three regions. Each region roughly coincided with a major ethnic category: the Hausa-Fulani in the North, the Yoruba in the West, and the Igbo in the East. This divide-and-conquer strategy was the legacy for a new state that carried ethnic animosities to their natural climax in the Hausa-Fulani pogroms against the Igbo living among them, and the Biafra War in response to the Igbo attempt to secede.

This rather simplistic view of colonial history should not mask the extraordinary impact of European control. After all, Nigeria was not a political entity until it was invented by European powers at the turn of the century. Without taking the time to offer a detailed and more complex view of Nigerian history, there are, however, two aspects of this tripartite division that are worth describing. First, the division was not into three equal parts. The Northern Region was larger physically, and, presumably, in population size than the other two regions combined. The subsequent political domination by the North, and the politicization of demographic data, which resulted in false censuses or disqualification of accurate ones, are also the products of colonial strategies. Constitutional changes over the years have transformed the three regions into thirty-one states, and there is renewed promise that the next census will be both honest and publishable.[5]

Second, colonial administration differed in each of the three regions because of the differences the British found in Hausa-Fulani, Yoruba, and Igbo political systems. The Hausa-Fulani and the Yoruba conformed to a system of indirect rule, whereby the indigenous hierarchical structures could be kept intact by simply taking control of the head. The Yoruba were less stratified than the Hausa-Fulani, but their separate chiefdoms recognized a historic commonality in their allegiance to a single place of origin. The Igbo presented a problem to colonial administators because Igbo communities, which ranged in size from a few hundred to twenty thousand inhabitants, were largely organized in egalitarian fashion, with decisions made by consensus, and with no central administrative organization. The other, smaller, populations in these regions varied in degree of centralized authority along the continuum ranging from the traditions of the Hausa-Fulani to the Igbo.

In Somalia, a civil war ended in late January, 1991 with the overthrow of President Mohammed Siad Barre. No one replaced him initially, and the country was reported to be in near anarchy (NY Times, April 4, 1991). The roots of the conflict were also attributed to colonial rule, as in Nigeria, and, according to news reports, to "the most deeply felt [clan hostilities] on the continent."

During the colonial period present-day Somali was divided in two: Italian Somaliland to the south, and British Somaliland to the north. After World War II, Italy lost all its colonies, but in 1950 the former Italian colony was placed under a UN trusteeship administered by Italy (Hess 1966). British Somaliland retained its colonial status until independence, when the two colonies were united. For a nine-year period following independence, Somali practiced a parliamentary democracy that "was widely regarded as being derived from the traditional right of every man to be heard. The national ideal professed by the Somalis was one of political and legal equality in which historic Somali values and acquired Western practices appeared to coincide" (Nelson 1982:35). The colonial heritage, however, left two institutionally separate countries (Laitin and Samatar 1987). Italy and Britain had developed separate administrative, legal, and educational systems. Not only were there different exchange rates for their currencies, but the languages for public affairs, the police and taxes were also different (Nelson 1982:35, Laitin and Samatar 1977). After independence in 1960, "dissatisfaction at the distribution of power among the clan-families and between the two regions" resulted in a military coup in 1961 by British-trained junior army officers in the north. In 1969 another coup brought Major General Barre to the presidency.

Somali is seen as unique among Africa countries because of the inclusion of a single cultural entity within national boundaries. As I implied, however, by my references to clans, cultural commonalities do not preclude social divisions. The Somali are divided into two main branches, the Samaal and the Sab, which are different linguistically, socially, and politically. According to I. M. Lewis (1961), the Samaal nomads practice a "pastoral democracy" without permanent chiefs, and where all adult males in the clan or lineage group participate in reaching a consensus. The Sab confederated themselves under the leadership of a dominant lineage that held title to the land and defined themselves by the area in which they lived as well as by ties of kinship (Nelson 1982:9). The Samaal and the Igbo on the one hand, and the Sab and Yoruba on the other illustrate roughly parallel political processes.

Another source of conflict in Somali was the competition for land, either between herders and farmers, or between different groups of herders searching for new grazing areas for their animals. Conflicts were articulated by the lineage structure. Those involved recruited their support at the furthest point of descent that separated them. Six clans are the principal demarcators, or, to put it in political terms, are the non-state institutions for regulating social relations among its members and for waging war with others.

Quite clearly, Somali, like Nigeria and most of the rest of the continent, was not a reservoir of peaceful and contented people who arrived at their present state of political discontent solely through the machinations of colonial rule. The colonial experience of both countries undoubtedly exacerbated social divisions within each. For purposes of comparison and analysis we can see that these divisions, whether identified as ethnic, clan, race, or religion, are functionally similar even though each label may require specific consideration.

Ijo and Galim

Turning now from state comparisons to a more micro-societal level, I will sketch two communities that resemble the homogeneous versus heterogeneous ethnic constitutions of Nigeria and Somali. The Ijo in Nigeria consist of a relatively homogeneous population, with internal differences reminiscent of the Somali case; the chiefdom of Galim in the Cameroun seems more like the Nigerian case in general, and similar to some combination of the Hausa-Fulani and Yoruba societies in particular.

The Ijo are the eighth largest ethnic category in Nigeria, with a population of over one million people, who largely occupy the Niger Delta area. Linguistically and culturally they have a common origin that separates them from neighboring populations of Igbo, Urhobo, and Isoko. Political integration, however, never extended beyond village or clan boundaries. A major division in the population is found in the way Ijo polities in the eastern part of the delta developed into "city-states," in contrast to Ijo groups elsewhere that did not.

Hardly "cities," these island communities evolved from fishing settlements into economic and political organizations referred to as Houses. These entities used their geographical position to monopolize the trade with Europeans for slaves and, later, for palm nut products. This hierarchy of heads of Houses, and a royal head chosen from among them, was tempered in two respects. First, the basis for action rested on the need to derive communal consensus from the adult males, a value found throughout Ijo society, which continued to legitimize the decisions of the king and heads of Houses. Second, trading activities placed a premium on achievement, which, when combined with the Ijo practice of incorporating non-Ijo into their social system through cultural assimilation, enabled former slaves to become heads of Houses (Horton 1969; Jones 1963).

Cultural familiarity did not prevent Ijo houses from fighting each other in the eastern delta. In the central and other parts of the delta, villages and kin groups did not hesitate to settle a dispute with armed force. The Ijo looked with some trepidation at the coming of independence, as did many other minority groups in Nigeria. Groups that they had dominated, such as the Igbo, were now in a position to dominate them. Because of competition with other ethnic groups for political positions and economic rewards, the post-colonial period saw a striving for Ijo political unification that had not been manifested before (Hollos and Leis 1989).

Like Nigeria and Somalia, the United Republic of Cameroon also became independent in 1960. Cameroon is divided between north and south, as are so many other African countries. People in the north are predominantly Moslems; in the south they practice Christian or African religions. Islam is not only the dominant religion in northern Cameroon, but it also signifies a political tradition of conquest. The Fulani, carrying forward a *jihad*, established kingdoms wherever their calvary enabled them to subjugate the indigeous populations.

In Galim, a small community of a few thousand people on the Adamoua Plateau, the local population, called the Nyam-Nyam, was able to defend itself by retreating to nearby mountains. After the Germans and then the French established colonial control, the Nyam-Nyam were able to assume the headship of the territory of Galim. By then the Nyam-Nyam had acquired the political organization introduced by their enemies. Thus the *lamido* (the Fulani word for chief), and the appearances and rituals of the court were now performed by the Nyam-Nyam and accepted by the several ethnic groups, including the Fulani, occupying Galim. It is significant that the Nyam-Nyam *lamido* presented himself as a Moslem, but he still interacted with his own people in their language and ruled on breeches of customary law (Leis 1970).

The ethnic divisions within Galim included Nyam-Nyam, Fulani, Mbororo, and a number of others, and these were manifested not only in language but also in the division of labor. The Nyam-Nyam, male and female, were the sedentary farmers; the Fulani and Hausa were the traders and religious teachers; the Mbororo were the nomadic herders. The major conflict was between farmers and herders. Herders allowed their cattle to trample farms, or they set fire to fields to produce new sprouts for their herds to feed on, and burned the farmers' granaries in the process. Residents described these conflicts in the idiom of ethnic conflict because ethnicity and occupation were coincident. At the same time, within the domain of the colonial and independent nation regimes, the various populations gave their allegiance to the chiefdom in the person of the *lamido*.

Discussion

A few select examples cannot speak for much more than themselves. I am not pretending to use them to infer that they provide a sample of African societies *per se*. However, even on an anecdotal level at worst, and at a middle-range level of theory at best, limited comparisons of particular variables in special cases may enable us to reexamine and extend our understanding of ethnic conflict. The propositions I put forward earlier can now be restated. The first assigns the problem of national integration in African states to the pervasiveness of ethnic conflict. The second proposes that the configuration of past and present offers an evolutionary view of national integration in terms of the adaptiveness of culture.

These two propositions touch on a long-standing argument over whether ethnicity should be accepted as a "primordial" principle in human relations; or whether ethnicity is a product of those relations, especially conflicting relations; or whether ethnicity is a false consciousness for class and material interests.

Clifford Geertz defines "primordial attachment [as] one that stems from the...assumed 'givens' of social existence: immediate contiguity and kin connection mainly...These congruities of blood, speech, custom, and so on, are seen to have an ineffable, and at times overpowering, coerciveness in and out of themselves" (1963:109). Although he acknowledges that primordial sentiments are stimulated by the state itself because of the rewards the state offers, those sentiments are inherently contradictory to "the doctrine that legitimate authority is but an extension of the inherent moral coerciveness such sentiments possess...[T]o permit oneself to be ruled by men of other tribes, other races, or other religions is to submit not merely to oppression but to degradation..."(Gertz 1963:127).

Barth (1969), Abner Cohen (1969), Parkin (1974), Joseph (1987) and others take a contrary view. They see ethnicity as a cultural system that sets group boundaries. Ethnicity is the product rather than the cause of conflict. The colonial regimes of Nigeria and Somalia did more, in other words, than stimulate latent hostilities; the regionalization of both countries produced conflicts which, indeed, used categorical cultural differences, but elevated them to the arena of divisive ethnic politics.

The difference between primordial sentiments and cultural systems is perhaps more exaggerated than it needs to be. The term "primordial" is an unfortunate one because it conjures up the image of a pre-cultural condition in human evolution. In fact, Geertz is stressing that the human condition is a cultural one, whereby the "givens" are as symbolically constructed as any other facet of human behavior, only more so, because the symbols are treated as natural facts. In *Ethnic Groups in Conflict* (1985), Horowitz offers the social-psychological basis for such a construction by emphasizing the human striving for identity and security. A similar thesis found in political psychology states that human societies "need" enemies in the same way that individuals need others to develop the self (Volkan 1985). From this point of view, the emphasis is on societal divisions, whether called ethnic, religious, or by some other label. The Somalia case, in other words, is analytically similar to the Nigerian one because of the oppositions found within the Somalia segmentary lineages. At first blush, it would appear that the cases I have presented here offer contradictory examples for determining the relationship between ethnicity and conflict. Ethnic pluralism could be said to induce conflicts, as in the case of Nigeria, but not in the case of Galim; whereas ethnic singularity does not avoid conflict, as in the cases of Somalia and the Ijo.

If Horowitz helps clarify what is meant by primordial sentiments, and thereby softens the distinction between them and cultural systems as ways of understanding ethnic conflicts in nation-states, he strengthens the objection to linking ethnic conflict to class consciousness. Instead of treating ethnic competition as a "false consciousness," manipulated by colonial administrations and the elite in African independent countries to hide their economic motives, Horowitz argues that ethnic competition for psychic status does not always promote a people's economic self-interest. In this sense, unlike the cultural system theorists, ethnic competition is not just a strategy for defining boundaries and competing for valued goods; there is an intensity to ethnic conflict and a continuity that requires explanation.

The explanation I wish to advance refers to the cultural system interpretation, but it adds an historical dimension to it that satisfies the established condition of an ethnocentric orientation. The way information about social relations in a political context is processed, whether defined by ethnicity *per se*, or by religion, language, or so on, gives it its effective strength. This processing, which I referred to in the second proposition I mentioned earlier, occurs within an ever-changing interpretation of the present through history, and of history from the present.

We can look at the effects of history in two ways. One is to examine the evolution of political systems in Africa. The other is to trace the continuity of particular systems. The two examine the same events but at different levels of analysis. From an evolutionary point of view, the question is how and why nation-states develop in the first place. In Africa the quest for the origins of pre-colonial states has invoked a corpus of scholarly research, and a strong rejection of such endeavors because of the unreliability of historical data.

In place of conjectures, scholars have substituted a comparative approach that lists the social structural conditions associated with state formation. Fortes and Evans-Pritchard (1940), comparing eight African societies in one of the earliest such classifications, found that total population, rather than population density, identified centralized societies and their use of administrative organizations and coercive force in contrast to non-centralized societies. They found no support for what they called "mode of livelihood," or for conquest as significant conditions. The other contrasting variables tended to describe the constituent characteristics of the dual typology rather than to suggest conditions pursuant to state formation. Another difference they offer between the two types of political systems is the way in which they responded—or might be expected to respond—to colonial rule. They hypothesized that societies with paramount rulers would remain stable since the colonial power reinforced traditional authority. Non-centralized societies, on the other hand, which they identify as societies with segmentary lineages, whose structure of mutually balancing segments is exercised by the conflicts between lineage segments, would collapse because of the colonial powers' restraint on the direct resort to force. They saw such societies as readily accepting bureaucratic European structures and becoming "more like that of a centralized state" (Fortes and Evans-Pritchard 1940: 16). This prediction has not been fulfilled, but I believe it has an important bearing on the development of the modern African state, which I shall turn to in a moment.

Much more recent studies of early states, one by Shifferd (1987) comparing twenty-two early states, most of them in Africa, and one by Tymowski (1987) on the early state in the western Sudan, put forward a challenge-and-response kind of hypothesis. They are reminiscent of Toynbee's thesis that the environmental challenge of the flooding Nile produced the social and religious innovations that gave rise to the Egyptian administrative hierarchies. Thus the African states that rose and fell over a period of a thousand years are seen as responding, or not responding, to pressures of the natural environment, demographic pressures, and the opportunities afforded for controlling local markets and long-range trading (Tymowski 1987:63). One challenge Shifferd finds that is important to our investigation is that of a diverse population (1987:42). The incorporation of ethnic groups, in other words, rather than dividing the society, was an impetus to the development of centralizing socio-political structures.

Summarizing these comparative-evolutionary studies we find: (1) there were broad differences in the types of political systems found in Africa before colonial control; (2) centralized systems may develop because of, rather than despite, ethnic diversity; and (3) segmentary lineage systems may be more prone than centralized systems to adapt to the modern form of the bureaucratic state.

The significance of particular histories for shaping modern-day responses is illustrated by Richard Joseph's *Democracy and Prebendal Politics in Nigeria* (1987). He defines the term "prebendal" as "patterns of political behaviour which rest on the justifying principle that such offices should be competed for and then utilized for the personal benefit of office holders as well as of their reference or support group" (1987:8). Joseph finds that prebendal politics describes not only the national Nigerian scene, but also the kind of domain that operates within certain ethnic groups. In this respect he quotes J.D.Y. Peel's study (Peel 1983) of the Ijesha people of the Yoruba: "...while the material ends of politics are so contemporary, the framework of action within which they are sought show continuity with the past. The Ijesha have, as it were, chosen to make their history relevant to their politics" (Joseph 1987:197). Joseph concludes that "the predicament of African states can thus be seen to be the fact that the conduct of public affairs has deep historical and social roots, which reflect a rationality of thought and action which becomes distorted and destructive in the wider political arenas" (Joseph 1987:197).

In combining Joseph's analysis with the evolutionary conclusions I mentioned earlier, I find that the problem in developing viable African nation-states can be attributed in no small part to colonial regimes. However, the thesis I put forward here is that the problem was not regionalism and its attendant stimulation of primordial sentiments. Rather, colonialism, and the neo-colonialisms which followed independence, are more supportive, morally and politically, of the Hausa-Fulani, Yoruba, and Galim type of political systems, than of the egalitarian—"democratic"—type found in Igbo, Ijo, and Somalia societies. The prebendal domain common to the former type worked for the pre-colonial states. Perhaps they succeeded too well and contributed to their failure to evolve into what has been referred to as the Mature State, otherwise known as an idealized form of the European nation-state.

The transformation of stateless societies to democratic, modern-day rational-bureaucratic ones was anticipated, theoretically, by Fortes and Evans-Pritchard. Somalia came close to illustrating the possibility on a state level, the Ijo on a more communal level. Colonial competition between Britian and Italy, and post-colonial competition between the United States and the Soviet Union helped ensure that Somalia would not fulfill its democratic potential. The dominance in Nigeria of societies that interpret modern day politics through the historical structures of prebendal domains provide a formidable barrier to a historical conception of politics based on democratic relations.

Notes

1. A preliminary version of this paper was read to the Working Group: Race, Ethnicity, and Demography of a conference titled, North-South/East-West: Establishing a Common Agenda; Thomas J. Watson Jr. Institute for International Studies, Brown University, April 9, 1991. I am grateful for the critical comments offered by the participants, but I am fully responsible for the final product. Socio-political changes after 1991 are not included.

2. Any generalization about "Africa" has to be qualified continuously. I shall attempt to be geographically specific in all of my discussion.

3. There are exceptions to this dismal picture. In early 1991, two countries, The Republic of Cape Verde and Mauritius, had their presidents replaced by heads of opposition parties in free elections, although both of these countries are islands off the coast of the continent. Since this paper was presented, successful government transitions have occurred in Benin, Sao Tome and Principe, and Zambia. An even more emphatic exception to the crisis viewpoint is offered by Pierre Pradervand, based on his study of five countries, Senegal, Zimbabwe, Burkina Faso, Mali, and Kenya, during 1977 to 1987. He believes "the overwhelmingly positive development in African villages have, for years, remained the best-kept secret in the world development arena" (1989: xvi). However, this exception, like those illustrated by awards to the communal farmers of Zimbabwe and the Iringa of Tanzania from The Alan Shawn Feinstein World Hunger Program at Brown University, seem to prove the rule that the viable social-political units in Africa do not extend beyond the village or regional level. These units succeed in promoting food production or nutritional support programs despite the crisis of state formation.

4. The 1991 Nigerian Census, announced after the Working Group met earlier that year, revealed a total population of 88.5 million people, approximately 20 million fewer than had been estimated.

5. Ibid.

References

Barth, Frederick. 1969. *Ethnic Groups and Boundaries: The Social Organization of Culture Difference.* Boston: Little, Brown and Co.

Bernstein, Henry and Bonnie Campbell. 1985. "Introduction." In *Contradictions of Accumulation in Africa,* edited by Henry Bernstein and Bonnie Campbell. Beverly Hills: Sage Publications.

Cassanelli, Lee V. 1982. *The Shaping of Somali Society: Reconstructing the History of a Pastoral People, 1600-1900.* Philadelphia: University of Pennsylvania Press.

Cohen, Abner. 1969. *Custom and Politics in Urban Africa.* London: Routledge and Kegan Paul.

Fortes, M. and Evans-Pritchard, E.E. 1940. "Introduction." In *African Political Systems,* edited by M. Fortes and E.E. Evans-Pritchard. London: Oxford University Press :1-23.

Geertz, Clifford. 1963. "The Integrative Revolution: Primordial Sentiments and Civil Politics in the New States." In *Old Societies and New States,* edited by Clifford Geertz. London: Free Press of Glencoe.

Graf, William D. 1988. *The Nigerian State.* London: James Currey.

Hess, Robert L. 1966. *Italian Colonialism in Somalia.* Chicago: University of Chicago Press.

Hollos, Marida and Philip E. Leis. 1989. *Becoming Nigerian in Ijo Society.* New Brunswick: Rutgers University Press.

Horowitz, Donald L. 1985. *Ethnic Groups in Conflict.* Berkeley: University of California Press.

Horton, Robin. 1969. "From Fishing Village to City-State: A Social History of New Calabar." In *Man in Africa,* edited by Mary Douglas and Phyllis M. Kaberry. London: Tavistock Publications.

Jones, G.I. 1963. *The Trading States of the Oil Rivers.* London: Oxford University Press.

Joseph, Richard A. 1937. *Democracy and Prebendal Politics in Nigeria: The Rise and Fall of the Second Republic.* Cambridge: CUP.

Laitin, David D. and Said S. Samatar. 1977. *Politics, Language, and Thought: The Somali Experience.* Chicago: University of Chicago Press.

Laitain, David D. and Said S. Samatar. 1987. *Somalia: Nation in Search of a State.* Boulder: Westview Press.

Leis, Philip E. 1970. "Accommodation in a Plural Chiefdom Cameroun." *Man* 5 : 671-685.

Lesthaeghe, Ron J. 1989. *Reproduction and Social Organization in Sub-Saharan Africa.* Berkeley: University of California Press.

Lewis, I.M. 1961. *A Pastoral Democracy: A Study of Pastoralism and Politics among the Northern Somali of the Horn of Africa.* London: Oxford University Press.

_____. 1988. *A Modern History of Somalia; Nation and State in the Horn of Africa.* Revised. Boulder: Westview Press.

Nelson, Harold D. (ed.) 1982. *Somalia, a Country Study*. American University: Foreign Area Studies.

Parkin, David. 1974. "Congregational in Interpersonal Ideologies in Political Ethncity." In *Urban Ethnicity*, edited by Abner Cohen. London: Tavistock Publication: 119-157.

Parpart, Jane L. and Kathleen A. Staudt. 1989 . "Women and the State in Africa." In *Women and the State in Africa*, edited by Jane L. Parpart and Kathleen A. Staudt. Boulder: Lynne Rienner : 1-19.

Peel, J.D.Y. 1983. *Ijeshas and Nigerians: The Incorporation of a Yoruba Kingdom, 1890s-1970s*. Cambridge: Cambridge University Press.

Pradervand, Pierre. 1989. *Listening to Africa: Developing Africa from the Grassroots*. NY: Praeger.

Selassie, Bereket Habte. 1980. *Conflict and Intervention in the Horn of Africa*. New York: Monthly Review Press.

Shifferd, Patricia A. 1987. "Aztecs and Africans: Political Processes in Twenty-Two Early States." In *Early State Dynamics*, edited by Henri J.M. Claessen and Pieter Van De Velde. Leiden: E.J. Brill: 39-53.

Tymowski, Michal. 1987. "The Early State and After in Precolonial West Sudan; Problems of the Stability of Political Organizations and the Obstacles to Their Development." In *Early State Dynamics*, edited by Henri J.M. Claessen and Pieter Van De Velde. Leiden: E.J. Brill: 54-69.

Volkan, Vamik D. 1985. "The Need to Have Enemies and Allies: A Developmental Approach." *Political Psychology* 6, no. 2: 219-247.

5

Fact and Myth: Discovering
a Racial Problem in Brazil[1]

Thomas E. Skidmore

Every Brazilian and every perceptive visitor knows that racial terms are not clearly defined in that society. The lesson is especially striking for North Americans and Europeans, who are used to a conventional black/white (or, at least, white/nonwhite) dichotomy. That polarization was institutionalized in U.S. racial segregation, a polarity that Europeans, unused to home-country contact with nonwhites in the modern era, instinctively understood.

But Brazil, like most of Latin America, is different. In the Caribbean and Latin America the European colonizers left a legacy of multi-racialism, in spite of early attempts to enforce racial endogamy, i.e., the prohibition of marriage outside the same racial category. Multiracial meant more than two racial categories—at a minimum, three. The mulatto and the mestizo became the "middle caste," with considerable numbers attaining free legal status, even under slave systems. The result was a system of social stratification that differed sharply from the rigid color bifurcation in the U.S. (both before and after slavery) and in Europe's African colonies. There was and is a color (here standing for a collection of physical features) spectrum on which clear lines were often not drawn. Between a "pure" black and a very light mulatto there are numerous gradations, as reflected in the scores of racial labels (many pejorative) in common Brazilian usage.

This is not to say that Brazilian society is not highly color conscious. In fact, Brazilians, like most Latin Americans, are more sensitive to variations in physical features than white North Americans or Europeans. This results from the fact that variations along the color spectrum, especially in the middle range, are considered significant, since there is no clear dividing line.

The question of accurate color terminology is especially difficult when discussing Brazil. The terms used in the Brazilian census—*preto, pardo* and *branco*—translate literally as "black," "brown," and "white." The principal distinction in this paper will be between white and nonwhite, the latter including *preto* and *pardo*. To designate the latter, i.e., nonwhite, the term used here will be "Afro-Brazilian" rather than "black," since *preto* (the literal Portuguese translation of "black") is a far more restrictive (often pejorative) label in Brazil. The increasingly common term used in Brazil (in the mass media, for example) for nonwhite is *negro,* but the English equivalent is archaic for an English-speaking audience. It should also be noted that *negro* is the label which Afro-Brazilian militants use in their campaign to convince all Brazilian nonwhites, above all mulattos, to "assume" their color and not succumb to the belief, à la the whitening ideology, that a lighter nonwhite can hope for greater social mobility.

In sum, Brazil is multiracial, not biracial. This makes its race relations more complex than in the U.S. and more complex than most Europeans expect. The most important fact about this multiracial society, from the standpoint of those wishing to study it, is that until fifteen years ago there were virtually no quantitative data with which to analyze it. Between 1890 and 1940 neither the Brazilian government nor Brazilian social scientists considered race to be a significant enough variable to justify recording it in the national census. Even when race was later included, as in 1950 and 1960, until the 1976 household survey Pesquisa Nacional por Amostra de Domicílios (PNAD) there were no data by race on income, education, health, and housing (there were limited data on marriage, fertility and morbidity).

Discussion about Brazilian race relations was therefore invariably based on "soft" data. History and anthropology were the two main intellectual approaches used. Historians dwelt on laws, travellers' accounts, memoirs, parliamentary debates, and newspaper articles. They avoided researching police records, health archives, court records, personnel files and other sources from which they might have constructed time series. When they did consult such sources, it was usually to study slavery. They seldom studied race relations in the larger society.

TABLE 5.1 Racial Composition of the Brazilian Population

Year	Branco (white)	Pardo (brown)	Preto (black)
1835	24.4	18.2	51.4
1872	38.1	42.2	19.7
1890	44.0	41.4	14.6
1940	63.5	21.2	14.7
1950	61.7	26.5	11.0
1960	61.0	29.5	8.7
1980	54.8	38.4	5.9

Source: Fiola 1990. "Pardo" is often taken to mean "mulatto" in Brazil but not always. It is also sometimes used to refer to other mixed bloods.

The telling anecdote remained the accepted form of evidence. Nonetheless, historians did not hesitate to draw conclusions about the historical nature of race relations. But to do so they had to lean heavily on "qualitative" evidence.

Anthropologists produced a rich literature describing many dimensions of relations among and within distinguishable racial categories, often emphasizing the subtle distinctions. Inevitably, however, their picture remained particularistic. They could not tell us whether race made a macro difference in educational attainment, or income, or professional advancement. They were not, after all, sociologists. We cannot consult their monographs for statistics on which to base verifiable judgements about relative social welfare in Brazil.

Sociologists, demographers, economists, and political scientists, from whom we might expect such analysis, were disarmed. They had no data. The government collected no information and analysts made virtually no effort to generate their own. Why?

The answer lies in the way Brazilians have looked at their own society. We begin with certain facts about that society in the last century and a half. First, as we have seen, it was multiracial. There was no clear-cut racial line, either legally or in social practice. For someone from the U.S. or South Africa (or virtually any European colony in Africa), the chief defining feature was the lack of a "descent rule."[2] Racial category was not defined exclusively by ancestry, but by a combination of factors, including physical appearance, apparent station in life, and, to a limited extent, ancestry.[3] This contrasts with the U.S. or South Africa, where race was defined by descent and certified in legal records. The latter were then used to enforce racial endogamy with such laws only being declared unconstitutional in the U.S. in 1967.[4] No such laws existed in modern Brazil.

Second, despite the lack of a clear "color line," Brazilian society was based on an explicit belief in white superiority, although not white supremacy. The distinction is crucial. To understand it we must go back to the colonial era.

Although Portuguese racial attitudes in the colonial era need more study, we can say that white stood at the apex of the social scale and African at the bottom. But the Portuguese in Brazil differed from the English in North America. In the English continental colonies the colonists transformed the social superiority into a doctrine of moral superiority (later "white supremacy") and institutionalized it in legalized rules enforcing racial endogamy. This structure hardened after the Civil War into the Jim Crow system, which became easy to enforce because of the rigid biracial categorization that had become fixed long before abolition. It was also reinforced by the rise of scientific racism, which came to dominate U.S. and European academic and elite circles after the mid-nineteenth century. These "scientific" theories purported to prove, by physical, historical, biological, or behaviorial evidence, the superiority of whites. This prejudice was later to produce a politically significant backlash in the U.S. as white guilt—the product of a religious perfectionism and a philosophical egalitarianism, both absent in Portuguese America—led white U.S. citizens eventually to accept racial integration for an Afro-American minority one quarter proportionally the size of Brazil's.

Brazil never had the option, at least after the mid-colonial era, to enforce racial endogamy, or its implicit biracial assumptions, because too many persons of color (primarily mixed bloods) had entered free society—by birth or manumission. Relatively few had penetrated to the top of the society (the exact pattern of such mobility cries out for research and analysis), yet the moral and social legitimacy for drawing a sharp color line was already lost. Enforced racial endogamy and segregation were practical impossibilities.

To deal with this reality, the Brazilian elite had developed an assimilationist ideology to rationalize their *de facto* multiracial society. Although they believed in white superiority, as could be clearly seen in the parliamentary debates over the slave trade in the early nineteenth century, they did not express the same deep fears of being overwhelmed demographically (and eventually politically) by nonwhites as did their U.S. counterparts. This is ironical, since by the mid-nineteenth century the nonwhite proportion of the population in Brazil was far larger than in the U.S. (Table 5.1).

This *de facto* assimilationist ideology faced a severe challenge when the doctrines of scientific racism struck Brazil, especially after 1870.5 How could the Brazilians reconcile their multiracial society and its implicit assimilationist assumptions with the "new truth" that white was not only absolutely superior, but that it faced a mortal challenge from what white supremacists in North America and Europe called "mongrelization?"

The Brazilian elite offered an ingenious response. They turned on its head the basic assumption of the white supremacists. They accepted the doctrine of innate white superiority, but they then argued that in Brazil the white was prevailing through miscegenation. Instead of "mongrelizing" the race, racial mixing was "whitening" Brazil. Miscegenation, far from a menace, was Brazil's salvation. Since they had no means of proving this scientifically, Brazilians simply asserted that Brazilian experience substantiated their claim. It gained its most famous rationale in Gilberto Freyre's claim6 that the unique cultural legacy of the Portuguese had turned Brazilians into a new race (which in practice had precious few dark-skinned at or near the top).

This assimilationist ideology, commonly called "whitening" by the elite after 1890,7 had taken hold by the early twentieth century, and continues to be Brazil's predominant racial ideology today. In effect, the Brazilian elite argued that Brazil, unlike the U.S. to which they frequently (and unfavorably) compared it, had no racial problem: no U.S. phenomena of race hatred (the logical product of the white supremacy doctrine), racial segregation and, most important, racial discrimination. In a word, Brazil had escaped racism. It was on the path to producing a single race through the benign process of miscegenation. The unrestrained libido of the Portuguese, along with his cultural "plasticity," had produced a fortuitous racial harmony. Brazil, thanks to historical forces of which it had not even been conscious, had been saved from the ugly stain of racism.8

The implication of this ideology was that color did not matter in Brazil. Racial difference was on its way to extinction. Leading Brazilian scientists in the early twentieth century freely predicted that their country was headed toward total whiteness. In a paper presented in London in 1911, the Brazilian anthropologist João Batista de Lacerda9 estimated it would take no more than another century. Upon returning to Brazil he was attacked for being too pessimistic.

In practice, the assimilationist assumption led the government to take a revealing step: it omitted race from the census. Although race had been included in the census of 1872 (the first) and of 1890, it was omitted in 1900 and 1920 (there was no census in 1910 and 1930), only reappearing in the 1940 census. From 1890 to 1940, therefore, the basic data collection ignored racial categories in the New World country which had received more African slaves than any other.10

Since there were no data, there could be no discussion of the facts of race relations. Exactly how did relations among people of different color proceed? Even if the color spectrum were blurred, even if there was no legally enforced racial endogamy, even if there was no segregation, was race—despite all the subtleties of its definition—insignificant in Brazilian lives? Could the largest slave population in the New World (total abolition came only in 1888, latest in the Americas) have left no legacy of racial antagonism?

The Social Reality: 1890-1976

How could slavemaster and government violence—amply documented by Brazilian historians—have been transformed into such a benign scene? Historians have by and large avoided even investigating the question. One can count on the fingers of one hand the Brazilian authors who have done serious research on post-abolition race relations. It is as if the topic of race ceased to have any relevance in Brazil after slavery ended in 1888.

Yet evidence for such research is readily at hand. Virtually every court record, police blotter, personnel file, driver's license and voter's registration card has, at least until recently, included a racial category. Newspaper stories have routinely identified Afro-Brazilians (whites do not need identification). There have even been separate beauty contests for mulattos. In truth, Brazil has remained a highly race conscious society. Popular music, television, folklore, humor, and literature are saturated with references to race. For anyone who has lived in Brazil in this century, there can be little doubt that awareness of racial categories is a staple of everyday life.

But historians have focused virtually all their attention on the institution of slavery and its abolition. Even race relations (in the broadest sense) *before* abolition have come in for little attention. The all-important topic of free coloreds in slave-holding Brazil, for example, has not been researched extensively. Yet it is the key to understanding the emergence of the most important feature of modern Brazilian race relations: its multiracial nature. A prime example is the attempt to explain how the middle racial category emerged in Brazilian history. The U.S. historian Carl Degler pointed to the "mulatto escape hatch"11 as the essential difference between North American and Brazilian race relations. Yet when it came to explaining why this "escape" developed in one society and not the other, he chose to emphasize, in what was necessarily a speculative manner, the inferior status of women of the slave-holding class in Portuguese America and therefore of their supposed inability to prevent the acceptance (or even legitimation) of their husbands' illicit mixed-blood offspring.

From the historians we have only a few glimmerings of Brazilian social reality after abolition. Nonetheless, from other sources we know that race mattered greatly. One cannot read the tortured poetry of the late nineteenth-century symbolist poet João da Cruz e Souza without feeling his anguish over the pain of being black. One cannot read the novels of Lima Barreto without being moved by the hypocrisy and contempt with which a talented and ambitious mulatto was treated by early twentieth-century Rio de Janeiro society.[12] One cannot read without shock the graphic accounts of the brutal suppression of the all-black enlisted men's 1910 rebellion against the still standard practice of whipping in the navy[13] or the accounts of relentless police raids against Afro-Brazilian religious cults in the Northeast in the 1920s. In this context one is not surprised to read that one of the first groups to suffer repression at the hands of dictator Getúlio Vargas's police after the coup of 1937 was the fledgling *Frente Negro Brasileiro*.[14]

There can be no doubt that color correlated highly with social stratification in Brazil. No sensible Brazilian would have denied this in 1900 and no sensible Brazil would deny it today. The question is why.

The predominant answer from the elite, and from the social scientists, has been a simple application of the assimilationist thesis. Nonwhites languish far down in the social hierarchy, it is argued, because of class, not race. They are the victims not of discrimination but of their disadvantaged socio-economic background. That, in turn, stems from a combination of factors: the legacy of deprivation under slavery, the resulting disadvantage vis-à-vis the European immigrants who streamed into Brazil after abolition, and the liability of being concentrated in the poorest sector (the countryside) of the poorest region (the Northeast). This has combined to weaken the Afro-Brazilian in the increasingly competitive capitalist economy. It is therefore not surprising, by this logic, that Afro-Brazilians are disproportionately represented at the bottom of the economic and social scale.

The solution, by this reading of the problem, is a logical extension of the assimilationist thesis. Nonwhite poverty will decline as poverty in general declines. The solution to the misfortune of Afro-Brazilians is the same as the solution for all Brazilians: rapid economic growth.

We thus face an interesting paradox when looking at post-1888 Brazilian society. On the one hand, the elite succeeded in imposing its assimilationist ideology, expressed not only in official census policy, but also in the academic research, as we shall see below. On the other hand, Brazilian society exhibited to its writers and its artists, especially the Afro-Brazilians, a social structure that bore the marks of something deeper than mere class. Furthermore, on the functional level—police reports and personnel records—the elite was always careful to track racial categories.

The Debate over Race: 1890-1976

The assimilationist ideology of "whitening" for the last century permeated the rhetoric of politicians, social philosophers and literary mandarins. It has also been common currency among social scientists. It reached its apogee in the widely read writings of Oliveira Vianna, the lawyer-historian who produced an extended apologia for the supposedly superior role of the "Aryan" in Brazilian history.[15] He was echoed in the words of Fernando de Azevedo, doyen of Brazilian sociologists, who in his preface to the 1940 census described Brazil's future thus:

> If we admit that Negroes and Indians are continuing to disappear, both in the successive dilutions of white blood and in the constant process of biological and social selection, and that immigration, especially that of a Mediterranean origin, is not at a standstill, the white man will not only have in Brazil his major field of life and culture in the tropics, but be able to take from old Europe—citadel of the white race—before it passes to other hands, the torch of western civilization to which the Brazilians will give a new and intense light—that of the atmosphere of their own civilization.[16]

Against these prophets of a whitening Brazil there arose a band of (white) articulate dissenters in the 1900-1930 era. In the face of the formidable prestige of North Atlantic scientific racism, these dissenters had the courage to denounce the doctrine of white superiority, as well as white supremacy (the latter having long been anathema in Brazil). Such writers as Manoel Bomfim and Alberto Torres directly challenged racist doctrine.[17] In so far as they defended Brazil against the charge of racial degeneracy, they were welcomed. But they had little effect in undermining the underlying elite faith in whitening. Even the pioneering anthropologist Edgar Roquette-Pinto, who fought to promote the environmentalist concept of "culture" in refutation of the prevailing scientific racism, made little dent on the academic world's underlying endorsement of whitening.

The most interesting voice in this dialogue was Gilberto Freyre, a Northeast-born sociologist-historian-writer who produced the apologia par excellence for the virtues of miscegenation. He argued eloquently, often in response to Oliveira Vianna, for the beneficial and creative effects of the Portuguese colonizer's mixture with the Indian and African. In the 1930s and 1940s he applied with great skill the precepts of his anti-racist mentor, the Columbia University anthropologist Franz Boas (with whom he had studied), to refute the now waning claims of scientific racism. But in the end Freyre's eloquence served primarily to reinforce the whitening ideal by showing how the overwhelmingly white elite had acquired valuable cultural assets from their intimate mixing with the non-European, especially the African. For both Brazilians and non-Brazilians, Freyre became the high priest of racial assimilation in the Portuguese-speaking world. He has remained to this day the intellectual talisman to whom the Brazilian elite turns when refuting any suggestion their society might be racist.

It should be clear why the whitening ideology led politicians and academics alike to believe that race merited little attention either in data collection or in formal discussions about their society. Indeed, one might ask whether their eagerness to ignore race might have masked a fear of facing an obvious doubt: with Brazil's huge nonwhite population (56 percent in the 1890 census) how could they be so certain it would whiten? Might it not go in the opposite direction? In any case, to control the collection of data was to control the society's knowledge of itself. That, in turn, meant control of the nation's public policy agenda.

The indifference to race as a variable gained strength also from explicitly antiracist social scientists who concluded, on the basis of their (primarily anthropological) field research, that race, as it operated in the North American context, had no comparable role in Brazil. One of the earliest was the U.S. sociologist Donald Pierson, whose research in the 1940s on the heavily Afro-Brazilian region of Salvador, Bahia, led him to stress the fluidity of color lines and the mobility of the mulatto.[18] The most outspoken of these researchers was the U.S. anthropologist Marvin Harris, who in the early 1960s argued that Brazilians were so inconsistent in their application of racial categories that no meaningful pattern could be established.[19] This was a skeptical extreme that went well beyond the more scholarly respectable concept of "social race" which he and Charles Wagley had elaborated in the early 1950s in their explanation of Brazilian reality.[20]

But in his hyperbole Harris had merely lapsed into the standard Brazilian excuse for eliminating race from the census: the lack of agreement on the definition of racial categories. This rationalization has been repeatedly invoked to justify abandoning any effort at mapping the complexities of Brazilian racial relations. It was the official explanation for the omission of race in the 1970 census, a decision undoubtedly influenced also by the military government's often expressed aversion to any criticism of Brazil's "racial democracy."

This mentality dies hard in Brazil. In preparing for the 1980 census, authorities attempted once again, despite the easing of military rule, to omit race from the official count. Only vigorous protest from demographers, academics (a new mood and a new generation had emerged, as explained below), Afro-Brazilian militants, and elements of the press forced a reconsideration. Officials backtracked, allowing the inclusion of two questions about color in the 25 percent sample.

In 1983, census researchers in the central government institute Instituto Brasileiro de Geografia e Estatística (the IBGE) produced a highly revealing analysis of this data, the first ever collected on race as a variable in the labor force.[21] The results showed a clear pattern of discrimination against Afro-Brazilians. The president of IBGE refused to allow publication of the study. It did not appear until two years later, on the decision of a new president.[22] This establishment mentality—shared by virtually all politicians, most technocrats and many academics—rovoked three main lines of dissent: (1) the São Paulo school led by anthropology professor Florestan Fernandes; (2) Afro-Brazilian militants; and (3) a new generation of (virtually all white) social scientists, especially demographers.

The São Paulo school was the label given to the Paulista anthropologist Florenstan Fernandes and his students and fellow researchers, Fernando Henrique Cardoso and Octávio Ianni. Their work grew out of a UNESCO-sponsored research project that was the first systematic large-scale analysis of modern day Brazilian race relations. The project also included the Bahian anthropologist Thales de Azevedo and such foreign Brazilianists as Charles Wagley of the U.S. and Roger Bastide of France.

The project began with the objective of investigating the realities of what the outside world had perceived (usually via Gilberto Freyre's writings) as Brazil's "racial democracy." The results of the research were mixed. Wagley, and his students Marvin Harris and Harry Hutchinson, produced monographs that substantiated their concept of "social race," which was perfectly compatible with the assimilationist ideology. Thales de Azevedo's portrait of Bahia,[23] the largest Northeastern state and the area of Brazil's greatest African influence, emphasized the mediating role of the mulatto in that still highly traditional society. Fernandes and his students were critical of the established myth of "racial democracy." This resulted in part from their more radical intellectual background. Both Fernandes and Ianni started from Marxist assumptions, while Cardoso, if sympathetic to Marxist analysis, assumed a more Weberian approach.

Within the São Paulo school, Fernandes (whose principal book in this project was co-authored with Roger Bastide) went farthest in contesting the assimilationist dogma. All these researchers' work began with the assumption that "color prejudice" *did* exist in Brazil. Yet the bulk of the research was historical, mostly concentrating on slavery or the decade immediately thereafter. Even when most critically minded, they seemed reluctant to shift their gaze from the panorama painted by Gilberto Freyre to look extensively at the twentieth century. In 1951, for example, Fernandes and Bastide published a detailed "study project" on "racial prejudice in Sao Paulo." They laid out the guidelines for an ambitious opinion survey, but they took care to qualify their document as on "a purely abstract level."[24] There is no record the project was ever carried out.

Fernandes went on to become the best-known and most influential Brazilian academic critic of the dogma of Brazil's "racial democracy."[25] He coined the memorable phrase that Brazilians exhibit "the prejudice of having no prejudice."[26] He became the most authoritative Brazilian voice arguing that race *was* a significant variable in determining a Brazilian's life chances. Yet neither he nor any of the São Paulo school conducted empirical research to document the message for which they became famous.

The politically motivated dismissal of Fernandes, Cardoso, and Ianni from their University of São Paulo teaching posts in 1968 precluded further research. And there can be no doubt that the cloud of repression imposed by the military after 1968 made field research on race relations virtually impossible. Not only was race omitted from the 1970 census, but government censorship precluded any criticism in the mass media of the image of Brazil's "racial democracy." The U.S. government's Inter-American Foundation, which had made grants to several Afro-Brazilian communities (for consciousness raising and social activism), was unceremoniously expelled from the country.[27]

Interestingly, much of the left, although bitterly opposed to the military regime, also regarded the question of race as strictly secondary. Whatever might appear as racial discrimination was, by this view, a result of socio-economic stratification. A revolutionary attack on the capitalist system was the key to achieving social justice, and nonwhites would benefit more or less automatically from the adoption of more egalitarian policies. Racism, according to this view, was simply not an independent variable.

Holders of this view were not dupes of the Freyre myth, properly speaking, but rather devotees of an economistic world view. Economic injustice rules the capitalist world and attacking it would lift all boats, whatever their color. In truth, these intellectuals may have been more deeply influenced by the myth of racial democracy than they would like to admit. But the rationale for their position differed significantly and must be seen as such.

The second group to challenge the establishment doctrine of assimilation through "whitening" were the Afro-Brazilian militants.[28] These were the black and mulatto Brazilians who not only said racial discrimination was pervasive, but who rejected outright the alleged white superiority that had underlain the assimilationist consensus. They argued implicitly that African traditions were as valuable as European traditions.

These voices were tiny in number. Their strains could be heard occasionally in the nineteenth century, and again in the 1920s and 1930s, when an Afro-Brazilian press and Afro-Brazilian political movement arose, centered primarily in São Paulo.[29] It was snuffed out during the Estado Novo (1937-1945) but reappeared after 1945 in the person of its best-known spokesman, Abdias do Nascimento.[30] The return of authoritarianism in 1968 once again silenced the Afro-Brazilian militants, who resurfaced with the gradual political opening of the late 1970s.[31]

The relative lack of militant Afro-Brazilian protest in twentieth-century Brazil, in the face of now-documented discrimination, is a phenomenon worth studying. How can it be explained? One reason is the whitening ideology, which operated to co-opt mulattos. A second reason is a corollary of the first. Because there was no legal segregation, there were no parallel nonwhite institutions, such as the U.S. all-black Protestant churches, which in the U.S. furnished most of the leadership for the civil rights movement.[32]

In the late 1970s a new generation of Afro-Brazilians—small in number but outspoken in their militancy—arose to contest in an unprecedented way the "myth" of Brazil's racial democracy. In several major cities, primarily in the industrialized Southeast, they organized protests against police brutality and mistreatment at the hands of public agencies, as well as discrimination in the job market and in public places. The movement enjoyed a flurry of publicity in the late 1970s and early 1980s and provoked greater interest among foreign academics than their Brazilian counterparts.33 The militants never enjoyed broad support in the Afro-Brazilian community, although they argued that their potential support went deep. The movement was bedeviled by factionalism and a barrage of animosity from the political and cultural establishment. The latter termed them "un-Brazilian," "racist" and mindless imitators of the U.S. civil rights activists.

Notwithstanding the limitations of the militants' political movement, they were significant as a social phenomenon. It was one expression of a wave of Afro-Brazilian consciousness stronger than had ever appeared in twentieth century Brazil. It could be seen in the outpouring of Afro-Brazilian literature, much of it published in modest editions at the author's expense.34 It could be seen in the highly militant Afro-Brazilian action groups within a leading national labor confederation and among domestic employees in São Paulo. It could be seen in the increasing willingness of prominent blacks and mulattos (especially in the arts and entertainment) to speak out about their experiences of discrimination.35

Yet it would be rash to argue that Afro-Brazilian protest has had any significant impact either on the prevailing assimilationist ideology or on social behavior (although the fact that our earliest data dates from 1976 makes documented discussion of trends impossible). It is true that the 1988 Constitution (the eighth since 1824) for the first time in Brazilian constitutional history outlawed racism, declaring that "the practice of racism constitutes a crime that is unbailable and without statute of limitation and is subject to imprisonment according to the law."36 But the necessary enabling law has never been passed, and Brazilian civil rights lawyers have found it difficult in practice to establish a legal basis for their criminal complaints.37

It should be added that Afro-Brazilian militants regard their battle as only in its preliminary stages. One of their greatest challenges is the fact the pervasiveness of the assimilationist ideology. It has penetrated into every layer of Brazilian society. Militant Afro-Brazilians see their country's ambiguous racial terminology as their greatest obstacle to creating solidarity among nonwhites. They have appropriated the Portuguese term *negro* as their identifying label—a term meant to proclaim the oneness of *preto* and *mulatto*. They challenge nonwhites to "assume" their true color, directing their fire above all at those who believe they can "whiten" themselves by "correct" attitudes and behavior. The latter are disparaged as the *negros de alma branca* ("blacks with a white soul"), or the nonwhites who have fallen for the concept of "social race" articulated by the anthropologists.

The final group dissenting from the assimilationist ideology is the new generation of (almost entirely white) social scientists, intellectuals, and social activists who have become convinced that racial discrimination is a pervasive reality in Brazil. It was inevitable that this revisionist initiative would require a full-scale attack on Gilberto Freyre, as the leading spokesman for the myth of "racial democracy." One of the first salvos was fired by a young São Paulo historian.[38] These new dissenters included demographers, journalists, social workers and labor union and church activists[39] who have had the courage to denounce both racial discrimination and the assimilationist ideology that befogs public discussion of race relations in Brazil. They, along with the Afro-Brazilian militants, form the backbone of the historically most serious challenge of establishment practice and ideology.

1976: Some Brazilians Discover a Race Problem

The National Household Survey (PNAD) of 1976 marked the first time the Brazilian government had ever collected and published data on employment and income by race. The results showed unmistakably that race *was* an independent variable in determining life outcomes. Suddenly all the previous generalizations about race relations had become obsolete. Researchers could no longer get by with citing anecdotal evidence. Now there was hard data (Table 5.2). The "class vs. race" thesis had been put to the test and found wanting. Even when education, age and sex were controlled, race turned out to be the only explanation for significant variations in income.[40]

In fact, the disparity grew with educational attainment. This data seemed to refute the "social race" hypothesis. The more the nonwhite approximated what the Brazilian elite assumed to be the ultimate noninheritable marker, i.e., education, the greater the income disparity vis-à-vis the white. The pattern reappeared in the data from the 1980 census and the 1982 PNAD.

What could one conclude about these findings? Most important, racial discrimination did exist despite the absence of the descent rule and despite the absence of legal segregation. In short, the absence of the key markers of institutuionalized racism in the U.S. did not mean the absence of systematic discrimination. Second, mulattos did better than blacks, in general, in earnings.Within an overall pattern of discrimination, therefore, multi-racialism still operated. Exactly how remains to be explained.

TABLE 5.2 Urban Nonwhite Earnings as a Proportion of Urban White Earnings by Sector

1976 PNAD	Pardos (Brown)	Pretos (Black)
Professional	49.6	36.9
Semi-professional	72.4	80.8
Manufacturing	76.4	60.9
Construction	82.8	77.4
Commerce	82.8	51.0
Transport	82.7	81.0
Services	66.2	64.6

Source: Oliveira, Lúcia E. Garcia de, et al, *O Lugar do Negro na Força de Trabalho.* Rio de Janeiro: Departmento de Estudos e Indicadores Sociais, IBGE, 1985.

What has been the effect of these revelations? Minimal. Perhaps we should not expect much in the short run. But these data have given ammunition to the dissenters—the Afro-Brazilian militants and the white iconoclasts and activists. It was much in the air at the Constituent Assembly that drafted the 1988 Constitution.[41] And it is much cited by the activists who are fighting for change at the level of unions, courts, employers and the media.

Social scientists tell us that the data base on Brazilian race relations is still very thin. There is much more we need to know about health, housing, education, family structure, etc. Little of this is covered in the bare bones questionnaires of the census data. Indeed, researchers have had to fight even to get access to the data already collected. Much of the most important information has never been published and is available only on tapes, which the census bureau refused to release for years and then only at great cost to users. Official policies have been so obstructionist that some researchers have organized a pressure group to force the census authorities to release future data (as of mid-1992 the 1990 census is yet to be completed!) on a timely and accessible basis. Even more interestingly, activists have organized a campaign to convince Afro-Brazilians to respond accurately when the census ennumerator asks their race. The objective is to counteract the "whitening" ideology by getting mixed bloods not to identify themselves as white, which would distort the census data.

The fact of the matter is that the new facts about racial discrimination in Brazil have yet to register any significant impact upon the elite, the politicians, or the scholarly community. In a word, the

Brazilian establishment still does not believe its society has a racial problem. Gilberto Freyre, not Florestan Fernandes, still dominates enlightened Brazilian public discussion. The antiracist article in the Constitution of 1988, like the Affonso Arinos Law of 1951 (which outlawed racial discrimination in public accommodations), is rhetoric, not a societal commitment. The efforts of such progressive state governors as Franco Montoro in São Paulo and Leonel Brizola in Rio de Janeiro (his first term) to move against racial discrimination have largely aborted. Their successors sabotaged their initiatives, sometimes blatantly.

What is most interesting from the standpoint of this paper is the lack of reaction among academics. The occasion of the centenary of abolition in 1988 was an important indicator. That would have seemed the ideal opportunity to do a stock-taking of progress in race relations in the century since the end of slavery. Instead, there was a flood of self-congratulation as befitting a racial democracy that had allegedly escaped unscathed from the trauma of slavery. Brazil even witnessed the scene of the imperial heir of Princess Isabella, the benefactress of the "Golden Law" of abolition, receiving obsequious thanks from an awed delegation of black and mulatto Brazilians.

Militant Afro-Brazilians sought to make their case against the myth of racial democracy in 1988. But they were largely drowned out by the civic ceremonies celebrating Brazil's genius in having liquidated slavery without such traumas as the U.S. Civil War.

No social scientist rose to the challenge to produce an in-depth portrait of contemporary Brazilian racial relations. We are still without any comprehensive, well documented overview based on the post-1976 data. The Brazilian academic community has been notably slow to assimilate, or even to acknowledge, the new reality.

We do start with some guideposts and research instruments. One is the bibliographical guide to publications in Portuguese on slavery and race relations in Brazil.[42] A second is the two-volume guide to archival sources in Brazil on Africa, slavery and the Afro-Brazilian.[43] A third is the source collection documenting the Brazilian observation of the 1988 centennial of the abolition of slavery at CIEC of the Federal University of Rio de Janeiro.[44]

There is also a series of recent bibliographical surveys, of which only a sample can be mentioned here: Carlos A. Hasenbalg, "Notas Sobre Relações de Raça no Brasil e na América Latina" (Trabalho apresentado no I Encontro sobre Gênero e Raça, Fundação Memorial de América Latina, Centro Brasileiro de Estudos de América Latina, São Paulo, 13 a 15 de agosto de 1990), Hasenbalg, "A Pesquisa Sobre

Migrações, Urbanização, Relações Raciais e Pobreza no Brasil: 1970-1990" (Trabalho apresentado no seminário "Temas e Problemas de Investigação de Ciências Sociais: Brasil e América Latina," IDESP, Campos do Jordão, SP, 5 a 7 dezembro de 1990), and Ciro Flamarion S. Cardoso, "A Historiografia Brasileira Sobre a Abolição: Análise de uma Seleção de Obras Publicadas Entre 1979 e 1987." An interesting recent overview by a non-Brazilian highly critical of establishment opinion in Brazil is given in Jan Fiola.[45] The first major overview to be done after the late 1970s was the collaborative volume edited by Pierre-Michel Fontaine.[46]

Among the important volumes of papers produced for recent conferences in Brazil are *Desgualdade Racial no Brasil*,[47] which contains a wealth of demographic data, and *100 Anos Depois: Perspectivas dos Discursos sobre "Raça" e "Diferença"*[48] which resulted from an October 1989 conference that looked at both race and gender.

Yet there has been little social science research drawing on the new official data or attempting to generate any new data. Take political science. There is not a single published monograph on race in Brazilian politics. One article by Amaury de Souza[49] remained the only substantial scholarly paper until Glaucio Soares and Nelson do Valle Silva[50] debunked the myth of "moreno socialism" ("mulatto socialism") than had grown up around Rio de Janeiro Governor Leonel Brizola. Three mulattos won state governorships in 1990 but we await any political science analysis of the role race may or may not have played in their election.[51] What of the five Federal Deputies who identify themselves as Afro-Brazilians? How have they organized to defend Afro-Brazilian interests in the Congress? What special problems do they face in representing their constituents, white and nonwhite? These and many more questions await investigation.

Economics has produced even less. One searches in vain for any academic economics center devoting any attention to the variable of race. It is a non-subject for economists. Researchers in education have at least made a start. The key institution here has been the Fundação Carlos Chagas in São Paulo.[52]

Sociology is the social science discipline that has produced most quantitative research on race relations, virtually all of it by demographers. The fundamental work based on pre-1976 data is by Carlos Hasenbalg.[53] The only book-length studies drawing on post-1976 data are by Lúcia E. Garcia de Oliveira, et. al.,[54] Charles Wood and J. M. Carvalho,[55] Carlos Hasenbalg and Nelson do Valle Silva,[56] the Instituto Brasileiro de Analises Sociais e Economicas,[57] and P. A. Lovell.[58] The most important of the principal article-length studies are by Nelson do

Valle Silva,[59] Carlos Hasenbalg[60] and Hasenbalg and Silva.[61] Most of the more technical studies by demographers are to be found in the *Anais* of the annual meetings of ABEP (Asociação Brasileira de Estudos Populacionais), especially the VI Encontro Nacional de Estudos Populacionais at Olinda, Pernambuco, 1988.

History and anthropology are the two disciplines which have produced the most extensive research on race relations. The overwhelming quantity of the historical research and publication has been on slavery and the struggle for abolition. This tendency was only reinforced by the funding generated for the 1988 centennial of abolition. Research on slavery and race relations before 1888 has certainly been enriched by recent work, with its focus on the wide rural-urban variations in slavery, the frequency of slave resistance, the paths to manumission, the fate of ex-slaves and free coloreds (before 1888), and the comparison of Brazilian slavery and pre-abolition race relations with other major slave-holding regions in the Americas.[62] Historical research on post-1888 race relations is however, almost non-existent, although the beginnings of research are apparent.[63] The first major study (on São Paulo, 1888-1988) is by a North American scholar, Reid Andrews.[64] Most of his documentation comes from original research, since the previous scholarly secondary literature is so sparse. The leading centers of historical research, such as the University of São Paulo, the University of Campinas and the Fluminense Federal University, continue to focus on pre-1888. Such historical studies as are done come most often from scholars in other disciplines, such as education, demography or literature.

Anthropology is the other discipline, along with history, that has produced the research in African-Brazilian Studies. This is what one would expect, since anthropology takes race and ethnicity as central themes. Anthropologists have produced a rich monographic literature that concentrates on religion, folklore, language, music, art and dance.[65] But it has focused primarily on the African "survivals," the elements of Afro-Braziliana that show the continuing influence of some "pure" African origins. The pioneering work of Roger Bastide[66] on Afro-Brazilian religion is the supreme example of this genre. It is duplicated in the present-day work of SECNEB (*Sociedade de Estudos da Cultura Negra no Brasil*) group in Bahia. To such researchers we owe the large body of literature on *candomblé, macumba, capoeira,* along with Afro-Brazilian folklore, music, cuisine and art.

The problem with this scholarship, as with the study of slavery and pre-1888 race relations, is that it rarely connects to contemporary race relations. The practical effect, although far from the intention of the scholars, is to produce a predominant cultural mindset well captured by Carlos Hasenbalg when he analyzed a slick magazine ad sponsored by a metallurgical firm which showed "a photograph of a Negro *mestre-sala* and mulatta *porta bandeira* (lead couple in a samba parade) presenting themselves to the "sambadrome" stands. The ad suggested the contrast between two Brazils:

> One is the eternal Brazil, "blessed and tropical," represented by Negroes parading in their samba school. The other is the spectators, looking on from their strong steel bleachers. The latter is the new Brazil, changing and progressive. We thus have a counterpoint between the idea of development, seen positively, and its negative: the merely folkloric, represented by the Negroes. The ad is a perfect example of the appropriation of Negro cultural production, presented as typically Brazilian, into its most folklorized and commercialized form.[67]

Even the most innovative of the social anthropologists, such as the highly creative faculty at the *Museu Nacional* (Rio), have made little progress in looking at contemporary race relations. Indeed, it is hardly on their agenda as an explicit topic, although it enters tangentially in their research on such themes as urban neighborhoods, sport, middle class sexual mores, political symbolism and syncretistic religious practices.

The fact is that quantifiable studies with policy relevance will not come from the anthropologists because it is not what they are trained to do nor what they are most interested in. That is not to say that they will not continue to contribute rich insights or that their collaboration with other social scientists will not be vital for success in developing the field. On the contrary, their participation will be vital. But they will not *themselves* produce the kind of research and training most relevant to policy debates over how to deal with Brazil's racial problem.

The fields of literature, art, art history, dance, theater, film, and communications suffer from the same limitations as anthropology, yet they also have a vital contribution to make. All have enriched and will continue to enrich our understanding of race and race relations in Brazil, although they have received less emphasis in this overview. To take but one example, discourse analysis can greatly illuminate the mentalities—both elite and non-elite—with which Brazilians approach race.[68]

A Research Agenda

It is not difficult to assemble a list of promising topics for research in Afro-Brazilian Studies. Insofar as scholars accept the fact that racial discrimination is a reality to be investigated, the areas for investigation become obvious. The following is merely a tentative list (drawn primarily from agendas suggested by leading researchers such as Carlos Hasenbalg, Luiz Felipe de Alencastro and Elza Berquó) which practicing researchers could quickly adapt and revise:

1. Basic population dynamics: the demographic profile by race. The population growth by race, broken down by gender, income level, education, location, etc. What are the facts behind the much discussed "browning" of Brazil? What explains this phenomenon?

2. What are the recent changes, especially during the 1980s, in socio-economic stratification by race? By indicators such as income, education, occupation and housing?

3. Education merits special attention, since it has often been seen as the most ready instrument for social mobility. What is the evidence for differential access to education, especially secondary and university education, by race? How does this vary by type of institution (public vs. private, etc.) and region?

4. What are the variations by race in access to other social services, such as health care, employment training, government pensions, subsidized housing, labor courts and civil and criminal justice?

5. What is the effect of race in the labor market? How does it influence the behavior of employers, labor unions, Ministry of Labor and Labor Court officials, etc?

Conclusion

It must be stressed that there is still no consensus among the Brazilian elite, or even among Brazilian social scientists, that Brazil suffers from significant and systematic racial discrimination. Yet evidence to prove it is rapidly accumulating. What matters, however, is how Brazilian society reacts to that information. That, in turn, depends on two factors.

The first is whether Afro-Brazilians come to see their life situation as being determined to a significant degree by racial discrimination. If so, will they translate this consciousness into collective action? In doing so, they could become politically powerful, since they are virtually half the population (and since illiterates, who are disproportionately numerous among Afro-Brazilians, have recently been enfranchised).

The second factor is whether white Brazilians choose to accept the facts about discrimination and are prepared to take remedial action. In short, will they honor their country's commitment to democracy, which can never be realized under conditions of racism?

Finally, will Brazilian social scientists take the lead in acknowledging and documenting the facts about racial behavior in their country? And how will they choose to act on that knowledge? Their response will have much to do with the fate of democracy in Latin America's largest and most misunderstood multi-racial society.

Notes

1. Reprinted with permission of the Helen Kellogg Institute for International Studies, University of Notre Dame, Notre Dame, IN 46556. Originally appeared in *Working Paper* #173 in April, 1992.

2. Harris, Marvin, *Patterns of Race in the Americas* (New York: Walter, 1964).

3. Nogueira, Oracy, *Tanto Preto Quanto Branco: Estudos de Relações Raciais* (São Paulo: TA Queiroz, 1985).

4. *The New York Times* (December 2, 1991).

5. Skidmore, Thomas E., *Black Into White: Race and Nationality in Brazilian Thought* (New York: Oxford University Press, 1974).

6. Freyre, Gilberto, *New World in the Tropics: The Culture of Modern Brazil* (New York: Alfred Knopf, 1959), and *The Masters and the Slaves* (New York: Alfred Knopf, 1956).

7. Skidmore, Thomas E., *Black Into White: Race and Nationality in Brazilian Thought* (New York: Oxford University Press, 1974).

8. DaMatta, Roberto, *Relativizando: Uma Introdução à Antropologia Social* (Rio de Janeiro: Rocco, 1987).

9. Lacerda, João Batista de, "The Métis, or Half-breeds, of Brazil," *Papers on Inter-Racial Problems Communicated to the First Universal Races Congress held at the University of London, July 26-29, 1911*, G. Spiller, ed. (London, 1911), 377-382.

10. Fiola, "Race Relations in Brazil: A Reassessment of the 'Racial Democracy' Thesis," (Amherst: Occasional Papers Series Number 24, University of Massachusetts at Amherst, Program in Latin American Studies, January 1990).

11. Degler, Carl N., *Neither Black Nor White: Slavery and Race Relations in Brazil and the United States* (New York: MacMillan, 1971).

12. Barbosa, Francisco de Assis, *A Vida de Lima Barreto*, 3rd ed. (Rio de Janeiro: Editora Civilização Brasileira, 1964).

13. Morel, Edmar, *A Revolta da Chibata* (Rio de Janeiro, 1963).

14. Andrews, George Reid, *The Afro-Brazilians of São Paulo, 1888-1988* (Madison: The University of Wisconsin Press, 1991).

15. Vianna, Francisco José de Oliveira, *Evolução do Povo Brasileiro* (Rio de Janeiro, 1922).

16. Azevedo, Fernando de, *Brazilian Culture: An Introduction to the Study of Culture in Brazil* (New York: MacMillan, 1950), 40-41.

17. Skidmore, Thomas E., *Black Into White: Race and Nationality in Brazilian Thought* (New York: Oxford University Press, 1974).

18. Pierson, Donald, *Negroes in Brazil* (Chicago: University of Chicago Press, 1942).

19. Harris, Marvin, "Racial Identity in Brazil," *Luso-Brazilian Review* 1:2 (1964), 21-28.

20. Wagley, Charles, ed., *Race and Class in Rural Brazil* (Paris: UNESCO, 1952).

21. Oliveira, Lúcia E. Garcia de, et al, *O Lugar do Negro na Força de Trabalho* (Rio de Janeiro: Departmento de Estudos e Indicadores Sociais (DEISO), (IBGE, 1985).

22. *Veja* (August 28, 1985).

23. Azevedo, Thales de, *Les Élites de Couleur das une Ville Brésilienne* (Paris: UNESCO, 1953).

24. Bastide, Roger and Florestan Fernandes, *Brancos e Negros em São Paulo* (São Paulo: Companhia Editora Nacional, 1959), 271.

25. Fernandes, Florestan, *Significado do Protesto Negro* (São Paulo: Cortez Editora, 1989).

26. Fernandes, Florestan, *The Negro in Brazilian Society* (New York: Columbia University Press, 1969).

27. Skidmore, Thomas E., "Race and Class in Brazil: Historical Perspectives," *Race, Class and Power in Brazil*, Pierre-Michel Fontaine, ed. (Los Angeles: Center for Afro-American Studies, UCLA, 1985).

28. Moura, Clovis, *Rebeliões da Senzala: Quilombos, Insurreiçoes, Guerrilhas* (São Paulo: Edições Zumbi, 1959).

29. Andrews, George Reid, *Blacks and Whites in São Paulo, Brazil: 1888-1988* (Madison: The University of Wisconsin Press, 1991).

30. Nascimento, Abdias do. 1968. *O Negro Revoltado*. Rio de Janerio: Edições GRD; and 1979. *Mixture or Massacre? Essays in the Genocide of a Black People*. Buffalo: Puerto Rican Studies and Research Center, State University of New York.

31. Turner, Michael, "Brown Into Black: Changing Racial Attitudes of Afro-Brazilian University Students, *Race, Class and Power in Brazil*, Pierre-Michel Fontaine, ed. (Los Angeles: Center for Afro-American Studies, UCLA, 1985), 73-94.

32. Skidmore, Thomas E., "Toward A Comparative Analysis of Race Relations Since Abolition in Brazil and the United States," *Journal of Latin American Studies* 4:1 (1972), 1-28.

33. Mitchell, Michael, "Blacks and the 'Abertura Democrática,'" *Race, Class and Power in Brazil*, Pierre-Michel Fontaine, ed. (Los Angeles: Center for Afro-American Studies, UCLA, 1985), 95-119.

34. Camargo, Oswaldo de, *A Razão da Chama: Antologia de Poetas Negros no Brasil* (São Paulo: Ediçoes GRD). *Cadernos Negros* 10: Contos (Sao Paulo: Edição dos Autores).

35. Costa, Haroldo, *Fala, Crioulo: Depoimentos* (Rio de Janeiro: Editora Record, 1982).

36. Article 5, XLI.

37. "Racismo em SP Motiva 64 Processos em 2 Anos," *Folha de Sao Paulo* (January 27, 1991).

38. Mota, Carlos Guilherme, *Ideologia da Cultura Brasileira: 1933-1974* (São Paulo: Editora Atica, 1978).

39. CNBB (Conferencia Nacional dos Bispos do Brasil), *Ouvi o Clamor deste Povo: Manual* (Brasília: Centro de Pastoral Popular, 1988).

40. Silva, Nelson do Valle, "Updating the Cost of Not Being White in Brazil," *Race, Class and Power in Brazil*, Pierre-Michel Fontaine, ed. (Los Angeles:UCLA, Center for Afro-American Studies, 1985).

41. Santos, Lourdes Fiuza dos and José Antonio Carlos Pimenta, "O Negro e a Ordem Social," *Constituinte: Temas em Análise*, Vania Lamonaco Bastos and Rania Moreira da Costa, eds. (Brasília: Universidade de Brasília, n.d.), 107-122.

42. Luiz Claudio Barcelos, et. al., *Escravidão e Relações Racais no Brasil: Cadastro da Produção Intelectual, 1970-1990* (Rio de Janeiro: (Centro de Estudos Afro-Asiáticos, 1991).

43. Arquivo Nacional, *Guia Brasileiro de Fontes para a História da Africa, da Escravidão Negra e do Negro na Sociedade Atual*, 2 volumes (Rio de Janeiro: Departamento de Imprensa Nacional, 1988).

44. Maggie, Yvonne, *Catálogo: Centenário da Abolição* (Rio de Janeiro: CIEC/Nucleo da Cor/Universidade Federal do Rio de Janeiro, 1989).

45. Fiola, "Race Relations in Brazil: A Reassessment of the 'Racial Democracy' Thesis," (Amherst: University of Massachusetts at Amherst, Program in Latin American Studies: Occasional Papers Series Number 24, January 1990).

46. Fontaine, Pierre-Michel, ed., *Race, Class, and Power in Brazil* (Los Angeles: UCLA, Center for Afro-American Studies, 1985).

47. Lovell, Peggy A., ed., *Desigualdade Racial no Brasil Contemporâneo* (Belo Horizonte: CEDEPLAR/Universidade Federal de Minas Gerais, 1991).

48. CIEC (Centro Interdisciplinar de Estudos Contemporâneos)-UFJR. Forthcoming. *100 Anos Depois: Perspectivas dos Discursos Sobre "Raça e Diferença."*

49. Souza, Amaury de, "Raça e Política no Brasil Urbano," *Revista de Administraçao de Empresas* 11:4 (1971), 61-70.

50. Soares, Glaucio Ary Dillon and Nelson do Valle Silva. 1987. "Urbanization, Race and Class in Brazilian Politics," *Latin American Research Review* 22:2, 155-176.

51. "Albuíno se elege apesar do preconceito racial," *Jornal do Brasil* (December 12, 1990); *Veja* (December 5, 1990).

52. Rosemberg, Fulvia, "Pesquisas sobre Relaçoes Raciais e Educaçao" (1991) - typescript.

53. Hasenbalg, Carlos, *Discriminação e Desgualdades Raciais* (Rio de Janeiro: Edições Graal, 1979).

54. Oliveira, Lúcia E. Garcia de, et al, *O Lugar do Negro na Força de Trabalho* (Rio de Janeiro: Departamento de Estudos e Indicadores Sociais (DEISO), (IBGE, 1985).

55. Wood, Charles H. and José Alberto Magno de Carvalho, *The Demography of Inequality in Brazil* (Cambridge: Cambridge University Press, 1988).

56. Hasenbalg, Carlos and Nelson do Valle Silva. 1988. *Estrutura Social, Mobilidade e Raça*. São Paulo: Vértice.

57. IBASE, *Negros no Brasil: Dados da Realidade* (Petrópolis: Vozes, 1989).

58. Lovell, Peggy A., ed., *Desigualdade Racial no Brasil Contemporâneo* (Belo Horizonte: CEDEPLAR / Universidade Federal de Minas Gerais, 1991).

59. Silva, Nelson do Valle, "Cor e o Processo de Realização Sócio-Econômica," DADOS 24:2 (1981) 391-409; Silva, Nelson do Valle, "Updating the Cost of Not Being White in Brazil," *Race, Class, and Power in Brazil*, Pierre-Michel Fontaine, ed. (Los Angeles: UCLA, Center for Afro-American Studies, 1985).

60. Hasenbalg, Carlos, "Race and Socioeconomic Inequalities in Brazil," Pierre-Michel Fontaine, ed. (Los Angeles: UCLA, Center for Afro-American Studies, 1985), 25-41.

61. Hasenbalg, Carlos and Nelson do Valle Silva, "Raça e Opportunidades Educacionais no Brazil," *Estudos Afro-Asiáticos* 18 (1990), 73-91.

62. Lara, Silvia Hunold, ed., "Escravidão: Número Especial," *Revista Brasileira de Historia* 8:16 (1988); *Luso-Brazilian Review* 25:1, (1988) Issue on slavery and race relations, reprinted as Scott, Rebecca J., et al, *The Abolition of Slavery and the Aftermath of Emancipation in Brazil* (Durham: Duke University Press, 1988).

63. Maciel, Cleber da Silva, *Discriminações Raciais: Negros em Campinas, 1888-1921* (Campinas: UNICAMP, 1987).

64. Andrews, George Reid, *Blacks and Whites in São Paulo, Brazil: 1888-1988* (Madison: The University of Wisconsin Press, 1991).

65. Braga, Julio, *O Jogo de Búzios: Um Estudo da Adivinhação no Candomblé* (São Paulo: Brasiliense, 1988); Carneiro, Edison, Candomblés da Bahia (Rio de Janeiro, 1961).

66. Bastide, Roger, *The African Religions of Brazil: Toward a Sociology of the Interpenetration of Civilizations* (Baltimore: Johns Hopkins, 1978).

67. Hasenbalg, Carlos and Nelson do Valle Silva, *Estrutura Social, Mobilidade e Raça* (São Paulo: Vértice, 1988), 187.

68. Azevedo, Celia Maria Marinho de, *Onda Negra, Medo Branco: O Negro no Imaginário das Elites: Século XIX* (Rio de Janeiro: Paz e Terra, 1987); Vainfas, Ronaldo, *Ideologia e Escravidão: Os Letrados e a Sociedade Escravista no Brasil Colonia* (Petrópolis: Vozes, 1986).

References

Andrews, George Reid. 1991. *Blacks and Whites in São Paulo, Brazil: 1888-1988*. Madison: The University of Wisconsin Press.

Arquivo Nacional. 1988. *Guia Brasileiro de Fontes para a História da Africa, da Escravidão Negra e do Negro na Sociedade Atual*. Rio de Janeiro: Departamento de Imprensa Nacional. 2 vols.

Azevedo, Celia Maria Marinho de. 1987. *Onda Negra, Medo Branco: O Negro no Imaginário das Elites: Século XIX*. Rio de Janeiro: Paz e Terra.

Azevedo, Fernando de. 1950. Brazilian Culture: *An Introduction to the Study of Culture in Brazil*. New York: MacMillan.

Azevedo, Thales de. 1953. *Les Élites de Couleur das une Ville Brésilienne*. Paris: UNESCO.

Barbosa, Francisco de Assis. 1964. *A Vida de Lima Barreto*. Rio de Janeiro: Editora Civilização Brasileira (3rd. ed.).

Bastide, Roger. 1978. *The African Religions of Brazil: Toward a Sociology of the Interpenetration of Civilizations*. Baltimore: Johns Hopkins.

Bastide, Roger and Florestan Fernandes. 1959. *Brancos e Negros em São Paulo*. São Paulo: Companhia Editora Nacional.

Braga, Julio. 1988. O Jogo de Búzios: Um Estudo da Adivinhaçao no Candomblé. São Paulo: Brasiliense.

Cadernos Negros 10: Contos. n.d. São Paulo: Edição dos Autores.

Camargo, Oswaldo de. 1986. *A Razão da Chama: Antologia de Poetas Negros Brasileiros*. São Paulo: Edições GRD.

Carneiro, Edison. 1961. *Candomblés da Bahia*. Rio de Janeiro: 1961.

Centro de Estudos Afro-Asiáticos. 1991. *Escravidão e Relações Raciais no Brasil: Cadastro da Produção Intelectual, 1970-90*. Rio de Janeiro: FAPERJ.

CIEC (Centro Interdisciplinar de Estudos Contemporâneos)-UFRJ. Forthcoming. *100 Anos Depois: Perspectivas dos Discursos sobre "Raça e "Diferença"*.

CNBB (Conferencia Nacional dos Bispos do Brasil). 1988. *Ouvi o Clamor deste Povo: Manual*. Brasília: Centro de Pastoral Popular.

Costa, Haroldo. 1982. *Fala, Crio lulo: Depoimentos*. Rio de Janeiro: Editora Record.

DaMatta, Roberto. 1987. *Relativizando: Uma Introdução à Antropologia Social*. Rio de Janeiro: Rocco.

Degler, Carl N. 1971. *Neither Black Nor White: Slavery and Race Relations in Brazil and the United States*. New York: MacMillan.

Fernandes, Florestan. 1969. *The Negro in Brazilian Society*. New York: Columbia University Press.

_____. 1989 *Significado do Protesto Negro*. São Paulo: Cortez Editora.

Fiola, Jan. 1990. "Race Relations in Brazil: A Reassessment of the 'Racial Democracy' Thesis," Program in Latin American Studies: Occasional Papers Series No. 24 (University of Massachusetts at Amherst).

Folha de São Paulo. 1991. "Racismo em SP Motiva 64 Processos em 2 Anos," January 27.

Fontaine, Pierre-Michel, ed. 1985. *Race, Class, and Power in Brazil.* Los Angeles: Center for Afro-American Studies, UCLA.

Freyre, Gilberto. 1959. *New World in the Tropics: The Culture of Modern Brazil.* New York: Alfred Knopf.

_____. 1963 *Casa-Grande e Senzala: Formação da Família Brasileira sob o Regime Patriarcal.* Brasília: Universidade de Brasília (12th ed.).

Harris, Marvin. 1964a. *Patterns of Race in the Americas.* New York: Walter.

_____. 1964b. "Racial Identity in Brazil," *Luso-Brazilian Review* 1: 2, 21-28.

Hasenbalg, Carlos. 1979. *Discriminação e Desigualdades Raciais.* Rio de Janeiro: Edições Graal.

_____. 1985. "Race and Socioeconomic Inequalities in Brazil." In Fontaine, 25-41.

Hasenbalg, Carlos and Nelson do Valle Silva. 1988. Estrutura Social, Mobilidade e Raça. São Paulo: Vértice.

_____. 1990. "Raça e Oportunidades Educacionais no Brasil," *Estudos Afro-Asiáticos* 18, 73-91.

IBASE. 1989. *Negros no Brasil: Dados da Realidade.* Petrópolis: Vozes.

Jornal do Brasil. 1990. "Albuíno se elege apesar do preconceito racial," December 12.

Lacerda, João Batista de. 1911. "The Métis, or Half-breeds, of Brazil." In *Papers on Inter-racial Problems Communicated to the First Universal Races Congress held at the University of London, July 26-29, 1911* (ed. G. Spiller), London, 377-382.

Lara, Silvia Hunold, ed. 1988. "Escravidão: Número Especial," *Revista Brasileira de Historia* 8:16.

Lovell, Peggy A., ed. 1991. Desigualdade Racial no Brasil Contemporâneo. Belo Horizonte: CEDEPLAR/ Universidade Federal de Minas Gerais.

Luso-Brazilian Review. 1988. (Issue on slavery and race relations) 25:1.

Maciel, Cleber de Silva. Discriminações Raciais: Negros em Campinas, 1888-1921. Campinas.

Maggie, Yvonne. 1989. *Catálogo: Centenario da Abolição.* Rio de Janeiro: CIEC/ Nucleo da Cor/ Universidade Federal do Rio de Janeiro.

Mitchell, Michael. 1985. "Blacks and the 'Abertura Democrática,'" in Fontaine, 95-119.

Morel, Edmar. 1963. *A Revolta da Chibata.* Rio de Janeiro.

Mota, Carlos Guilherme. 1978. *Ideologia da Cultura Brasileira: 1933-1974.* São Paulo: Editora Atica.

Moura, Clovis. 1959. *Rebeliões da Senzala: Quilombos, Insurreições, Guerrilhas.* São Paulo: Edições Zumbi.

Nascimento, Abdias do. 1968. *O Negro Revoltado.* Rio de Janeiro: Ediçoes GRD.

_____. 1979. *Mixture or Massacre? Essays in the Genocide of a Black People.* Buffalo: Puerto Rican Studies and Research Center, State University of New York.

New York Times. 1991. December 2.

Nogueira, Oracy. *Tanto Preto Quanto Branco: Estudos de Relações Raciais.* São Paulo: T.A. Queiroz.

Oliveira, Lúcia E. Garcia de, Rosa Maria Porcaro, and Tereza C. N. Araújo. 1985. *O Lugar do negro na Força de Trabalho.* Rio de Janeiro: Departamento de Estudos e Indicadores Sociais (DEISO), IBGE.

Pierson, Donald. 1942. *Negroes in Brazil.* Chicago: University of Chicago Press.

Rosemberg, Fulvia. 1991. "Pesquisas sobre Relações Raciais e Educação."

Santos, Lourdes Fiuza dos and José Antonio Carlos Pimenta. n.d. "*O Negro e a Ordem Social,*" in *Constituinte: Temas em Análise* (ed. Vania Lamonaco Bastos and Tania Moreira da Costa; Brasília: Universidade de Brasília), 107-112.

Scott, Rebecca J., et. al. 1988. *The Abolition of Slavery and the Aftermath of Emancipation in Brazil.* Durham: Duke University Press.

Silva, Nelson do Valle. 1981. "Cor e o Processo de Realização Socio-Econômica," *DADOS* 24:2.

Silva, Nelson do Valle. 1985. "Updating the Cost of Not Being White in Brazil," in Fontaine, 42-55.

Skidmore, Thomas E. 1972. "Toward a Comparative Analysis of Race Relations Since Abolition in Brazil and the United States," *Journal of Latin American Studies* 4:1, 1-28.

_____. 1974. *Black Into White: Race and Nationality in Brazilian Thought.* New York: Oxford University Press.

_____. 1985. "Race and Class in Brazil: Historical Perspectives," in Fontaine, 11-24.

Soares, Glaucio Ary Dillon and Nelson do Valle Silva. 1987. "Urbanization, Race and Class in Brazilian Politics," *Latin American Research Review* 22:2, 155-176.

Souza, Amaury de. 1971. "Raça e Política no Brasil Urbano," *Revista de Administraçao de Empresas* 11:4, 61-70.

Turner, Michael. 1985. "Brown into Black: Changing Racial Attitudes of Afro-Brazilian University Students," in Fontaine, 73-94.

Vainfas, Ronaldo. 1986. *Ideologia e Escravidão: Os Letrados e a Sociedade Escravista no Brasil Colonial.* Petrópolis: Vozes.

Veja. 1985. August 28.

_____. 1990. December 5.

Vianna, Francisco José de Oliveira. 1922. *Evolução do Povo Brasileiro.* Rio de Janeiro.

Wagley, Charles, ed. 1952. *Race and Class in Rural Brazil.* Paris: UNESCO.

Wood, Charles H. and José Alberto Magno de Carvalho. 1988. *The Demography of Inequality in Brazil.* Cambridge: Cambridge University Press.

6

Ethnicity and Nation-Building in Israel: The Importance of Demographic Factors

Calvin Goldscheider

Significant ethnic differences continue to characterize social life in Israel, even as ethnic groups have been integrated into the national society and polity. National policy and cultural ideology favor not only the integration but the total assimilation of Jews from many countries of origin into the new Jewish state. So the central analytic questions are: What are the contexts that reinforce ethnic distinctiveness? Which contexts are most likely to reduce ethnic differences in Israeli society?

The analysis of these contexts begins with the sources of ethnic group formation. I shall argue that demographic factors, in particular the timing and selectivity of immigration and continuing patterns of residential concentration, have been critical in shaping the ethnic mosaic in Israel; are central to the ways in which ethnicity has changed over the last several decades; and are linked directly to the perpetuation of ethnic differentiation and inequalities. As a result, ethnic differences are embedded in the structure of social life in Israel, of which population processes have been, and continue to be, an integral part. Moreover, while there were sharp ethnic differences in fertility and mortality within Israel in the past, these differences have narrowed considerably as exposure to Israeli society has increased. So these demographic factors are no longer the critical sources of ethnic distinctiveness and inequality. Demographic factors that mainly reflect origins and socioeconomic factors have diminished in importance over time in shaping ethnicity; factors that have emerged in Israeli society tend to perpetuate ethnic distinctiveness.

Ethnic Categories: Constructions and Definitions

In examining ethnic factors in nation-building in Israel, we shall include both the ethnic divisions within the Jewish population as well as differences between Jewish and Arab populations. Ethnicity captures an odd mixture of religion and ethnic-national origins in Israel and goes to the heart of who is a member of the society. Ethnic differentiation in Israel does not derive from ideological sources or explicit policies. To the contrary, the national ideology, Zionism, denies the prominence of ethnicity as a continuing factor for the Israeli Jewish population. National origin differences among Jews are viewed as the product of the long-term dispersal of the Jewish people in the Diaspora; returning to the homeland, it is argued, will result in the emergence of a new Jew— untainted by the culture and psychology of the Diaspora and freed from the constraints and limitations in places of previous (non-Israel) residence.

Zionism's construction of peoplehood, therefore, involves the assignment of ethnic origin to the experiences of Jews as minorities in places outside of Israel, and hence requires its devaluation. Zionism rejected both the assimilation of Jews and the retention of ethnic minority status as solutions to the position of Jews in modernizing societies. The long Diaspora of 2,000 years is viewed simply as an empty interlude between the origins of Jews as a nation in the land of Israel and the return of Jews to their land of origin. Hence, Zionist ideology posits that Israel is the national origin of Jews. Their countries of "interlude," that is, their ethnicities, are not the source of their Jewish-national identity; Israel is. It follows that the recognition of ethnic origins as the country of ancestry would be, in part, a denial of the "return" home to Israel. To recognize ethnicity is to treat coming to Israel as immigration in the normal demographic sense, not as *aliya*, the imperative "ascent" to Israel of Zionist ideology. To deny "returning" to Israel would be ideologically and politically awkward, as would the acknowledgment of the value and importance of ethnic origins. The continuing distinctiveness of ethnicity among Jews in Israel is perceived as temporary, reflecting the past, diminishing in the present, and expected to disappear in the future. Hence, Zionist ideology in the past, along with the national ideology-culture of contemporary Israeli society, views Jewish ethnic differences in Israel as transitional and largely irrelevant to the longer term goals of national Jewish integration.

The consensus within Israel about the value of bringing Jews to Israel from diverse countries of origin and the resulting policies encouraging it are consistent with Zionist ideology, as is the anticipated integration of immigrants with these diverse ethnic backgrounds into the national culture and polity. To hasten this latter goal, explicit policies have been designed and implemented to "absorb" Jewish immigrants into Israeli society. Policymakers fully expect that as the third-generation Israeli Jew emerges, far from his ethnic origins; socialized into the national polity and culture by exposure to educational institutions and the military; and raised by native–born Israeli parents, little should remain of ethnicity except nostalgic cultural remnants of no economic or social significance. Nation-building in the ideological and policy contexts of Israeli society is expected to remove the diversity of ethnic origins, as new forms of loyalty to the Jewish nation emerge.

Nowhere is the ideology that denies the importance of ethnicity more symbolically poignant than in the way ethnic origin is treated in government statistical publications. Ethnic origin among Jews in Israel is almost always categorized in terms of the place of birth of the person (i.e., some "objective" fact that is ascriptive and unchanging). For the Israeli-born, place of birth of parent (usually father), also an unchanging characteristic, is obtained. In that context, ethnic origin is simply limited by time (until the third generation) and it describes the immediate past. Using this definition, generational distance from foreignness or exposure to Israeli society marks the progress toward the end of ethnicity and ethnic self-identification. The question of the ethnic origins, or, in the Western sense, of the "ancestry" of the third generation (the native-born of native-born parents) has not been addressed in Israel. Indeed, to judge solely by the official way government bureaus in Israel in the 1990s present their texts, this third generation has no differentiating ethnic origins of significance.

Information collected on specific ethnic origins is re-categorized into broad divisions by continents: Europe-America and Asia-Africa (with a third category, Israeli-born of Israeli-born parents). This ethnic categorization is constructed for Jews only in the state of Israel, reflecting a distinction between "Western" and "Middle East" origins. It is a clear rejection of the more widely used and historically more complex division between "Sephardic" and "Ashkenazic" Jewries. This latter distinction has been retained only to identify the political designations of the two Chief Rabbis of Israel, which is the only legitimate, governmentally recognized and reinforced arena for Jewish diversity. Thus, whether ethnic origin in Israel is rooted in specific countries (e.g., Poland or Yemen), broad regions of origin (e.g., Eastern Europe or Asia), or whether new forms of ethnic categories are becoming salient in Israel (e.g., Europe-America or Asia-Africa) remain empirical questions.

Differences between Jews and Arabs are another framework of "ethnicity" within Israel. As constructed in government documents and in politics, these are differences of religious affiliation, reflecting variations among Judaism, Islam, and Christianity. Arab-Jewish differences are not viewed as based on national origins or ethnic characteristics. The distinction between "religion" and "ethnicity" as the basis of the Arab-Jewish differentiation within Israel lies centrally in the quagmire of a series of political and ideological debates: Are Jews a nation or a religion? What constitutes Arab nationalism? What is the relevance of commonalities among religiously diverse Arabs—Moslem, Christian, and Druze? The treatment of Arabs in Israel as religious categories symbolically denies their "Palestinian" identity and their political relationships to Arabs (or Palestinians) elsewhere in the region.

The Arab-Jewish distinction is designated on the identity card carried by all adults in Israel, and it characterizes all transactions between Arabs and others in Israel. The Arab-Jewish distinction is therefore clearer publicly and socially than are the ethnic differences among Jews. Arabs are often identified by the majority population as the "other," and the category "non-Jew" is used explicitly in official government publications. The formal designation of "minority" in Israel is a category allocated to non-Jewish "religious" groups; their communities have their own "religious" organizational character, with appropriate religious leadership positions.

Some might argue that Arab-Jewish differences are not another case of ethnic differentiation because of the unique history and political status of Arabs in Israel and the particular forms of tensions that have characterized Arab-Jewish relations for so long. However, Arabs within the state of Israel are citizens largely without political constraints and with recognized rights enunciated in the declaration of independence. Of course, the politics of the region result in less than full rights of participation (e.g., in the military), and create powerful informal rules about geographic mobility and residence, marriage and social activities, and hence about access to opportunity, social integration, and education. Nevertheless, we shall treat ethnic variations among Jews and between Arabs and Jews under the rubric "ethnic" in order to make comparisons among the variety of groups within Israel; to isolate the important features that are unique for each sub-population; and to generalize about what is shared among groups. We focus on the demographic processes underlying the distinctiveness of ethnic groups in Israel, even as we recognize the unique culture of particular groups, their special histories, and the specific economic, political, and social dimensions of their contemporary circumstances.

The Changing Ethnic Mosaic in Israel

Despite the ideological and political denial of ethnicity in Israel, and the concomitant assumption that religion is the only basis of cleavage, there is significant ethnic differentiation (at one point in time) and stratification (over time, between the generations) within the Jewish group. There is also substantial evidence of convergences among Jewish ethnic groups in some areas of social life. Focusing on both the Jewish and Arab populations, we will review how some forms of ethnic differentiation diminish and how new forms of distinctiveness, the product of new contexts in which Israelis find themselves, emerge. Underlying and reflecting these emerging ethnic patterns are complex and changing demographic processes that have been the sources of ethnic convergences and the basis of ethnic continuity.

As a prelude to investigating the demographic sources of ethnicity in Israel, we sketch the ethnic composition of the Israeli population and outline the major changes that have occurred. A snapshot, cross-sectional view of ethnicity in Israeli society reveals a complex mosaic of ethnic groups. Out of a total 1990 population size of 4.8 million, Jews are the dominant sub-population, representing 82 percent of the total, with a rather even split between those of European-American and those of Asian-African origins. Of the first- and second- generation Jewish-Israeli population, 24 percent were from Asia (of whom 35 percent were from Iraq and 22 percent from Yemen); 26 percent were from Africa (of whom 62 percent were from Morocco); and 49 percent were from Europe, America, and Oceania (32 percent were from the USSR, 18 percent were from Poland, and 18 percent were from Rumania). The population size of the third generation (Israeli-born of Israeli-born parents) is increasing, and was 22 percent of the Jewish population in 1990. Its ethnic origins can only be estimated but, given past immigration patterns, third-generation Israelis are dominated by Jews of Eastern European origins. About four decades earlier, when the state of Israel was established at the end of 1948, there were 716,700 Jews; about 82 percent of the total population was from approximately the same land area; and most were of European origins (85 percent).

There were 678,000 Moslems within the State of Israel at the end of 1990, almost all of them members of the Sunni branch of Islam. Moslem Israelis were 14 percent of the nation's total population of 4.8 million persons. Additionally, 114,700 people were Christian (2.4 percent of the total), and 82,600 (1.7 percent) were Druze or persons of other religions. The Arab population has become more Moslem over time, increasing from less than 70 percent of Israeli Arabs in 1948 to 78 percent in 1990 (Table 6.1).

TABLE 6.1 Ethnic and Religious Composition of Israel's Population, 1948-1990

	Total Jewish Population (000s)	Percent Foreign Born/ Jewish	Percent Europe- America Origin/ Jewish	Percent Jewish/ Total	Percent Moslem/ Arab
1948	717	65	88	82	xx
1961	1,932	62	56	89	69
1972	2,687	53	50	85	76
1983	3,350	42	50	83	77
1990	3,947	38	49	82	78

Note: The ethnic data relate to the ethnic origin (father) of the native-born of foreign-born parents and an estimate of the ethnic composition of the third-generation, native-born of native-born parents. There are no ethnic origin data and no data on the divisions among the Arab population in 1948; the data are estimates for census years (except for 1990) for the month when these were taken or are end-of-the-year estimates.

Source: Statistical Abstract of Israel, 1991, Table 2.22.

How have demographic factors shaped the emergence of ethnic groups and the processes of ethnic group integration in the context of nation-building in Israel? Snapshots four decades apart reveal some of the story about ethnic compositional changes, but omit most of what has happened demographically in the society, and miss all of the processes underlying these changes. For example, there has been a rather stable Jewish-Arab population ratio over the four-decade period, despite rapid population growth. This stable ratio reflects the growth of the Jewish population through immigration combined with the indirect effects of the fertility of the immigrants; the growth of the Arab population has been largely by natural increase (Friedlander and Goldscheider, 1984). These different processes have important implications for the nature of political, social, and cultural change.

The dynamics of the demographic processes characterizing Israeli society are well known, since they parallel demographic transitions in

Western and Third World countries (Goldscheider, 1992b). These include: Declines in mortality along with improvements in, and the extension of, public health services; the transition to a nuclear family structure; the increasing use of efficient contraception and the emergence of smaller families; the urban concentration of the population and the expansion of metropolitan areas; population aging, along with the expansion of welfare and service needs; and the increasing role of the state in the formulation and implementation of a broad range of population policies. Along with the convergence of basic demographic processes among ethnic and religious groups, these trends are part of the demographic transformations of Israeli society. They have shaped the social, economic, cultural, and political landscape of Israel, as they have in other societies. Demographic transformations in Israel and elsewhere have been linked to the expansion of economic opportunities; the changing roles of women; the growing diffusion of Western technology to developing nations; and the increasing political and economic dependencies of small periphery nations on a number of large, powerful, core countries. Our central question is: How have these complex demographic transformations been connected with the formation of the ethnic mosaic and with the ethnic change processes that have emerged in Israel over the last several decades?

Immigration, Nation-Building, and Ethnicity

The ethnic mosaic and the ethnic processes in Israeli society have been shaped directly by immigration patterns. Immigration has been a major strategy of nation-building in the state of Israel: The Zionist movement since the nineteenth century, and the state of Israel from its establishment, have sought to gather in one country the multitude of populations around the world that considered themselves Jewish by religion or ancestry. The processes, patterns, and policies of immigration to the state of Israel have been unique. The conditions preceding and following the Holocaust and World War II in Europe; the emerging nationalism among Jews around the world; the conditions of Jews in Arab-Moslem countries; the existence of an expanding Jewish community in pre-state Palestine; and the radical changes in the 1990s within eastern Europe together with the breakup of the Soviet Union all have influenced the immigration of Jews to Israel from a wide range of countries. The emergence of a large and integrated American Jewish community that has not participated significantly in immigration to

Israel is another element in understanding the selectivity of worldwide Jewish immigration to Israel.

Immigration to Israel is also special because of its ideological centrality; the socio-cultural diversity of the immigrants; its overwhelming importance in the formation and development of Israeli society; the high rates of immigration in the first three years after the establishment of the state; and, in the 1990s, the fact that Jews "returning" to the state of Israel had not lived there for almost 2,000 years. Immigration—in its ideological, policy, and behavioral forms— has symbolized the renewal of Jewish control over their own national development and has been one of the core symbols of the conflicts between Jews and Arabs in the Middle East (Goldscheider, 1990; Friedlander and Goldscheider, 1979; Smooha, 1992; Al Haj, 1992. For parallels to other countries see Goldscheider, 1991; Goldscheider, 1992b; Alonso, 1987). Not surprisingly, immigration has been perceived very differently by Jewish and Arab populations within Israel (Al Haj, 1992). The establishment of the state and its Jewish demographic expansion has profoundly affected the Arab population, converting it from a majority population before the establishment of the state to a minority group when the new boundaries and its population were drawn in 1948 (Al Haj, 1987). Immigration not only shaped the ethnic composition of the Jewish population of Israel, but also redefined the position of the Arab Israeli population.

Understanding the basic contours of who immigrated to Israel, when they arrived, from which areas of the world, and what happened to them in their integration into Israel are indispensable bases for clarifying the changes in the society over the last half century, particularly the evolution of ethnic factors. Pick up any thread of social life in Israel—family, social and geographic mobility, education, politics, religion, gender, stratification, culture—and the role of immigration and the ethnic origins of the Israeli population will be important. Identify any social problem—Arab-Jewish relationships, inequality, economic dependencies, crime, religious conflict—and the past and continuing effects of immigration and ethnic composition will become clear. Here, we focus on the basics of immigration and the role of immigration in shaping the ethnic development of Israeli society, including Arab-Jewish demographic patterns.

Jewish Immigration to Israel: Four Major Streams—1948-1991

From the establishment of the state of Israel in 1948 until the 1990s, the rates of immigration and the countries of origin of the immigrants have fluctuated. They can be divided roughly into four main periods (Table 6.2).

A very high volume and rate of Jewish immigration from diverse countries in the three years after the establishment of the state of Israel doubled the size of the Jewish population. Initially, the immigrants were Jewish refugees coming to a predominantly European origin society; in 1948, 85 percent of the 100,000 immigrants to Israel were of European origin. This pattern changed as Jewish immigrants from Middle Eastern countries joined this stream. In 1949 and 1950 only about half of the immigrants were from Europe. By 1951, over 70 percent of the immigrants were from Asian and North African countries, mainly Iraq, Iran, and Libya. The primary determinants of this migration were political and economic, with some elements of religious messianism among Jews from the traditional communities of Asia and North Africa. The period of mass immigration, 1948-1951, established some of the basic socio-demographic, economic, and political contours in Israeli society.

The second major stream of immigration to Israel began in the mid-1950s, when over half the immigrants were from North African countries, particularly from Morocco, Tunisia, and Egypt.

Between 1955 and 1957, 165,000 immigrants arrived. The occupational skills and educational background of these immigrants differed significantly from the earlier European origin streams. The migrants arrived with fewer occupational skills and lower levels of education and were not easily integrated into the labor market.

The third major immigration wave began after the 1967 war, coming mostly from Eastern Europe (the Soviet Union and Rumania) and from Western countries, mainly the United States. These areas continue to be the largest Jewish population centers outside of Israel, and therefore the major potential sources of Jewish immigration. Between 1972 and 1979, 267,582 immigrants arrived in Israel, including 51 percent from the Soviet Union and 8 percent from the United States. Of the 153,833 immigrants to Israel between 1980 and 1989, 65 percent were from Europe and America; 11 percent were from Ethiopia; and 6 percent were from Iran. Restrictions on the emigration of Jews from the Soviet Union and the option of alternative destinations (particularly to the United States) reduced the flow of Russian immigrants to Israel until 1989.

TABLE 6.2 Immigrants by Origin and Period of Immigration, 1948-1991: Israel

	All Countries (000s)	Percent	Asia	Africa	East Europe	Central Europe Balkan	Other West
1948	101.8	100	5	9	54	29	3
1949	239.6	100	31	17	28	22	3
1950	170.2	100	34	15	45	4	2
1951	175.1	100	59	12	26	2	1
1952-54	54.1	100	25	51	12	5	8
1955-57	164.9	100	6	62	23	6	3
1958-60	75.5	100	18	18	56	2	6
1961-64	228.0	100	9	51	32	1	6
1965-68	81.3	100	19	31	37	2	11
1969-71	116.5	100	17	10	41	2	29
1972-74	142.8	100	4	5	71	1	19
1975-79	124.8	100	10	5	60	1	24
1980-84	83.6	100	8	19	43	1	30
1985-89	70.2	100	12	13	42	1	33
1990	199.5	100	3		95	1	1
1991	169.2	100	11		87	1	1

Note: East Europe includes USSR, Latvia, Lithuania, Poland, Rumania; Central Europe includes Germany, Austria, Czechoslovakia, Hungary; Balkan includes Greece, Bulgaria, Yugoslavia; Other West includes other European countries, America, South Africa, and Oceania.

Source: D. Friedlander and C. Goldscheider, *The Population of Israel*, Columbia University Press, 1979, Table 2.6; Statistical Abstract of Israel, various years. For 1991, Jewish Telegraph Agency, 2/92.

A fourth immigration stream to Israel began in 1989 and continued through 1991, as large numbers of Russian Jewish immigrants emigrated from the former Soviet Union. (Immigration restrictions reduced the number of Russian Jews entering the United States). An estimated 370,000 Jewish immigrants arrived in Israel during the two-year period of 1990 to 1991, mostly from Russia. The number of immigrants (although not the number relative to the population of Israel) is the largest since the period of mass immigration forty years earlier. It is the largest ever to enter Israel from any one country during such a brief period. During this period an additional 15,000 Ethiopian Jews were airlifted to Israel in a few days. While small in size, this group symbolized Israel's continuing commitment to be the political haven for refugee Jews around the world. The potential for more immigrants from Russia is great, given the large number of Jews still living there and their uncertain economic and political conditions under the Confederation of Independent States that emerged in place of the Soviet Union in December, 1991.

Changes over time in the rate and composition of immigration to Israel have reverberated throughout the society in terms of the integration of the immigrants themselves and their impact on previous immigrant streams, as well as on the social-demographic structure of the whole society. Several demographic implications are highlighted: (1) The role of immigration in the relative growth of Jewish and Arab populations, which maintains the demographic dominance of the Jewish population and the link between population growth and nation-building; (2) changes in residential distribution and ethnic composition that resulted from immigration; and (3) socioeconomic changes and generational continuities (marriage and family) among ethnic-immigrant communities, their national integration, residential segregation, and changes in ethnic inequalities.

The most conspicuous and direct effect of immigration was on the increase in the population of the country. The size of the population doubled between 1948 and 1951, and doubled again between 1951 and 1971, increasing to almost five million by the end of 1991. The Jewish population component increased more than five-fold between 1948 and 1990, from 717,000 to almost four million. Had there been no immigration, the size of the Jewish population of Israel in the 1970s would have been less than one million instead of 2.7 million, and the proportion of Jews in the state of Israel would have been 65 percent instead of the actual proportion of 85 percent (Friedlander and Goldscheider, 1979, Table 7.6). In contrast, the Arab minority within the state of Israel has grown by natural increase, since immigration has remained in large part restricted to the Jewish population. Almost half of the total growth of the Jewish population between 1948 and 1990 was a direct function of immigration, while 98 percent of the growth of the Arab population was due to natural increase.

Population Growth and the Arab Minority

Demographic issues have been in the forefront of the conflict between Arabs and Jews in Palestine-Israel since the end of the nineteenth century (Friedlander and Goldscheider, 1979; Goldscheider, 1991; Goldscheider, 1992b). The relative size and growth rates of Arab and Jewish populations; their geographic distribution; the number of Jews permitted or subsidized to enter the country (relative to economic opportunities and rates of Arab demographic growth); the different sources of their population growth (high fertility among Arabs and immigration among Jews); and the "optimum" size of the Jewish and Arab populations (relative to resources, territory, and political control) have been among the more conspicuous demographic concerns over the last century, under several political regimes and within different territorial configurations. As a result, the analysis of Arab demographic patterns often has been limited to its role in the Arab-Jewish conflict, rather than serving as a basis for understanding Arab social structure.1

The issue that has been at the core of the demographic history of Arab Israelis has been the changing Arab-Jewish population ratio within Israel. This often has been considered the key or only demographic issue of the Arab-Israel conflict, with powerful political, economic, and ideological implications for the emerging Jewish state. The relative size and the implied growth rates of Jewish and Arab populations were recognized by all three political actors (Jews, Arabs, and the British) before the establishment of the state. This became a different but no less critical issue in the years following the mass immigration of 1948 to 1951, after the Arab population had been converted into a minority group, and in later periods, when the volume and rates of Jewish immigration to Israel fluctuated. The Arab-Jewish demographic balance emerged in more dramatic form after the 1967 war with the inclusion of Arab areas and populations under Israeli administration and control (see the extensive discussions and analyses in Friedlander and Goldscheider, 1974; 1979; 1984; Goldscheider, 1991; Goldscheider, 1992b. On the general theme of the sociological significance of the relative size of minority and majority populations, see Lieberson, 1980).

The Arab-Jewish population growth rates and their different demographic sources have been viewed in the traditional framework of demographic transition theory. It is argued that the Arab demographic situation has reached the stage of "transition," with low levels of mortality and continuing higher rates of fertility that began to decline only during the 1970s. In contrast, the Jewish demographic pattern already has reached a later evolutionary stage of low levels of both fertility and mortality, and hence, low population growth rates due to natural increase. This pattern first characterized the European Jewish population in Israel and currently describes second-generation Israeli Jews of Asian and African origins. While the younger cohorts of Jewish Israelis are moving toward zero population growth, the Arab Israeli population remains in the high population growth stage. It does not take much demographic orientation to imagine (and often exaggerate) the socio-political consequences of a rapidly growing minority population and a relatively slow-growing majority population.

However, the issue of the relative number of Israeli Jews and Arabs and the implied demographic threat of Israeli Arab population growth rates to the political control of the Jewish majority is a profound ideological construction with little demographic basis. Since the establishment of Israel, the Arab proportion of the total population of the state has fluctuated around a narrow and low range. No reasonable assumption of future demographic dynamics would lead to an Arab Israeli demographic threat to the Jewish majority. Only the political incorporation of Arab populations that are not Israeli citizens—e.g., those living on the West Bank and Gaza—or the mass emigration of Jewish Israelis would lead to this result. When considering only Arab Israelis, not Palestinians living outside the current boundaries of the state, and assuming that mass emigration of Jews from Israel or mass immigration of Arabs to Israel are very unlikely events, it is unambiguously clear that the Arab population will remain a permanent demographic minority in both the short and long runs at the national level.

Arab-Jewish population size differences are most striking at the regional and community levels, where residential concentration patterns have emerged between them. There are regions within Israel with a majority Arab population, and areas within regions that have high levels of Arab population concentration and segregation. It is at the local level that changes in Arab population size shape the labor supply and demand in an economic market, and create the potential for local market expansion as well as the retention of some specialized skilled labor and professionals. The regional-community demography of Arab-Israeli population change emerges, with importance far beyond that of the national Jewish-Arab population ratio.

Immigration and Ethnic Compositional Changes

While Jewish immigration maintained a Jewish majority population, the most conspicuous change associated with immigration has been the emergence of Jewish ethnic compositional diversity. In the years between 1948 and 1990, over two million Jewish immigrants entered Israeli society, for an annual average of about 45,000 per year. Of this total, 40 percent were from Asian-African countries and 60 percent were from European-American countries. The proportion of immigrants from

Asian and African countries has shifted, from over 70 percent in the period 1952 to 1957 to a low of less than 10 percent in the early 1970s.

The changing immigration patterns by specific countries of origin translate into important shifts in the ethnic composition of the population over time, from an overwhelming Western-origin population to a balanced composition of those from Western and Middle East origins. Given the overlap of ethnic origin with social and economic resources, political orientations, and culture, the ethnic compositional shifts have had and will have major implications for the social, economic, and demographic development of Israeli society. The ethnic dimension is primarily based on the relative economic and educational status of ethnic groups; the different access of ethnic groups to economic opportunities and networks; and the generational transmission of ethnic stratification.

Immigration to Israel has resulted in the convergence of ethnic differences in some areas of social life as well as ethnic continuities in others (Schmelz et al., 1990). The key questions are the relative balance of these changes and their implications for the next generation and for the factors that sustain ethnic distinctiveness. On the one hand, all groups have assimilated linguistically as the national language of Hebrew has developed and expanded, linking Jews of different national origins and with diverse linguistic backgrounds. Educational and military institutions have been almost universal experiences for the Jewish population; external hostilities and continuous wars with Arab countries also have unified the Jewish population of Israel.

Nevertheless, ethnic communities in Israel are marked by continuing differential socioeconomic advantage and access to resources that are reinforced by discrimination and culture. They have different life-styles and differential relationships with the Arab minorities living in Israel and in the territories administered by Israel (Smooha, 1978; Lewin-Epstein and Semyonov, 1992; Goldscheider, 1986; Goldscheider, 1992a; Goldscheider, 1992b). It is also clear that new Jewish Israeli patterns have emerged that are neither fully "Western" nor "Oriental." At the same time, Israel has generated new forms of ethnicity through its institutions and the ways immigrants of various waves have been integrated into Israeli society, particularly when associated with ethnic residential concentration. These new ethnic forms are Israeli-made products, not simply the legacy of origins, background, and immigrant selectivity. These new forms are symbolized by the use of the designations "European-American" and "Asian-African" for the two major ethnic origin populations of Jews and the application of the term "non-Jews" or Arabs to designate the Moslem, Christian, and Druze segments of the Arab Israeli population. Jewish ethnic differences in education and in family patterns, for examples, are more tied to these emerging groups than to the specific countries of origin within them (Friedlander, et al., 1979; Nahon 1987).

Although ethnic cultural differences remain prominent, and distance from the immigrant generation continues to be an important factor in understanding social change in Israel, the critical issues are still the structural features of Israeli society that differentiate ethnic groups in Israel. There is a substantial overlap of ethnic origin with educational attainment, residential concentration, and political orientation (Goldscheider and Zuckerman, 1985). Higher levels of education and occupation continue to characterize European origin populations of the third generation. Ethnic residential concentration continues by region (e.g., living in a development town versus a major urban center), which, in turn, is linked to occupational and educational opportunities. Ethnic concentration also characterizes residential patterns among the neighborhoods of large metropolitan centers. Continuing high rates of intra-ethnic marriages and ethnic self-identity may be observed, despite some increases in inter-ethnic marriages over time (Goldscheider, 1983; Eisenbach, 1992; Schmelz, et al., 1991). The selectivity of inter-ethnic marriages by education, for example, reinforces ethnic differentiation, since it is the more educated Asian-African origin persons who marry out. Paradoxically, as inter-ethnic marriage rates increase, the ethnic-social class overlap is reinforced. This pattern contrasts sharply with the assumption that intermarriage among groups is the quintessential indicator of assimilation (cf. Gordon, 1964; Eisenbach, 1992 on Israeli inter-ethnic marriage; Goldscheider, 1983; Goldscheider, 1986).

Ethnicity and Residential Concentration

A major source of continuing ethnicity is the residential concentration of ethnic groups within Israel. This is reflected in regional variation in ethnic Jewish composition, with high levels of continuous Asian-African concentration in development towns, and high levels of European-American populations in wealthier suburbs of cities and in older areas of settlement (Kirshenbaum, 1992). These regional patterns are echoed by ethnic Jewish population concentrations within cities. Evidence from the early 1960s through the 1980s points to an initial segregation by immigrant origins and a continuing segregation by broader ethnic categories. For the recent period, there are trends toward both segregation and integration within Israeli cities. Within the European-American origin population there has been a general decline in the level of segregation, because of mobility of Asian- and African-origin families into the higher-status, inner areas of cities. At the same time, small clusters of European-American origin populations in new garden suburban neighborhoods have been joined by people of Asian and African origins. The residential integration trends for Asian and African origin groups have been limited to some geographic areas; some have observed that Asian and African sub-populations increasingly have been segregated within pockets of poverty. Those who have been left behind in the social mobility process have become a hard core poverty group, segregated not only from the Europeans but from the upwardly mobile second-generation Asian and Africans (Klaff, 1977; Gonen, 1985; Kirshenbaum, 1992).

As a result, the ethnic residential map has become more complex over the last several decades. The overlap between ethnicity and poverty is a clear national pattern. Segregation at the development town level has had, and continues to have, negative consequences for some ethnic groups by increasing the socioeconomic gap in Israel through the differential availability of local educational institutions, jobs, and access to the other institutions of society (Spilerman and Habib, 1976; Lipshitz, 1991). The dispersion of immigrants to the national periphery of Israel in the 1950s tended to spread out the population more evenly, but resulted in increased polarization in the distribution of development (Lipshitz, 1991).

A similar process of residential concentration along with a reinforcement of ethnic distinctiveness characterizes the Arab population. Political control over internal migration limited voluntary movements through the mid-1960s; informal constraints continue to limit internal migration.2 Residential segregation among Arab Israelis is nearly total, and much more extensive than among ethnic Jewish groups. There are over 100 communities listed in the Israeli census; all but seven are either totally Arab (35) or totally Jewish (61). The proportion of Arabs in the seven mixed localities ranges from 6 percent to 30 percent (Semyonov and Tyree, 1981; Lewin-Epstein and Semyonov, 1992). The places where Arabs are segregated reveals the differential opportunity structure of Jews and Arabs, and their access to economic markets. Most of the Arab communities are small and rural, where opportunities are scarce and economic development and infrastructure limited. The ecological distribution of health facilities, educational opportunities, and other social and economic investments, combined with geographic isolation and small size, conspire to maintain women's dependency on men and the relative economic dependency of men on the Jewish economic sector. Through its impact on educational and occupational opportunities, segregation limits efforts by the next generation of young adults to improve its standard of living and reinforces the general scarcity of opportunity for an expanding population base.

The "integration" of the Arab Israeli population within the Jewish economy has thus resulted in its increased economic and political dependency and continuing social and economic inequality. The residential segregation of Israeli Arabs has been a key factor in this process. Dependency is used in the sociological sense of the power exercised by the majority population and its control over the social, economic, and political opportunities available to the minority population. Dependency does not necessary reflect legal or political inequalities, but implies the continued social structural asymmetries and differential access to opportunities for the Arab minority within Israel. The structural sources of discrimination against Arab Israelis are reflected in the income and occupational returns to education and in the costs of residential segregation in limiting access to economic opportunity. Data from the 1983 Israeli census show that Arabs working in the Jewish economic sector experience both occupational and income inequality. In contrast, Arabs working in Arab communities are occupationally advantaged, reflecting group competition in local labor markets. While segregation into ethnic enclaves excludes minorities from equal access to broader opportunities and rewards, it provides temporary protection from discrimination generated by competition (Nahon 1987; Semyonov and Cohen, 1990; Lewin-Epstein and Semyonov, 1992).

The system of economic dependency among Arab Israelis permeates the system of stratification among Arabs, particularly their economic and political powerlessness. Dependency is integral part of the educational system and the curricular orientation of Arab schools; of the Israeli values that inform their lives; the national character of their communities; and the general feeling that their communities are linked to an Israeli society that dismisses their culture as merely political and views their strength only as potential for terrorism. The dependence of the Arab population has increased in direct relation to the rise in the standard of living within Arab communities (Al Haj, 1987; 1992).

The economic and labor force consequences of residential concentration for Arab men and women have been critical in maintaining their disadvantaged economic status. The dependency of the Arab communities on the Jewish economic sector is a direct outcome of state policies and the subsequent increased discrimination in the labor market. These outcomes are part of the costs of the external Arab-

Israel conflict and they reinforce internal ethnic tensions within the state of Israel. While there may be short-term economic benefits to segregation, in the long run the increasing educational attainment of Arab men and women raises a new cohort of young men and women whose opportunities are constrained both by residential segregation and by economic dependence on the Jewish sector.

As it has become clear among black Americans (Massey, 1990; Wilson, 1987), segregation, disadvantage, and dependency are often the result of the changing nature of the economy in post-industrial societies. Levels of racial segregation in large urban areas of America are high and show little signs of decline; as education and income rise the degree of black segregation has not declined. Similar processes appear to characterize Arab Israelis. Neither black Americans nor Arab Israelis can escape the high economic, social, educational, and unmeasured social psychological costs of residential segregation and regional concentration. The vulnerability of Arab Israelis stems from the fact that segregation intensifies and magnifies any economic setback and builds deprivation structurally into the socioeconomic environment (Goldscheider, 1992b). It is also likely that the residential concentration of Asian-African origin Jews in development towns experience similar kinds of disadvantage and economic deprivation.

Residential concentration in this structural context results, therefore, in the continuing economic powerlessness of Arab Israelis, leading to an Arab underclass, as it leads to poverty among some Jewish ethnics. The expanded work opportunities that occurred in Israel in the post-1967 period did not change the status of Arab Israelis. Their increased segregation, resulting from increased population growth and limited expansion of the area where they could live, led to increased levels of economic disadvantage precisely at the time when objective conditions were becoming better. These processes of residential segregation have made the Arab minority vulnerable and conspicuous: vulnerable in the sense of being subject to economic changes, not just to political harassment; conspicuous in the sense of being located where a distinctive quality of life characterizes their community and identifies them in clear ways.

Their increased level of educational attainment, the availability of jobs in the Jewish sector, and their traditional family structure have spared Arab Israelis some of the dire consequences of their residential segregation. The presence of West Bank and Gaza Palestinians in the market also may have reduced their level of disadvantage. Nevertheless, the consequences of segregation for the quality of life of Arab Israelis are as profound as they have been for black Americans, even though the reasons behind the residential concentration are different. The longer term disadvantage for Israeli Arabs may be as powerful as the "apartheid" residential situation that has been described for black Americans.

In the short run, there may be a need for Arabs and Jews to develop opportunities within separate economic sectors. Ethnic segregation within Israel may be necessary, given the evidence that shows that there is a great deal of mistrust between the communities (Smooha, 1992). Greater segregation may work to the benefit of both Jewish and Arab communities if it includes greater symmetry between them, with freedom of internal economic and political controls, and linked in important ways to the national entitlement programs. However, such segregation is likely to reinforce distrust between the communities.

By the standards of ethnic assimilation, in Israel and in other pluralistic societies, the Arab Israeli distinctiveness is embedded in the social and residential structure of Israeli society, its values and political culture. The disadvantage associated with continued distinctiveness is not likely to change until the wider set of Israel-Arab issues is resolved. Although concrete steps were being taken by mid-1992 toward a peaceful resolution of the Arab-Israel conflict, initiated by a newly formed Labor-dominated government, the disadvantage of Arabs within Israel is unlikely to be resolved without major internal changes within the society, its institutions, values, and political system. Barring fundamental changes within the Jewish state of Israel, the segregation of Arab Israelis will continue and the consequences for socioeconomic inequality will persist at least for another generation.

Ethnicity and Demographic Convergences

Unlike the continuing residential concentration among Jews and between Jewish and Arab sub-populations, which perpetuates ethnic distinctiveness and disadvantage, there are clear indications of demographic convergences in the vital processes of mortality and fertility. This is clear evidence that similarities in levels of fertility and mortality do not necessarily imply the end to ethnic stratification or the decline of ethnic communities.

Along with government policy, immigration and ethnic compositional shifts have had a major impact on the reduction of mortality differentials, which were a powerful indicator of social inequality. The initial differential mortality by ethnic origin initially reflected the range of mortality levels among places of origin. Taking a simple illustration, Jews from Yemen had rates of mortality that were similar to less-developed countries of the 1950s, with life expectancies of less than 40 years, and with infant mortality claiming about 33 percent of all births within a year. In contrast, the European immigrants had much lower levels of mortality, similar to Western levels. By the 1980s, life expectancy of Jews in Israel was 73 years, with almost no variation by ethnic origin. The decline in mortality and the convergence among ethnic groups can be attributed in large part to changes in the basic health infrastructure; the control over environmental conditions; the increased access to education; the development of an entitlement system of an emerging welfare state that created health clinics and medical personnel; and the accessibility of these resources to the population.

It is also clear that the system of entitlements that was designed to overcome the liability of origin could not provide perfectly equal entitlements. Differences in the location of services and the continuing, although strongly reduced, ability to purchase even better access and resources have an effect on differential mortality (Zadka, 1989; Peritz, 1986). Mortality differentials by ethnic origin in contemporary Israel should be viewed another way: what would have been the mortality levels if there had been no system of entitlement and no attempt to reduce the health-welfare gap among immigrant groups from diverse places of origin? While it is likely that the mortality differences would have declined over several decades, the rapid decline and the clear-cut convergence among ethnic origin groups can be understood only as an attempt to build the society on the basis of health and welfare services for all. To the extent that there are pockets of higher mortality that are ethnically based, the sources of these differences are likely to be socioeconomic and locational (Friedlander et al., 1990). So the health and entitlement system could overcome the resource differentials among ethnic groups, at least among Jews.

Have these entitlements been extended to the Arab-Israeli population? An examination of Arab mortality shows significant declines beginning before 1948 that gained momentum later. In the 1920s, the infant mortality rate of Moslems was around 17 percent of all births compared to around 12 percent for Jews. By the 1930s, the infant mortality rate of Jews declined to around 6 percent of all births, while Moslem infant mortality remained over 12 percent until the 1940s. By 1955, the Jewish level was around 3 percent compared to 6 percent among Moslems. The relative infant mortality rates per 1,000 births were 8 for Jews and 15 for Moslems by the late 1980s. So the decline was slower for Moslems and the mortality levels have remained almost twice as high as for Jews. The extension of health care and public health facilities within Arab communities accounts for most of the reduction of Arab mortality. However, residential segregation continues to result in the unequal distribution of health care in more isolated Arab communities in Israel and their differential access to the more extensive health care facilities in large Jewish areas (Anson, 1992). Thus, for Israeli Arabs, and to a lesser extent for Israeli Jews in development towns and in poorer neighborhoods of cities, continuing residential concentration has resulted indirectly in the unequal distribution of life chances.

Ethnic convergences in fertility have taken place as all groups within Israel have moved toward the small family. The transition from large to small family size, in Israel and around the world, has been linked to the decreasing value of children as farm laborers; the changing role of women; the increasing investments of parents in their children together with the higher costs of raising children; the returns to small family size as the opportunity structure expands; and the greater ability of couples to control their reproductive decisions. Indeed, one manifestation of the increasing choice that accompanies modernization is the revolutionary change in fertility (Goldscheider, 1992c).

The fertility of Israelis of European-American origins has remained low, with a slight increase over time; in contrast, there has been a steady decline in Christian fertility and a significant reduction in Moslem Israeli fertility over the last two decades. Over time, major reductions have occurred in the high fertility levels of migrants from Asian and African countries: total fertility rates dropped by 50 percent in the 30 years to the 1980s and to 2.8 in 1990. (See Table 6.3 for various measures of fertility over time.) These several fertility transitions have resulted in substantial ethnic convergences.

As with mortality differentials, specific country of origin differences in fertility have diminished. The remaining ethnic differences reflect socioeconomic differences between the two broad Israeli-created groups—European-American and Asian-African. Recent analyses (Friedlander and Feldman, 1993; Kupinsky, 1992) suggest that religion has become the major remaining differentiator of Jewish-Israeli fertility. This factor probably is linked to a series of values about family and the role of women that have been less responsive to change in socio-economic contexts.

The fertility transition was slower among Arabs than Jews. Fertility declines have characterized the Moslem Israeli population since the 1970s (see Eisenbach, 1986) and even earlier among Christian Arab Israelis (see Friedlander, et al, 1979).

TABLE 6.3 Selected Measures of Fertility by Ethnicity: Israel 1955-1990

	1955	1960	1965	1970	1975	1980	1985	1990
Total Fertility Rates								
TOTAL	4.03	3.95	3.99	3.97	3.68	3.14	3.12	3.02
Jews	3.64	3.49	3.47	3.41	3.21	2.76	2.85	2.69
EA Born	2.63	2.38	2.60	2.84	2.82	2.76	2.79	2.31
AA Born	5.68	5.10	4.58	4.07	3.77	3.04	3.21	3.09
Moslem	7.96	9.31	9.87	8.95	7.75	5.98	4.86	4.70
Christian	4.85	4.61	4.74	3.62	3.35	2.66	2.12	2.57
Druze	6.58	7.88	7.61	7.46	6.85	6.09	4.47	4.05
Proportion with Five or More Live Births								
TOTAL	23	29	27	22	17	15	14	16
Jews	19	24	21	15	10	8	9	12
Moslem	49	50	51	50	45	40	32	28
Christian	39	40	33	25	19	16	9	7

Age Specific Fertility Rates

	1955-1959	1965-1969	1975-1979	1985-1989
JEWS				
Europe-America Born				
<Age 19	43.4	33.3	58.3	34.0
20-24	168.1	172.0	166.3	135.6
40-44	8.4	5.5	6.8	10.7
45-49	0.8	0.5	0.2	0.7
Asian-African Born				
<Age 19	89.3	61.0	47.6	38.8
20-24	289.9	234.4	202.1	163.4
40-44	50.2	33.2	17.5	15.1
45-49	15.8	8.7	1.9	1.2
Moslem				
<Age 19	119.6	113.8	91.8	53.9
20-24	375.8	383.9	334.0	236.9
40-44	107.8	154.9	90.0	47.4
45-49	41.1	55.8	20.6	5.8
Christian <Age 19	58.7	45.5	30.3	18.0
20-24	227.9	224.7	189.5	154.4
40-44	29.8	29.6	15.8	7.6
45-49	5.5	4.4	1.3	0.6

Source: Statistical Abstract of Israel, Various Issues.

An analysis of ideal family size by marriage cohort (as viewed in the 1970s) documented significant change in the fertility expectations of Arab women (Friedlander and Goldscheider, 1978). While Christian women who were married before 1955 had an ideal family size of around six children, the younger cohorts married in the post-1967 period had an average ideal family size of four children. Moslem women of the older cohort had an ideal family size of around eight children, declining among those married in the 1970s to five children. Viewed in the cross-section, the fertility of Israeli Moslems reached 9.9 births per women in the 1960s and dropped in the last two decades to 4.7 children per women, one of the lowest among Moslem populations in the Middle East. In the last 15 years, fertility reductions occurred even among women at shorter marriage durations and spread to all socioeconomic segments of the population (Eisenbach, 1989).

The importance of Arab-Jewish differences in fertility for population growth is unmistakable. There are also costs of high fertility for Arab women within their communities and families. Large family size also imposes costs by limiting the socioeconomic opportunities available for the next generation. The traditional role of Arab women is not only a factor sustaining high fertility (Friedlander, et al., 1979) but large family size has reinforced the family-oriented roles of Arab-Israeli women (Al Haj, 1987). The trend toward lower fertility reflects a combination of factors, including declining mortality, increased female educational attainment, and greater female labor force participation, particularly among the more educated (Eisenbach, 1989).

The economic integration of Arabs within the Jewish economy has also had an impact on the role of women and on their fertility. Women and men have left agriculture to commute to jobs within the Jewish sector; standards of living have increased in real terms, as has consumption (Eisenbach, 1989). These overall economic changes, along with the benefits from the welfare state and the increased role of the Jewish economic sector in generating opportunities, suggest that the power of the extended family (the *Hamulah*) has declined, particularly among younger couples. Thus, from the point of view of the Arab community, large family size reinforced the family-economic connection intergenerationally in the past, but this is changing for young couples. Fertility change is an important reflection of the changing social organization of Arab Israeli communities (Eisenbach, 1989; Friedlander et al., 1979; Al Haj, 1987).

Is Ethnicity Transitional?

Have the ethnic convergences in fertility and mortality resulted in the declining significance of ethnicity and of ethnic communities? Is the increasing demographic homogeneity among ethnic groups paralleled by increasing cultural and social homogeneity? Put analytically, under what conditions do ethnic communities retain their importance and what are the contexts that facilitate ethnic assimilation, particularly under a regime of demographic convergence?

The occupational skills, educational background, family and ethnic ties, and earlier entry into Israeli society of the European immigrants facilitated their relatively successful rise and their access to power, resources, and opportunity. European immigrants could take advantage of their connections to the European-dominated society and economy. Asian-Africans came from societies that were less modern and were less able to compete with the European-origin groups in Israel. The timing of immigration and the cultural differences between groups reinforced these structural factors as well as community links that divided Israeli Jews. Immigration created new ethnic communities among Jews in Israel, even as the specific country of origin differences declined in significance.

The timing of immigration along with the ethnic composition of immigrant streams created the contexts of residential concentration among Jews. These ethnic residential patterns, not the legacy of social and cultural origins, shape what ethnicity means in the process of nation-building in Israel. Residential concentration forged from political considerations is the key process underlying the Jewish-Arab distinctiveness. New Israeli patterns have emerged that are neither fully "Western" nor "Oriental." Although ethnic cultural differences remain prominent, and distance from the immigrant generation continues to be an important factor in understanding social change in Israel, the structural features within Israel, particularly residential segregation and its implication for access to opportunity, are critical in retaining ethnic distinctiveness. Higher levels of education and occupation continue to characterize European origin populations of the third generation. Ethnic residential concentration regionally and in metropolitan areas is linked to educational opportunities and to jobs. High rates of intra-ethnic marriages and ethnic self-identity remain, despite some increases in inter-ethnic Jewish marriages over time. Marriage patterns reinforce the ethnic-family network connection. Again, these patterns are almost total between Jews and Arabs and characterize most third-generation Jews when examined by the two broad Jewish ethnic categories.

Intergenerational mobility has not closed the educational or occupational gap between immigrant Jewish groups. While every ethnic group has been characterized by social mobility, the ethnic gap has not diminished and has, at times, widened. Thus, inequalities have persisted even with rapid development and economic growth and the opening up of new opportunities within a relatively open stratification system (Kraus and Hodge, 1990). Ethnic differences in economic, social, cultural, and political spheres extend to the second and third generations born in Israel. These differences relate primarily to the different socioeconomic background of these populations, reinforced by the residential segregation of groups within Israel.

Israeli society has been shaped by immigration, its selectivity and ethnic composition, and the demographic transitions that have occurred. Israel has been characterized by patterns of change and transformation of ethnic-immigrant groups among the Jewish population and its minority Arab populations. On the one hand, there are clear indications of ethnic convergences in fertility and mortality and in other spheres of activity. National integration has taken place politically, if not socially. Yet other indicators show that along with integration, and often because of it, new forms of ethnic community patterns are emerging and new forms of minority distinctiveness have appeared. Such patterns are likely to persist for at least another generation. The emerging patterns in Israel suggest that the economic integration of ethnic populations may result in continuing forms of ethnic distinctiveness; that social mobility does not necessarily result in greater equality; and that ethnic residential concentration perpetuates divided societies.

In reviewing the political and demographic contexts of Israeli society, it becomes clear that some ethnic demographic differences diminish in importance and ethnic convergences occur over time. Ethnic convergences result when differences are primarily the result of the background of immigrants and the legacy of the past. So with each passing generation, mortality and fertility differentials by ethnic origin are reduced. In contrast, when the sources of ethnic differences are embedded in the society of destination, perhaps as a result of the timing of immigration and the ethnic-economic selectivity of immigrant streams, ethnic communities remain prominent. Ethnic residential concentration among Jews and between Jews and Arabs reinforces the overlap of ethnicity and socioeconomic factors through the impact of locational factors on access to educational and economic opportunities. As a result, residential concentration shapes the continuing importance of ethnic distinctiveness in Israel. Where groups (primarily ethnic

Jewish groups) are integrated residentially, ethnic differences have become marginal in their social, economic, and political importance. Where residential segregation within Israel has persisted, it has become the primary engine of ethnic persistence and inequality.

The social, political, and economic structure of Israeli society will continue to reflect the fundamentals of its demography. At both the societal and the community levels, Israel's demographic patterns may be viewed as a microcosm of general population patterns in Western and Third World countries. In their detail, these patterns reflect the historical legacy of Israel's formation as a new state in the post World War II era, the distinctive demographic patterns that have characterized its development from the turn of the century in Palestine, and the influence of demographic, social, political, and cultural events around the world at the end of the twentieth century. Indeed, Israel is an extraordinary illustration of the dynamic interplay among population processes, nation-building, and ethnicity.

Notes

1. The Arab population of Israel is heterogeneous with regard to religion, social class, and region of residence, as well as in terms of demographic processes. We focus on Moslem Israelis, who represent 78 percent of the Arab population of Israel in 1990. Christian Arabs in Israel have lower rates of mortality and fertility than either Moslem or Druze Israelis, are more urbanized and more educated. "Arab Israeli" will be treated as approximately equivalent to "Moslem Israeli" or "Palestinian Israeli."

2. While some internal migration has occurred over time in selected areas, including movements toward cities and internal movements among Arab communities, the major form of mobility, which is rarely captured and almost always underestimated by standard official migration data sources, is commuting—the daily movements of Arabs to work in Jewish areas. This circular or daily commuting pattern has replaced other, more permanent migration forms, and has been one factor slowing down changes that would have occurred under a more open internal migration policy. The absence of large scale internal migration reinforces the sharply differentiated status of Arabs vis-a-vis Jews and the status of women and men within the Arab community. There are also economic consequences of population growth without migration, which tends to reinforce the economic dependency of the Arab Israeli population (Goldscheider, 1992b).

References

Al Haj, Majid. 1987. *Social Change and Family Process: Arab Communities in Shefar A'm*. Boulder: Westview Press.

Al Haj, Majid. 1992. "Soviet Immigration as Viewed by Jews and Arabs: Divided Attitudes in a Divided Country." In *Population and Social Change in Israel*, edited by Calvin Goldscheider. Boulder: Westview Press.

Alonzo, William. 1987. "Introduction: Population North and South." In *Population in an Interacting World*, edited by William Alonzo. Cambridge: Harvard University Press.

Anson, Jon. 1992. "Mortality, Ethnicity, and Standard of Living: A Minority Group Effect?" In *Population and Social Change In Israel*, edited by Calvin Goldscheider. Boulder: Westview Press.

Berelson, Bernard. 1979. "Foreword." In *The Population of Israel*, edited by Dov Friedlander and Calvin Goldscheider. New York: Columbia University Press, 1979.

DellaPergola, Sergio. 1986. "Aliya and Other Jewish Migrations: Toward an Integrated Perspective." In *Studies In the Population of Israel*, edited by U.O. Schmelz and G. Nathan. Jerusalem: Magnes Press 1986.

Eisenbach, Zvi. 1986. "Family Planning Among the Muslim Population of Israel." In *Studies in the Population of Israel*, edited by O. Schmelz and G. Nathan. Jerusalem: Magnes Press, 1-14.

Eisenbach, Zvi. 1989. "Changes In the Fertility of Moslem Women In Israel in Recent Years." *HaMizrach Hahadash* : 86-102 (Hebrew).

Eisenbach, Zvi. 1992. "Marriage and Fertility In the Process of Integration: Intermarriage Among Origin Groups In Israel." In *Population and Social Change in Israel*, edited by Calvin Goldscheider. Boulder: Westview Press.

Friedlander, Dov and Calvin Goldscheider. 1974. "Peace and the Demographic Future of Israel." *Journal of Conflict Resolution* 18 : 486-501.

Friedlander, Dov and Calvin Goldscheider. 1978. "Immigration, Social Change and Cohort Fertility in Israel." *Population Studies* 32: 299-317.

Friedlander, Dov and Calvin Goldscheider. 1979. *The Population of Israel*. New York: Columbia University Press.

Friedlander, Dov and Calvin Goldscheider. 1984. *Israel's Population: The Challenge of Pluralism*. Population Bulletin, Population Reference Bureau.

Friedlander, Dov and Carole Feldman. 1993. "The Modern Shift to Below-Replacement Fertility: Has Israel's Population Joined the Process." *Population Studies* 47, no. 2 (July).

Friedlander, Dov, E. Ben-Moshe, J. Schellekens, and C. Feldman. 1990. *Socioeconomic Change, Demographic Processes, and Population Aging In Israel's Cities and Towns: Implications for Welfare Policies*. The Jerusalem Institute for Israel Studies, Research Studies 37.

Friedlander, Dov, Z. Eisenbach and C. Goldscheider. 1979. "Modernization Patterns and Fertility Change." *Population Studies* 33 : 239-254.

Goldscheider, Calvin. 1983. "The Demography of Asian and African Jews in Israel." In *Ethnicity, Identity, and History,* edited by J. B. Maier and C.I. Waxman. New Brunswick, N.J.: Transaction Books.

Goldscheider, Calvin. 1986. "Family Change and Variation among Israeli Ethnic Groups." In *The Jewish Family,* edited by Steve Cohen and Paula Hyman. New York: Holmes and Meier.

Goldscheider, Calvin. 1990. "Israel." In *Handbook on International Migration,* edited by W. J. Serow, C. Nam, D. Sly and R. Weller. New York: Greenwood Press.

Goldscheider, Calvin. 1991. "The Embeddedness of the Arab-Jewish Conflict in the State of Israel: Demographic and Sociological Perspectives." In *Israeli Politics in the 1990s,* edited by B. Reich and G. Kieval. New York: Greenwood Press : 111-132.

Goldscheider, Calvin. 1992a. *Population and Social Change in Israel.* (Edited) Boulder: Westview Press.

Goldscheider, Calvin. 1992b. "Demographic Transformations in Israel: Emerging Themes in Comparative Context." In *Population and Social Change in Israel,* edited by Calvin Goldscheider. Boulder: Westview Press.

Goldscheider, Calvin. 1992c. *Fertility Transitions, Family Structure, and Population Policy.* (Edited) Boulder: Westview Press.

Goldscheider, Calvin and Alan Zuckerman. 1984. *The Transformation of the Jews.* Chicago: University of Chicago Press.

Goldscheider, Frances and Calvin Goldscheider. 1989. *Ethnicity and the New Family Economy.* Boulder: Westview Press.

Goldscheider, Frances and Zara Fisher. 1989. "Household Structure and Living Alone In Israel." In *Ethnicity and the New Family Economy,* edited by Frances Goldscheider and Calvin Goldscheider. Boulder: Westview Press.

Gonen, Amiram. 1985. "The Changing Ethnic Geography of Israeli Cities." In *Studies In Israeli Ethnicity,* edited by Alex Weingrod. Gordon and Breach.

Gordon, Milton. 1963. *Assimilation in American Life.* Oxford University Press.

Klaff, Vivian. 1977. "Residence and Integration In Israel: A Mosaic of Segregated Groups." *Ethnicity* 4 : 103-121.

Kirshenbaum, Avi. 1992. "Migration and Urbanization: Patterns of Population Redistribution and Urban Growth." In *Population and Social Change in Israel,* edited by Calvin Goldscheider. Boulder: Westview Press.

Kupinsky, Shlomo. 1992. "Jewish Fertility Patterns: Norms, Differentials, and Policy Implications." In *Population and Social Change in Israel,* edited by Calvin Goldscheider. Boulder: Westview Press.

Kraus, Vered and Robert Hodge. 1990. *Promises in the Promised Land: Mobility and Inequality in Israel.* Westport, Conn.: Greenwood Press.

Lewin-Epstein, Noah and M. Semyonov. 1992. "Local Labor Markets, Ethnic Segregation and Income Inequality." *Social Forces* 70 : 1101-1119.

Lieberson, Stanley. 1990. *A Piece of the Pie: Blacks and White Immigrants Since 1880.*Berkeley: University of California Press.

Lipshitz, Gabriel. 1991. "Immigration and Internal Migration as a Mechanism of Polarization and Dispersion of Population and Development: The Israel Case." *Economic Development and Cultural Change*: 391-408.

Massey, Douglas. 1990. "American Apartheid: Segregation and the Making of the Underclass." *American Journal of Sociology* 96 : 329-357.

Nahon, Yaacov. 1987. Dfusei Hitrahavot Hahaskalah UMivneh Hahizdomnut Hataasukatit: Hammemad HaAdati. (Types of Educational Expansion and the Structure of Occupational Opportunities: the Ethnic Dimension). Machon Yerushalyim L'hekar Yisrael (Hebrew).

Peritz, Eric. 1986. "Mortality of African Born Jews in Israel" In Studies in the Population of Israel, edited by O. Schmelz and G. Natan. Jerusalem: Magnes Press, 229-242.

Schmelz, U.O., S. DellaPergola and U. Avner. 1990. "Ethnic Differences Among Israeli Jews: A New Look." American Jewish Yearbook 90 : 3-204.

Semyonov, Moshe and A. Tyree. 1981. "Community Segregation and the Costs of Ethnic Subordination." Social Forces 59 : 649-666.

Semyonov, Moshe and Y. Cohen. 1991. "Ethnic Discrimination and the Income of Majority Group Workers." American Sociological Review 55 : 107-114.

Smooha, Sammy. 1978. Israel: Pluralism or Conflict. Los Angeles: University of California Press.

Smooha, Sammy. 1989. Arab and Jews In Israel 1. Boulder: Westview Press.

Smooha, Sammy. 1991. Arab and Jews In Israel 2. Boulder: Westview Press.

Spilerman, Seymour and Jack Habib. 1976. "Development Towns In Israel: The Role of Community In Creating Ethnic Disparities in Labor Force Characteristics." American Journal of Sociology 81 : 781-812.

Statistical Abstract of Israel. Various issues.

Wilson, William Julius. 1987. The Truly Disadvantaged: The Inner City, the Underclass and Public Policy. Chicago: University of Chicago Press.

Zadka, Pnina. 1989. "Infant Mortality of the Jewish Population in Israel: Trends over Two Decades" In Papers In Jewish Demography: 1985, edited by O. Schmelz and S. DellaPergola. Jerusalem : 219-228.

7

Demographic Sources of the Changing Ethnic Composition of the Soviet Union[1]

Barbara A. Anderson
Brian D. Silver

Among the most dramatic phenomena in the Soviet Union after the beginning of the period of *perestroika* (restructuring) in 1985 was the increase in the open assertion of rights by ethnic minorities. Among non-Russian ethnic groups, claims of cultural autonomy and the establishment of local languages as official languages were related to concerns about loss of their distinctive ethnic heritages and patrimonies, the despoiling of the environment, and the lack of economic and political autonomy. Many of these claims focused on the policies of the central Party and government in Moscow as well as on the Russianization of the non-Russian regions.[2] Some of the most serious and violent instances of intergroup conflict occurred between non-Russian ethnic groups, such as between Uzbeks and Meskhetian Turks in Uzbekistan, between Armenians and Azerbaijanis in Nagorno-Karabakh, and between Abkhazians and Georgians in Soviet Georgia.

All of those events reminded us that the Soviet Union was a multi-ethnic country and that ethnic loyalties were an enduring aspect of society. More than 90 nationalities ("ethnic groups," in common English usage) had their historic homelands within the Soviet Union. According to the 1989 Soviet census, twenty-two nationalities had populations of one million or more. Table 7.1 provides some information about the nationalities that had more than one million members in 1989. These nationalities varied greatly in their population size and rates of growth.

TABLE 7.1.Demographic Characteristics of Nationalities in the USSR with a Population Greater than One Million in 1989a

Nationality	Population in 1989 (thousands)	Average annual growth rate (in percent)			Change in Population		Status of Titular Area	Population of Group Living in Titular Area in 1989 (thousands)	Percent of Group Living in Titular Area
		1959-70	1970-79	1979-89	1989 minus 1959	1989 divided by 1959			
USSR Total	285,743	1.3	0.9	0.9	76,916	1.37			
Russians	145,155	1.1	0.7	0.5	31,041	1.27	SSR	119,866	82.6
Ukrainians	44,186	0.8	0.4	0.4	6,933	1.19	SSR	37,419	84.7
Uzbeks	16,698	3.9	3.4	2.9	10,683	2.78	SSR	14,142	84.7
Belorussians	10,036	1.2	0.5	0.6	2,123	1.27	SSR	7,898	78.7
Kazakhs	8,136	3.5	2.4	2.2	4,514	2.25	SSR	6,535	80.3
Tatarsc	6,931	2.0	0.7	0.9	2,150	1.45	ASSR	1,765	25.5
Azerbaidzhanis	6,770	3.6	2.5	2.2	3,830	2.30	SSR	5,805	85.7
Armenians	4,623	2.2	1.7	1.1	1,836	1.66	SSR	3,084	66.7
Tadzhiks	4,215	4.0	3.5	3.5	2,818	3.02	SSR	3,172	75.3
Georgians	3,981	1.7	1.1	1.1	1,289	1.48	SSR	3,787	95.1
Moldavians	3,352	1.8	1.1	1.2	1,138	1.51	SSR	2,795	83.4
Lithuanians	3,067	1.2	0.7	0.7	741	1.32	SSR	2,924	95.3
Turkmenians	2,729	3.8	3.2	2.9	1,727	2.72	SSR	2,537	93.0
Kirgiz	2,529	1.7	3.0	2.8	1,560	2.61	SSR	2,230	88.2
Germans	2,039	1.2	0.5	0.5	419	1.26	Foreign		
Chuvash	1,842	1.3	0.4	0.5	372	1.25	ASSR	906	
Latvians	1,459	0.2	0.1	0.1	59	1.04	SSR	1,388	49.3

Jews[d]	1,450	-0.5	-1.9	-2.2	-817	0.64	AO	9	0.6
Bashkirs	1,449	2.1	1.1	0.6	460	1.47	ASSR	864	59.6
Mordvinians	1,154	-0.2	-0.6	-0.3	-799	0.63	ASSR	313	27.1
Poles	1,126	-1.5	-0.2	-0.2	-254	0.82	Foreign	963	93.8
Estonians	1,027	0.2	0.1	0.1	38	1.04	SSR		

a *Source:* Population figures for each year are from the Soviet censuses. Population counts for 1959 and 1970 are the "present (*nalichnoe*) population"; counts for 1979 and 1989 are the "permanent" (*postoiannoe*) population. Although the populations of the Daghestani nationalities together total more than 1 million persons, none of the separate populations reaches that size.

b SSR: Soviet Socialist Republic (union republic)
ASSR: Autonomous Soviet Socialist Republic (autonomous republic)
AO: Autonomous Oblast' (autonomous province)

c For the sake of continuity in calculating growth rates between censuses, both Volga Tatars and Crimean Tatars are included in the totals for Tatars in this table. See Table 7.2 for further information about the number of Crimean Tatars and other Tatars in Soviet Censuses.

d See the notes to Tble 7.2 regarding subpopulations of Jews. The Jewish Autonomous Oblast' is an official homeland of Soviet jews, thereby making them officially "indigenous" rather than foreign. But this region, which was established by Stalin in the early 1930s in the Soviet Far East, has never been the main homeland of Soviet Jews.

In the aftermath of the aborted *coup d'etat* of August 1991, the Soviet Union split apart in December 1991. Few people had forecast such a sudden and nonviolent end to the Soviet Union. The country broke up along ethnically-defined territorial boundaries, the borders of the federal republics of the USSR, which had delimited the historic homelands of major nationalities. The internal borders of the major Soviet federal republics now serve as the external borders of the successor states. Because of the dictatorial nature of the Soviet state, however, some of the federal territorial boundaries had been arbitrary and all had been permeable. As a result, the republics were ethnically diverse, and no regional government in the federal system could openly resist immigration by people of different ethnic groups. Just after the dissolution of the Soviet Union, 25 million Russians resided in the fourteen newly independent non-Russian states. And 20 million persons whose titular homelands became the fourteen new non-Russian states resided in independent Russia (the Russian Federation).

In this chapter, we discuss the changing ethnic composition of the Soviet population as a whole and by region between 1959 and 1989, the dates of the first and last post-War censuses of the population. We examine the proximate demographic sources of change for different regions of the country, with a special emphasis on fertility and migration. We show that the ethnic makeup of the Soviet population was very dynamic. Differences in population growth rates and in migration during the last 30 years led to marked changes in the ethnic composition of the USSR as a whole as well as the 15 union republics.[3] We focus on the populations of those union republics rather than the entire set of federal units and nationalities. The titular nationalities of these republics—the nationalities for which the republics are named— comprised 90.3 percent of the population of the Soviet Union in 1989.[4]

Our examination of the ethnic composition and distribution of the Soviet population during the three decades leading up to the break-up of the Soviet Union shows that an ethnically based territorial sorting out process had long been under way. It was not simply a product of rising nationalist feelings during the period of *perestroika* in the late 1980s.

Moreover, at the end of the 1980s, the long-dominant numerical position of Russians in the Soviet Union was on the verge of disappearing. At the time of the 1989 census, Russians comprised just 50.8 percent of the Soviet population. Before these data appeared, many observers had speculated that the 1989 census would show that Russians had become a numerical minority of the Soviet population. In fact, Russians outnumbered non-Russians by 4.6 million. This compares to a difference of 12.7 million in 1979,[5] 16.3 million in 1970, and 19.4 million in 1959. Russians might have fallen to a numerical minority in

1989 had there been a sudden and sharp reversal of assimilation of non-Russians by Russians. About 2.4 million people who called themselves Russians in the 1989 census would have had to have indicated a different ethnic affiliation to the census takers. This is less than 2 percent of the Russian population in 1989. We think it is likely that some such reversal did occur but that it was not large enough to reduce Russians to a numerical minority in 1989.

Components of Demographic Change

Four components of demographic change affect the composition of the population: migration, assimilation, mortality, and fertility. Of these, fertility and migration are the most important factors accounting for the changing ethnic composition of the Soviet population. In principle, one can examine each of these components to show their effect on the changing ethnic composition of the population.

A major limitation to studying the components of change in the ethnic composition of the Soviet population is that published data on fertility, mortality, and migration by ethnic group were scarce.[6] Almost all of the published data on these demographic processes refer either to the USSR as a whole or to regional units of the Soviet federation. For this reason, and owing to the absence of age data by nationality for 1979 and 1989, use of standard cohort component methods to project the changing ethnic composition of the Soviet population is difficult.

Migration

For the USSR as a whole, international migration—whether emigration or immigration—had only a negligible effect on the composition of the population in the last few decades before the USSR was dissolved in December 1991, although it had a large effect on the size of the migrating groups. Emigration mainly involved three groups: Jews, Germans, and Armenians.[7] The level of emigration was determined by internal political factors (the willingness of the Soviet government to grant exit visas to applicants wishing to leave), by the willingness of intended destination countries to receive immigrants from the Soviet Union, and by the attitudes and desires of populations from which emigrants come. Similarly, immigration had a negligible effect on the composition of the Soviet population as a whole, although it had an appreciable effect for some groups; for example, more than 100,000 Armenians were repatriated to Soviet Armenia after World War II, mostly from countries in the Middle East and the Mediterranean.

Internal migration had a large effect on the ethnic composition of particular regions. Such migration was a source of intergroup friction and a spur to debate over population policy, particularly among groups within the non-Russian regions that had experienced a large amount of immigration from other republics. Unfortunately, most Soviet official statistics did not include data on the ethnic affiliation of migrants. But available data permit us to estimate the impact of immigration of Russians on the ethnic composition of non-Russian regions.

Assimilation

Assimilation is another component of the changing ethnic composition of the population. No official data or estimates of assimilation were published in the USSR,[8] nor did Soviet researchers publish such estimates. Soviet censuses gathered information on the self-identified nationality of the population on the census date but did not ask whether individuals had identified themselves with a different nationality or whether their parents belonged to another nationality.

Elsewhere, we have attempted to measure the extent of assimilation of non-Russian ethnic groups (Anderson and Silver, 1983). We estimated that between 1959 and 1970, Russians gained a net 600,000 persons aged 11 to 49 years in 1970 due to ethnic self-identification of non-Russians. This amounts to about 1 percent of the number of 11 to 49 year-old Russians enumerated in the 1970 census. Although to our knowledge no researchers have made analogous estimates of assimilation for later dates, it is important to recognize assimilation as a source of change in the ethnic composition of the population, especially for many of the smaller and middle-sized nationalities, some of which have declined in absolute population size. Some of the larger nationalities, especially Ukrainians and Belarussians, also appear to have experienced moderate losses due to assimilation, though not as large as some observers have supposed (Anderson and Silver, 1983).

Another aspect of assimilation, one that does not strictly affect the ethnic composition of the population, is language. "Native language" was an important ethnic marker, closely tied to an individual's ethnic self-concept, yet also distinct from it. For most people, the change of native language was a fundamental, though not definitive, indication of change in ethnic self-concept, fairly easily followed by ethnic re-identification. "Second language," on the other hand, does not appear in general to be as fully imbued with the emotional component of ethnic identity. Whether non-Russians learned Russian as a second language depended heavily on more pragmatic considerations: the availability of schools in Russian and the non-Russian languages, and the extent of contact between Russians and non-Russians in the residential environment, work places, other day-to-day activities, and during military service. Thus, both for Russians and non-Russians living in non-Russian areas, the extent of bilingualism indicated the degree of mutual accommodation of ethnic groups. The extent of accommodation was not only due to attitudes and values; it also reflected practical incentives and opportunities to learn the other language. But in contrast to change in native language, learning a second language did not necessarily connote a serious change in ethnic self-concept.[9]

Mortality

Differential mortality also affected the ethnic composition of the population, although in the case of Soviet nationalities and the composition of Soviet regions the effect was much less than that of differential fertility and migration. As noted above, the Soviet government published virtually no data on mortality by ethnic group. Data for regions are an imperfect substitute and probably understate ethnic differences in general, because regions were not ethnically homogeneous. Also, Soviet mortality data were subject to substantial error (Anderson and Silver, 1986b, 1989, 1990b, 1993; Dmitrieva and Andreev, 1987; Sinel'nikov, 1988). Although regional comparisons of indicators as infant mortality rates and life expectancy at birth can show differences in the overall health conditions of the population, use of Soviet regional mortality schedules to measure or project the contribution of mortality to population change would be problematic even if the data were meant to represent ethnic groups rather than regions. Indirect estimation of mortality rates from age distributions in successive Soviet censuses is also risky, because a major source of the error in mortality data appears to be age overstatement (Garson, 1987).

Fertility

Fertility differences were a major source of the changing ethnic composition of the Soviet population as a whole and by region. Some data on fertility by ethnic groups have been published by selected years (Bondarskaia and Darskii, 1988). Soviet fertility data were also subject to considerable error, due to under-registration of births (Coale, Anderson, and Härm, 1979; Anderson and Silver, 1985a, 1986b, 1988; Anderson, Silver, and Liu, 1989). The most severe underregistration occurred in Central Asia (Coale, Anderson, and Härm, 1979). For some purposes, it was safer to infer birth rates from census counts than from vital registration figures. Census counts of young children were also subject to error, however. In the 1959, 1970, and 1979 Soviet censuses, approximately 3 to 4 percent of preschool children were not counted (Anderson and Silver, 1985a; Kingkade, 1985).

The foregoing discussion of the components of population change indicates some of the data limitations on the study of the ethnic demography of the Soviet Union. The increasing openness of Soviet official statistics after 1985 helped to lessen these limitations. However, very few new data on ethnic groups appeared, and we even lack some fundamental indicators from earlier years.

Nonetheless, the available data allow us to study many aspects of change in the ethnic composition of the Soviet population, including the two most important ones: fertility and migration. Fertility contributes most strongly to the changing ethnic composition of the Soviet population as a whole. Fertility and migration together account for most of the change in the ethnic composition of the population by region. Fertility is the most important factor in the Asiatic parts of the Soviet Union; migration is the most important factor in the European parts.

Data and Definitions

The main sources of data for this study are the Soviet censuses of 1959, 1970, 1979, and 1989. Additional data come from vital statistics on births and deaths. None of these sources is infallible. Elsewhere, we have shown systematic patterns of error in Soviet census and vital statistics data, most of which are the result of administrative difficulties in assuring accurate and complete counts of the population and of vital events, not of deliberate manipulation of statistics (Anderson and Silver, 1985a, 1986b, 1988, 1989, 1990b; Silver, 1986).

The data that we use from the 1959 and 1970 Soviet censuses are for the "present" (*nalichnoe*) population; the data for 1979 and 1989 are for the "permanent" (*postoiannoe*) population, which is slightly smaller for the USSR as a whole. The Soviet central statistical office changed its method of reporting on population between censuses.[10] In figures from the 1989 census, the present population exceeded the permanent population by about 1 million persons.[11]

Our discussion of regional patterns will focus on the 15 union republics of the USSR and on the titular nationality of the republics. We shall sometimes group the republics by region, using conventional categories: (1) Baltic (Estonia, Latvia, Lithuania), (2) West (Belarus, Moldavia, Ukraine), (3) Russia (RSFSR), (4) Transcaucasia (Armenia, Azerbaijan, Georgia), and (5) Central Asia (Kyrgyzstan, Tajikistan, Turkmenistan, Uzbekistan) and Kazakhstan.[12] In some of the graphs and tables, we will use abbreviations for the regions and the titular nationalities.[13] We shall refer to the Baltic, West, and RSFSR together as "European," and to Transcaucasia, Central Asia, and Kazakhstan as "non-European."[14]

Soviet censuses asked people to name their nationality (in Russian, *natsional'nost'*).[15] The answers were supposed to reflect the individual's subjective ethnic identity or affiliation. All people in the census had a "nationality," which was meant as an ethnic designation, not one of citizenship.[16] It was possible for a person to name any nationality that he or she chose as a census nationality, and therefore it was also possible to change self-designated nationality between census dates. We refer to such a change as "ethnic re-identification."

The Soviet statistical office sometimes changed its procedures for identifying and labelling ethnic groups, and for this reason the population totals of some nationalities can be volatile from one census to the next.[17] As an illustration, no separate number of Crimean Tatars was listed in the 1959, 1970, or 1979 Soviet census reports. Instead, Crimean Tatars appear to have been grouped with Volga Tatars into "Tatars." Data from the 1989 census, however, reported the number of Crimean Tatars for both 1979 (132,000) and 1989 (269,000), while the reported number of Tatars in 1979 is reduced from the previously reported figure by the exact number of reported Crimean Tatars in 1979. Two things that are important to note about the new figures are that they marked the first time that an official count of the Crimean Tatars had been reported in the Soviet Union[18] and that the doubling of the reported number of Crimean Tatars between 1979 and 1989 reflected a substantial gain through "ethnic re-identification"—not simply through natural increase of Crimean Tatars.[19]

Most Soviet citizens (age 16 or over) had an internal passport that listed their nationality. Also, other identity papers and official documents, such as school records, military records, and work records, listed the individual's nationality. Unlike the "subjective" nationality that the census was supposed to record, this was an "official" nationality, presumably based on the individual's ethnic heritage. The rules stated that an individual could choose as his or her nationality for the internal passport the nationality of either one of the parents, and that once nationality had been determined in this way, it could not be changed (for further discussion, see Silver, 1986). In principle, it was possible for an individual's subjective nationality (such as on the census) to differ from his or her official nationality. Census enumerators were not supposed to check identity papers to establish the nationality of respondents. We are aware of no studies published in the USSR that examined the empirical relation between these two aspects of nationality group membership.[20]

TABLE 7.2 Population of the Soviet Union and of its Nationalities, by Population in 1959, 1970, 1979, and 1989. Traditional Religion, and Classification into Subgroups of Nationalities Used in the Analysis[a]

	Population 1959 (thousands)	Population 1970 (thousands)	Population 1979 (thousands)	Population 1989 (thousands)	Predominant Traditional Religion	Subgroup Used in Analysis	Region Group of Union Republics
USSR	208,827	241,720	262,085	285,743			
UNION REPUBLIC (SSR)							
Russians	114,114	129,015	137,397	145,155	Orthodox	Slavic	RSFSR
Ukrainians	37,253	40,753	42,348	44,186	Orthodox	Non-Russ. Slavic	West
Uzbeks	6,015	9,195	12,456	16,698	Sunni Muslim	Muslim	Cent. Asia
Belorussians	7,913	9,052	9,463	10,036	Orthodox	Non-Russ. Slavic	West
Kazakhs	3,622	5,299	6,556	8,136	Sunni Muslim	Muslim	Kazakhstan
Azerbaidzhanis	2,940	2,380	5,477	6,770	Shiite Muslim	Muslim	Transcaucasia
Armenians	2,787	3,559	4,151	4,623	Armen. Christian	Other Non-Muslim	Transcaucasia
Tadzhiks	1,397	2,159	2,898	4,215	Sunni Muslim	Muslim	Cent. Asia
Georgians	2,692	3,245	3,571	3,981	Georgian Orth.	Other Non-Muslim	Transcaucasia
Moldavians	2,214	2,698	2,968	3,352	Orthodox	Other Non-Muslim	West
Lithuanians	2,326	2,665	2,851	3,067	Roman Catholic	Other Non-Muslim	Baltic
Turkmenians	1,002	1,525	2,028	2,729	Sunni Muslim	Muslim	Cent. Asia
Kirgiz	969	1,452	1,906	2,529	Sunni Muslim	Muslim	Cent. Asia
Latvians	1,400	1,430	1,439	1,459	Lutheran	Other Non-Muslim	Baltic
Estonians	989	1,007	1,020	1,027	Lutheran	Other Non-Muslim	Baltic
AUTONOMOUS REPUBLIC (ASSR)							
Tatars[b]	4,765	5,931	6,185	6,649	Sunni Muslim	Muslim	
Daghestan Peoples[c]	944	1,365	1,657	2,044	Sunni Muslim	Muslim	

Chuvash	1,470	1,694	1,751	1,842	Orthodox	Other Non-Muslim
Bashkirs	989	1,240	1,371	1,449	Sunni Muslim	Muslim
Mordvinians	1,285	1,263	1,192	1,154	Orthodox	Other Non-Muslim
Chechens	419	613	756	957	Sunni Muslim	Muslim
Udmurts	625	704	714	747	Orthodox	Other Non-Muslim
Mari	504	599	622	671	Orthodox	Other Non-Muslim
Ossetians	413	488	542	598	Orthodox	Other Non-Muslim
Karakalpaks	173	236	303	424	Sunni Muslim	Muslim
Buriats	253	315	353	421	Orth./Buddhist	Other Non-Muslim
Yakuts	233	296	328	382	Orthodox	Other Non-Muslim
Komi	287	322	327	345	Orthodox	Other Non-Muslim
Ingush	106	158	186	237	Sunni Muslim	Muslim
Tuvinians	100	139	166	207	Buddhist	Other Non-Muslim
Kalmyks	106	137	147	174	Buddhist	Other Non-Muslim
Karelians	167	146	138	131	Orthodox	Other Non-Muslim
Abkhazians	65	83	91	105	Sunni Muslim	Muslim

AUTONOMOUS PROVINCE (AO)

Jewsd	2,267	2,151	1,811	1,450	Jewish	Other Non-Muslim
Kabardinians	204	280	322	391	Sunni Muslim	Muslim
Karachai	81	113	131	156	Sunni Muslim	Muslim
Adygei	80	100	109	125	Sunni Muslim	Muslim
Khakasy	57	67	71	80	Orthodox	Other Non-Muslim
Altais	45	56	60	71	Orthodox	Other Non-Muslim
Balkars	42	60	66	85	Sunni Muslim	Muslim
Cherkess	30	40	46	52	Sunni Muslim	Muslim

AUTONOMOUS DISTRICT (AD)

Komi-Permiaks	144	153	151	152	Orthodox	Other Non-Muslim
Evenks	24	25	27	30	Orth./Shamanist	Other Non-Muslim
Nenets	23	29	30	35	Orth./Shamanist	Other Non-Muslim
Khanty	19	21	21	23	Orth./Shamanist	Other Non-Muslim
Chukchi	12	14	14	15	Orth./Shamanist	Other Non-Muslim
Mansi	6	8	8	8	Orth./Shamanist	Other Non-Muslim
Koriaks	6	7	8	9	Orth./Shamanist	Other Non-Muslim
Dolgans	4	5	5	7	Orth./Shamanist	Other Non-Muslim

TABLE 7.2 (Continued)

	Population 1959 (thousands)	Population 1970 (thousands)	Population 1979 (thousands)	Population 1989 (thousands)	Predominant Traditional Religion	Subgroup Used in Analysis	Region Group of Union Republics
OTHER INDIGENOUS							
Crimean Tatarsb	…	…	132	269	Sunni Muslim	Muslim	Muslim
Gagauz	124	157	173	197	Orthodox	Other Non-Muslim	Non-Muslim
Abaza	20	25	29	34	Muslim	Muslim	Muslim
Muslim Tats	11	17	22	31	Sunni Muslim	Muslim	Muslim
Talysh	…	…	…	22	Sunni Muslim	Muslim	Muslim
Shors	15	16	16	17	Orth./Shamanist	Other Non-Muslim	Other Non-Muslim
Evens	9	12	13	17	Orth./Shamanist	Other Non-Muslim	Other Non-Muslim
Vepps	16	8	8	13	Orthodox	Other Non-Muslim	Other Non-Muslim
Nanai	8	10	11	12	Orth./Shamanist	Other Non-Muslim	Other Non-Muslim
Udins	4	7	4	9	Sunni Muslim	Muslim	Muslim
Nivkhi	4	4	4	5	Orth./Shamanist	Other Non-Muslim	Other Non-Muslim
Sel'kups	4	4	4	4	Orth./Shamanist	Other Non-Muslim	Other Non-Muslim
Karaims	6	5	3	3	Jewish	Other Non-Muslim	Other Non-Muslim
Ul'chi	2	2	3	3	Orth./Shamanist	Other Non-Muslim	Other Non-Muslim
Saams	2	2	2	2	Orth./Shamanist	Other Non-Muslim	Other Non-Muslim
Udegei	1	1	2	2	Orth./Shamanist	Other Non-Muslim	Other Non-Muslim
Itel'mens	1	1	1	2	Orth./Shamanist	Other Non-Muslim	Other Non-Muslim
Izhora	1	1	1	1	Orthodox	Other Non-Muslim	Other Non-Muslim
Kety	1	1	1	1	Orth./Shamanist	Other Non-Muslim	Other Non-Muslim
Orochi	1	1	1	1	Orth./Shamanist	Other Non-Muslim	Other Non-Muslim
Tofa	1	1	1	1	Sham./Muslim	Other Non-Muslim	Other Non-Muslim
Negidals	…	1	1	1	Orth./Shamanist	Other Non-Muslim	Other Non-Muslim
Iukagirs	0.4	1	1	1	Orth./Shamanist	Other Non-Muslim	Other Non-Muslim
Aleuts	0.4	0.4	1	1	Orth./Shamanist	Other Non-Muslim	Other Non-Muslim

NONINDIGENOUS

Nationality	1959	1970	1979	1989	Religion	
Germans	1,620	1,846	1,936	2,039	Cath./Lutheran	Other Non-Muslim
Poles	1,380	1,168	1,151	1,126	Roman Catholic	Non-Russian Slavic
Koreans	314	358	389	439	Buddhist	Other Non-Muslim
Bulgarians	324	351	361	373	Orthodox	Non-Russian Slavic
Greeks	309	337	344	358	Orthodox	Other Non-Muslim
Uighurs	95	173	211	263	Sunni Muslim	Muslim
Gypsies	132	175	209	262	Christian	Other Non-Muslim
Turks	...	...	93	208	Sunni Muslim	Muslim
Hungarians	155	166	171	171	Roman Catholic	Other Non-Muslim
Rumanians	106	119	129	146	Orthodox	Other Non-Muslim
Kurds	59	89	116	153	Sunni Muslim	Muslim
Dungans	22	39	52	69	Sunni Muslim	Muslim
Finns	93	85	77	67	Lutheran	Other Non-Muslim
Persians	21	28	31	40	Shiite Muslim	Muslim
Beluchi	8	13	19	29	Sunni Muslim	Muslim
Assyrians	22	24	25	26	Christian	Other Non-Muslim
Czechs	25	21	18	16	Roman Catholic	Non-Russian Slavic
Chinese	26	...	12	11	Buddhist	Other Non-Muslim
Slovaks	15	12	9	9	Roman Catholic	Non-Russian Slavic
Afghans	2	4	4	7	Sunni Muslim	Muslim
Albanians	5	4	4	4	Orthodox	Other Non-Muslim
Khalkha-Mongols	2	5	3	3	Buddhist	Other Non-Muslim

a Totals for 1959 and 1970 are the "present (*nalichnoe*) population." Totals for 1979 and 1989 are the "permanent (*postoiannoe*) population."

b The figures for Tatars in 1959 and 1970 given in this table include all enumerated "Tatars" in the Soviet censuses for those years. These totals include the Crimean Tatars as well as other Tatars. The figures for "Crimean Tatars" in 1979 and 1989 exclude the reported number of Crimean Tatars. The figures for "Tatars" in 1979 and 1989 come from preliminary unpublished data from the 1989 Soviet census report.

c The "Daghestani" nationalities consist of a large number of groups, for less than ten of which separate population totals are listed in recent Soviet census reports. The largest groups are the Avars, Dargin, Laks, Lezgians, Nogai, and Tabasaran. The total for 1989 represents the sum of the reported populations of those six groups plus the Rutul'tsy, Aguly, and Tsakhury.

d The figures for Jews include those identified as "Jews", Georgian Jews, Central Asian Jews, Mountain Jews (Jewish Tats), and Crimean Jews (*Krymchaki*). They do not include the Karaims, who are listed separately in this table.

All Soviet censuses also ascertained the individual's "native language" (in Russian, *rodnoi iazyk*). This designation, too, was subjective. Census respondents were not given a test of language ability at their doorstep. Although "native language" was supposed to register the language that people knew best, survey research conducted in the USSR showed that sometimes an individual did not know how to speak his or her "native language." "Native language" may have been more a marker of ethnic background than language use or language preference.

The Soviet censuses of 1970, 1979, and 1989 also asked people what "other language of the peoples of the USSR" they could "freely command." Although the term "freely command" was supposed to be equivalent to "freely converse," no test of language competence was given. The question was added to the censuses primarily as a way to find out how many non-Russians knew the Russian language as a second language, that is, were bilingual (Silver, 1975, 1986).

Perhaps as a result of this special purpose of the second-language question, the answers were unstable. For example, between 1970 and 1979, the proportion of Estonians who claimed Russian as a second language declined from 29 to 24 percent (it increased to 34 percent in 1989). This improbable result apparently reflected a popular referendum of attitudes toward the political leadership of the republic.[21] A similar improbable shift occurred for Lithuanians between 1979 and 1989: the proportion who claimed to command Russian freely as a second language dropped from 52.1 to 37.9 percent (it had been 35.9 percent in 1970). Whether the figure for 1979 or for 1989 (or perhaps for 1970) is the more nearly correct is impossible to determine from available information. In the 1970-1979 intercensal period, the proportion of Uzbeks who claimed Russian as a second language rose sharply from 14 to 49. This rise, too, is improbable, and could reflect the fact that in 1979 census enumerators were encouraged to be very generous in listing knowledge of Russian as a second language.[22] This percentage dropped to a more plausible figure of 23.8 in 1989.

Analysis

The Soviet Union as a Whole

Table 7.2 lists the population sizes of more than 100 nationalities, grouped by the official status of the nationality in the Soviet federal system. To simplify later discussion, we also classify the nationalities into subgroups.

TABLE 7.3 Characteristics of Major Subgroups of Nationalities in the Analysis

Year	Russians	Non-Russian Slavs	Other Non-Muslims	Muslims	Total USSR
Population Size (thousands)					
1959	114,114	46,910	23,440	24,286	208,827
1970	129,015	51,357	26,590	34,619	241,720
1979	137,397	53,352	28,050	43,267	262,085
1989	145,155	55,746	29,917	54,885	285,743
Percentage of USSR Population					
1959	54.7	22.5	11.2	11.6	100.0
1970	53.4	21.3	11.0	14.3	100.0
1979	52.4	20.4	10.7	16.5	100.0
1989	50.8	19.5	10.5	19.2	100.0
Average Annual Growth Rate (percent)					
1959-70	1.12	0.82	1.15	3.22	1.33
1970-79	0.70	0.42	0.59	2.48	0.90
1979-89	0.55	0.44	0.64	2.38	0.86
Growth of Population Between Censuses (thousands)					
1959-70	14,901	4,447	3,150	10,333	32,893
1970-79	8,382	1,995	1,460	8,648	20,365
1979-89	7,758	2,348	1,867	11,618	23,658
Percentage of Soviet Population Growth in Each Subgroup					
1959-70	45.4	13.5	9.6	31.5	100.0
1970-79	40.9	9.7	7.1	42.2	100.0
1979-89	32.9	10.0	7.9	49.2	100.0

a In every Soviet census report, a small part of the population was not identified by nationality (listed among members of "other nationalities"). This ranges from 0.008 percent in the 1979 census to 0.058 percent in the 1970 census. In this table, the "Total USSR" population size and the intercensal growth figures in this table are for the total USSR population, including persons belonging to an "other nationality"; however, the distribution of the Soviet population among subgroups and the allocation of the share of intercensal growth among subgroups are relative only to the population that was identified by nationality.

Table 7.3 gives information about the size and growth of four subgroups between 1959 and 1989: Russians, Non-Russian Slavs, other non-Muslims, Muslims.

This information is also reflected in Figures 7.1, 7.2, and 7.3. Figure 7.1 shows the population in each of the four subgroups according to the Soviet censuses of 1959, 1970, 1979, and 1989. Each subgroup grew in every intercensal interval. Nationalities within each of the groups differed in their rates of growth. A few nationalities experienced negative growth, due to international emigration (the primary explanation for the declining number of Jews) or assimilation (the primary explanation for the declining number of Mordvinians and Karelians and also perhaps of Poles).

FIGURE 7.1 Size of Four Major Subgroups of the Soviet Population: 1959, 1970, 1979, 1989

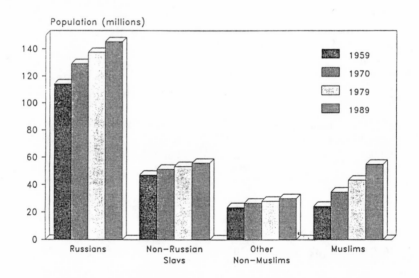

Figure 7.2 shows the proportion of the total Soviet population that each of the four subgroups comprised at each of the census dates. Although all four subgroups increased in absolute size over time, all except Muslims declined as a proportion of the Soviet population.

FIGURE 7.2 Proportion of the Total Soviet Population Accounted for by Four
Major Subgroups: 1959: 1970, 1979, and 1989

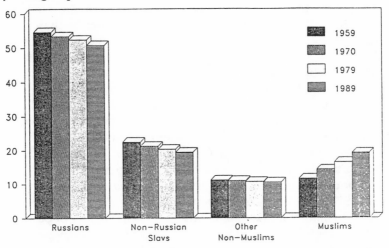

FIGURE 7.3 Average Annual Rates of Growth of the Soviet Population and
Four Major Subgroups: 1959-70, 1970-79, 1979-1989

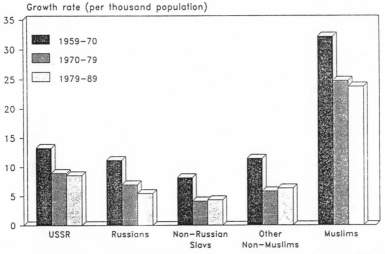

Figure 7.3 shows the average annual growth rates of each of the four
subgroups for each of the three intercensal periods.[23] The growth rate
of each subgroup was lower in later intercensal intervals than in earlier
ones. The decline in the growth rate of Russians in the three intercensal
periods is consistent with an increase in their population doubling time
from 62 years, to 99 years, to 128 years; the decline in the growth rate of

Muslims is consistent with an increase in their population doubling time from 22 years, to 28 years, to 29 years.

The growth rate of Muslims far exceeded that of the other three groups during all three intercensal periods. Moreover, as shown in the bottom panel of Table 7.3, the Muslim share of the total growth in population of the Soviet Union has risen sharply over the last 30 years. Muslims contributed 31.5 percent of the Soviet Union's population increase between 1959 and 1970, 42.2 percent between 1970 and 1979, and 49.2 percent between 1979 and 1989. Also during that last intercensal period, Muslims contributed 75 percent of the net increment to the labor force of the Soviet Union (Anderson and Silver, 1990a).

The Russian share of population growth of the USSR declined commensurately. Russians contributed 45.4 percent of the Soviet Union's population increase between 1959 and 1970, 40.9 percent between 1970 and 1979, and 32.9 percent between 1979 and 1989. Thus, although Muslims comprised only one-sixth of the Soviet population in 1979, they contributed almost half of the entire increase in the population of the Soviet Union between 1979 and 1989; and although Russians comprised 52 percent of the Soviet population in 1979, they contributed less than one-third of the population increase between 1979 and 1989.

It would be possible to project future changes in the ethnic composition of the Soviet Union—the proportion of the total Soviet population comprised of Russians, all Slavs, and Muslims—assuming a continuation of the 1979 to 1989 average annual growth rates of each group (as well as survival of the USSR itself) indefinitely into the future. However, the growth rates of each group would certainly change.[24] If the growth rates were to remain as they were between 1979 to 1989 (an admittedly mechanistic assumption), then Russians would have ceased to be a majority of the population of the Soviet Union by the year 1994 and the Soviet Union would have ceased to be a predominantly Slavic country by 2051. Muslims would have outnumbered Russians in the USSR by the year 2042, they would have outnumbered Slavs by the year 2059, and they would be a majority of the Soviet population by the year 2066. This implied a very different future ethnic composition of the Soviet population.

It bears emphasis that the dates mentioned are not meant as predictions, but only as an aid to understanding the implications of the prevailing differential growth rates of population subgroups. If we had reliable nationality-specific data on fertility, mortality, assimilation, and age distributions for recent dates, we could make cohort component projections. By estimating fertility, mortality, and age distributions for nationalities, Kingkade (1988, 1989) made such cohort component projections under a variety of assumptions. Under the set of assumptions that Kingkade considered the most likely (his median variant), Russians would have lost their majority status in the USSR very early in the 1990s.

An important aspect of projecting the future ethnic composition of the Soviet population is assimilation. Our projection takes assimilation into account implicitly, because the growth rate of Russians between 1979 and 1989 reflects the consequences of all four components described earlier: fertility, mortality, net emigration, and assimilation (ethnic re-identification). Based on change between the 1959 and 1970 Soviet censuses, we projected that "if Russians were not gaining through re-identification, they would decline to only half of the Soviet population in 1994; because they are gaining through re-identification, they will not decline to half of the Soviet population until 2003—nine years later" (Anderson and Silver, 1983: 480).

The rise in ethnic awareness and assertiveness among the Non-Russian nationalities in the late 1980s could have affected assimilation rates in two ways. Both involve the changing relative attractiveness of different ethnic self-designations. First, the propensity of members of some Non-Russian groups to re-identify themselves subjectively as Russians could have slowed down or stopped. In the last few decades of the USSR, the ethnic groups that were changing most rapidly to Russians were Non-Russians who were of Orthodox traditional religion and whose titular areas in the Soviet federation were at a lower status than that of union republic.25 Also, Non-Russian Slavs (mainly Ukrainians and Belarussians), though not showing an especially high rate of re-identification to Russian, contributed more than half of the estimated total number of ethnic re-identifiers between 1959 and 1970 (Anderson and Silver, 1983). In addition, the children of Non-Russ.s who married Russians living outside of the titular area of nationality of the Non-Russian spouse were quite likely to choose Russian as their nationality on their internal passport—and presumably also in the census.26

A second way in which the rise of ethnic self-awareness of Non-Russians could have affected assimilation rates is that many individuals who in the 1979 census called themselves Russians could have identified with a different nationality in 1989. A large pool of people were likely candidates for such a step. Persons who had previously switched from a Non-Russ. self-identification to Russian (in 1959, 1970, or 1979) could have switched back in 1989, especially if they retained knowledge of the language of their former nationality.

In the context of the census conducted in January 1989, it is possible that Russians experienced some net population loss as a result of a reversal of historical tendencies toward assimilation. Had the latest census been scheduled for January 1990 rather than 1989, it is likely that increased ethnic self-awareness among such groups as the Ukrainians— which found expression in large public demonstrations and the formation of a popular front movement after the mid-January census date—could have further reduced the size of the Russian majority.

The shifting future ethnic balance of the Soviet population had implications for many aspects of social welfare policy, regional development strategies, manpower policy, and language and cultural policy.27 The reduction of Russians to a numerical minority of the population of the USSR would have been especially important as a political event, since the USSR would have then become a country of minorities. No single ethnic group could have claim to represent the interests of a majority of the population, in an era in which public opinion and majority rule were increasingly perceived as ways to legitimate government decisions.

Based on their shared history and culture, the other major Slavic nationalities (Belarussians and Ukrainians) were often considered a part of the "Slavic majority" and they often comprised a significant part of the "Russian-speaking" population in Non-Russ. parts of the Soviet Union. But the greater ethnic assertiveness of Non-Russ. Slavs, accompanied by the reduction of Russians to less than half of the Soviet population, would likely have sharpened perceptions of the differences in background and orientations of the Slavic groups.

The Union Republics

Overall Population Growth

Although changes in the ethnic composition of the Soviet population as a whole are interesting, changes in particular regions were probably more salient to most Soviet citizens. Table 7.4 describes some aspects of the ethnic composition of the 15 union republics in 1989. The republics differed greatly in population size, with the population of the RSFSR being nearly three times as large as that of the second largest union republic, the Ukrainian SSR. In 1989, the three Baltic republics— Estonia, Latvia, and Lithuania—together comprised less than 3 percent of the total Soviet population.

TABLE 7.4 Composition of the Union Republics in 1989 by Population of Titular Nationalities and Russians

Republic	Number of Persons (thousands)				Percentage Distribution		
	Total	Titular	Russian	Other	Titular	Russian	Other
RSFSR	147,022	119,866	119,866	27,156	81.5	81.3	18.5
Baltic							
Estonia	1,565	963	475	127	61.5	30.4	8.1
Latvia	2,667	1,388	906	373	52.0	34.0	14.0
Lithuania	3,675	2,924	344	407	79.6	9.4	11.0
West							
Belorussia	10,152	7,905	1,342	905	77.9	13.2	8.9
Moldavia	4,335	2,795	562	978	64.5	13.0	22.6
Ukraine	51,452	37,419	11,356	2,677	72.7	22.1	5.2
Transcaucasia							
Armenia	3,305	3,084	52	169	93.3	1.6	5.1
Azerbaijan	7,021	5,805	392	824	82.7	5.6	11.7
Georgia	5,401	3,787	341	1,273	70.1	6.3	23.6
Central Asia							
Kirgizstan	4,258	2,230	917	1,111	52.4	21.5	26.1
Tadjikistan	5,093	3,172	388	1,533	62.3	7.6	30.1
Turkmenistan	3,523	2,537	334	652	72.0	9.5	18.5
Uzbekistan	19,810	14,142	1,653	4,015	71.4	8.3	20.3
Kazakhstan	16,464	6,535	6,228	3,701	39.7	37.8	22.5

Figure 7.4 shows the population of each of the 15 union republics at each of the four most recent Soviet census dates. Every republic grew in population size during each intercensal period.

FIGURE 7.4 Total Population of the Union Republics, 1959, 1970, 1979, 1989

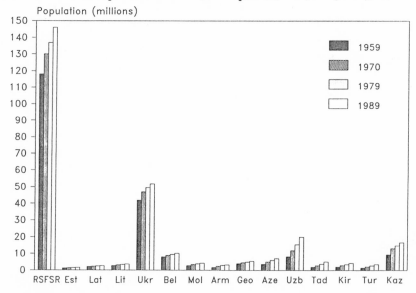

Differences in Growth by Nationality within Republics

None of the republics was ethnically homogeneous. Figure 7.5 shows the percentage of each republic's population comprised of that republic's titular nationality in 1959, 1970, 1979, and 1989. In 1989, this proportion ranged from a low of 40 percent for Kazakhs in Kazakhstan to a high of 93 percent for Armenians in Armenia. In all of the non-European republics, the proportion of the population from the titular nationality increased in each successive census. In all of the European republics except Lithuania, the proportion of the population from the titular nationality declined in each intercensal period. The proportion of Lithuania's population comprised of Lithuanians increased between 1959 and 1970 and then declined slightly over the 1970-1979 and 1979 to 1989 intercensal periods. Estonia and Latvia show especially rapid declines in the proportion of their populations of the titular nationality.

FIGURE 7.5 Proportion of Each Republic's Population that Belongs to the Titular Nationality: 1959, 1970, 1979, 1989.

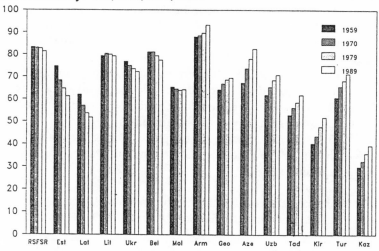

FIGURE 7.6 Proportion of Each Republic's Population that Belongs to the Russian Nationality: 1959, 1970, 1979, 1989.

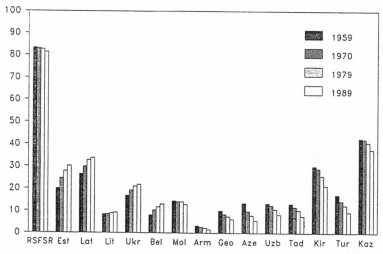

As shown in Table 7.4, in most cases the bulk of the population of a republic that was not from the titular nationality were Russians. In Latvia, Lithuania, and Moldavia in 1989, the "other" category was comprised primarily of Ukrainians and Belarussians. In the non-European republics, the "other" category was comprised mainly of

Ukrainians along with members of other ethnic groups from the same region, such as Armenians in Georgia, and Tajiks in Uzbekistan.

Figure 7.6 shows the percentage of the population of each republic comprised of Russians in 1959, 1970, 1979, and 1989. Among the Non-Russian republics in 1989, the share of the Russian population ranged from 2 percent in Armenia to 38 percent in Kazakhstan. In Kazakhstan at the first three census dates, Russians outnumbered Kazakhs. In 1989, however, the number of Kazakhs overtook the number of Russians. Russians did not outnumber the titular nationality in any other Non-Russian union republic at any of the census dates.

Table 7.5 shows the average annual growth rates between 1979 and 1989 of each union republic population and of major ethnic groups within the republics.

TABLE 7.5 Intercensal Growth Rates of Population of Union Republics and Titular Nationalities and Russians in Union Republics, 1979-1989

	Average Annual Growth Rate (%)				Percentage of Growth Due to Titular Nationality
	Total Population	Titular Nationality	Russians	Others	
RSFSR	0.7	0.5	0.5	1.4	63.0
Baltic					
Estonia	0.7	0.2	1.5	2.2	14.2
Latvia	0.7	0.3	1.0	1.4	24.4
Lithuania	0.8	0.8	1.2	1.2	71.0
West					
Belorussia	0.7	0.4	1.7	1.5	49.4
Moldavia	0.9	1.0	0.0	1.4	67.8
Ukraine	0.4	0.2	0.8	1.2	42.1
Transcaucasia					
Armenia	0.8	1.2	-3.1	-4.8	133.6
Georgia	0.9	1.0	-0.9	1.1	78.2
Azerbaijhan	1.5	2.1	-1.9	-0.1	108.9
Central Asia					
Kirgizstan	2.0	2.8	0.1	2.2	70.4
Tadzhikistan	2.9	3.5	-0.2	2.8	71.3
Turkmenistan	82.2	2.5	2.9	-0.4	2.5
Uzbekistan	2.6	2.9	-0.1	2.7	78.7
Kazakhstan	1.2	2.1	0.4	1.0	67.0

The republics differ considerably in the relative contribution of the titular nationality and other nationalities to population growth. The titular nationality contributed only 14.2 percent of the population increase in Estonia between 1979 and 1989, and 24.4 percent in Latvia. In two other republics the titular nationality also contributed less than half of the population increase between 1979 and 1989: Ukraine (42.1 percent) and Belarus (49.4 percent). In two republics, however, Azerbaijan and Armenia, the titular nationality contributed more than 100 percent of the population increase as a result of heavy emigration of members of non-titular nationalities from these republics between 1979 and 1989. In the two Transcaucasian republics, the increase in the number of members of the titular nationality between 1979 and 1989 exceeded the total growth in the population of each republic.

Figure 7.7 shows the average annual growth rates of the total population in the USSR as a whole and in each republic for the three last intercensal periods. In every republic, as in the Soviet Union at large, the growth rates declined from 1959 to 1970 to 1970 to 1979. In all republics except Russia and Georgia, growth rates also declined from 1970 to 1979 to 1979 to 1989.

FIGURE 7.7 Average Annual Rates of Growth of USSR and Union Republic Populations: 1959-70, 1970-79, 1979-89

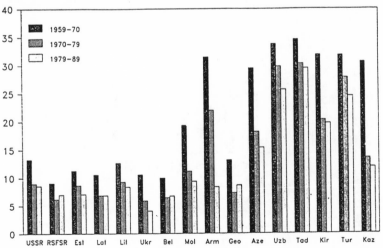

Republic growth rates were the result of a combination of different growth rates for the constituent nationalities. Figure 7.8 shows the average annual intercensal growth rate for the titular nationality in its own republic in 1959 to 1970, 1970 to 1979, and 1979 to 1989. Figure 7.9 shows comparable information for Russians within union republics.

FIGURE 7.8   Average Annual Growth Rate of Titualr Nationalities in Union Republics: 1959-70, 1970-79, 1979-89

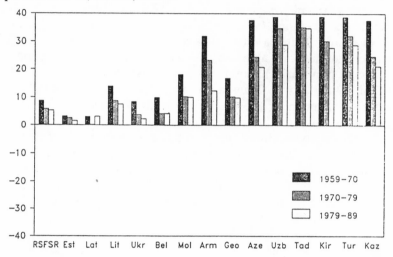

FIGURE 7.9 Average Annual Growth Rate of Russians in Union Republics: 1959-70, 1970-79, 1979-89

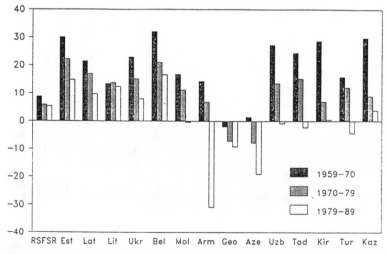

The titular nationalities of the union republics experienced growth in every republic in all three intercensal periods. The annual intercensal growth rate of the titular nationalities in 1979 to 1989 ranged from a low of 1.62 per thousand population for Estonians in Estonia (a population doubling time of 426 years), to a high of 34.80 per thousand for Tajiks in Tajikistan (equivalent to a population doubling time of 20 years).

FIGURE 7.10 Difference Between Growth Rates of Titular Nationalities and Russians: 1959-70, 1970-79, 1979-89

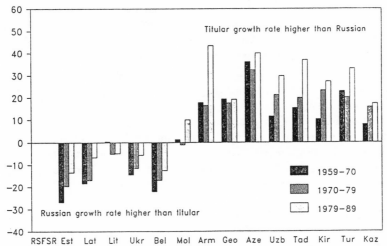

In the first two intercensal periods, the Russian population of every republic except Georgia and Azerbaijan experienced a positive growth rate. In the last intercensal period—1979 to 1989—the Russian growth rate was negative in six republics: the three Transcaucasian republics, as well as Tajikistan, Turkmenistan, and Uzbekistan. Moreover, in every Non-Russian republic (and, indeed, also in the RSFSR), the growth rate of Russians declined between 1979 to 1989 compared with the previous intercensal period. We will show that the negative growth rates of Russians in Transcaucasia and parts of Central Asia in the most recent intercensal period were the result of substantial emigration by Russians.

In 1979 to 1989, the average annual growth rate of Russians per thousand population ranged from a high of 16.8 in Belarus (equivalent to a population doubling time of 41 years) to a low of -31.0 in Armenia (a rate that, if maintained, would reduce the size of the Russian population of Armenia by 50 percent in 22 years). Such a rate implies a remarkably high level of emigration of Russians from Armenia.

Some implications of the differential growth rates by nationality for the future ethnic mix of Soviet republics are suggested in Figure 7.10. The figure shows the growth rate of the titular nationality minus the growth rate of persons of Russian nationality in a given republic. A positive number means that the population of the titular nationality was increasing more rapidly than that of Russians in the republic; a negative number means that the number of Russians was increasing more rapidly than the titular nationality. Note that although in 1979 Russians outnumbered Kazakhs in Kazakhstan, the number of Kazakhs overtook the number of Russians before the 1989 census.

In every non-European republic, the titular nationality grew more rapidly than the Russian nationality in all three intercensal periods. The situation is very different in the European republics. In 1959 to 1970, the Russian population grew more rapidly than the titular nationality in every European republic except Lithuania and Moldavia; in 1970 to 1979, the Russian population grew more rapidly than the titular nationality in every European republic; and in 1979 to 1989, the Russian population grew more rapidly than the titular nationality in every European republic except Moldavia. Thus, the non-European republics had become less Russianized over time, while the European ones had become more Russianized.

The Effects of Natural Increase

The changing ethnic composition of Soviet republics resulted primarily from a combination of differential fertility and differential net migration. We examine fertility first. Figure 7.11 shows the total fertility rate (TFR) of the Soviet Union as a whole and of the Soviet republics in 1958-59, 1969-70, 1978-79, and 1986-87.[28] In Central Asia, the TFR declined after 1969-70. In the European republics, the TFR was lower than in the non-European republics, but the TFR increased in all the European republics between 1978-79 and 1986-87.

As with the growth rate, a republic's TFR is a result of the different fertility levels of the various resident nationalities. Figure 7.12 shows the TFR of the titular nationality of each republic in 1958-59, 1969-70, and 1978-79 as reported by Bondarskaia and Darskii (1988).[29]

We do not have direct information on the TFR of Russians within Soviet republics (other than within the RSFSR itself). We wanted an indication of the size of the gap between the fertility level of the titular nationality of a given republic and the fertility level of Russians in that republic. An approximation of this gap, based on the assumption that the TFR of the Russian population in every republic is the same as the TFR of the Russian population in the RSFSR, is shown in Figure 7.13. As can be seen, in 1969-70 and in 1978-79 in every republic the TFR of the titular nationality exceeded that of Russians, although in every republic

except Latvia the size of the differential decreased between 1969-70 and
1978-79.

FIGURE 7.11 Total Fertility Rates, USSR and Union Republic Populations: 1958-
59, 1969-70, 1978-79, 1986-87

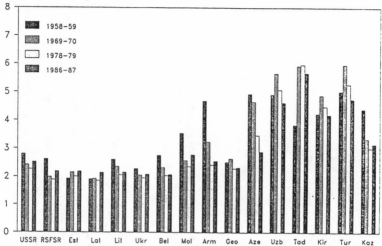

FIGURE 7.12 Total Fertility Rates of Titular Nationalities in Union Republics,
1958-59, 1969-70, 1978-79

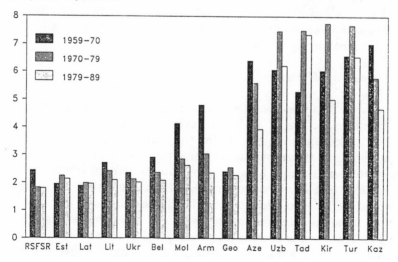

FIGURE 7.13 Difference Between TFR of Titular nationalities and of Russians in RSFSR, 1958-59, 1969-70, 1978-79

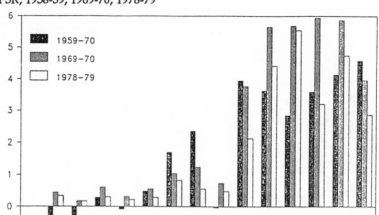

The fertility of the titular nationality in Estonia, Latvia, Ukraine, and Georgia was lower than that of Russians in the RSFSR in 1958-59. That situation reversed by 1969-70, and the fertility of the titular nationality still exceeded that of Russians in the RSFSR in 1978-79. Hence, it is unlikely that fertility differences contributed to the increasing Russianization of Estonia and Latvia over time; in fact, higher fertility of the titular nationality probably slowed that trend.

The Effects of Migration

We next examine the effects of migration on the ethnic composition of republics, using a variation on the residual approach to the estimation of net migration. In the residual approach, the growth of a group within a geographic area between two dates is calculated. Then the growth that would have occurred due to natural increase alone is calculated. The difference between the actual increase in the group and the predicted increase due to natural increase alone is an estimate of the net immigration of the group into the area between the two dates.

We cannot fully implement the residual approach because we do not have information on the natural increase (crude birth rate minus crude death rate) of *nationalities* either in the Soviet Union as a whole or within particular geographic areas. Therefore, we must estimate the contribution of natural increase to the growth of ethnic groups within geographic areas.

As mentioned earlier, with few exceptions the size of Soviet ethnic groups was virtually unaffected by international migration since 1959. Hence, in the Soviet Union as a whole, the change in the size of Soviet ethnic groups was mainly the result of natural increase.[30] We use this fact to estimate the growth that would have occurred to an ethnic group within a republic due to natural increase alone.

To obtain such an estimate for a given intercensal period, we divide the number of members of an ethnic group in the Soviet Union as a whole at the second census date (such as 1970) by the number of members of the same ethnic group in the Soviet Union as a whole at the first census date (such as 1959). We then multiply this ratio by the size of the same ethnic group in a given republic at the first census date to obtain the predicted size of that ethnic group in that republic at the second date due to the effects of natural increase. We subtract the predicted size of the group at the second date (reflecting the effect of natural increase alone) from the reported size of the ethnic group at the second date to obtain an estimate of net immigration of the group into the republic between the two dates (for a similar approach, see Silver 1983).

This method of estimation has limitations, but the overall picture that we derive is probably a reasonable reflection of the relative contribution of migration to the population growth across different republics. These estimates will attribute too much of the growth in a republic to natural increase and too little to net immigration if the rate of natural increase of the group in the republic is less than that of the nationality in the Soviet Union at large. This will generally be true for Russians, since the fertility of Russians outside of the RSFSR was likely to be lower than that of Russians in the RSFSR. These estimates will also be affected by differences in ethnic re-identification inside and outside a given republic. Members of a given nationality are more likely to re-identify as Russians if they live outside the nationality's titular republic than if they live in the group's titular republic. The combined effects of higher fertility and less ethnic re-identification of members of a Non-Russian group in their titular republic than outside of that republic would be to underestimate the emigration of the ethnic group from its titular republic.

Figure 7.14 shows estimated net immigration rates of the titular nationality in each of the republics between 1959 and 1970, 1970 and 1979, and 1979 and 1989.[31] These rates were obtained by dividing the estimated amount of net migration between two census dates by the size of the population of the titular nationality in the republic in question at the first date. In other words, the figure depicts the proportions by which each titular nationality would have increased or decreased between successive censuses in its own republic due to its own migration into and out of that republic.

FIGURE 7.14 Net Intercensal In-migration Rate of Titular Nationalities into Their Own Republics, 1959-70, 1970-79, 1979-89

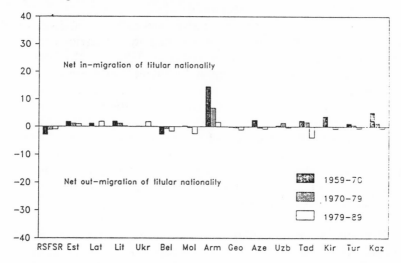

FIGURE 7.15 Net Intercensal Migration Rates of Russians into Union Republics, 1959-70, 1970-79, 1979-89

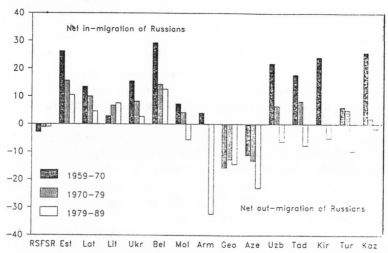

The most striking result in Figure 7.14 is the high rate of immigration of Armenians to Armenia in the first two intercensal periods. We estimate that the number of Armenians in Armenia would have increased by 15 percent between 1959 and 1970 due to immigration. In 1959 to 1970, part of the immigration could have been the result of the continued repatriation of Armenians from abroad. But it is likely that the bulk of the Armenian immigrants to Armenia both between 1959 and 1970 and between 1970 and 1979 came from other parts of the Soviet Union, probably mainly from Georgia and Azerbaijan, which experienced extremely low growth in the number of Armenian inhabitants between 1970 and 1979 and between 1979 and 1989. Between 1979 and 1989, the number of Armenians in Georgia declined by 2.5 percent, and the number in Azerbaijan declined by 17.8 percent.

A large portion of the recent emigration of Armenians from Azerbaijan has probably resulted from the outbreak of violent conflict between Armenians and Azerbaijanis in February 1988. Data on migration by ethnic group (USSR, Goskomstat, 1989) show that in 1988, 43,555 Armenians migrated from cities within Azerbaijan. While some of these migrants may have been destined for other cities or for rural places in Azerbaijan, most probably left for Armenia. The decline in the number of Armenians in Azerbaijan between 1979 and 1989 is especially noticeable for areas outside the disputed territory Nagorno-Karabakh Autonomous Republic (which is located within the Azerbaijan SSR), in which Armenians comprised 77 percent of the population in 1989. Within Nagorno-Karabakh, the number of Armenians increased by 18.2 percent between 1979 and 1989, while outside Nagorno-Karabakh the number of Armenians in Azerbaijan decreased by 30.5 percent during the same time.

The exodus of Armenians from Azerbaijan was paralleled by a departure of Azerbaijanis from Armenia. The number of Azerbaijanis in Armenia decreased by 47.2 percent between 1979 and 1989. Most of these emigrants probably moved to Azerbaijan, especially after the eruption of conflict with Armenians in 1988.[32]

Other nationalities also migrated into their titular republics, although at a less dramatic rate than did Armenians. There was considerable net immigration of Estonians into Estonia, especially between 1959 and 1970. This was largely due to return of Estonians from Siberia. Members of various Central Asian nationalities also tended to move back to their home republics, especially between 1959 and 1970. But this tendency reversed in many republics between 1979 and 1989. For example, whereas in the 1959 to 1970 and 1970 to 1979 intercensal periods Tajiks tended to resettle into Tajikistan, between 1979 and 1989 more Tajiks appear to have migrated out of Tajikistan than into it.[33]

Figure 7.15 shows similar information concerning the net immigration of Russians into republics between censuses. Migration of Russians out of the Russian Republic has decreased in each successive census interval. Between 1979 and 1989, the net migration of Russians from the RSFSR was close to zero. But there was still considerable net movement of Russians into and out of other republics during all three intercensal periods.

There was substantial net emigration of Russians from Azerbaijan and Georgia in all three intercensal periods, and from all three Transcaucasian republics in the last intercensal period. In addition, although more Russians migrated into than out of Kazakhstan and the Central Asian republics in both the 1959 to 1970 and 1970 to 1979 periods, their net migration into Central Asia was much smaller in the second period and then turned negative between 1979 and 1989. The net immigration of Russians into Kazakhstan has decreased greatly over time. The estimated number of Russian net immigrants decreased from 1,029,000 in 1959 to 1970 to 111,000 in 1970 to 1979 and then became negative between 1979 and 1989. The immigration of Russians in 1959 to 1970 reflects the effects of settling and cultivating 42 million hectares of land under the Virgin and Idle Lands Program (Grandstaff, 1980).

Net immigration of Russians into all of the Non-Russian European republics occurred in the 1959 to 1970 and 1970 to 1979 intercensal periods. In every European republic except Lithuania, however, the rate of Russian immigration decreased between the two periods, and in 1979 to 1989 it decreased further in each of those republics. Moldavia experienced net emigration of Russians in the last intercensal period. Lithuania was the only Non-Russian republic to experience a larger net immigration of Russians between 1979 and 1989 than in the previous intercensal period. In Estonia and Latvia, the immigration of Russians slowed in each of the last two intercensal periods. While in 1970 to 1979, the rate of Russian immigration was higher to Estonia than to any other Non-Russian republic, in 1979 to 1989 it was highest to Belarus.

Effects of Natural Increase and Immigration to Population Change

Figure 7.16 apportions the increase in each republic's population between successive censuses to four factors: (1) natural increase of the titular nationality, (2) net immigration of the titular nationality, (3) natural increase of the Russian population, and (4) net immigration of Russians. The contribution of other ethnic groups is not shown.

Panel A shows the results for 1959 to 1970, Panel B for 1970 to 1979, and Panel C for 1979 to 1989. The figures reflect the number of persons added relative to the size of the population in the republic at the beginning of each intercensal period. By expressing the changes in terms of the effect on the proportionate increase of the population of the republic, we avoid confusing a large absolute increase with a large relative increase due to a given source.

FIGURE 7.16-A Contribution of Natural Increase and Migration of Titular Group and Russians to Population Growth, 1959-70

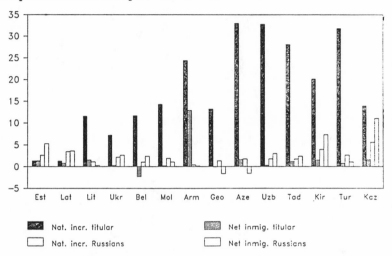

FIGURE 7.16-B Contribution of Natural Increase and Migration of Titular Group and Russians to Population Growth, 1970-79

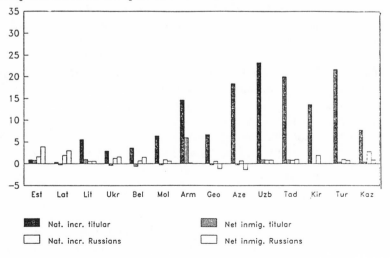

FIGURE 7.16-C Contribution of Natural Increase and Migration of Titular Group and Russians to Population Growth, 1979-89

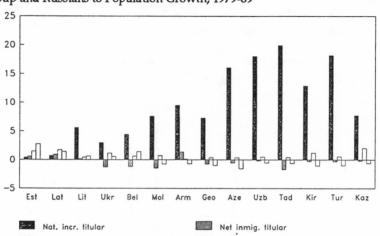

In all three intercensal periods the major source of population increase in every republic except Estonia and Latvia was natural increase of the titular nationality. In Estonia and Latvia, in contrast, the largest source of population increase usually was net immigration of Russians. In Latvia in 1979 to 1989, the largest source was the natural increase of Russians.

Net immigration of the titular nationality constitutes a substantial proportion of the increase in the republic population only for Armenia. Elsewhere, net immigration of the titular nationality makes the smallest proportionate contribution to the republic's population increase.

The natural increase of Russians is generally the second largest contributor to the population growth of the republics. In Estonia and Latvia, however, its contribution exceeds that of natural increase of the titular nationality.[34]

Immigration of Russians has played a modest role in the population increase of the union republics, except for Estonia and Latvia during all three intercensal periods, and of Kazakhstan and Kirgizia between 1959 and 1970.

Language Patterns

Figure 7.17 shows the proportion of the members of the titular nationality of each republic who reported Russian as their native language in 1959, 1970, 1979, and 1989.[35] In most republics, the proportions are very low. In Ukraine and Belarus, however, the proportions were large, especially in 1979 and 1989. Adoption of Russian as native language by a Non-Russian was often a first step toward changing his or her self-reported nationality to Russian (Anderson, 1979; Anderson and Silver, 1985b).[36] Figure 7.17 shows a large potential for re-identification of Ukrainians and Belarussians as Russians.

FIGURE 7.17 Pct. of Titular Group With Russian Native Language, 1970, '79, '89

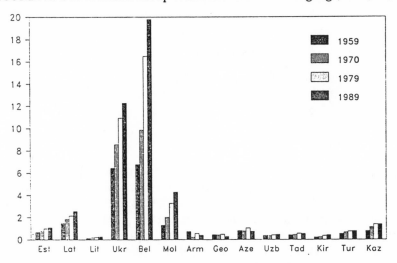

FIGURE 7.18 Pct. of Titular Group in own Republic with Russian as Native or Second Language, 1970, 1979, 1989

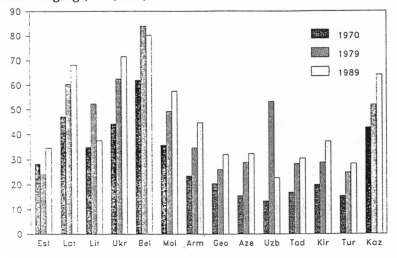

FIGURE 7.19 Percent of Russians in SSR's With Titular Language as Native or Second Language, 1970, 1979, 1989

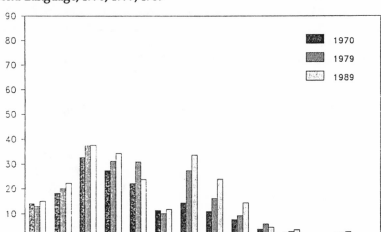

Figure 7.18 shows the proportion of the members of the titular nationality of a republic who reported Russian as either their native language or their second language in 1970, 1979, and 1989.[37] This generally can be interpreted as the proportion of the members of the titular nationality who knew the Russian language reasonably well.[38] But we should also recall that some of the intercensal changes in this proportion, such as those in Uzbekistan, Estonia, and Lithuania, result from implausible changes in the proportion of persons who reported that they freely command the Russian language.

Nonetheless, it is clear that members of the European nationalities were more likely to report knowledge of Russian than were members of the non-European nationalities. Among the titular nationalities of the union republics, knowledge of Russian was most common in Ukraine and Belarus, and most rare in Central Asia. Kazakhs in Kazakhstan were also very likely to know the Russian language. This is probably because Kazakhs in Kazakhstan needed to interact with Russians. In 1970, over half of the rural population of Kazakhstan was comprised of Russians and Ukrainians.

Figure 7.19 shows the proportion of Russians in each republic who reported the language of the titular nationality as their native language or a second language in 1970, 1979, and 1989. Russians in Central Asia and Kazakhstan rarely knew the language of the titular nationality. Russians in Transcaucasia and in the European republics were much more likely to know the language of the titular nationality. This was especially true in Ukraine and Belarus. However, some of those "Russians" in Ukraine and Belarus who reported Ukrainian or Belarussian as second language probably had formerly identified themselves as members of those nationalities.

That Russians in several of the Non-Russian republics became more likely to claim knowledge of the titular language in successive censuses might also be caused by other factors. First, especially in later years, it could be caused by increased pressure to use the local language. Second, it could result from selective migration: since many of these republics experienced reduced Russian net immigration, and some experienced net Russian emigration, those Russians who came to a Non-Russ. area or who chose to remain there may increasingly have been those who had adapted to the local culture or learned the local language.

Issues of language policy are often critical in debates over regional autonomy. In addition to the question whether Non-Russians should be required to study the Russian language in schools (as they were required to do in all republics), in the late 1980s leaders of political movements as well as regional government and party institutions in several republics proposed requiring members of non-titular nationalities to learn the language of the titular nationality. In some republics, such as Estonia and Lithuania, this had been the official policy for many years. In others, such as Moldavia and Ukraine, it had not been official policy. Inspection of Figure 7.19 suggests that although the policies proposed in some republics to require knowledge of the language of the titular nationality as a prerequisite for full civil rights would be difficult to implement in the European republics, they would be virtually impossible to implement in Central Asia and Kazakhstan.

Conclusions

The impending decline of ethnic Russians to a minority within the Soviet Union had greater political and symbolic significance than demographic significance. Nevertheless, differential growth rates of Russians, Slavs, other non-Muslims, and Muslims portended more dramatic changes in the ethnic composition of the USSR over the longer term if the USSR itself had survived. Although fertility had been rising among the European populations in the latter years, while it had been falling among Muslims, Muslim fertility was still so much higher than non-Muslim fertility that the level of Muslim fertility as well as the very young age structure of the Muslim populations was the major factor influencing the likely future balance of Muslims and non-Muslims in the Soviet population.

The patterns of ethnic composition of Soviet regions were not only changing but also very diverse. While the non-European republics were becoming more homogeneous, the European republics were becoming more Russianized, though the pace of Russianization had slackened in the 1980s. Briefly, the patterns within particular regions were as follows.

Central Asia and Kazakhstan

This region was becoming more indigenized over time. This was mainly due to higher fertility of the indigenous nationalities compared with Russians, and partly due to net emigration by Russians. Russians and the indigenous nationalities typically lived in very different settings and, compared to other regions of the USSR, each group had very little knowledge of the other group's language.

Kazakhstan had become more indigenized, due to a combination of higher fertility of Kazakhs than that of the Russian population and large declines in the net immigration of Russians. By 1989, this had led to the Kazakhs outnumbering Russians in the republic.

Transcaucasia

This region was also becoming more indigenized over time. This is partly due to higher fertility among the indigenous population than among Russians but primarily due to an acceleration of Russian emigration. In Armenia, net immigration of Armenians, especially from Georgia and Azerbaijan, was also a significant factor.

Baltic Republics

Estonia and Latvia were becoming increasingly Russianized over time as a result of net immigration of Russians. However, the level of Russian immigration had declined in the last two intercensal periods. The effect of Russian net immigration was countered to some extent by fertility differentials by nationality-slightly higher fertility among the titular nationality than among Russians.

Lithuania witnessed almost no change in the proportion of the titular nationality within the total population between 1959 and 1989. This was due to the higher fertility of Lithuanians than of Russians, which offset net immigration of Russians. In contrast to Estonia and

Latvia, however, the level of immigration of Russians to Lithuania increased in each of the last two intercensal periods.

The level of knowledge by Russians and by the titular nationalities of each other's languages in the Baltic republics was generally higher than in Central Asia and somewhat higher than in Transcaucasia.

The Soviet West

Ukraine and Belarus saw a small decline over time in the proportion of the population represented by the titular nationality. This near steady state was a result of the higher natural increase of the titular nationality than of Russians, which was offset by the tendency of the indigenous nationalities to re-identify as Russians or to migrate from these republics. Both republics had a substantial potential for members of the titular nationality to change to Russian ethnic self-identification. Also, there were higher levels of knowledge by titular nationalities of Russian and of the titular language by Russians than elsewhere in the USSR. But the growth of indigenous popular front movements, which focused on preservation of the culture and language as well as on economic and political autonomy, was likely to retard the rates of ethnic Russification.

Moldavia also had very little change in the proportion of the titular nationality in the total population between 1959 and 1989. This was due to substantially higher fertility of Moldavians than of Russians, which countered the immigration of Russians and others. Moreover, in the late 1980s popular movements and public demonstrations sought greater local autonomy and for recognition of the cultural and linguistic identity of Moldavians with Rumanians.

Analysis of Demographic Change in a Social and Political Context

In a book review published in the journal *Sotsiologicheskie issledovaniia* (Social Research) in January 1988, Ia. I. Rubin criticized Brian Silver for his explanation of the trends in migration in Transcaucasia between 1970 and 1979. Writing in 1983, Silver had concluded:

> In the absence of a primary investigation of the motives of migrants, we can only speculate about the motives for the cross-migration of Armenians and Azeris. One plausible explanation is that the historic antipathy between members of the two groups has crystallized in recent years to encourage mutual avoidance and resettlement. Despite cultural policies in the Transcaucasian republics that have been aimed

at reducing ethnic tension...an unfavorable cultural, administrative, or work environment for Armenians in Azerbaijan and for Azeris in Armenia may have encouraged resettlement to their official homelands.

Alternatively, perhaps the cross-migration in Transcaucasia has another, less nationalistically tinged explanation. Namely, the very rapid rate of urbanization of Armenia in recent years, which has advanced that republic's level of urbanization ahead of the USSR as a whole, may have created significant opportunities for urban Armenians in Georgia and Azerbaijan to move out of those republics to Armenia... (Silver, 1983: 377-378).

Rubin commented on Silver's argument as follows:

B. Silver sees the causes [of the resettlement of Armenians and Azerbaijanis from neighboring republics to their own republics] in "historically formed antipathies," in the still existing mutual hostility of Caucasian peoples, which "became aggravated to such a degree that they sought to flee from one another." The farfetchedness and tendentiousness of such an explanation is partly revealed by the sovietologist himself. It is possible, he confesses, that the cause is the rapid urbanization of Armenia, the desire of people to take on an urban way of life (Rubin, 1988: 132).

Rubin's comment was published in January 1988. The massive outbreak of violence between Azerbaijanis and Armenians in Nagorno-Karabakh, Sumgait, and elsewhere occurred in February 1988, accompanied by a large-scale emigration of Armenians from Azerbaijan and of Azerbaijanis from Armenia. Relations between the two nationalities in Transcaucasia remained very tense after that time and eventually deteriorated into a virtual war between Azerbaijan and Armenia.

Examination of long-term demographic trends is useful for understanding and interpreting the past. As the preceding example illustrates, however, examining underlying demographic processes is also instrumental for anticipating likely future events and problems.[39]

Other, less dramatic changes in the ethnic demography of the USSR also stimulated continuing discussion of public policies. Examination of the nature of these changes makes the issues more understandable. For example, leaders in the Baltic republics focused on pronatalist policies (aimed mainly at the titular nationalities) as well as regulating immigration and cultural policies to foster the preservation of indigenous languages and cultures. These actions are not surprising in light of the patterns of demographic change in the Baltic republics that we have shown.

In contrast to the Baltic republics, most other republics experienced increasing ethnic indigenization for an extended period prior to the demise of the USSR. The move toward greater dispersal of governmental autonomy within the federal system, accompanied by the growth of local popular movements and parties, meant that, even if the USSR had survived, the trend toward indigenization of these Non-Russian republics was not likely to be reversed in the near future.

Notes

1. This study was supported by NICHD Grant Nos. RO1 HD-19915 and P30 HD-10003. The authors are grateful to Douglas Johnson for research assistance and to Richard Hovannisian and Lee Schwartz for helpful comments on an earlier draft. Earlier versions were presented at the General Conference of the International Union for the Scientific Study of Population, 20-27 September 1989 (New Delhi), and at the Annual Meeting of the American Association for the Advancement of Slavic Studies, 2-5 November 1989 (Chicago). This chapter is adapted from an article published in *Population and Development Review*, Volume 15 (December 1989): 609-656. The authors thank the Population Council for permission to republish.

2. Following Aspaturian (1968), we use the term "Russianization" to refer to the spread of Russian people and Russian language in an area. It is distinguished from "Russification," which is change in the ethnic attachment or self-identification of Non-Russian to Russian. Soviet scholars have eschewed use of the term "Russification" as well as of "assimilation" as implying a deliberate official policy. In using terms such as assimilation, Russification, and re-identification, we do not imply anything about official policy. Instead, we use the terms to describe important aspects of change in ethnic self-identification.

3. "Union republics" were also referred to as Soviet Socialist Republics, or SSRs. See Table 7.1 for a listing of the fifteen SSR nationalities. Autonomous Soviet Socialist Republics and Autonomous Oblasts were located within SSRs. Autonomous Districts were also the titular geographic units of some Soviet ethnic groups with small population size, such as Komi-Permiaks.

4. The remaining population consists of persons who belong to an ethnic group that lacks an official homeland (titular area) in the Soviet federation, or who belong to a nationality whose titular area is of lower status than union republic. Some ethnic groups, such as the Gagauz, that lacked an official territory in the Soviet Union, were nonetheless considered indigenous to the

Soviet Union. Other ethnic groups that lacked a homeland in the USSR, such as Poles and Germans, were considered foreign.

5.   Figures for 1979 and 1989 refer to the "permanent" (*postoiannoe*) population.   Figures for 1959 and 1970 refer to the "present" (*nalichnoe*) population. For discussion of this distinction, one of minor importance in the context of the present analysis, see Anderson and Silver (1985c) and the section in this article on "Data and Definitions."

6.   An exception is the age-specific fertility data published by Bondarskaia and Darskii (1988). Similar data were published earlier by Karakhanov (1983). We have also estimated total fertility rates and infant mortality rates of the titular nationalities of the six Soviet Muslim republics (Anderson, Silver, and Liu, 1989).

7.   Kingkade (1988) reports that between 1970 and 1985, the number of those who emigrated from the USSR in the three nationalities were: Jews—264,451; Germans—70,777; Armenians—17,846.

8.   The closest approximation to such estimates is an unusual article by the director of the demography department of the Scientific Research Institute of the USSR State Committee on Statistics (Volkov, 1989), which examined the dynamics of ethnic intermarriage based on census data from 1959, 1970, and 1979. For additional discussion of ethnic intermarriage in the USSR, see Silver (1978a).

9.   For elaboration of the arguments in this paragraph, see Silver (1974, 1976, 1978b) and Anderson and Silver (1983, 1985b).

10.   There are some implications of these differences for our analysis. The urban permanent population is always smaller than the urban present population, and the permanent population of Russians and members of other non-indigenous nationalities in Non-Russian areas is always smaller than the present population of these groups.   The change from a present population basis to a permanent population basis thus will tend to depress the urban population in 1979 and will depress the Russian population in 1979, compared to 1970, in the Non-Russian republics. We think that the change of definitions is not a major source of the estimated changes in the proportion of the Non-Russ. republic populations who are Russians, but it nevertheless should be kept in mind.

11.   This difference is much larger than that for earlier Soviet censuses. For example, in the 1979 census, the present population exceeded the permanent population by 350,000. We do not know the reason for the increase in this difference between 1979 and 1989.

12.   Some scholars think that Kazakhstan should not be considered part of Central Asia, since it lies primarily in the Steppe zone. The Kazakhs, however, have close historical and cultural links to the titular nationalities of Central Asia, and the Kirgiz language is very similar to the Kazakh language.

13. Estonia=Est; Latvia=Lat; Lithuania=Lit; Belarus=Bel; Moldavia=Mol; Ukrain=Ukr; Armenia=m; Azerbaijan=Aze; Georgia=Geo; Kyrgyzstan=Kir; Tajikistan=Tad; Turkmenistan=Tur; Kazakhstan=Kaz.

14. This is more a matter of convention than good geography, since much of the RSFSR (east of the Urals) lay in Asia. Also note that the distinction between European and non-European union republics is not identical to a distinction between those republics in which the traditional religion of the titular nationality was not Muslim and those in which the traditional religion of the titular nationality was Muslim; Armenia and Georgia are non-European union republics, but Armenians and Georgians are traditionally Christian.

15. *Natsional'nost'* was the term used in the Soviet censuses of 1939, 1959, 1970, 1979, and 1989. In the 1926 census, the term *narodnost'* ("people") was used, purportedly in the interest of obtaining a more complete and accurate ethnographic picture of the Soviet population. For further discussion, see Silver (1986).

16. Unlike the censuses in Yugoslavia, which allowed designation of a category "Yugoslav," Soviet censuses did not provide for a "Soviet" nationality.

17. This may not be limited only to smaller nationalities. For discussion of the Ukrainian case, see Silver (1986), and Zeimal' (1988).

18. In the 1926 Soviet census, the number of Crimean Tatars can be approximated reasonably well by counting all those enumerated as Tatars who lived in the Crimean Autonomous Region. This total probably includes some Tatars who were not Crimean Tatars.

19. This does not mean that non-Crimean Tatars changed their ethnic self-identification to Crimean Tatar. More likely it means that people with Crimean Tatar ethnic background were more likely to call themselves Crimean Tatars in the 1989 census than in the 1979 census. This would reflect the more favorable climate for claiming such an affiliation in 1989 than in 1979. A similar trend is apparent for the Vepps (who increased by 65 percent between 1979 and 1989), Mountain Jews (who more than doubled), Georgian Jews (up by 91 percent), and Turks (who more than doubled). The "Turks" were most likely Meskhetian Turks, who have resided primarily in Uzbekistan and Kazakhstan after being deported there during World War II. The figures for the Turks may represent the first official tally of Meskhetian Turks in any Soviet census.

20. Kozlov (1969, 1982) has argued that the existence of an official nationality on the internal passport and other documents retarded the shifting of self-identified nationality. For further discussion, see Anderson and Silver (1983, 1985b).

21. The interpretation that we have heard in Estonia is that the 1979 census occurred shortly after a new First Secretary of the Communist Party of the Estonian SSR was installed. This First Secretary was regarded by many Estonians as too Russified; their responses to the census question on second language thus represented a covert political protest.

22. It has been speculated that in 1979 all Uzbeks who had a secondary education or who used machinery in their work were counted as freely commanding Russian as a second language (Voronitsyn, 1989). The absence of age-specific data on native and second language from the 1979 census precludes the exploration of alternative explanations of the patterns of change in language between 1970 and 1979.

23. An average annual growth rate assumes exponential growth between two dates, calculated according the formula $P2 = e^{rt}.P1$, where $P2$ is the population at Time 2, e is the base of the natural logarithm, r is the average annual rate of growth, t is the number of years between Time 1 and Time 2, and $P1$ is the population at Time 1. A population growing at a rate of 1 percent per year would double in 69 years, a population growing at 2 percent would double in 35 years, and a population growing at 3 percent would double in 23 years.

24. The growth rates are a product of each of the components of change mentioned earlier as well as of the age structure of the population.

25. See Anderson (1979) and Anderson and Silver (1983). Other historical factors help to account for this phenomenon (Anderson and Silver, 1985b).

26. See Gantskaia and Terent'eva (1965) and Terent'eva (1969). In contrast, in a majority of cases when a Russian and a Non-Russ. married inside the titular area of ethnic group of the Non-Russ. spouse, the children were likely to choose the nationality of the Non-Russ. parent as their passport nationality (Ievstigneev, 1971, 1972). Also see Volkov (1989).

27. For commentary on the manpower and regional development issues, see especially Feshbach and Rapawy (1973, 1976) and Rapawy and Baldwin (1982).

28. The total fertility rate (TFR) is the number of children that a woman would have in her reproductive life if she followed a given age-specific fertility schedule, such as that of all women in a given year.

29. A reading of the age-specific fertility schedules that Bondarskaia and Darskii (1988) report strongly suggests that the authors inadvertently transposed age-specific fertility figures above age 30 for the Kirgiz and Tajik nationalities in 1978-79. The data in Figure 7.12 correct this apparent error.

30. There are two other sources of the difference in the number of persons of a given nationality reported in successive censuses: differential undercount and assimilation. We cannot make corrections for either of these factors. We have no evidence on which to base estimates of differential census undercount by nationality. On the other hand, in principle it would be possible to take assimilation into account, at least between 1959 and 1970, for which we have made estimates (Anderson and Silver, 1983). But these estimates could be made only for the population of the nationality in the Soviet Union as a whole, whereas what we would need to know for present purposes is the amount of assimilation within a given republic.

31.   Strictly speaking, these are not *rates* because there is no defined "population at risk" of net migration. But this kind of estimate is conventionally referred to as a migration "rate."

32. A special note of caution is in order about the 1989 Soviet census data for Azerbaijan and Armenia. The outbreak of inter-ethnic violence and the subsequent large-scale migrations probably reduced the accuracy of census enumerations in both republics. In addition, the Armenian earthquake in 1988 not only caused serious loss of life but disrupted the census count among survivors, many of whom were living in temporary quarters at the time of the 1989 census.

33. We are skeptical about the apparent emigration of Tajiks from Tajikistan. It is possible that some of the results shown in Figure 7.14 are artifacts of changes in the accuracy of the data. For example, if Tajiks living in the Tajik SSR were undercounted in the 1959 census but counted more or less completely in 1970, they could appear to have been migrating into Tajikistan when they were not in fact doing so. Such a result would also appear if Tajiks living outside the Tajik SSR were counted more completely in 1959 than in 1970. We think the accuracy of counting of Tajiks at various dates deserves closer scrutiny. The number of Tajiks living in Uzbekistan reportedly increased 56.7 percent between 1979 and 1989, while the number of Tajiks living in Tajikistan increased by 41.6 percent. In the previous two intercensal periods, the rate of increase in the number of Tajiks living in Uzbekistan was substantially lower than the rate of increase in the number of Tajiks living in Tajikistan. It is possible that some Tajiks in Uzbekistan who were previously counted as Uzbeks were counted more often as Tajiks in 1989. We are grateful to Lubko Hajda for calling our attention to this discrepancy.

34. This relative contribution partly reflects the older age distribution of the Estonian and Latvian population compared to that of the Russian population, which leads to higher crude death rates among Estonians and Latvians than Russians. The fertility of Estonians and Latvians has exceeded that of Russians since at least the late 1960s (Bondarskaia and Darskii, 1988).

35. The data on the percentage who claimed Russian as their native language in 1989 are an approximation. We know the percentage of the population of each nationality that claimed their own nationality's language as native, but not the percentage of the members of a Non-Russ. nationality that claimed Russian as native language. We approximate the latter figure by using information from the 1979 census. We assume that of those who did not claim their own nationality's language as native, the same percentage claimed Russian as their native language in 1989 as in 1979. Similarly, we do not know what proportion of Russians in a given Non-Russ. republic claimed the language of the republic's titular nationality as native language in 1989. We use an analogous approach to estimate this proportion.

36. On the factors that account for the spread of Russian as a second language and for the shift of native language to Russian, see Anderson and Silver (1984, 1985b) and Silver (1974, 1976, 1978a).

37. Since this is the sum of those who claimed Russian as their native language and those who claimed Russian as a second language, for 1989 we again rely on an approximation of the first value.

38. We are aware that some Non-Russ.s who claimed the language of their nationality as their native language may not actually have spoken it well, if at all. It seems less likely, however, that Non-Russ. who claimed Russian as their native language would not speak it. For further discussion, see Silver (1986).

39. For a similar point, see Goble (1987).

References

Anderson, Barbara A. 1979. "Some Factors Related to Ethnic Re-identification in the Russian Republíc," In *Soviet Nationality Policies and Practices*, edited by Jeremy R. Azrael. (New York: Praeger): 309-333.

Anderson, Barbara A., and Brian D. Silver. 1983. "Estimating Russification of Ethnic Identity Among Non-Russ.s in the USSR." *Demography* 20 (November): 461-489.

____. 1984. "Equality, Efficiency, and Politics in Soviet Bilingual Education Policy: 1934-1980." *American Political Science Review* 78 (December): 1019-1039.

____. 1985a. "Estimating Census Undercount from School-Enrollment Data: An Application to the Soviet Censuses of 1959 and 1970," *Demography* 22 (May): 289-308.

____. 1985b. "Demographic Consequences of World War II on the Non-Russ. Nationalities of the USSR." In *The Impact of World War II on the Soviet Union*, edited by Susan J. Linz. Totowa, NJ: Rowman & Allanheld : 207-242.

____. 1985c. "'Permanent' and 'Present' Populations in Soviet Statistics," *Soviet Studies* 37 (July): 386-402.

____. 1986a. "Sex Differentials in Mortality in the Soviet Union: Regional Differences in Length of Working Life in Comparative Perspective," *Population Studies* 40 (July): 191-214.

____. 1986b. "Infant Mortality in the Soviet Union: Regional Differences and Measurement Issues," *Population and Development Review* 12 (December): 705-738.

____. 1988. "The Effects of the Registration System on the Seasonality of Births: The Case of the Soviet Union," *Population Studies* 42 (July): 303-320.

____. 1989a. "The Changing Shape of Soviet Mortality, 1958-1985: An Evaluation of Old and New Evidence," *Population Studies* 43 (July): 243-265.

____. 1989b. "Patterns of Cohort Mortality in the Soviet Population," *Population and Development Review* 15 (September): 471-501.

____. 1990a. "Growth and Diversity of the Population of the Soviet Union," In *World Population: Approaching the Year 2000*, edited by Samuel H. Preston, Vol. 510 of *The Annals of the American Academy of Political and Social Science* (July): 155-177.

____. 1990b. "Trends in Mortality of the Soviet Population," *Soviet Economy* 6 (July-September): 191-251.

____. 1993. "Mortality Trends in the Working Ages: Soviet Regions in Comparative Perspective, 1959-1988," In *Demographic Trends and Patterns in the Soviet Union Before 1991*, edited by W. Lutz, S. Scherbov, and A. Volkov. (London: Routledge): 291-334.

Anderson, Barbara A., Brian D. Silver, and Jinyun Liu. 1989. "Mortality of Ethnic Groups in Soviet Central Asia and Northern China," University of Michigan, Population Studies Center, *Research Reports*, No. 89-158 (September).

Aspaturian, Vernon V. 1968. "The Non-Russ. Nationalities," In *Prospects for Soviet Society*, edited by Allen Kassof. (New York: Praeger): 143-198.

Bondarskaia, G., and L. Darskii. 1988. "Etnicheskaia differentsiatsiia rozhdaemosti v SSSR" (Ethnic differentiation of fertility in the USSR), *Vestnik statistiki*, No. 12 (December): 16-21.

Coale, Ansley J., Barbara A. Anderson, and Erna Härm. 1979. *Human Fertility in Russia Since the Nineteenth Century* (Princeton: Princeton University Press).

Dmitrieva, R., and Ie. Andreev. 1987. "O srednei prodolzhitel'nosti zhizni naseleniia SSSR" (On the average length of life of the population of the USSR), *Vestnik statistiki*, No. 12 (December): 31-39.

Feshbach, Murray, and Stephen Rapawy. 1973. "Labor Constraints in the Five-Year Plan," in *Soviet Economic Prospects for the Seventies*, U.S. Congress, Joint Economic Committee (Washington, D.C.: Government Printing Office): 485-563.

____. 1976. "Soviet Population and Manpower Trends and Policies," in *Soviet Economy in a New Perspective*, U.S. Congress, Joint Economic Committee (Washington, D.C.: Government Printing Office): 113-154.

Gantskaia, O. A., and L. N. Terent'eva. 1965. "Etnograficheskie issledovaniia natsional'nykh protsessov v Pribaltike" (Ethnographic research on ethnic processes in the Baltic), *Sovetskaia etnografiia*, No. 5: 3-19.

Garson, Lea Keil. 1986. *The Centenarian Question: Old Age Mortality in the Soviet Union 1897-1970*. Unpublished Ph.D. dissertation, Princeton University.

Goble, Paul A. 1987. "Gorbachev and the Soviet Nationality Problem," In *Soviet Society under Gorbachev*, edited by Maurice Friedberg and Heyward Isham. (Armonk, NY: Sharpe): 76-100.

Grandstaff, Peter A. 1980. *Interregional Migration in the U.S.S.R.: Economic Aspects, 1959-1970*. Durham: Duke University Press.

Ievstigneev, Iu. A. 1971. "Natsional'no-smeshannye braki v Makhachkale" (Ethnically mixed marriages In Makhachkala), *Sovetskaia etnografiia*, No. 4: 80-85.

_____. 1972. "Mezhetnicheskie braki v nekotorykh gorodakh severnogo Kazakhstana" (Inter-ethnic marriages in some cities of northern Kazakhstan), *Vestnik Moskovskogo universiteta, Seriia istorii*, No. 6: 73-82.

Karakhanov, M. K. 1983. *Nekapitalisticheskiy put' razvitiia i problemy narodonaseleniia* (The noncapitalist path of development and problems of human population). Tashkent: FAN.

Kingkade, W. Ward. 1985. "An Evaluation of Selected Soviet Population Statistics," U.S. Bureau of the Census, Center for International Research, *CIR Staff Paper* No. 9 (November).

_____. 1988. "USSR: Estimates and Projections of the Population, by Major Nationality, 1979 to 2050," U.S. Bureau of the Census, Center for International Research, *CIR Staff Paper* No. 41 (May).

_____. 1989. "The Future Population of the Soviet Union," Manuscript, U.S. Bureau of the Census, Center for International Research (September).

Kozlov, V. I. 1969. *Dinamika chislennosti narodov (Metodologiia issledovaniia i osnovnye faktory)* Dynamics of the Numbers of Peoples [Methodological research and basic factors]). Moscow: Nauka.

_____. 1982. *Natsional'nosti SSSR: Etnodemograficheskii obzor* (Nationalities of the USSR: Ethnodemographic overview). Second Edition. Moscow: Finansy i statistika.

Rapawy, Stephen, and Godfrey Baldwin. 1982. "Demographic Trends in the Soviet Union: 1950-2000," In *Soviet Economy in the 1980's: Problems and Prospects*, Vol. II, U.S. Congress, Joint Economic Committee (Washington, D.C.: Government Printing Office): 265-322.

Rubin, Ia. I. 1988. Book review published in *Sotsiologicheskie issledovaniia*, No. 1 (January-February): 131-133.

Silver, Brian D. 1974. "Social Mobilization and the Russification of Soviet Nationalities," *American Political Science Review* 68 (March): 45-66.

_____. 1975. "Methods of Deriving Data on Bilingualism from the 1970 Soviet Census," *Soviet Studies* 27 (October): 574-597.

_____. 1976. "Bilingualism and Maintenance of the Mother Tongue in Soviet Central Asia," *Slavic Review* 35 (September): 406-424.

_____. 1978a. "Ethnic Intermarriage and Ethnic Consciousness Among Soviet Nationalities," *Soviet Studies* 30 (January): 107-116.

_____. 1978b. "Language Policy and the Linguistic Russification of Soviet Nationalities," In *Soviet Nationality Policies and Practices*, edited by Jeremy R. Azrael. (New York: Praeger): 250-306.

_____. 1983. "Population Redistribution and the Ethnic Balance in Transcaucasia," In *Nationalism and Social Change in Transcaucasia*, edited by Ronald G. Suny. (Ann Arbor: University of Michigan Press): 373-396.

____. 1986. "The Ethnic and Language Dimensions in Russian and Soviet Censuses," In *Research Guide to the Russian and Soviet Censuses*, edited by Ralph S. Clem, (Ithaca: Cornell University Press): 70-97.

Sinel'nikov, A. B. 1988. "Dinamika urovnia smertnosti v SSSR" (Dynamics of the level of mortality in the USSR), In *Naselenie SSSR za 70 let*. (Population of the USSR over the last 70 years), edited by L. L. Rybakovskiy. (Moscow: Nauka): 115-133.

USSR, Tsentral'noe Statisticheskoe Upravlenie. 1962-63. *Itogi vsesoiuznoi perepisi naseleniia 1959 goda* (Results of the all-union census of population of 1959). Moscow. Gosstatizdat.

____. 1972-73. *Itogi vsesoiuznoi perepisi naseleniia 1970 goda* (Results of the all-union census of population of 1970). Moscow: Statistika.

____. 1980. *Naselenie SSSR (Po dannym vsesoiuznoi perepisi naseleniia 1979 goda)* (Population of the USSR [According to data of the all-union census of population of 1979]). Moscow: Politizdat.

USSR, Goskomstat. 1988. *Naselenie SSSR 1987: Statisticheskii sbornik* (Population of the USSR 1987: Statistical Collection). Moscow: Finansy i statistika.

____. 1989. *Statisticheskii press-biulleten'* (Statistical press-bulletin) No. 4. Moscow: Goskomstat.

____. 1991. *Natsional'nyi sostav naseleniia SSSR (Po dannym vsesoiuznoi perepisi naseleniia 1989 g.)*. (Nationality composition of the population of the USSR [According to data of the all-union census of population of 1989]). Moscow: Finansy i statistika.

Volkov, A. 1989. "Etnicheski smeshannye braki v SSSR: dinamika i sostav" (Ethnically mixed marriages in the USSR: dynamics and composition), *Vestnik statistiki*, No. 7: 12-22, and No. 8: 8-24 (two parts).

Voronitsyn, Sergei. 1989. "Questions Surrounding the 1989 Census," *Report on the USSR* (Munich: Radio Liberty), 20 January 1989: 13-14.

Zeimal', Ie. 1988. "Narodnosti i ikh iazyki pri sotsializme" (Peoples and their languages under socialism), *Kommunist* 15 (October): 64-72.

8

The Cultural Partitioning of Canada: Demographic Roots of Multinationalism[1]

Edward T. Pryor

Canada, a nation-state for some 125 years, has evolved around a considerable array of concepts, often contradictory, that are intended to accommodate the diverse origins of its people. These concepts have developed as conquest and various sources of immigrants forced the sharing of the country by factions and regional parties along language and ethnic lines. Complicating the formation of Canada as a single nation-state was the regionalism that arose from the marked diversity in the demographic and economic evolution of different parts of the country. The concerns of preserving heritages, not merely British vis-à-vis French, but those of each maritime province, Quebec, and Ontario, were early issues to be resolved (McNaught, 1969: 124-137). The Confederation that emerged in 1867 was most definitely a compromise, with a clear differentiation in the Constitution (British North America Act) between federal and provincial powers. To this day, the issues of powers, centralization versus decentralization, provincial autonomy, and "special status" persist in attempts to change the regional balance of power.

Although not constitutionally explicit and therefore debatable, the Confederation established in 1867 attempted to give Lower Canada (French) and Upper Canada (British) a certain rough equity. In a sense, this trade-off attempted to gloss over the fact that French Canada continued to feel like a defeated "nation" under victorious British domination. This reality has generally been submerged by the so-called English side of Canada. But it remains a deeply embedded part of the cultural memory ("Je me souviens") in Quebec and among Francophones elsewhere in Canada. From the beginnings of Confederation, the notion of Quebec's having only provincial status in a larger nation-state was only partially accepted.

A basic theme of Canada has been how to maintain this fragile relationship, politically, socially, economically, and culturally. Canada has developed over time an elaborate set of federal policies and legislation to accommodate this duality. Canada commenced with this notion of two "founding peoples." That solid beginning was all well and good as far as it went. However, over the 125 years that followed, Canada did not remain a nation of two peoples. With massive immigration over its history, the complexion of the country changed, and continues to change. Table 8.1 illustrates the dramatic changes in the origins of immigrant Canadians over time, with Asia replacing Europe as the dominant source of immigrants. In fact, immigration data by country of last permanent residence show that by 1991 over half (52.1 percent) of all immigrants to Canada came from Asia, while Europe's share dropped to about 21 percent of all immigrants.

Obviously, the Canada based on two founding peoples has been transformed. Federal and provincial laws and policies have had to evolve to accommodate this changing cultural reality. Canada now must juggle the two founding peoples as the base of its nationhood, while recognizing various other ethnic and racial groups that continue to increase as a proportion of the population (Table 8.2). In addition, in recent years, aboriginal rights and nationhood have emerged as another political force cross-cutting the cultural "mosaic" (as Canadians say) of the nation (Breton, 1986: 32-37). The resulting nomenclature can be confusing because of these attempts to absorb and amalgamate these various people. Therefore, Canadian nationalism is not completely covered by the two peoples concept. Cultural duality also must take into account "multiculturalism," aboriginals as "first nations," and the maintenance and preservation of all of Canada's cultures. This dilution of precision and duality of cultural origin is a threat to Quebec in that the growth of Canada's population has reduced the influence of the French dimension of this duality. Thus, the central theme of this paper is that understanding the demographic roots and evolution of Canada is fundamental to comprehending the particular brand of nationalism portrayed by Canada.

TABLE 8.1 Immigrant Population by Place of Birth, Showing Period of Immigration, Canada, 1986

	Period of Immigration (% of population)						
Place of Birth	Before 1961	1961-65	1966-70	1971-75	1976-80	1981-86*	Total
Europe	87.7	76.1	62.7	38.3	30.3	28.8	62.3
USA	7.3	6.5	7.0	8.2	6.7	7.0	7.2
Africa	0.5	3.3	3.3	6.0	5.0	4.5	2.9
Caribbean, Central, South America	1.2	5.2	10.6	17.8	16.0	15.4	8.7
Asia	2.8	7.8	15.0	27.9	40.4	43.0	17.7
Other	0.5	1.0	1.5	1.9	1.7	1.4	1.1
Total	100.0	99.9	100.1	100.10	100.1	100.1	99.9
N =	(1,543)	(305)	(574)	(578)	(462)	(445)	(3,908)

* First five months of 1986 only.

Source: Census of Canada.

TABLE 8.2 Distribution of the Population by British, French, and Other Ethnicities, Canada, 1951 - 1986*

Ethnic Origin	Census Year (%)				
	1951	1961	1971	1981	1986
British	47.9	43.8	44.6	43.7	42.6
French	30.8	30.4	28.7	27.3	25.7
Other	21.3	25.8	26.7	29.0	31.7
Total	100.0	100.0	100.0	100.0	100.0
N =	(14,009)	(18,238)	(21,568)	(24,083)	(25,022)

* 1981 and 1986 multiple responses are assigned proportionately.

Source: Census of Canada.

The Demographic Infrastructure

A brief look at the population evolution of Canada is crucial to understanding the current attempts to preserve nationhood via constitutional changes. Even in the early 1990s, the prevailing theme is to constitutionally preserve the notion of "two founding peoples or nations." This foundation is being challenged now by the Assembly of First Nations, which represents some half-million reserve and non-reserve Indians, who insist that aboriginal people be recognized as the third founding people. In a recent book, Lyse Champagne states it well:

> Canada has not one history but many histories, some of which have been ignored, some of which have been overemphasized. By continuing to foster the two-founding-nations myth, we perpetuate a history that excludes more Canadians than it includes. (Champagne, 1990:48)

Although not a "myth" in the founding days of Canada, the current demographic reality has radically changed this rather simple view.

Ethnicity

This mind-set of Canadian duality continues to be held despite the demographic evidence. The changes in Canadian ethnic composition, especially since World War II, confirm the obsolescence of this notion of duality. Since 1951, the proportion of the population from these "two founding peoples" (Table 8.2) has continued to decline. In 1951, some 48 percent of the population was of British (Welsh, Scottish, Irish, English, etc.) origins. Thirty-one percent claimed French origins. Only some 21 percent of Canada's population in 1951 was from "other" (i.e., non-British, non-French) roots. By 1986, almost one-third (32 percent) of all Canadians had "other" origins. Even this change in distribution is somewhat misleading, because regional differences are not taken into account. The initial evidence here for the cultural partitioning of Quebec vis-a-vis the rest of Canada is presented in Table 8.3. Looking at the province of Quebec over this same 35-year period (1951-1986), this "dichotomizing" is apparent. Ethnically, the French held their own at some 82 to 79 percent of the population. On the other hand, people of British origins gradually are being replaced by other ethnicities. By 1986 British origins account for less than 7 percent, and other ethnicities grew from 6 percent to over 14 percent of the Quebec population. The story outside of Quebec mirrors that situation. Both British and French have a considerably smaller share of the population, as other ethnicities have increased from 27 percent to over 37 percent of the population. As the French population share declines to about 7 percent outside Quebec, it reflects the similar decline of the British population in Quebec to about 7 percent.

TABLE 8.3   Distribution of the Population by British, French, and Other Ethnicities, Quebec vis-à-vis Canada, 1951 - 1986*

Region and Ethnic Origin			Census Year(%)		
	1951	1961	1971	1981	1986
Quebec					
British	12.1	10.8	10.6	8.0	6.7
French	82.0	80.6	79.0	80.5	79.0
Other	5.8	8.6	10.4	11.5	14.3
Total	99.9	100.0	100.0	100.0	100.0
N =	(4,055,681)	(5,259,211)	(6,027,765)	(6,369,070)	(6,454,485)
Rest of Canada					
British	62.	57.2	57.8	56.6	55.1
French	10.0	10.0	9.1	8.1	7.2
Other	27.6	32.7	33.0	35.3	37.7
Total	100.1	99.9	99.9	100.0	100.0
N =	(9,953,748)	(12,979,036)	(15,540,545)	(17,714,425)	(18,567,520)

* 1981 and 1986 multiple responses are reassigned to single responses on a proportional basis.
Source: Census of Canada

Even this brief look at provincial differences tells only part of the story of ethnic distribution. Major Canadian cities, especially Toronto and Vancouver, are approaching the day when British and French together will account for a minority share of the population. Not only is the partitioning of English and French Canada taking place, but the significance of this traditional duality is decreasing, especially outside Quebec. On the other hand, the concentration of French in Quebec, combined with French attrition outside, is one demographic factor leading to a nationalistic stance. The evolution of a view that contrasts against cultural duality, and an official policy of multiculturalism in Canada is understandable from the recent trends in ethnic composition. But this also illustrates the contradictions that have emerged in efforts to promote both French-British duality and multiculturalism. Adding the growing aboriginal consciousness of autonomy (self-government vs. sovereignty) sets the stage for multi-dimensional ethnic and nationalistic conflict.

Language

This is not the place for any comprehensive review of the rich language history of Canada. The interest here is in a brief look at language (mother tongue and bilingual) trends as these pertain to the partitioning thesis. An abbreviated resume of what has happened to the distribution of English, French, and other mother tongues is shown in Table A in the Appendix. Again, the further dichotomization of English and French is apparent.   Between 1941 and 1986 there were parallel declines of English in Quebec and French in the rest of the country, along with a slight increase in the proportion of French in Quebec and a considerable growth of English in the rest of Canada (Lachpelle, 1989: 9-11). Table B of the Appendix, using "home language" as the measure, shows a similar pattern between 1971 and 1986.

Table 8.4 attempts to capture both English-French language trends in recent times and to determine the reality of bilingualism as a national trend. In general, the trends in English-French both within Quebec and outside Quebec reflect what was found for ethnic patterns. Bilingualism has come to be viewed as a symbolic, if not real, cultural bridge between the so-called "two solitudes" of "English" and "French" Canada. Although a great deal has been made recently of the increase in bilingual abilities outside Quebec, Table 8.4 shows that bilingualism still remains the "burden," or responsibility, of Quebec's population, which accounted for 55 percent of all bilingual Canadians in 1986. Looking at the situation by mother tongue, 59 percent of all bilingual Canadians possessed French mother tongue in 1986. Although the trends suggest eventual convergence, the ability to speak both official languages remains in the hands of a Quebec, Francophone majority.

TABLE 8.4 Who and Where are the Bilingual* (English and French speaking) Populations in Canada, 1971 - 1986

| Region | MotherTongue**(%) | | | |
	English	French	Other	Total
1971				
Quebec	10.0	43.1	4.3	57.4
Rest of Canada	14.5	24.8	3.3	42.6
Total	24.5	67.9	7.6	100.0
1981				
Quebec	10.1	40.9	5.2	56.2
Rest of Canada	20.2	19.9	3.8	43.9
Total	30.3	60.8	9.0	100.1
1986				
Quebec	9.7	40.4	4.8	54.9
Rest of Canada	23.2	18.4	3.5	45.1
Total	32.9	58.8	8.3	100.0

* Refers to the ability, as measured in the census, to conduct a conversation in English and French, the official languages of Canada.
** Refers to the first language learned in childhood and still understood by the individual at the time of the census.

Source: Census of Canada

Share

An important concept underlying the nationalistic view within Quebec is "share" of Canada's population and to what extent Quebec is maintaining its share of Canada's population. That concept has placed demographic change and its causes front and center in the discussions of Quebec's cultural and political future. Simply, nationalism and sovereignty have demographic underpinnings that inevitably have influenced the stance of Quebec governments and institutions. The basic argument is that the decline of Quebec's population share vis-à-vis the rest of Canada has been a major, if underlying, contributor to Quebec nationalism and to Quebec's demands for greater control over traditionally central government powers like immigration policy.

Quebec's Population Share

In 1951 Quebec contained 28.9 percent of Canada's population. By 1991 this share had declined to 25.3 percent. Looking back over this period, the trend (Table 8.5) is dramatically clear. The annual growth rate both inside and outside Quebec declined steadily through the 1961 to 1966 period. However, there was an increase in population during 1986-91 in both Quebec and the rest of Canada. Quebec is certainly not alone in slow growth (Table 8.6). The greatest increases have taken place in British Columbia, Alberta, and Ontario. More significant is that Quebec's below-average growth has persisted for so long. Why?

TABLE 8.5 Average Annual Rate of Population Growth, Quebec and the Rest of Canada, 1951-56 to 1986-91

| Period | *Rate of Growth (%)* | |
	Quebec	Rest of Canada
1951-56	2.68	2.84
1956-61	2.59	2.53
1961-66	1.91	1.86
1966-71	0.84	1.77
1971-76	0.68	1.52
1976-81	0.65	1.33
1981-86	0.31	1.00
1986-91	0.92	1.38

Source: Statistics Canada, Demography Division, Catalogue 91-210, Vol. 9.

TABLE 8.6 Population for Canada, the Provinces and Territories, Jan. 1, 1992*

	Population	*Annual Growth Rate (%)*
Canada	27,243,000	1.5
Newfoundland	574,200	0.4
Prince Edward Island	129,800	-0.4
Nova Scotia	906,100	0.8
New Brunswick	726,700	0.3
Quebec	6,895,400	1.2

TABLE 8.6 *(continued)*

	Population	*Annual Growth Rate (%)*
Ontario	10,018,900	1.8
Manitoba	1,094,200	0.4
Saskatchewan	992,300	0.0
Alberta	2,549,500	1.9
British Columbia	3,273,000	2.6
Yukon	27,400	3.4
Northwest Territories	55,600	2.6

* Preliminary postcensal estimates.
Source: Statistics Canada, Demography Div., Catalogue 91-002, Vol. 5, No. 4.

Fertility

The past generation has brought a revolution in Quebec in terms of fertility. (Romaniuc, 1984: 14-18). Although historically it had the highest fertility levels in Canada, Quebec in recent times has produced the lowest fertility rates in the country (Table 8.7). By 1987, the total fertility rate in Quebec had declined to the lowest ever. Since that time, the Quebec government has taken a number of steps to shore up fertility, including baby bonuses, tax credits, baby allowances, and some subsidized child care. The effectiveness of these new policies is a subject of debate. Nonetheless, after 1987, the total fertility rate has risen in Quebec, although Quebec's rate is among the lowest in Canada. As for the usefulness of Quebec government's fertility incentives, some observers would say these have worked; others would assign the rise in fertility in the latter 1980s in Canada generally to "catching up" by women over the age of 30. Looking at the 1987-89 period in Quebec, Dumas concludes that "....fertility among relatively older women has increased the most" (Dumas, 1984:40). In any case, below-replacement fertility rates in Quebec remain a crucial concern to both federalists and separatists.

TABLE 8.7 Total Fertility Rate in Quebec and the Rest of Canada, 1926 - 1989*

| Year | Total Fertility Rate | | Ratio Quebec/Canada (without Quebec) |
	Quebec	Canada (without Quebec)	
1926	4.2054	2.9705	141.6
1927	4.1726	2.9308	142.4
1928	4.0932	2.9210	140.1
1929	3.9098	2.8875	135.4
1930	3.9464	2.9611	133.3
1931	3.8953	2.8696	135.7
1932	3.7144	2.7767	133.8
1933	3.4128	2.5908	131.7
1934	3.3494	2.5297	132.4
1935	3.2769	2.4944	131.4
1936	3.2717	2.4253	134.9
1937	3.1828	2.3839	133.5
1938	3.1790	2.4599	129.2
1939	3.1318	2.4070	130.1
1940	3.2156	2.5334	126.9
1941	3.3215	2.5812	128.7
1942	3.4230	2.7243	125.6
1943	3.5066	2.7973	125.4
1944	3.5856	2.7228	131.7
1945	3.6093	2.7233	132.5
1946	3.7785	3.1599	119.6
1947	3.8487	3.4511	111.5
1948	3.7557	3.2717	114.8
1949	3.7522	3.2978	113.8
1950	3.7698	3.2873	114.7
1951	3.7350	3.3726	110.7
1952	3.8664	3.5135	110.0
1953	3.8880	3.6174	107.5
1954	3.9831	3.7301	106.8
1955	3.9287	3.7603	104.5
1956	3.9423	3.8116	103.4
1957	4.0386	3.8653	104.5
1958	3.9621	3.8326	103.4
1959	3.9472	3.9197	100.7
1960	3.7310	3.9606	94.2

TABLE 8.7 *(continued)*

| Year | Total Fertility Rate | | Ratio Quebec/Canada (without Quebec) |
	Quebec	Canada (without Quebec)	
1961	3.6685	3.9100	93.8
1962	3.5476	3.8437	92.3
1963	3.4425	3.7643	91.5
1964	3.3034	3.5807	92.3
1965	2.9693	3.2126	92.4
1966	2.6214	2.9304	89.5
1967	2.3444	2.7389	85.6
1968	2.1703	2.6136	83.0
1969	2.0940	2.5700	81.5
1970	1.9687	2.5162	78.2
1971	1.8744	2.3524	79.7
1972	1.7156	2.1878	78.4
1973	1.6820	2.0770	81.0
1974	1.6636	2.0087	82.8
1975	1.7197	1.9366	88.8
1976	1.7319	1.8783	92.2
1977	1.7387	1.8422	94.4
1978	1.6869	1.7880	94.3
1979	1.7251	1.7761	97.1
1980	1.6662	1.7652	94.4
1981	1.6223	1.7552	92.4
1982	1.5185	1.7705	85.8
1983	1.4842	1.7719	83.8
1984	1.4777	1.7827	82.9
1985	1.4524	1.7712	82.0
1986	1.4302	1.7543	81.5
1987	1.4235	1.7392	81.8
1988	1.4830	1.7593	84.3
1989	1.5958	1.8175	87.8

* Index calculated on the female population 15 to 44 years of age, derived from the population estimates as of June 1, between 1926 and 1980. The female population is estimated using the average of the two successive first days of January. Between 1966 and 1989, except for 1975, the rates for Canada included Newfoundland. It must be kept in mind that in the mid-1970s, the total fertility rate in Quebec is under-estimated because of an under-registration of births.
Source: Statistics Canada, Canadian Centre for Health Information and Demography Division.

Internal Migration

Obviously, regions of any country can gain and lose population share depending on the ebb and flow of inter-regional migration. Such shifts, especially over the long run, can have important consequences for population growth or decline. Quebec's experience with net inter-regional migration in the past 40 years has been unambiguous. In only one of the last forty years, 1961-1962, has Quebec experienced a net gain in inter-provincial migration (Table 8.8). Quebec's net loss has had its peaks and valleys over that period, with net losses of some 38,000 in 1970 to 1971 (probably pushed predominantly by economic factors) and over 46,000 in 1977 to 1978 (the beginnings of the Parti Québécois's government). Clearly, no one explanation is adequate to explain this forty-year pattern. Cultural pressures, political change, and relative economic opportunities elsewhere all have played a part. The past decade has brought a closer balance of in-and-out migration for Quebec, even though the net effect is negative. In recent years, the net losses have been modest. During the tumultuous decade from 1975 to 1984 internal migration was a major contribution to Quebec's loss of population share. During the 1976 to 1986 period, there was a significant out-migration of two hundred thousand persons with English as their mother tongue. Roughly four Anglophones departed for every immigrant to Quebec. French mother tongue net losses were about 30,000, while persons of neither English nor French mother tongue were also net emigrants by about four to one. The general result, whether intended or not, was to enhance the demographic partitioning of Quebec in terms of language.

Immigration

One of the proposals spelled out in a constitutional reform package, the 1991 Meech Lake Accord, which later failed to be ratified, was the increased assignment of immigration control to the Quebec provincial government. The wording was as follows:

2. The Government of Canada will, as soon as possible, conclude an agreement with the government of Quebec that would:

(a) Incorporate the principles of the Cullen-Couture agreement on the selection abroad and in Canada of independent immigrants, visitors for medical treatment, students and temporary workers, and on the selection of refugees abroad and economic criteria for family reunification and assisted relatives,

TABLE 8.8 Net Interprovincial Migration, Quebec, 1951-1952 to 1989-1990

Year	Net Migration	Year	Net Migration
1951-52	-6,191	1971-72	-20,461
1952-53	-9,891	1972-73	-20,072
1953-54	-11,079	1973-74	-15,135
1954-55	-6,032	1974-75	-9,299
1955-56	-4,994	1975-76	-12,643
1956-57	-7,447	1976-77	-26,366
1957-58	-5,063	1977-78	-46,429
1958-59	-8,313	1978-79	-30,884
1959-60	-7,184	1979-80	-29,976
1960-61	-683	1980-81	-22,841
1961-62	1,659	1981-82	-25,790
1962-63	-504	1982-83	-24,678
1963-64	-5,978	1983-84	-17,417
1964-65	-6,130	1984-85	-8,020
1965-66	-8,906	1985-86	-5,349
1966-67	-14,478	1986-87	-4,088
1967-68	-15,726	1987-88	-7,693
1968-69	-18,695	1988-89	-7,618
1969-70	-35,841	1989-90	-8,642
1970-71	-37,996		

Source: Statistics Canada, Demography Division, unpublished data for 1951-1952 to 1960-61 and Catalogues 91-208, 91-210, Vol. 9.

(b) Guarantee that Quebec will receive a number of immigrants, including refugees, within the annual total established by the federal government for all of Canada proportionate to its share of the population of Canada, with the right to exceed that figure by 5 percent for demographic reasons, and

(c) Provide an undertaking by Canada to withdraw services (except citizenship services) for the reception and integration (including linguistic and cultural) of all foreign nationals wishing to settle in Quebec where services are to be provided by Quebec, with such withdrawal to be accompanied by reasonable compensation, and the government of Canada and the government of Quebec will take the necessary steps to give the agreement the force of law under the proposed amendment relating to such agreements.

In fact, since the accord failed, some resolution of this issue has been achieved between Quebec and Ottawa, giving Quebec a greater say over immigration policy and entrants. Generally, the ability of Canada's provinces to attract immigrants is highly skewed. In 1986, the census showed this wide variability, (Table 8.9) with 22 to 23 percent of Ontario's and British Columbia's populations composed of immigrants, compared to only 2 percent in Newfoundland. Of the largest provinces, Quebec has usually trailed Ontario, Alberta, and British Columbia in recent times in the proportion of the population who are immigrants.

TABLE 8.9 Immigrants as a Percent of Provincial and Territorial Population, Canada, 1986

	Total Population	Total Immigrant Population	Percentage
Canada	25,022,010	3,908,150	15.6
Newfoundland	564,005	8,925	1.6
Prince Edward Island	125,090	4,325	3.5
Nova Scotia	864,150	40,465	4.7
New Brunswick	701,855	26,950	3.8
Quebec	6,454,485	527,135	8.2
Ontario	9,001,170	2,081,200	23.1
Manitoba	1,049,320	142,220	13.6
Saskatchewan	996,695	71,990	7.2
Alberta	2,340,265	368,755	15.8
British Columbia	2,849,585	630,670	22.1
Yukon	23,355	2,675	11.5
Northwest Territories	52,025	2,840	5.5

Source: Census of Canada

Another important demographic drama is portrayed by the past forty-year trend in Quebec's small share of immigrants to Canada, and the general loss in population share within Canada (Table 8.10). Since 1951 there has never been a year when Quebec's immigration share approached its population share. Recent years have not shown any marked improvement. Obviously, Quebec has been emphasizing the search for new immigrants that would mesh best with the cultural and language environment of the province. That challenge is further encumbered by the possibility that new arrivals are tempted by the opportunities of not merely other regions of Canada but of North

America in general. Improving immigration into Quebec will remain an issue of importance in the struggle for Quebec to hold its own in the demographic environment of the continent.

TABLE 8.10 Quebec's Share of Immigration and Population, 1951-91*

	Total Population			Total Immigrant Population	Percentage
1951	28.9	24.5	1971	27.9	15.2
1952	28.9	19.8	1972	27.8	14.4
1953	28.8	20.0	1973	27.6	15.1
1954	28.7	19.1	1974	27.4	14.9
1955	28.8	19.9	1975	27.2	16.1
1956	28.8	19.4	1976	27.1	19.4
1957	28.7	20.6	1977	27.0	16.0
1958	28.7	22.5	1978	26.8	17.6
1959	28.7	23.3	1979	26.7	16.8
1960	28.8	22.9	1980	26.6	15.0
1961	28.8	24.8	1981	26.4	17.4
1962	28.9	25.5	1982	26.3	18.3
1963	29.0	23.8	1983	26.1	17.6
1964	28.9	22.3	1984	26.0	16.1
1965	28.9	20.4	1985	25.9	17.7
1967	28.8	19.7	1987	25.7	16.3
1968	28.6	19.1	1988	25.6	16.5
1969	28.5	16.5	1989	25.5	18.3(R)
1970	28.2	16.2	1990	25.4(PR)	20.6 (P)
			1991	25.4(PP)	

* Population is as of June 1 each year; immigration is by census year (early June).
R and PR: Updated postcensal estimates.
P and PP: Preliminary postcensal estimates.
Source: Statistics Canada, Demography Division, unpublished data and Catalogue 91-210, Vol. 9.

The Future

Given Quebec's experience in failing to maintain its demographic share of Canada's population, what does the near future have in store? Using Statistics Canada's most recent projections, Table 8.11 presents the Canadian situation under four projected scenarios, using different assumptions ("low" to "high") for fertility and net international migration, with mortality viewed as basically declining with various assumptions on the distribution of internal migrants (see Statistics Canada, Cat. No. 91-520, Methodology Section). Under any of these scenarios, Quebec's share of population would continue to decline (Table 8.12) from that of 1991. Simply, the yearly percent growth of Quebec's population would remain below the national average (Table 8.13).

TABLE 8.11   Distribution of the Population of Canada, the Provinces and Territories, June 1, 1991 and 2011

			Population (in thousands)		
			2011-Projections Series		
	1991 (PR)	1	2	3	4
Canada	27,000	29,340	30,324	31,690	32,388
Newfoundland	573	543	577	566	621
Prince Edward Is.	131	132	145	139	157
Nova Scotia	901	915	974	964	1,053
New Brunswick	726	707	756	741	832
Quebec	6,846	6,996	7,467	7,684	8,028
Ontario	9,914	11,062	11,795	11,843	12,231
Manitoba	1,093	1,125	1,216	1,224	1,342
Saskatchewan	994	1,061	1,001	1,125	1,246
Alberta	2,522	3,015	2,692	3,299	3,005
British Columbia	3,218	3,683	3,592	3,998	3,777
Yukon	27	34	29	37	30
Northwest Terr.	55	67	81	72	67

PR: Updated postcensal estimates.
Source: Statistics Canada, Demography Div., Catalogues 91-210, Vol. 9: 91-520.

Of course such projections may turn out to have missed the mark. However, even the most optimistic experts have not been able to develop a set of fertility and migration assumptions that plausibly show Quebec maintaining its population share over the next decade. Within such a pessimistic demographic setting, the urge to seek more innovative solutions is understandable. However, incentives to increase and retain immigrants; to encourage more births; and to attract internal migrants and reduce emigration requires a considerable infusion of funds and the development of conducive economic, social, and political conditions.

TABLE 8.12 Distribution of the Population of Canada, Provinces and Territories, June 1, 1991 and 2011

	1991(PR)	Population (%)			
		2011 - Projections Series			
		1	2	3	4
Canada	100.0	100.0	100.0	100.0	100.0
Newfoundland	2.1	1.9	1.9	1.8	.9
Prince Edward Is.	0.5	0.5	0.5	0.4	0.5
Nova Scotia	3.3	3.1	3.2	3.0	3.3
NewBrunswick	2.7	2.4	2.5	2.3	2.6
Quebec	25.4	23.8	24.6	24.2	24.8
Ontario	36.7	37.7	38.9	37.4	37.8
Manitoba	4.0	3.8	4.0	3.9	4.1
Saskatchewan	3.7	3.6	3.3	3.6	3.8
Alberta	9.3	10.3	8.9	10.4	9.3
British Columbia	11.9	2.6	11.8	12.6	11.7
Yukon	0.1	0.1	0.1	0.1	0.1
Northwest Terr.	0.2	0.3	0.3	0.2	0.2

PR: Updated postcensal estimates.
Source: Statistics Canada, Demography Division, Catalogues 91-210, Vol. 9: 91-520.

The Dilemma

The basic demographic trends for Quebec (inevitably seen vis-à-vis the rest of Canada) can be summarized as follows:

1. Quebec's share of Canada's population has been declining and is projected to continue in that direction for some time to come;
2. While fertility rates in Quebec have increased slightly in recent years, they remain below the replacement level;

TABLE 8.13 Average Annual Growth Rate of the Population of Canada, the Provinces and Territories, 1991-2011

| | Projection Series (%) | | | |
	1	2	3	4
Canada	0.4	0.6	0.8	0.9
Newfoundland	-0.3	0.0	-0.1	0.4
Prince Edward Is.	0.0	0.5	0.3	0.9
Nova Scotia	0.1	0.4	0.3	0.8
New Brunswick	-0.1	0.2	0.1	0.7
Quebec	0.1	0.4	0.6	0.8
Ontario	0.5	0.9	0.9	1.1
Manitoba	0.1	0.5	0.6	1.0
Saskatchewan	0.3	0.0	0.6	1.1
Alberta	0.9	0.3	1.4	0.9
British Columbia	0.7	0.6	1.1	0.8
Yukon	1.2	0.4	1.6	0.5
Northwest Terr.	1.0	2.0	1.4	1.0

Source: Statistics Canada, Demography Division, Catalogues 91-210, 91-520.

3. Quebec has not been able to attract and keep its share of immigrants over the past four decades although there is evidence of improvement in recent years;

4. Similarly, the long-term balance of internal net migration has contributed to the continuing drain on the population of Quebec compared to the rest of the country;

5. The increasing concentration of French (whether measured by ethnicity or language) in Quebec combined with the counterpart trend of non-French (British and others) increases outside Quebec has accentuated the dichotomy; and

6. Current projections of Canada's population show a decreasing proportion of the population in Quebec.

Quebec nationalism is a complex issue, but this movement cannot be properly understood if the demographic dimension is not incorporated into the formula.

Multinationalism

As a federal state, Canada is confronting various movements, major and minor, that have the potential to divide the country. These movements are generally along regional lines with culture (language, ethnicity, aboriginal status) forming one axis of disharmony. Along the other axis, the problems of slow economic growth; persistent regional disparities in income and economic growth; and trends of industrial and resource decline accentuate the problems of disunity. The general objective of these movements toward regionalism or nationalism is to establish greater regional autonomy or government decentralization (e.g., Quebec), or for greater geographic control over specific localities (e.g., Indian Reserve or Band sovereignty). The main premise behind these movements is that specific cultures and economies can be better protected and fostered if greater regional, provincial, or local autonomy prevails. Of course, this notion fuels the classic confrontations of nationalism versus federation of states. In Canada's case, the demographic partitioning of Quebec has enhanced the social and political reactions to this state of affairs with efforts to create policies to counter these trends (e.g., encouraging higher fertility, seeking greater provincial control of immigration, instituting language legislation that protects French). The long-run impact of these initiatives is yet to be demonstrated.

Autonomy has various definitions and degrees of independence from the federal state. Canadian confederation itself includes specific responsibilities assigned to provinces, and this modifies the notion of total central or federal control. For example, education and health care are provincial responsibilities, while national defense is a federal mandate. However, in some areas, such as immigration policies, new modes of federal-provincial sharing of control have emerged.

Multinationalism is an appropriate description of the current movements for autonomy in Canada. Quebec nationalists argue for sovereignty or "sovereignty association," with a range of nuances attached to these terms. Various ethnic groups across Canada, armed with their best numbers, push for greater protection and maintenance of their cultures and languages (the Canadian "cultural mosaic"), and aboriginal organizations argue for the delivery by the federal government of long-promised "self-government."

Demographic realities will catch up with some of these notions and force a reassessment of nationalism in Canada. Certain questions are unavoidable in the light of the current situation or projected demographic developments. For example:

1. what will it mean when most Canadians are neither French nor British by ethnicity?

2. what will be the consequences of the increasing dichotomy of French in Quebec and non-French in the rest of Canada?

3. what will be the impact of the increasing "multicultural" immigration to Quebec, especially to Montreal?

4. will the old English-French conflicts be a thing of the past submerged by the reality of a pan-ethnic Canada?

The demographic infrastructure of any society is quite intractable. Short of catastrophe, demographic trends are not easily reversed or changed. A more homogeneous Quebec is, for many people, an objective worth achieving. For others, such homogeneity signals restricted opportunities, greater remoteness or partitioning to the detriment of the Canadian state (Porter, 1975: 294-295). Wherever these past and current trends described here take the country, there is solid evidence that Canada is one more world example of the relevance of ethnicity, language and culture to the political agenda of the 1990s.

Appendix

TABLE 8.A Population by Mother Tongue, Quebec / Rest of Canada, 1941* and 1986**

Region and Mother Tongue	Percentage	
	1941	1986
Quebec		
English	14.1	10.4
French	81.6	82.8
Other	4.4	6.8
Total	100.1	100.0
N =	(3,331,882)	(6,532,460)
Rest of Canada		
English	73.6	80.0
French	7.8	5.0
Other	18.6	14.9
Total	100.0	99.9
N =	(8,174,773)	(18,776,880)

* Excludes Newfoundland. ** Based on adjusted data for multiple responses.
Source: Statistics Canada, Canada Yearbook 1992

TABLE 8.B Population by Home Language, Quebec/ Rest of Canada, 1971 and 1986*

Region and Home Language	Percentage	
	1971	1986
Quebec		
English	14.7	12.3
French	80.8	82.8
Other	4.5	4.9
Total	100.0	100.0
N =	(6,027,765)	(6,454,495)
Rest of Canada		
English	87.2	88.6
French	4.3	3.6
Other	8.4	7.8
Total	99.9	100.0
N =	(15,540,545)	(18,567,495)

* Based on adjusted data. *Source: Statistics Canada.*

Notes

1. The author thanks Jean Dumas, Réjean Lachapelle, Benoît Laroche, Margaret Michalowski, Lise Paquette, Ronald Raby, Viviane Renaud, and the staff of the Demography Division, all of Statistics Canada, for their indispensable help in preparing this paper. Appreciation is expressed also to Calvin Goldscheider for his persistent encouragement and fellow authors of this volume for their understanding. Of course, all interpretations herein are those solely of the author and cannot be attributed to any other person or organization.

References

Breton, Raymond. 1986. "Multiculturalism and Canadian Nation-Building." In *The Politics of Gender, Ethnicity and Language in Canada.* (Alan Cairns and Cynthia Williams, research coordinators). Toronto: University of Toronto Press: 27-66.

Champagne, Lyse. 1990. *Double Vision.* Toronto: Key Porter Books Ltd.

Dumas, Jean. 1991. *Report on the Demographic Situation in Canada 1991.* Cat. No. 91-209E, Ottawa: Statistics Canada.

Lachapelle, Réjean. 1989. "Evolution of Language Groups and the Official Languages Situation in Canada." In *Demolinguistic Trends and the Evolution of Canadian Institutions.* Montreal: Department of the Secretary of State, Office of the Commissioner for Official Languages, and the Association for Canadian Studies: 7-33.

Leacy, F.H. (Editor). 1983. *Historical Statistics of Canada.* Cat. No. CS11-516E, Ottawa: Statistics Canada, 1983.

McNaught, Kenneth. 1969. *The Pelican History of Canada.* Baltimore: Penguin, 1969

Porter, John. 1975. "Ethnic Pluralism in Canadian Perspective." In *Ethnicity: Theory and Experience,* edited by Nathan Glazer and Daniel P. Moynihan. Cambridge: Harvard University Press: 267-304.

Romaniuc, A. 1984. *Fertility in Canada: From Baby-boom to Baby-bust.* Cat. No. 91-524E, Ottawa: Statistics Canada.

Statistics Canada. *1986 Census Highlights, The Daily.* Ottawa.

_____, Demographic Statistics for Years Ending May 31, 1990 and 1991, Demography Division, March 1992.

_____, *Dictionary 1986 Census.* Cat. No. 99-101E, Ottawa: 1987.

_____, *Population Projections for Canada, Provinces and Territories, 1989-2011.* Cat. No. 91-520, Ottawa: 1990.

_____, *Postcensal Annual Estimates of Population by Marital Status, Age, Sex and Components of Growth for Canada, Provinces and Territories.* Cat. No. 91-210, Vol. 9, Ottawa, 1991.

_____, *Quarterly Demographic Statistics.* October-December, Cat. No. 91-002, Vol. 5, No. 4, 1991.

White, Pamela M. 1990. *Ethnic Diversity in Canada.* Cat. No. 98-132, Ottawa: Statistics Canada.

9

On the Structure of Ethnic Groups: Crisscrossing Ties of Ethnicity, Social Class, and Politics in Europe[1]

Alan S. Zuckerman

The large-scale processes of modernization—the creation of nation-states, the development of capitalist economies, and the formation of political movements—carved sources of division and cohesion into European societies. New occupations and industries; migrations from rural to urban areas; the spread of formal schooling and differences in educational attainment; variations in religiosity; differences in language; and the formation of political movements split societies into swirls of overlapping social class, ethnic, and political patterns. A kaleidoscope of diversity formed in the states, cultures, and industrial economies of Europe.

In an effort to simplify and understand these processes, scholars have emphasized the consequences of capitalist economic development for the various characteristics of European societies. Research has been conditioned by Marx's argument: (a) Capitalist development is the key to understanding social, economic, and political life in the modern world; (b) Classes, defined according to their relation to the means of production, form and divide the workers, or proletariat, from the capitalists, or bourgeoisie; (c) Over time, the proletariat grows in size while displaying social and political cohesion; living and working close to each other; forming political organizations; exhibiting class consciousness; and engaging in revolutionary political action. In this view, the cohesion of persons in the same class categories of a society is a necessary product of capitalist economic expansion.

Other scholars emphasize the importance of ethnic factors in the formation of nation-states and capitalist economies. According to Ernest Gellner, the development of nations and nationalism defines the contemporary world:

> It is the establishment of an anonymous, impersonal society, with mutually substitutable atomized individuals, held together above all by a shared [national] culture...in place of a previous complex structure of local groups, sustained by folk cultures reproduced locally and idiosyncratically by the micro-groups themselves. That is what *really* happens.[2]

Successful ethnic communities formed nations; other ethnic groups disappeared. In this process, the Jews of Europe suffered enormously. Gellner views the destruction of European Jewry as an example of the conflict among ethnic groups as nation-states and industrial economies emerged across Europe:

> These persecutions illustrate, better than any others, the kind of fate which is likely to befall culturally distinguishable, economically privileged and politically defenceless communities, at a time when the age of specialized communities, of the traditional form of organic division of labour, is over.[3]

In this perspective, the formation of nation-states and national cultures in Europe resulted from conflict among ethnic groups.[4]

Both analytic traditions—the scholars who emphasize class conflict and those who focus their attention on ethnic conflict—err by drastically oversimplifying complex patterns. They assume that persons who share membership in a class or ethnic category exhibit social and political cohesion. They do not demonstrate the conditions under which a set of persons interact regularly and peacefully with each other. Both sets of scholars assume that one or the other of these categories determines the general and particular characteristics of European societies, even though precise comparisons deny the power of their arguments. Each of these research traditions mistakenly places individuals into overly simple analytic categories; each replaces empirical proof with theoretical assertion.

In contrast to the claims of these research schools, there is strong reason to argue that the cohesion—the likelihood of regular and peaceful interaction—of a set of persons who share membership in an ethnic category or class category of a society always varies.[5] After reviewing the empirical difficulties that abound for analyses based on the Marxist perspective, Aristide Zolberg asks, "If capitalism is of a piece, why is the working class it called into existence so disparate?"[6] The same general question applies to ethnic categories: If the process of nation-building is uniform, why are the ethnic communities of Europe so disparate?

The elements of modernization produce many forces. As a result, ethnic, class, and political diversity, not cohesion, have been constant features of European societies over the past century. Those who share location in areas of life that cut wide swaths through a society, like occupation, language, religion, and ethnicity, show variations in the extent to which they live near each other; go to the same schools and obtain comparable levels of education; choose each other as friends and spouses; and join to vote for the same party, to march, and to riot. Frequently, class and ethnic ties intersect. The intersections may divide members of ethnic categories along lines of occupation, residence, and education, and separate members of class categories along lines of dialect, language, religion, and origin. Sometimes, class and ethnicity overlap; sometimes they do not; the extent of the overlap always varies. There are usually no more than pockets of ethnic, class, and political cohesion.

Political networks stand as separate dimensions of social interaction apart from those of ethnicity and class. Since they always influence voting decisions, political ties may also affect the ability to obtain jobs, educational opportunities, and friends. Individuals vary in the extent to which they join political parties and engage in party activities. They differ in the extent to which a political party seeks to influence their political views and electoral decisions. Individuals vary in the extent to which they are surrounded by persons who share their political preferences and activities. Political ties are not simply products of location in a class or ethnic category. Frequently, memberships in the networks of political parties cut additional lines through the social divisions, organizing subsets of the categories into blocs of voters and activists while separating them from others in the ethnic and class categories who do not share these political ties. In all cases, even where ethnic and class memberships overlap, the electoral cohesion of members of an ethnic or class category is heavily influenced by the activities of political parties.[7]

In this essay, I will contrast the analysis of electoral cohesion against the effort to detail the patterns of diversity. Various streams within the literature of network theory come together to specify the conditions for electoral cohesion. A series of general propositions stand at the heart of this theoretical orientation: The likelihood that a set of persons will vote consistently for the same political party is tied directly to the extent to which they share membership in multiple and reinforcing social and political networks. The greater the number of shared ties, the higher is the level of electoral cohesion. Furthermore, memberships in political organizations have particularly strong effects on voting decisions. These general propositions imply several more-precise claims: (1) Membership in an ethnic or class category by itself has no impact on electoral behavior; (2) Political appeals, by themselves, to the members of an ethnic or class category have no impact on electoral behavior; (3) Multiple and reinforcing ties, as in the case of persons who are members of an ethnic category and who live near each other, with similar levels of educational attainment, and with similar positions in the class structure; or members of a class category who live near each other and speak the same language, are necessary conditions for high levels of electoral cohesion; (4) Memberships in political organizations, such as political parties or party affiliated trade unions and ethnic associations, are sufficient conditions for high levels of electoral cohesion; (5) Ties to political organizations always increase the likelihood that persons who share social ties will vote consistently for the same political party.[8]

My analysis focuses on Vienna and Warsaw during the 1920s. Studying cities, rather than national aggregates, brings the analysis close to people's lives, permitting fine-grained comparisons. The era between the formation of new democracies out of the German, Hapsburg, and Tsarist Empires and the civil wars, coups, and invasions that marked the ascendancy of the Nazis abounded in class and ethnic conflicts. In the Austrian capital, the dominant Socialist party created what became known as "Red Vienna." Left-wing activists and workers battled the political right, adherents of the Christian Social Party, various veterans, battalions, German Nationalists, and Nazis. Political anti-Semitism played a central role in the city's politics. Warsaw exemplifies a city in which a wide chasm separated the members of the two ethnic groups, the Poles and Jews, who lived there. Ethnic and class ties defined the social and political lives of the citizens of Vienna and Warsaw.

This analysis shows that persons who shared membership in the ethnic or class categories of Vienna and Warsaw did not form unified blocs. In both cities, ethnic groups displayed relatively high levels of residential concentration, and ethnic ties induced persons who shared the same occupations to live near each other. Even so, the cities differed in the extent to which ethnicity and class reinforced each other. While Warsaw's Poles and Jews displayed different class characteristics, in Vienna the overlap between ethnicity and class appeared only in particular niches of the city's occupational structure. In both cities, the likelihood that children of the same ethnic category would attend the same schools was directly affected by the class attributes of their parents. The patterns of educational attainment did not relate simply to the extent to which the ethnic group's culture valued formal education. Furthermore, ethnic ties seem to have had a greater impact on electoral cohesion than class networks did. Members of each city's ethnic communities never voted for a political party purporting to represent one of the other ethnic groups, while the likelihood that they cast their ballots for a party of their own ethnic group was tied to the nature of the political competition. In contrast, members of a particular class category of Vienna and Warsaw split their votes among all parties. They voted for ethnic parties and they cast ballots for all the political parties claiming to represent the city's different social classes, not only their own class. Only when persons of a social class also belonged to the formal organizations of a political party did they exhibit electoral cohesion. In Vienna and Warsaw, there was a complex pattern of interaction among ethnicity, social class, and politics.

Division and Cohesion in Vienna (1920-30)

In the decades before World War I, Vienna was a city of extraordinary change and diversity. In 1890, the city's population exceeded 850,000, nearly double the number that had lived there in 1860. By 1910, the number of residents doubled again, reaching 1,800,000. At the turn of the century, 36 percent of the residents reported speaking German at home, 23 percent spoke Czech, 17 percent Polish, 13 percent Ruthenian, and the remainder conversed in several other languages of central and Eastern Europe.[9] In the 1850s, no more than 5,000 Jews resided in the capital of the Hapsburg Empire. In the following decades, Jews from Bohemia and Moravia and later on Galicia and other areas in the eastern reaches of the empire moved to Vienna. Their numbers reached 73,000 in 1880; nearly 100,000 in 1890; 175,000 in 1910.[10] A population explosion, fueled by the entrance of migrants from across eastern and central Europe, turned Vienna into a multi-ethnic and polyglot metropolis.

Carl Schorske's study[11] of the Hapsburg capital's culture and politics at the turn of the century depicts a world overturned. Citing the imagery used by Arthur Schnitzler and Hugo von Hofmannstahl, Schorske underlines the themes of confusion and incoherence:

Modern society and culture seemed to [Hofmannstahl], as to Schnitzler, hopelessly pluralistic, lacking in cohesion or direction. "[T]he nature of our epoch," he wrote in 1905, "is multiplicity and indeterminacy. It can rest only on das Gleitende [the moving, the slipping, the sliding], and is aware that what other generations believed to be firm is in fact das Gleitende."[12]

Challenges to accepted principles of music and art; the breakdown of social order; new sources of social status; strange people in a Hapsburg capital constantly expanding in population size and geography; the formation of a powerful Socialist organization seeking to organize a burgeoning class of industrial workers; increasingly visible Jews; and anti-Semitic attacks all were parts of processes that transformed Vienna at the turn of the century. Swirling patterns of diversity seemed to replace longstanding order.

The dislocations of World War I followed by floods of poverty-stricken immigrants, and the formation of the Austrian Republic out of the dismantled Hapsburg Empire increased the force and tempo of this transformation. In 1923, over two million persons lived in Vienna. Conflict, decline, and fear of catastrophe join Hoffmansthal's image of a world of order replaced by diversity:

In Die Freudlose Gasse, G. W. Pabst's brilliant film of 1925, postwar Vienna is portrayed with an unvarnished realism as a city in crisis: inflation is rampant; tough profiteers lord it over a declassed bourgeoisie; the poor hunger to satisfy their most basic wants; and a moral decay hangs over all.[13]

To this picture, Helmut Gruber adds:

revolutionary ferment and republican reform; Germans, Jews, Czechs, and others; domiciles, workplaces, and infrastructures; the new state's uncertain viability; political camps and trade union loyalties; titles, parades, uniforms, hatreds and other residues of the old regime, the Catholic Church, anti-Semitism, and Germanic Christianity; the identity of the Viennese, and psychological shocks to the metropolitan ego caused by the city's newly diminished status as a capital of alpine yokels.[14] (1990: 13).

Ethnic divisions remained; approximately 10 percent of the people were Czechs and 10 percent were Jews.[15] The census, joining persons of diverse ethnic origins, classified the remainder as Germans. Class divisions drew attention to dramatic variations in wealth, education, and status, but also hid differences that cut through the class categories. A militant and well-organized Socialist party (Social Demokratische Arbeiter Partei, or SDAP) controlled the city's government. The rhetoric of class, ethnic, and religious conflict resounded in the battles between workers, Socialists, and their allies against right-wing activists. "By the mid-1920s, political violence in the First Republic became a secondary political system, a state of latent civil war which became endemic with the rise of fascism in the early 1930s."[16] In 1934, a right-wing coup ended this democracy, and in 1938, the Anschluss joined Austria to Nazi Germany. Socialists, Christian Socials, and partisans of ties with Germany politicized and exacerbated Vienna's ethnic, religious, and class divisions.

An analysis of Vienna's social and political structures during the 1920s displays a pattern of crisscrossing complexity. Ethnic divisions cut across class categories and class ties split persons who shared membership in the city's ethnic and religious groupings. Additional differences sliced through these broad categories. At the same time, the Socialist party dominated the city's government and constructed a massive organization, drawing adherents across the city's class and ethnic lines. Even in "Red Vienna," membership in supporting political organizations was a necessary condition for electoral cohesion among the city's working class.

Ethnic Concentration in the Neighborhoods

Census data on the residential distribution of the city's ethnic groups permit the most detailed look at the Jewish community, whose members continued to display high levels of residential concentration. In 1923, nearly half the city's Jews resided in three districts, Innere Stadt, Leopoldstadt, and Alsergrund, where they composed between 25 percent and 40 percent of the population. On average, each Jew lived in a district in which nearly 20 percent of the other residents were Jews. Another way to display the high level of residential concentration is to note that 40 percent of the city's Jews would have had to move to various neighborhoods of the city in order for the geographic spread of the Jews to have mirrored that of the other residents.[17] During the inter-war years, the Jews of Vienna maintained a pattern of residential concentration that had characterized their community since its inception more than a century earlier. Available evidence depicts most of Vienna's Czechs living in three districts,[18] strengthening a pattern of high residential concentration for the city's ethnic communities.

Crisscrossing Ties of Ethnicity and Occupation

In Vienna, there was a complex arrangement between occupation and ethnicity. No simple generalizations apply to the city's kaleidoscopic population. Contemporary reports allow us to depict these patterns, by exploring the differences and similarities among the city's Jewish and German[19] populations:

> Jews and Germans displayed different occupational profiles. A little more than half the Jews were self-employed, independents, or managers, as were a little more than 33 percent of the Germans; a quarter of the Jews and slightly more than 10 percent of the Germans were white-collar or salaried employees; and 20 percent of the Jews and nearly half the Germans were industrial workers. More than 25 percent of the Jews and nearly 50 percent the Germans worked in industry, and nearly half the Jews and 14 percent of the Germans were in commerce.

> Given the relative size of the two communities, however, it follows that Jews were a minority in each of these categories, composing 12 percent of those who owned their own businesses, 16 percent of the salaried, and 4 percent of the workers. They were also 5 percent of all persons working in industry and 14 percent of those working in commerce.

> The distinctive place of Jews in the economic structure of Vienna derives primarily from their location in particular segments of each of the broad categories of the city's economy: a) Jews maintained their long-standing dominance in the textile trades (73 percent of the employed); in the production and distribution of wine and liquor (64 percent); and in the distribution of fuel oil (54 percent); as well as furs (68 percent), jewelry (40 percent), and garments (34 percent); b) Jews were 25 percent of the salaried persons in commerce and 17 percent of the shopkeepers; c) Even though the Austrian government and the Viennese municipality employed 20,000 residents of the capital, Jews composed 0.3 percent to 0.4 percent of the civil service employees;[20] d) Jews were more than 50 percent of the city's lawyers, physicians, and dentists, and 33 percent of the pharmacists; e. Jews worked almost exclusively for other Jews. As self-employed Jews clustered in the liberal professions and particular commercial enterprises and artisan shops, and as salaried Jews were hired only by other Jews, occupational divisions reinforced the ethnic and religious differences that separated the city's Jews and Germans.

The Interaction of Ethnicity, Social Class, and Education

Jews were more likely than other Viennese to send their children to institutions of higher education. In the academic year 1923 to 1924, 17 percent of the Jews between 18 and 22 years of age were in the university; 28 percent of those of high school age were in the gymnasia; and 33 percent were in a high school of any kind. In comparison, approximately 6 percent of the German children in the appropriate age groups attended the gymnasia; 12 percent went to a high school of any kind; and about 3 percent attended the university. As a result, Jews accounted for more than 33 percent of the gymnasia students and 25 percent of those attending the University of Vienna, continuing a pattern that existed in the decades before World War I.

In Vienna, as in other cities, parental position in the class structure strongly affected the probability of attending institutions of higher education. Members of the working class sent very few children to the gymnasia and universities; most students came from parents whose class position was in the liberal bourgeoisie and the upper reaches of the government. Given the divergent occupational characteristics of the city's Jews and Germans, it would seem that a significant portion of the high rate at which Jewish children attended institutions of higher learning derives from their parents' location in the city's class structure. Jews composed 20 percent to 25 percent of the salaried, self-employed, and managers in commerce, segments of Viennese society with the wherewithal to send their children to the gymnasia and university.

Variations in educational attainment provided new sources of cohesion within the Jewish community and reinforced the separation between most members of the city's German and Jewish communities:

> Given the relatively high levels of residential concentration among Vienna's Jews, these children attended schools in which most of the other students were Jewish. The level of ethnic concentration was particularly elevated for those who attended the institutions of higher education. In the pre-war era, on average, each Jewish child who went to a gymnasium attended a school in which half the other children were Jewish.[21]

> It follows from these patterns of educational and residential concentration that only 10 percent of the Germans, almost exclusively the children of the city's bourgeoisie, liberal professionals, and higher-level salaried and civil service classes,

went to school with Jews. Furthermore, hardly any children from German working-class homes went to the gymnasia or university. As a result, very few of these youngsters went to school with Jews.

Several more general characteristics of the relationship between ethnicity and social class in Vienna emerge from this discussion: a) Large portions of Vienna's German population lived in neighborhoods, worked, and spent the school years with little direct contact with Jews; b) The only contact that a German worker, or approximately half of the community's adult population and 75 percent of its employed males, was likely to have with Jews was in the role of employee or customer; c) In turn, the networks of the Jewish community brought Jews in frequent contact with each other and with portions of the German middle classes. Most members of the Jewish community of Vienna occupied a particular niche within the city's middle classes.

Class, Ethnic, and Religious Divisions in the Jewish Community

Even as Jews occupied a distinctive position in Viennese society, reinforced by ties of occupation, education, and residential concentration as well as friendship and family, significant divisions split their community. Consider some of the consequences of the occupational and educational characteristics of the community that I just outlined.

In the academic year 1923 to 1924, two-thirds to three-fourths of the Jews between 15 and 22 were not in school but in the work force.

Occupational divisions were present among Vienna's Jews: More than 25 percent of the Jews were self-employed in the liberal professionals; 22 percent were salaried workers in industry or commerce; 17 percent were independents or managers in commerce; and 22 percent were craftsmen, workers, or apprentices in industry. As a result, approximately 30 percent of the Jews labored outside the new and expanding areas of the city's economy.

Sharp differences in wealth existed within the Jewish community. Given the relative poverty among many shopkeepers, it would seem that no less than 25 percent and as much as 40 percent of the community worked in spheres with relatively low incomes. Relatively few paid the communal tax to the Jewish communal organization, the *kultusgemeinde*. As a result, no more than 33 percent of the Jews were eligible to vote in these elections. In 1931, 11,000 families, 25 percent of the community, received welfare relief from the organized Jewish community.

Differences in levels of religious observance appeared as well among the city's Jews:[22]

Approximately 20 percent of the households regularly purchased kosher meat and attended religious services each week. Indeed, there were enough seats in the city's synagogues to accommodate no more than 20,000 to 22,000 Jews, or 10 percent of the Jewish population. On *Rosh Hashana* and *Yom Kippur*, holidays that would have particularly high rates of attendance at public prayer services, temporary accommodations were found to seat 50,000 Jews. It would seem that more than half the adult Jews of Vienna—indeed, approximately 65 percent of them—were not in the synagogues on these holidays.

Marked differences in religious education marked Vienna's Jewish children. Most received only the amount mandated by government policy: Jews and Protestants were tutored outside the classroom one hour a week, while a Catholic priest came to the school to teach the Catholic children. Approximately 20 percent of the Jewish children of school age attended the formal afternoon schools provided by the Jewish community for their religious education. The same proportion attended the Sabbath services organized by the *kultusgemeinde*. The city's only *yeshiva*, all-day Jewish school, educated 370 children in the mid-1930s, accommodating approximately 4 percent of the Jewish children of Vienna.

Elections to the *kultusgemeinde* indicate that approximately 10 percent cast ballots for political organizations associated with Orthodox Judaism, the *Agudah* party and the *Mizrachi* wing of the Zionist movement. In the mid-1920s, each claimed 1,500 members.

At the same time, it is important to note that divisions sliced through Vienna's Orthodox Jews as well. Battles between the Mizrachi and the Agudah paralleled and overlapped conflicts among the "Polish," "Hungarian," and "Galician" segments of this subsector of Vienna Jewry.

It would seem that not more than 20 percent of Vienna's Jews were tied together by the bonds of religious observance, and these Jews separated themselves into even smaller segments. Thirty-three percent of Jews of Vienna appeared occasionally at services and may have sent some of their children some of the time for religious instruction, and about half never went to public prayer services and did not provide religious education for their children.

Consider as well that Vienna's Jews migrated to the city from across the Hapsburg Empire. While the first waves came from nearby Bohemia and Moravia, later migrants came from Galicia and eastern portions of the empire. The first arrivals and their descendants were particularly likely to speak German, to be part of the professional classes, and to obtain particularly high levels of education. The later arrivals spoke Yiddish, and filled the ranks of the poorly educated and the poor. Differences of origin, which were perceived by the Jews as differences in ethnicity, joined with variations in levels of religiosity, education, and occupation to cut lines through the Jewish community of Vienna, even as differences based on ethnicity, religion, and class separated Vienna's Jews and Germans.[23]

Class, Ethnic, and Religious Divisions in the German Community

Vienna's Germans displayed their own patterns of class and educational divisions. Differences in region of origin, language, and dialect are obscured by the official decision to label all non-Jews as Germans. Differences also emerged in the occupational characteristics of Viennese Germans, carving a distinct niche for the relatively few members of cultural and economic elite, and drawing attention to the industrial workers and artisans who composed the vast majority of the city's Germans. Religious differences also appeared among Vienna's Germans. Whereas almost 90 percent of the city's population was born into the Catholic Church, contemporary reports note that no more than 10 percent attended services every Sunday. Furthermore, apostasy from the Church grew. In 1927, the level of formal resignations reached 120,000 and in 1933 it totalled nearly 200,000.[24] There is also evidence that religious and class divisions reinforced each other, since most of these resignations came from the working class.[25] Furthermore, the presence of a massive Socialist party organization deepened the class and religious divisions in this population. Social class, religious, and political ties pulled Viennese Germans in different directions.

Those placed into the working-class category did display differences in income, education, housing, and social standing. Wegs's analysis of working-class neighborhoods of Vienna notes sharp lines that cut through this population:

> At the top were a group of lesser officials (*Beamte*), most artisan masters, journeymen, and transport workers. They could earn less than the skilled factory workers, but they were separated from them by the higher social prestige of their work and the greater security of their position.[26]

> Among the non-artisan workers a three-way division existed: a group of primarily skilled workers at the top, where normally only the father was employed; a poorer middle group in which the father had regular employment, but his low pay and unemployment forced his wife and children to work full- or part-time and the family had to take in subtenants; and the very poor and the day laborers at the bottom.[27]

Wegs underlines further problems for the second group, as language differences hampered Czechs and others who came from Slavic lands, and differences of dialect interfered with the educational achievements of those who came from German-speaking lands. Furthermore, Gruber maintains (in a personal communication) that fears of unemployment, which reached beyond 35 percent, increased the threat of poverty and downward mobility among the workers. Differences of status, wealth, language, and ethnicity cut through Vienna's Germans, distinguishing an elite based on wealth and education from the working classes, while also cutting sharp lines through the city's workers.

Ethnic Patterns at the Polls: Jews and Czechs versus Germans

By examining the results of the elections and by assuming that only Jews voted for Jewish parties and that only Czechs voted for the Czech party, it is possible to estimate the electoral cohesion of the ethnic categories during the 1920s. In the elections of 1920 and 1923, 50 percent of the Jews voted for the SDAP and, in the elections held in 1927 and 1930, 70 percent to 90 percent of the Jews who voted cast their ballots for the SDAP (Table 9.1).

TABLE 9.1 Ethnic Divisions in the Electorate of Vienna*

Political Party	Jews	Czechs	Germans	Total
		1920 Election		
Democratic Lists	.30	--	.02	.04
Socialists	.50	.50	.44	.47
Christian Socials	--	--	.38	.30
Greater Germans	--	--	.12	.09
Jewish Party	.20	--	--	.02
Czech Party	--	.50	--	.05
		1923 Election		
Democratic Lists	.15	--	--	.02
Socialists	.60	.70	.53	.56
Christian Socials	--	.30	.40	.34
Greater Germans	--	--	.06	.05
Jewish Party	.25	--	--	.02
		1927 Election		
Democratic Lists	.10	--	--	.01
Socialists	.80	.80	.56	.60
Christian Socials and Greater Germans	--	.20	.42	.36
Jewish Party	.10	--	--	.01
		1930 Election		
Democratic Lists	.08	--	--	.01
Socialists	.90	.80	.52	.60
Christian Socials and Greater Germans	--	.20	.27	.24
Nazis and Far Right	--	--	.19	.15
Jewish Party	.02	--	--	--

Source: The data on Viennese elections come from *Die Nationaratswahlen vom 24, April 1927, 9, November, 1930, Statistisches Jahrbuch der Stadt Wien, 1929,* and Simon (172).

*In the postwar era, Jews and Czechs with Austrian citizenship each composed approximately .10 of the electorate, while Germans accounted for the remaining .80 of the electorate. It is reasonable to assume that only Jews voted for the Jewish parties and only Czechs voted for the Czech party.

Similarly, in the first two elections 70 percent of the Czechs voted for the SDAP, as did 80 percent of the Czechs who voted in the last two elections. In turn, the Germans divided their votes among the Socialists and various right-wing and far-right parties. No Jews and hardly any Czechs cast their ballots for the Christian Socials, Greater Germans, or any of the far-right political parties. The city's Germans divided their support between the political left and right.

The Socialist Party as a Source of Division and Cohesion

The Socialist party dominated the city's social and political life. In 1929, there were approximately 425,000 members of the SDAP and 375,000 workers who belonged to one of the Socialist trade unions. Furthermore, 170,000 adults lived in the massive housing projects built by the city for the working class, and all of them were members of the Socialist-sponsored tenants association. In addition, Vienna's Socialists were renowned for their newspapers, libraries, lectures, and cultural activities. In 1932, 100,000 attended the International Workers Olympics and 200,000 filled the city's sports stadium to take part in the workers' festival. And 30,000 to 35,000 party functionaries, cadres, and employees of the Socialist municipal government supported this massive enterprise.

The Socialists strove to organize the city's workers, developing their loyalty to the party and movement, and creating the *neue menschen* as a first step in the Socialist revolution. Rather than viewing the Socialist movement as simply an extension of the working class, it is necessary to examine the relationships among the activists who controlled the party, many of whom were members of the middle classes, and the workers. Each group had radically different incomes. In 1927, the salaries of party functionaries were between two and a half and four times the level of most skilled workers, and one-third of all party members in that year were unemployed.[28] Gruber's study joins Wegs's social history to highlight the chasm between the cultural world of most of the workers and that of the Socialist activists. Indeed, Gruber identifies this gap as the source of the Socialists' failure among Viennese workers:

In the Vienna experiment the problem was not the loyalty of leaders but the cultural distance that separated them from the rank and file. The distance reinforced the paternalism of leaders toward the workers they hoped to transform and liberate. The tendency to infantilize is explicit and implicit in the preconceptions about the workers which underlay the diverse party organizations and programs. Paramount among these was the total denigration of the workers' existing subcultures. On the one hand, the workers were viewed as aping the worst aspects of petty bourgeois cultural forms and aspirations. On the other, they were regarded as uncivilized: disorderly, undisciplined, and even brutish in their daily lives.[29]

As a result of these cultural and status divisions between Socialist activists and the members of the working class, and the lines of language, status, income, and education that cut through the workers, no more than 40 percent belonged to the various Socialist organizations (Table 9.2).

By extension, and in apparent contradiction to Socialist programs and rhetoric, at least half the workers remained outside the Socialist movement.

Class Divisions at the Polls

Far from uniting the city's workers into a cohesive bloc and dividing Vienna's population along class lines, the Socialist movement provided yet another basis for division and cohesion in Vienna.

The results of elections among the city's German population display the absence of high levels of electoral cohesion among the class categories. In the election of 1927 (Table 9.3), at least 40 percent of the middle classes and artisans supported the Socialists, as did 60 percent to 70 percent of the working class.

At the same time, this analysis underscores the extent to which the electoral cohesion of the working class depends on the organizational efforts of political parties. Indeed, membership in the various Socialist organizations seems to have been a necessary condition for casting a ballot for the SDAP.

The Viennese working class divided into three distinct political sets:[30] a) Persons who were closely tied to the Socialist movement, especially the party itself, the trade unions, and the tenants organization; b) those who voted for the SDAP, but were not part of its political and social network; c) those who voted for the Christian Socials, the Greater Germans, and other right-wing and far-right political parties (Table 9.4).

TABLE 9.2   Class Divisions in the Social Democratic Party of Vienna (1927)

There were 425,000 members of the SDAP, 375,000 members of Socialist trade unions, and 170,000 members of the Socialist sponsored union of tenants of city housing projects.   About 20,000 to 25,000 SDAP members were party functionaries, cadres, or worked for the Socialist dominated municipal government (Gruber 53-54). Also following Gruber (1990: 220), this analysis assumes that the class divisions in the population were mirrored in the membership of the Socialist Party. From these data, it is possible to derive estimates of the portions of the Vienna's social classes in the SDAP.

1. Excluding the Jews and taking the broader definition of the working class, "Four-fifths of Viennese SDAP members in 1929 were workers (blue-collar workers, employees, housewives, pensioneers). One-fifth or 80,000 members were from the middle class" (Gruber 220). There were 320,000 workers and 80,000 members of the middle class who belonged to the SDAP. As a result,

> 0.40 of these workers were members of the SDAP; slightly more than .50 of these workers were members of the tenants organization and Socialist trade unions; and .50 of them were members of the trade unions but not the tenants association.

> 0.40 of the middle class were members of the SDAP, and as many as .07 of the city's middle class and .15 of the middle class members of the SDAP had patronage connections to the party.

2. Excluding the Jews and taking the more narrow definition of the working class (based on the 1934 census, Heinrich and Wiatr report that 54 percent of the population were blue-collar workers; 30 percent were employees; and 16 percent were self-employed). Thus, .55 percent of the members of the SDAP were workers (220,000); .10 percent were artisans (40,000), and .35 percent (140,000 members of the SDAP) were members of the middle class. As a result,

> 0.40 percent of the workers were members of the SDAP, 0.77 percent of whom were also members of a tenants association a Socialist trade union, and 0.23 percent were union members but outside the tenants association. Put differently, no more than 0.30 percent of the workers were members of all three Socialist institutions, the tenants organization, trade unions, and the SDAP.

> 0.40 percent of the artisans were members of the SDAP.

> 0.40 percent of the middle class were members of the SDAP, and no more than 0.02 percent percent of the city's middle class and 0.07 percent of the middle class members of the SDAP had patronage connections to the party.

TABLE 9.3 Class Divisions in the General Electorate of Vienna (1927)

Approximately 1,160,000 persons voted; 693,893 voted for the Social Democrats (of which approximately 93,000 were Jews), and approximately 420,000 voted for the Right parties. It is reasonable to assume that all members of the SDAP voted for the Socialists and that no Jews voted for the Christian Socials and Greater Germans. Given these data and assumptions and the data and assumptions noted in Table 9.2, it is possible to derive estimates of the electoral cohesion of the social classes among the general population of Vienna, i.e., its non-Jews.

1. Given the broader definition of the working class (see Table 9.2) and the relative size of the classes in the electorate, and assuming that among the middle classes only members of the SDAP voted for that party:

> 0.40 of the middle classes (80,000) voted for the SDAP and the remaining 0.60 (120,000) voted for the Christian Right.

> 0.38 (300,000) of the workers voted for the Christian Right and 0.62 (500,000) supported the Socialists.

2. Given the more narrow definition of the working class and the relative size of these classes in the electorate and assuming that among the artisans and the middle classes only members of the SDAP voted for that party:

> 0.40 of the middle classes and 0.40 of the artisans (140,000 and 40,000 voters respectively) supported the SDAP and 0.60 of the these two social categories (60,000 artisans and 210,000 members of the middle classes) voted for the Christian Right.

> > 0.27 of the workers (150,000) supported the right, while 0.73 of the workers (400,000) supported the Socialists.

TABLE 9.4 The Political Cohesion of Workers* in Vienna (1927)

Taking the broader definition of the working class (see Table 9.2)

0.20 percent of the workers belonged to the SDAP, a Socialist trade union, and the Socialist tenants organization, and voted for the SDAP.

0.20 percent of the workers belonged to the SDAP and a Socialist trade union, and voted for the SDAP.

0.22 percent of the workers voted for the Socialists, but did not belong to any of the party's network of organizations.

0.38 percent of the workers were outside the Socialist party network of organizations and voted for the Christian Right parties.

Taking the more narrow definition of the working class (Table 9.2)

0.31 percent of the workers belonged to the SDAP, a Socialist trade union, and the Socialist tenants organization, and voted for the SDAP.

0.09 percent of the workers belonged to the SDAP and a Socialist trade union, but not the tenants organization, and voted for the SDAP.

0.24 percent of the workers belonged to a Socialist union, but did not belong to the SDAP and the tenants association, and voted for the Socialists.

0.27 percent of the workers were outside the Socialist party network of organizations and voted for the Christian Right parties.

---

*This analysis applies only to non-Jews.

All workers who were tied to the SDAP, as members of the party itself, as members of the tenants association or a trade union or both, voted for the SDAP. Workers who did not have any of these network ties to the Socialists were as likely to vote for one of the right-wing parties as for the SDAP. Among workers, support for the Socialists was not a simple extension of membership in a class category. Rather, it required organizational ties to the movement. The importance of membership in Socialist network as a determinant of voting for the SDAP is underscored by noting that organizational ties to the SDAP drew middle-class voters to the Socialists.

Patterns of Electoral Cohesion Among Vienna's Ethnic and Class Categories

As political ties crisscrossed Vienna, the city's ethnic and class divisions displayed variable levels of electoral cohesion. Table 9.5 displays the results of an analysis of the election of 1927.

TABLE 9.5 Electoral Cohesion of Viennese Social and Religious Groups, 1927
(Estimates of the percentage in each category voting for a political party)

Political Party	Jews	Workers*	Artisans	Middle Class	Total
Given the broader definition of the working class (see Table 9.2)					
Democratic Lists	.10	--	--	--	.01
Socialists	.80	.62	--	.40	.60
Christian Socials and Greater Germans	--	.38	--	.60	.36
Jewish Party	.10	--	--	--	.01
Category as % of voters	.10	.72	--	.18	.100
Given the more narrow definition of the working class (see Table 9.2)					
Democratic Lists	.10	--	--	--	.01
Socialists	.80	.73	.40	.40	.60
Christian Socials and Greater Germans	--	.27	.60	.60	.36
Jewish Party	.10	--	--	--	.01
Category as % of voters	.10	.50	.09	.31	.100

*This category includes only non-Jews.

The Germans and Jews who shared membership in the ranks of the city's white-collar workers, independents, managers, and self-employed voted for very different political parties. Most middle-class Germans supported the Christian Socials, German Nationalist, and other rightist and anti-Semitic political parties, while a significant minority supported the SDAP. None of the Jews supported the right-wing parties. In the years just after World War I, middle-class Jews supported the Democrats, Jewish parties, and the Socialists; by the end of the decade most of them cast their ballots for the Socialists. Among the working classes, traditional craftsmen, industrial workers, and the salaried in industry, most Germans and almost all the Jews supported the Socialist party. In all cases, organizational ties to the Socialist movement increased the rate by which persons voted for that party. Class and ethnicity intersected in complex ways in Viennese politics.

There is little reason to suggest that the Germans and Jews who supported the Socialists joined to form a separate niche in the class and ethnic kaleidoscope of the city. Ethnic, religious, residential, and social class differences separated the Germans and Jews who voted for the Socialists. Relatively few Jews belonged to the industrial unions affiliated with the Socialist parties; worked for the Socialist municipality; or lived in the city's housing projects. Furthermore, most of the Jews who supported the SDAP in national and municipal elections did not support the Socialist list in elections to the *kultusgemeinde*. While their shared political position brought portions of the Jewish and general communities together, these shared views and voting patterns did not supersede the ethnic, religious, and social class divisions that separated most members of these groups.

Class, ethnic, and political divisions separated and bound the population of Vienna during this period. The Jews occupied a distinctive niche in the occupational, residential, educational, and political structure of the city. Most Jews shared residence, education, and occupation with German members of the city's professional and salaried classes, but political, ethnic, and religious divisions separated Jews from the other segments of the middle class. At the same time, class and religious differences drew lines through each of the city's ethnic communities, and ethnic differences separated members of the city's class categories. A complex array of ethnic, class, and political lines joined and separated the Viennese.

Division and Cohesion in Warsaw (1920-30)

The creation of the Republic of Poland at the end of World War I formed a new state with deep and long-standing ethnic cleavages. Poles accounted for 65 percent of the population, while Jews, Germans, Ukrainians, Lithuanians, and members of other communities composed the remaining 35 percent. Leaders of the Polish nationalist political parties, led by the National Democrats, defined the state as the protector of the interests of ethnic Poles. The parties of the ethnic minorities battled to advance their rights. Ethnic conflict lay at the heart of Polish politics.[31]

The formation and collapse of new political parties and alliances, a crescendo of political crises, and, finally, a coup d'etat ended Poland's first attempt to establish a parliamentary democracy. None of the Polish parties entered the Republic with full-fledged organizations, centering around members, branches, meetings, and clearly articulated ideologies. The National Democrats were a loose association of Polish nationalists led by Roman Domowski. The Polish Socialist Party (PPS) was formed at the end of World War I by the merger of several smaller socialist parties, none of which displayed the organizational strength of the Socialist movements in central and western Europe. Dozens of other political parties competed for elections to the *Sejm*, the Polish Parliament; alliances among the parties formed and reformed; and cabinet crises abounded. In 1926, Josef Pilsudksi, the former leader of the PPS, marshal of Polish forces during the World War, and the first president of the Republic, led a coup d'etat, ending the rule of Poland's parties.[32]

In the new Republic, sharp residential and class divisions joined with language and religious differences to separate Poles and Jews.[33] Jews accounted for 10 percent of the national population and approximately 30 percent of the residents of Poland's towns and cities. Nearly 80 percent of those who declared Judaism as their religion attested that Yiddish was their mother tongue; 8 percent claimed to speak Hebrew; and 12 percent affirmed Polish as their language. Two-thirds of the Poles and 4 percent of the Jews worked the land, and 60 percent of the Jews and 5 percent of the Poles were self-employed artisans and shopkeepers in the towns and cities. Among those working outside of agriculture, sharp differences still applied: 56 percent of the Jews and 16 percent of the Poles were self-employed, and 60 percent of the Poles and 25 percent of the Jews were industrial workers. In the small towns and cities, Jews composed more than three-fourths of all persons engaged in commerce, continuing a long-standing pattern by which occupation and other economic differences reinforced ethnic, religious, and other cultural differences.

The Overlap of Ethnicity and Occupation in Warsaw's
Neighborhoods, Workplaces, and Schools

Poles and Jews divided the population of Warsaw between them. Consider the report of the novelist Alfred Doblin, who described his visit to Poland at this time:

> Three hundred fifty thousand Jews live in Warsaw, half as many as in all of Germany. A small number of them are strewn across the city, the bulk reside together in the northwest sector. They are a nation.... The Jews have their own costumes, their own language, religion, manners, and mores, their ancient national feeling and national consciousness.[34]

Doblin details his walks through various districts of the city:

I have crossed into a shabby neighborhood.... I skid too quickly
past churches, palaces. This is Praga. Peasant women in loose,
flowing linen skirts haul baskets. Jews in caftans....
A broad avenue leads off to the right. Woeful paving, small
houses with unclean fronts. A crack opens between two houses;
the entrance way to stalls..., for fruit, clothes, boots. The
peddlers are almost all Jews....
But to the south of Cracow Suburb, New World and
Ujazdowska Avenue stretch out, beautiful, modern with a
handful of stores, furniture, antiques. At the end, a park and a
chateau....[35]

Doblin proceeds through the Jewish neighborhood surrounding
Nalewki Street:

[The streets] are all filled and teeming with Jews. Trolleys run
along Nalewki Street. The houses have the same facades as
most of the houses in Warsaw, crumbling, unclean. Courtyards
submerge into all the buildings. I enter a courtyard; it's
rectangular and, like a marketplace, full of loud people, Jews,
mostly in caftans. The back wings contain furniture shops, fur
shops. And, after passing through a back wing, I stand in
another swarming courtyard full of crates, teams of horses,
Jewish porters loading and unloading. Nalewki Street has large
stores. Dozens of variegated signs indicate: hides, furs, ladies'
suits, hats, luggage.... Toward the city, in the southern part,
along the Dluga, large, open, modern stores: cosmetics, stamps,
textiles....Jewish women pass through the crowd; they wear
black wigs, small black veils on top, a kind of flower in front.
Black shawls. A tall young man in modern clothes with his
sister looks strange; he walks proudly, with a skullcap on his
head....A Polish policeman directs vehicular traffic in the
roadway. This contiguousness of two nations. Young girls
stroll arm in arm, they don't look very Jewish, they laugh, speak
Yiddish, their clothes are Polish down to the fine stockings....[36]

There was no way to miss Warsaw's Jews; they were omnipresent,
distinctive, and variegated. In 1925, they accounted for approximately
33 percent of the city's population and amounted to approximately 10
percent of the Jews of Poland. With few exceptions, only Poles and Jews

lived in Warsaw. Jews composed 80 percent of the residents of Nalewki and Muranow; in turn, the Jews of these districts accounted for half of the Jews of the Polish capital.[37] As a result, the average Jew lived in a district in which nearly half the residents were Jews. Nearly 40 percent of the Jewish population in Warsaw, as in Vienna, would have had to move in order for the distribution of Jews to have mirrored that of the total Polish population.

At the same time, there was a strong association between occupation and residence among the city's two ethnic groups. The correlation between the residential dispersion of Jewish and Polish members of the city's independents, managers, and self-employed was 0.67; for every increase of 10 percent of the population in a district who were Jewish members of this category, the proportion of Polish members increased by 3 percent. Among the salaried, the level of association was 0.98; for every increase of 10 percent of the population in a district who were Polish salaried, the proportion that Jewish salaried composed of the local population increased by 6 percent. Among the liberal professionals the correlation was 0.90, and for every increase of 10 percent of the population in a district who were Polish liberal professionals, the proportion that Jewish liberal professionals composed of the local population increased by 20 percent. Among the workers the correlation was 0.93; for every increase of 10 percent of the population in a district who were Polish workers, the proportion that Jewish workers composed of the local population increased by 5 percent. Pulls of ethnicity and social class dispersed Warsaw's residents into ethnic and class clusters.

In Warsaw, social class and ethnicity overlapped:

Jews and Poles displayed different occupational profiles. Forty-four percent of the Jews and 14 percent of the Poles were self-employed, independents, and managers; 33 percent of the Jews and more than half of the Poles were industrial workers; and 8 percent of the Jews and 20 percent of the Poles were salaried employees; 35 percent of the Jews and 13 percent of the Poles worked in commerce. Only industry, which contained 33 percent of the Jewish work force and 30 percent of the Poles, displayed a similarity of distribution between the two communities.

The ethnic communities clustered into distinct segments of these broad economic categories:

Given the relative size of the Jewish community and the large portion who were self-employed and who worked in commerce, Jews accounted for nearly three-fourths of the self-employed businessmen in the city.

Nearly 60 percent of the Jews in industry worked in the needle trades and hardly any labored in heavy industry. Forty percent of the Jews and 25 percent of the Poles could be classified as artisans, pursuing traditional forms of manufacture in small shops.

Almost no Jews and 15 percent of the Poles worked for the municipal and national governments.

As was the case in Vienna, only Jews hired Jews to work for them. As a result, Jewish industrial workers labored for Jewish bosses, and salaried members of the Jewish community found employment in firms owned by Jews.

Patterns of residential and economic concentration meant that almost all Jewish shopkeepers and artisans pursued their trades within the Jewish community and that members of the Jewish salaried classes worked for other Jews. Conversely, while Jews and Poles both worked in industry, they did not labor together in the same shops. Jews worked in relatively small workshops owned by other Jews, and Poles usually worked in more mechanized factories owned by Poles or Jews. Poles who were employed by the municipal and national governments had no Jewish colleagues. Because most Poles and most Jews lived in different neighborhoods, most Polish shopkeepers and artisans rarely did business with Jews. When the Jews of Warsaw went to work, they worked among and for other Jews. When Poles went to work, they worked for Jews and Poles, but only alongside other Poles. When Jews shopped, they bought their personal and household goods from other Jews, and when Poles shopped they made their purchases from Poles or Jews. Class divisions strongly reinforced the city's ethnic cleavage.

In Warsaw, differences in level and kind of education further separated members of the Jewish and Polish communities.[38] Warsaw's Jews were not especially likely to attend institutions of higher education. Indeed, they were less likely than Poles to obtain an elementary education in Poland. According to the law of the newly established state, Polish children between ages seven and thirteen were required to attend schools. Among children of the minority groups, like

the Jews, education was voluntary.[39]   As a result, attendance among
Polish children in Warsaw exceeded 90 percent, while 69 percent of the
Jewish children went to school. Furthermore, Jews accounted for less
than 30 percent of the school children of the capital and only 30 percent
of Jewish children who were in school attended the public schools. As a
result, Jews composed 20 percent of the children in Warsaw's public
schools.

Given the residential concentration of Jews, it would seem: (a) most
Jews receiving public elementary education attended schools in which
almost all their classmates were Jews; (b) a small number of Jews
attended public schools in which there were hardly any Jews; (c) almost
all Polish children attended schools with no Jews; (d) a small number of
Poles went to school with a small number of Jewish children.

Ethnic Concentration at the Polls

Political divisions, as they appeared in the three elections held in
Warsaw before the end of democratic rule, reflected the wide gap
between the city's Jews and Poles.[40] Table 9.6 displays the results of the
two elections to the parliament and one contest for Warsaw's city
council, held in 1919 and 1923.

Poles and Jews displayed sharp differences in electoral behavior.
None of the Poles and nearly all the Jews voted for one of the several
Jewish political parties, and only Poles voted for the right-wing alliance
led by the National Democrats. In Warsaw, the overlap among class,
ethnicity, religion, and politics carved a deep fissure between the city's
Jews and Poles.

Class and Political Divisions Among Warsaw's Poles

At the same time, class and political divisions appeared within each
of the two communities. In order to explore these patterns, it is
necessary to examine the Polish and Jewish communities separately.

Warsaw's Poles displayed social class and political divisions:

Twenty-five percent of the Poles were self-employed, half of
them as artisans and 25 percent as shopkeepers; 20 percent were
salaried and worked in the private sphere, and 10 percent were
salaried and found employment in the municipal and national
government; 18 percent were workers in industry; 12 percent
were domestics; 6 percent worked for the government, and 6
percent worked in commerce.

TABLE 9.6 Electoral Results in Warsaw (1919-1922)

Political Parties	Sejm Election 1919	Municipal Election 1919	Sejm Election 1922
Polish Socialist Party	.15	.18	.21
Polish Communist Party	--	--	.07
National Democrats and other right-wing parties	.54	.47	.46
Democratic parties	.02	.05	.02
Other	.04	.11	--
Jewish Parties	.25	.24	.23
Orthodox	.05		
Merchants	.02		
Orthodox, Merchants		.07	
Zionists	.06	.04	
Orthodox, Merchants, and Zionists			.13
Assimilationists	.01	.02	
Folkists	.10	.04	.06
Bund		.05	.05
Poalei Zion	.01	.02	--
% Jews voting for Jewish parties	.94	.88	.88
% Jews voting for non-Jewish parties	.06	.12	.12
Jews as % of those voting	.27	.27	.27
Jews as % of Electorate in Metropolitan Warsaw	.33		.30

Source: Hass, Ludwik, *The Political Attitudes of Warsaw's Residents as Reflected in the Results of Elections to Representative Bodies* (Warsaw: Panstwowc Wydawnictwo Nankowe, 1972, in Polish), Tables 2, 15, 18, 19.

Within the Polish community, the choice of where one lived was closely tied to occupation. Workers resided near other workers, so that for each 10 percent increase in the proportion of Polish workers in a district, there was a 5 percent decrease in the proportion of salaried and a 4 percent decrease in the proportion of self-employed.

Once again, class divisions manifested themselves in the distribution of support for the political parties in the national and municipal elections. Given the election results (see Table

9.6), it would seem that most workers supported the Socialist and Communist parties, and that almost all members of the Polish salaried and self-employed classes voted for the National Democrats, the party most closely associated with political anti-Semitism.

Table 9.7 presents an analysis that combines the votes obtained by the parties in the national elections of 1919 and 1923 and the municipal election of 1919.

The results display a strong association between the presence in a district of members of the Polish working class, support for the parties of the political left, and decreased support for the right-wing alliance of the National Democrats and various Christian parties. Indeed, for every 10 percent increase in the proportion of workers in a district there was a concomitant rise of 6 percent in the support for the Socialist party and a 5 percent decrease in support for the Polish right-wing parties. In addition, the National Democrats and Christian parties drew their support from across all the class categories. For every 10 percent increase in the proportion of Polish salaried and liberal professionals in a district, there was an 11 percent rise in the vote for the political right. Furthermore, given the class characteristics of the Polish citizens and the results of these elections (Table 9.6), all or almost all of the Polish shopkeepers, artisans, and other members of the self-employed, managers, and independents voted for the National Democrats and the Christian parties, as did a large portion of the working class.

These results underscore two critical points with regard to the electoral cohesion of the Polish social classes. Because the pre-war Czarist regime shackled the ability of the Polish Socialists to organize and to develop a mass movement, the PPS entered the new Polish Republic without the organizational strength displayed by the SDAP in Vienna. As a result, a significantly smaller portion of Warsaw's workers supported the city's Socialists compared to their counterparts in Vienna. Equally important, in the relative absence of these organizational and political ties to the Socialists, most of Warsaw's Poles supported the standard-bearers of Polish statehood in the first years of the Polish Republic, the parties of the political right.

TABLE 9.7 Social Class and Vote Among Warsaw's Poles (1919-1922)*

The Electoral Effect of the Salaried
>Vote for the National Democrats and other right-wing parties was positively related to the percentage of Poles in the district who were salaried. CORRELATION (R) .59623; R SQUARED .35549; SIGNIFICANCE .0003; STD ERR OF EST .16161; INTERCEPT (A) .24451; SLOPE (B) 1.21815.

>Vote for the Democratic parties was a direct positive function of the percentage of Poles in the district who were salaried. CORRELATION (R) .71016; R SQUARED .50433; SIGNIFICANCE .00000; STD ERR OF EST .01579; INTERCEPT (A) -.00506; SLOPE (B) .16167.

>Vote for the Socialist Party was inversely related to the percentage of Poles in the district who were salaried. CORRELATION (R) -.35805; R SQUARED .12820; SIGNIFICANCE .0408; STD ERR OF EST .10730; INTERCEPT (A) .26713; SLOPE (B) -.41759.

The Electoral Effect of the Liberal Professionals
>Vote for the National Democrats and other right-wing parties was positively related to the percentage of Poles in the district who were liberal professionals. CORRELATION (R) .63009; R SQUARED .39701; SIGNIFICANCE .0001; STD ERR OF EST .15632; INTERCEPT (A) .36660; SLOPE (B) 13.02002.

>Vote for the Democratic parties was a direct positive function of the percentage of Poles in the district who were liberal professionals. CORRELATION (R) .71516; R SQUARED .51146; SIGNIFICANCE .0000; STD ERR OF EST .01568; INTERCEPT (A) .01168; SLOPE (B) 1.64668.

The Electoral Effect of the Workers
>Vote for the Socialist Party was a direct positive function of the percentage of Poles in the district who were workers. CORRELATION (R) .71669; R SQUARED .51365; SIGNIFICANCE .00000; STD ERR OF EST .08014; INTERCEPT -.18134; SLOPE (B) .59784.

>Vote for the Democratic parties was negatively related to the percentage of Poles in the district who were workers. CORRELATION (R) -.42236; R SQUARED .17839; SIGNIFICANCE .0143; STD ERR OF EST .02033; INTERCEPT (A) .06587; SLOPE (B) -.06877.

---

*Because it is not possible to distinguish the electoral effects of the Jewish self-employed, managers, and independents, from the Poles, the analysis omits the Poles in this category.

Class and Political Divisions Among Warsaw's Jews

Differences in occupation, residence, and education affected the Jews of Warsaw:

Most of those in the work force clustered into five categories: 6 percent were liberal professionals; 8 percent were salaried; 20 percent were industrial workers; 15 percent were self-employed persons in industry (most of them artisans); and 25 percent were self-employed in commerce.

Relatively few Jews may be classified as members of Warsaw's liberal bourgeoisie: Self-employed and salaried teachers predominated among the Jewish liberal professionals, and rabbis added another 5 percent; physicians and lawyers composed 30 percent of the liberal professionals, less than 2 percent of the Jews in the work force. In 1913, Jews owned 357 industrial factories in the city, so that only a relative handful of the self-employed Jews in industry could be classified as industrialists.[41]

Most of Warsaw's Jews worked outside the advanced segments of Warsaw's economy: None of the teachers worked for the public schools and half were *melamdim* in the city's *hederim*, the traditional Jewish schools. Most of the Jewish members of the work force labored in small shops. Sixty-seven percent of those in commerce and 40 percent of those in industry worked in their own business or for a member of their family. As with most other residents of Warsaw, more than half lived in one- or two-room apartments without indoor toilets.[42]

Occupational characteristics overlapped closely with residential clustering among Warsaw's Jews: a) For each 10 percent increase in the percentage of the Jewish population in a district who were workers, there was a concomitant decline of 5 percent who were self-employed and 4 percent who were salaried; b) As noted earlier, many Jewish workers lived near Polish workers. The relatively small number of industrial and salaried workers among Warsaw's Jews tended to live apart from the other Jews of the city.

Patterns of educational achievements provide additional detail for a picture of Warsaw's Jews. Recall that 30 percent of the Jewish children between the ages of 7 and 13 were not in school and 30 percent attended public elementary schools. In addition, 25 percent went to private elementary schools in which all the children were Jewish, and 15 percent attended *hederim*. Relatively few of Warsaw's Jewish children were on track to obtain high levels of secular education; approximately 25 percent were too poor to attend school, and the rest were children of parents eking out livelihoods in Poland's capital. In the absence of a large class of professionals and members of the liberal bourgeoisie, relatively few Jewish children in Warsaw obtained anything more than an elementary school education.

An examination of the results of voting in national, municipal, and communal elections displays the murky swirl of political division and cohesion among the city's Jews (Table 9.6). In 1919, in the first contest for the Polish parliament, six Jewish political parties, the Orthodox, Merchants, Zionists, Folkists (cultural autonomists), Assimilationists, and *Poalei Zion* (Zionist revolutionaries) ran candidates, while the Bund (the inheritors of the Jewish revolutionary workers movement) abstained. During the municipal elections of that year, the Orthodox and the Merchants merged and the *Bund* entered the fray. These political movements coalesced and fought each other again in the parliamentary election of 1923 and the communal elections of 1924 and 1931.

Variation in the presence of self-employed, independents, and managers among the Jews of a district had a strongly positive effect on the proportion voting for the Orthodox, Merchants, Zionists, Folkists, and *Bund*; a weak positive effect on votes for the *Poalei Zion*; no relationship to any of the other Jewish political parties; and strongly negative or no relationship with voting for each of the Polish political parties. Almost all of these Jews casts their ballots among the Orthodox, Merchants, Zionists, and Folkists, the parties of the Jewish center and right.

Variation in the presence of salaried and liberal professionals among the Jews of a district had a strong positive effect on the proportion voting for the Assimilationists and Democrats; was inversely related to vote for the Socialist party; and had no relationship to the vote obtained by any of the other Jewish political parties. Most of these Jews divided their electoral support among the Jewish Assimilationist party and the Polish Democrats; approximately 20 percent to 25 percent voted for one of the other Jewish parties.

Table 9.8 displays the relationship between social class and voting for the Jewish parties across the districts of Warsaw:

TABLE 9.8 Social Class and Vote for Jewish Political Parties By Warsaw's Jews (1919-1922

Electoral Effect of the Jewish Self-Employed, Managers, and Independents

Vote for the Orthodox, Merchants, and Zionist Parties was a direct function of the percentage of Jews in a district who were self-employed, independents, or managers.

CORRELATION (R) .84535; R SQUARED .71462; SIGNIFICANCE .00000; STD ERR OF EST .07640; INTERCEPT (A) -1.12669; SLOPE (B) 2.40419

Vote for the Folkists was a direct function of the percentage of Jews in a district who were self-employed, independents, or managers.

CORRELATION (R) .74309; R SQUARED .55219; SIGNIFICANCE .00000; STD ERR OF EST .05377; INTERCEPT (A) -.55171; SLOPE (B) 1.18743

Vote for the Poalei Zion was weakly related to the percentage of Jews in a district who were self-employed, independents, or managers.

CORRELATION (R) .41014; R SQUARED .16821; SIGNIFICANCE .00888; STD ERR OF EST .01742; INTERCEPT -.06943; SLOPE (B) .15582.

Vote for the Bund was positively related to the percentage of Jews in a district who were self-employed, independents, or managers (pooled results of Municipal elections in 1919 and Sejm elections in 1922).

CORRELATION (R) .50099; R SQUARED .25099; SIGNIFICANCE .00877; STD ERR OF EST .04606; INTERCEPT (A) -.22817; SLOPE (B) .52162.

The Electoral Effect of the Jewish Salaried

Vote for the Assimilationists was a direct function of the percentage of Jews in a district who were salaried (pooled results of both elections in 1919).

CORRELATION (R) .77202; R SQUARED .59601; SIGNIFICANCE .00001; STD ERR OF EST .00765; INTERCEPT (A) -.00526; SLOPE (B) .15937.

The Electoral Effect of the Jewish Liberal Professionals

Vote for the Assimilationists was a direct function of the percentage of Jews in a district who were liberal professionals (pooled results of both elections in 1919).

CORRELATION (R) .70904; R SQUARED .50274; SIGNIFICANCE- .00011; STD ERR OF EST .00849; INTERCEPT (A) .00285; SLOPE (B) .39714.

The Electoral Effect of the Jewish Workers

Vote for the Orthodox, Merchants, and Zionist Parties was inversely related to the percentage of Jews in a district who were workers.

CORRELATION (R) -.37505; R SQUARED; .14066; SIGNIFICANCE .01575; STD ERR OF EST .13258; INTERCEPT (A) .38401; SLOPE (B) -.68623.

Vote for the Folkists was inversely related to the percentage of Jews in a district who were workers.

CORRELATION (R) -.27459; R SQUARED .07540; SIGNIFICANCE .06099; STD ERR OF EST .07727; INTERCEPT (A) .17386; SLOPE (B) -.28230.

Vote for the Assimilationists was inversely related to the percentage of Jews in a district who were workers (results of both elections in 1919).
CORRELATION (R) -.74112; R SQUARED .54927; SIGNIFICANCE .00004; STD ERR OF EST .00808; INTERCEPT (A) .05060; SLOPE (B) -.11231.

---

*Because of the tendency for Jews and Poles of the same class category to live near each other, this analysis only examines Jewish voting for Jewish parties.

Variation in the presence of workers among the Jews of a district was inversely related to the vote for the Orthodox, Merchants, Zionists, Folkists, and Assimilationists; had no relationship to vote for the *Poalei Zion*, and the *Bund*; and had a strong positive relationship with the proportion voting for the Socialist and Communist parties. Jewish workers in industry behaved very differently than other Jews: about 25 percent cast ballots for the Polish Socialist and Communist parties; another 25 percent voted for the *Bund*, and the remainder (about half) spread their vote among the other Jewish parties.

At the same time, it is important to note that most Jews had relatively weak ties to any of the political parties. Individual Jews frequently switched their vote choice among the political parties. If one assumes that the Zionists, Orthodox, and Merchants should be treated as a political bloc, and that aggregate stability in the results of elections implies stability in each person's electoral choice, then at least half the Jews who supported Jewish parties voted for different political parties in the two parliamentary elections. Since the second assumption is far from reality and the proportion of Jews voting for other parties varied, it follows that well over half the Jewish voters changed their votes between these two elections.

Data from the communal elections reaffirm the view that most Jews were indifferent to any particular political movement. In these contests, as in the national and municipal elections, approximately 60 percent exercised their right to vote. In 1924, 11 political parties shared the community's 50 seats, five of whom disappeared after that election. In 1931, twelve lists shared power, five of which were new lists. Only the *Agudah* party and the Zionist bloc displayed relative stability in the proportion of the vote they obtained. In 1924 and 1931, 20 percent of the voters supported the *Bund*, as did 21 percent in 1924 and 16 percent in 1931.[43] The Jews of Warsaw divided their votes among several political lists and usually changed their selection from one election to the next. The political divisions did not cut deep fissures into the Jewish community of Warsaw.

In the absence of direct information on levels of religiosity among Warsaw's Jews and Poles, these data on voting may serve as crude indicators of the kinds of religious divisions that were present. Note that the political parties associated with Orthodox Judaism, the *Agudah* and the *Mizrachi*, obtained about 25 percent of the votes cast in each of the elections. Jews who voted for the *Bund* and the Socialist and Communist parties, staunch opponents of Orthodoxy, gathered another 25 percent of the Jews. Among Warsaw's Poles, no more than 25 percent voted for these parties. Electoral results highlight the presence of a relatively small segment of each community whose political views separated them from the religious activities of most of their fellow Jews or Poles.

The Interaction of Social Class, Ethnicity, and Voting in Warsaw

Shared positions in the class structure of Warsaw separated and drew Jews and Gentiles together: (a) Almost all Jewish independents and self-employed supported Jewish parties, and almost all Polish independents and self-employed supported the National Democrats and the Christian parties; (b) large portions of the salaried and liberal professionals among Jews and Poles joined in supporting the Polish Democrats; but (c) members of the Polish salaried and liberal professionals who worked for the government supported the Polish right-wing parties; (d) broad segments of the Jewish and Polish working classes supported the Polish Socialist and Communist parties, but (e) no more than half of the Polish workers and 25 percent of the Jewish workers supported these parties.

In the absence of strong organizational ties, hardly any voters were bound to particular parties. Fewer members of the Polish working class supported the Socialists in Warsaw than in Vienna. By itself, location in the working class does not determine vote for a Socialist party. Similarly, in the absence of ties to a particular movement, most Jewish voters moved among the city's many Jewish political parties.

Social class, ethnic, and political divisions separated and bound the population of Warsaw during this period. The Jews, most of whom spoke Yiddish, occupied a distinctive niche in the occupational, residential, educational, and political structure of the city. Religious differences separated the city's Jews and Poles. Most of the Jewish people struggled to maintain themselves as tradesmen and artisans, greeting their customers as owners of small shops and peddlers.

Occupational, residential, and political differences appeared but did not cut wide swaths through Warsaw's Jews.

The examination of election results summarizes the complex interplay between class and ethnicity in Warsaw (Table 9.9).

TABLE 9.9 The Electoral Cohesion of Warsaw's Social Classes and Ethnic Divisions (Percentage in Each Category Voting for a Political Party)

	Political Parties	Independents	White Collar	Workers
	1919 Sejm Election			
Jews	Polish Socialist Party	--	--	.13
	National Democrats, right	--	--	--
	Democratic parties	--	.10	--
	Jewish Parties	.99	.90	.87
Poles	Polish Socialist Party	--	--	.36
	National Democrats, right	.99	.94	.64
	Democratic parties	--	.06	--
	Jewish Parties	--	--	--
	1922 Sejm Election			
Jews	Polish Left	--	.18	.26
	Socialist Party			
	Communist Party			
	National Democrats, right	--	--	--
	Democratic parties	--	.27	--
	Jewish Parties	.99	.73	.74
Poles	Polish Left	--	--	.66
	Socialist Party			
	Communist Party	--		
	National Democrats, right	.99	.97	.37
	Democratic parties	--	.03	--
	Jewish Parties	--	--	--

Relatively few were members of the city's tiny liberal bourgeoisie and no more than 20 percent of the Jews could be classified as part of Warsaw's industrial proletariat. Relatively few were so tied to a political party as to vote consistently for the party in governmental and communal elections. As a result, overlapping class, ethnic, and residential ties encircled most of Warsaw's Jews.

In the absence of a well-organized Socialist movement and in the presence of a political movement representing national independence, most members of the Polish working classes and all other Poles supported the right-wing political parties. Not only were there no ethnic divisions among Warsaw's Christians, but neither social class nor political divisions cut a sharp line through this population. As a result, overlapping ties of ethnicity, religion, and politics encircled Warsaw's Poles.

In the absence of strong ties that cut across the city's ethnic divisions, conflict between Jews and Poles emerged at the center of Warsaw's politics. Most Jews and Poles in Warsaw spoke different languages and observed the obligations of different religions. Class ties joined few members of these distinct communities; shared educational experiences brought few of them together; and hardly any of them worked together in the same political movements. Most of the city's Jews and Poles inhabited different worlds.

Conclusions

The analysis of Vienna and Warsaw during the 1920s underscores the variable character of ethnicity, social class, and political ties. Even where there is strong reason to expect to find class and ethnic categories to display the characteristics of unified wholes, kaleidoscopic swirls abound.

In both cities, class and ethnic groups were characterized by high levels of residential concentration. Jews distributed themselves across the neighborhoods of Vienna and Warsaw differently than did Germans and Poles in these cities. At the same time, members of the Jewish working class lived near members of the German and Polish working classes. Residential concentration reflected both class and ethnic factors.

Occupation and ethnicity interacted differently in each capital. In Vienna, large numbers of Jews were found in all of the broad categories of occupation and industry; only in specific economic niches do we find particularly heavy concentrations of Jews. In the Polish capital, most Jews were artisans, shopkeepers, and tradesmen, and most Poles were part of the industrial working class. As a result, differences with regard to wealth and education were much sharper among Vienna's Jewish community than among the Jews of the Polish capital. In Warsaw, members of the working class labored in work places that were segregated along ethnic lines; Polish and Jewish workers never labored side by side. Differences according to status of occupation, region of origin, dialect, and life-style split Vienna's German workers.

Ethnicity and education interacted differently in each of the cities as well. In the Austrian capital, Jews displayed particularly high levels of formal education. As a result, patterns of formal education drew together a particular segment of the Jewish community, separating them from almost all of the city's other residents. In Warsaw, Jews were even less likely than Poles to spend time in schools. Residential segregation, in turn, further reinforced the overlap between ethnicity and education.

In both cities, the amount of schooling obtained by members of the different ethnic groups was directly affected by their place in the class structure. Educational attainment did not simply reflect the extent to which the culture of an ethnic group valued formal education.

Even where ethnicity and religious affiliation overlapped, differences in levels of religious observance characterized members of ethnic communities. In Warsaw, Poles varied in their practice of Catholicism and Jews differed in the extent to which they observed their religion. Vienna displayed relatively low levels of religious observance among all the city's ethnic communities.

Ethnic cleavages emerged in electoral politics. In Vienna, Jews and Czechs voted very differently than did the city's Germans, and in Warsaw almost all Jews and Poles voted for different political parties.

Vienna and Warsaw exhibited different patterns of class-based politics. In both cities, most members of the working class supported the Socialist party, even as significant numbers of industrial workers voted for those who denied the centrality of class politics. In Vienna, a large segment of the city's middle class supported the Socialist party, and in Warsaw support for the Socialists and Communists remained confined to the city's industrial workers. Only workers who belonged to the networks of the Socialist movement were characterized by exceptionally high rates of voting for that party.

In all cases, membership in the organizations of a political movement appears to have been a necessary condition for consistent voting for the movement's political party.

The cohesion of a set of persons who share membership in a particular ethnic, social class, or political category always varies. Members of these categories vary in the extent to which they identify with each other; and they vary in the extent to which they regularly and peacefully interact with each other. Electoral cohesion rests directly on the patterns of network ties among sets of persons. Memberships in political organizations are particularly powerful determinants of consistent voting for the same political party. Each society is a complex array of interacting patterns of social class, ethnicity, and politics.

Notes

1. I am very happy to thank several persons and institutions who helped me gather and organize the data presented here. Danuta Dabrowska provided invaluable service at the archives at Yad Vashem, in Jerusalem. Mark Brilliant, Joshua Beiser, and my son, Ezra Zuckerman, were able research assistants. Michael Rich and Jack Combs helped me organize the material. Helmut Gruber and Calvin Goldscheider provided detailed readings and valuable comments. My research has been supported by grants from the Council for the International Exchange of Scholars, which awarded me a Fulbright Senior Research and Lecturer Award in the Department of Political Science, Tel-Aviv University, 1985 to 1986, and the Memorial Foundation for Jewish Culture, which awarded me a research grant, 1989 to 1990. I am pleased to thank both institutions for their generosity. The analysis here builds on Goldscheider and Zuckerman (1984, 1986 and see also Goldscheider, 1986; Goldscheider 1986, and Zuckerman, 1991). While I thank all of these persons and institutions, I stand responsible for the analysis.

2. Gellner, Ernest. *Nations and Nationalism*. Ithaca, NY: Cornell University Press, 1983: 57.

3. *Ibid*, 107.

4. In addition to Gellner, Ernest. *Nations and Nationalism*. Ithaca, NY: Cornell University Press, 1983, Smith, Anthony D. *The Ethnic Revival in the Modern World*. Cambridge: Cambridge University Press, 1981 and Horowitz, Donald L. *Ethnic Groups in Conflict*. Berkeley: University of California Press, 1985 exemplify this theoretical stance.

5. The classic source for this position is Max Weber's criticism of Marx's concept of social class; see *From Max Weber*, edited by H. H. Gerth and C. Wright Mills. New York: Oxford University Press, 1958 : 180-195. Note as well that Weber offers an extraordinarily strained view of Jews, insisting that they be analyzed as a caste, at a time when they were being transformed by the processes of modernization. For recent examples that develop the theme that class and ethnic categories are best analyzed as variables, see Brass, Paul. "Ethnic Groups and the State." *Ethnic Groups and the State*, edited by Paul Brass. Totowa, NJ: Barnes and Noble Books, 1985 : 1-56; Yancey, W. et al. "Emergent Ethnicity: A Review and a Formulation." *American Sociological Review* 41 1977 : 821-827; Katznelson, Ira. "Working-class Formation: Constructing Cases and Comparisons." In *Working-class Formation: Nineteenth Century Patterns in Western Europe and the United States*, edited by Ira Katznelson and Aristide R. Zolberg. Princeton, NJ: Princeton University Press, 1986 : 3-43; Kocka, Jurgen. "Problems of Working-class Formation in Germany: The Early Years, 1800-1875." In *Working-class Formation: Nineteenth Century Patterns in Western Europe and the United States*, edited by Ira Katznelson and Aristide R. Kolberg.

Princeton, NJ: Princeton University Press, 1986 : 273-358; Reddy, William M. *Money and Liberty in Modern Europe: A Critique of Historical Understanding.* Cambridge: Cambridge University Press, 1987; Zuckerman, Alan S. "New Approaches to Political Cleavage: A Theoretical Introduction." *Comparative Political Studies* 15 1982 : 131-144; Zuckerman, Alan S. "The Bases of Political Cohesion: Applying and Reconstructing Crumbling Theories." *Comparative Politics* 21 1989 : 473-495.

6. Zolberg, Aristide R. "How Many Exceptionalisms?" In *Working-Class Formation: Nineteenth Century Patterns in Western Europe and the United States,* edited by Ira Katznelson and Aristide R. Zolberg. Princeton, NJ: Princeton University Press, 1986, : 387.

7. Sources that emphasize this perspective include Brass, Paul. "Ethnic Groups and the State." In *Ethnic Groups and the State,* edited by Paul Brass. Totowa, NJ: Barnes and Noble Books, 1985, : 1-56; Huckfeldt, Robert and John Sprague. "Political Parties and Electoral Mobilization: Political Structure, Social Structure, and the Party Canvas." *American Political Science Review* 86 1992 : 70-86; Przeworksi, Adam and John Sprague. *Paper Stones: A History of Electoral Socialism.* Chicago: University of Chicago Press, 1986; Zuckerman, Alan S. "Political Cleavage: A Conceptual and Theoretical Analysis." *British Journal of Political Science 5* 1975 : 131-144; Zuckerman, Alan S. "New Approaches to Political Cleavage: A Theoretical Introduction." *Comparative Political Studies* 15 1982, : 131-144; Zuckerman, Alan S. "The Bases of Political Cohesion: Applying and Reconstructing Crumbling Theories." *Comparative Politics* 21 1989 : 473-495.

8. Zuckerman, Alan S. Nicholas Valentino, and Ezra W. Zuckerman. "A Structural Theory of Vote Choice: Social and Political Networks and Electoral Flows in Britain and the United States." Prepared for delivery at the 1992 Annual Meeting of the American Political Science Association, Palmer House Hilton September 3-6, 1992 synthesizes this vast literature especially Berelson, Bernard, Paul Lazarsfeld and William N. McPhee. *Voting: A Study of Public Opinion Formation in a Presidential Campaign.* Chicago: University of Chicago Press, 1954; Huckfeldt, Robert and John Sprague. "Networks in Context: The Social Flow of Information." *American Political Science Review* 81 1987 : 1197-1216; Huckfeldt, Robert and John Sprague. "Political Parties and Electoral Mobilization: Political Structure, Social Structure, and the Party Canvas." *American Political Science Review* 86 1992, 70-86; Lazarsfeld, Paul, Bernard Berelson and Hazel Gaudet, *The People's Choice.* New York: Duell, Sloan, and Pearce, 1944; Zuckerman, Alan S. "New Approaches to Political Cleavage: A Theoretical Introduction." *Comparative Political Studies* 15 1982: 131-144; and Zuckerman, Alan S. "The Bases of Political Cohesion: Applying and Reconstructing Crumbling Theories" *Comparative Politics* 21 1989 : 473-495; into a series of hypotheses applied to the analysis of voting decisions in adjacent elections in postwar Britain and the United States.

9. Gruber, Helmut. *Red Vienna: Experiment in Working-Class Culture 1919-1934.* New York: Oxford University Press. : 1991 : 194.

10. See, for e.g. Rozenblit, Marsha L. *The Jews of Vienna 1867-1914: Assimilation and Identity* Albany, NY: State University of New York Press, 1983.

11. Schorske, Carl. *Fin-De-Siecle Vienna: Politics and Culture* New York: Vintage Books, 1981.

12. *Ibid*, 19.

13. Gruber, Helmut. *Red Vienna: Experiment in Working-Class Culture 1919-1934*. New York: Oxford University Press, 1991 : 13.

14. *Ibid*, 13.

15. Gruber, in a personal correspondence, estimates that there were about 21,000 persons born of Jewish parents who were either in mixed marriages or who were legally categorized as "*Konfessionslos*." without religion. This brings the estimate of the total Jewish population to 221,650 12.3 percent of the population.

16. Rabinbach, Anson. *The Crisis of Austrian Socialism*. Chicago: University of Chicago Press, 1983 : 30.

17. The data on the number, residential distribution, occupations, and educational patterns of the Jews of Vienna for 1910 and 1924 come from Goldhammer, Leo *Die Juden Wiens: Eine Statistische Studie*, Vienna and Leipzig: R. Lowit Verlag, 1927. See also Simon, Walter. "The Jewish Vote in Austria." *Leo Baeck Institute Year Book* XVI 1971 : 97-121; Rozenblit, Marsha L. *The Jews of Vienna 1867-1914: Assimilation and Identity*. Albany, NY: State University of New York Press, 1983; Oxaal, Ivar. "The Jews of Young Hitler's Vienna: Historical and Sociological Aspects." In *Jews, Antisemitism and Culture in Vienna*, edited by Ivar Oxaal, Michael Pollak, and Gerhard Botz. London: Routledge and Kegan Paul, 1987 : 11-38; and Beller, Steven. "Class, Culture and the Jews of Vienna, 1900" In *Jews, Antisemitism and Culture in Vienna*, edited by Ivar Oxaal, Michael Pollak and Gerhard Botz. London: Routledge and Kegan Paul, 1987: 39-58; Freidenreich, Harriet P. *Jewish Politics in Vienna*. Bloomington: Indiana University Press, 1991 provides a detailed account of the Jewish community during the inter-war years. Note that the data provide information on the percentage in each district in the various occupations and religions, but they do not detail how these variables interacted, e.g., the occupations of members of the religious categories. As a result, one must estimate the interactions among ethnicity, class, and voting patterns.

18. Gruber, Helmut. *Red Vienna: Experiment in Working-Class Culture 1919-1934*. New York: Oxford University Press 1991 : 18.

19. Several points of definition need to be noted. Sources vary in how they define the various class categories and in the particular census from which the data are drawn. As a result, they differ in the proportion of the population that is to be assigned to each of the social classes. I have followed the rule of staying with the source that provides the most detail and that is closest in time to the point of analysis. As a result, the comparisons of the occupational characteristics of the city's ethnic categories relies on Goldhammer, Leo, *Die Juden Wiens: Eine Statistische Studie*. Vienna and Leipzig: R. Lowit Verlag, 1927, who draws on a census taken before World War I. The analysis of class and voting in 1927 draws on Gruber, Helmut. *Red Vienna: Experiment in Working-class Culture 1919-1934*. New York: Oxford University Press, 1991, and Heinrich, Hans-Georg and Slawomir Wiatr. *Political Culture in Vienna and Warsaw*. Boulder: Westview Press, 1991. Gruber provides estimates of the class

composition of the electorate and the membership of the Socialist Party. Heinrich and Wiatr draw on the census of 1934. See Table 9.2, for their estimates. In addition, following the usage in Vienna and the definitions presented in my sources and in recognition of the relative dearth of information on the Czechs, I will confine most of my discussion of the city's ethnic division to that which separated Jews and non-Jews, labelling all those in the second category as Germans. Where possible, I will provide separate discussion of Vienna's Czechs.

20. These calculations derive from pre-World War I data. Gruber, in a personal communication, estimates that there was a higher proportion of Jews in the civil service in the 1920s. For example, he notes there were 3,500 social workers, among whom were many Jewish women. No matter how many more Jews were employed in the civil service during this period, they were not likely to have exceeded 1 percent of the total.

21. Rozenblit, Marsha L. *The Jews of Vienna: 1867-1914: Assimilation and Identity*. Albany, NY: State University of New York Press, 1983.

22. The following descriptions have been taken from Freidenreich, Harriet P. *Jewish Politics in Vienna*, Bloomington: Indiana University Press, 1991.

23. See, for e.g., Rozenblit, Marsha L. *The Jews of Vienna: 1867-1914: Assimilation and Identity*. Albany, NY: State University of New York Press, 1983; and Beller, Steven. "Class, Culture and the Jews of Vienna, 1900." In *Jews, Antisemitism and Culture in Vienna*, edited by Ivar Oxaal, Michael Pollak, and Gerhard Botz. London: Routledge and Kegan Paul, 1987 : 39-58.

24. Gruber, Helmut. *Red Vienna: Experiment in Working-Class Culture 1919-1934*. New York: Oxford University Press, 1991 : 196-197.

25. *Ibid*, 28.

26. Wegs, J. Robert. *Growing Up Working Class: Continuity and Change Among Viennese Youth 1890-1933*. University Park, PA: Penn State University Press, 1989 : 28.

27. *Ibid*, 29-30.

28. Gruber, Helmut *Red Vienna: Experiment in Working-Class Culture 1919-1934*. New York: Oxford University Press, 1991 : 54.

29. *Ibid*, 8.

30. Similar patterns have been found among the working class of Berlin, (Hamilton, Richard. *Who Voted for Hitler?* Princeton, NJ: Princeton University Press, 1982) and Germany, (Falter, Juergen. "The First German Volkspartei: The Social Foundations of the NSDAP." In *Elections, Parties and Political Traditions: Social Foundations of German Parties and Party Systems, 1867-1987*, edited by Kerl Rohe. New York: Berg, 1990 : 53-81). Przeworski, Adam and John Sprague. *Paper Stones: A History of Electoral Socialism*. Chicago: University of Chicago Press, 1986 estimate variations in the electoral cohesion of the working classes across several countries and over many decades.

31. Davies, Norman. *God's Playground: A History of Poland in Two Volumes*. New York: Columbia University Press, 1982; and Polonsky, Antony. *Politics in Independent Poland 1921-1939: The Crisis of Constitutional Government*. Oxford: Clarendon Press, 1972.

32. Davies, Norman. *God's Playground: A History of Poland in Two Volumes.* New York: Columbia University Press, 1982; Polonsky, Antony. *Politics in Independent Poland 1921-1939: The Crisis of Constitutional Government.* Oxford: Clarendon Press, 1972; and Rothschild, Joseph. *Pilsudski's Coup D'Etat* New York: Columbia University Press, 1966.

33. The subsequent analysis centers on Warsaw, where Poles and Jews together accounted for almost all the residents. As a result, the discussion analyzes only Jews and Poles. The data on the number, residential distribution, languages, and occupations of the Jews of Poland come from Lestschinsky, Jacob. *The Social Classes of Polish Jews.* Berlin, 1931, in Yiddish, and Lestschinsky, Jacob. *Economic Writings II.* Vilna: YIVO, 1932, in Yiddish; Mahler, Raphael. *Jews in Poland Between the Two World Wars: A Socioeconomic History Based on Statistics.* Tel Aviv: Dvir, 1969, in Hebrew; Marcus, Joseph. *The Social and Political History of the Jews in Poland, 1919-1939.* Berlin: Mouton, 1983, and Shmeruk, Chone. "Hebrew-Yiddish-Polish: A Trilingual Jewish Culture." In *The Jews of Poland Between the Two World Wars,* edited by Yisrael Gutman, Ezra Mendelsohn, Jehuda Reinharz and Chone Shmeruk. Hanover, NH: The University Press of New England, 1989 : 285-311; and Tomaszewski, Jerzy "The Role of Jews in Polish Commerce, 1918-1939." In *The Jews of Poland Between Two World Wars,* edited by Yisrael Gutman, Ezra Mendelsohn, Jehuda Reinharz, and Chone Shmeruk. Hanover, NH: University Press of New England, 1989 : 141-157.

34. Doblin, Alfred. In *Journey to Poland,* edited by Heinz Graber. New York: Paragon, translated by Joachim Neugroschel, 1991 : 50.

35. *Ibid,* 13.

36. *Ibid,* 51.

37. The data on the number, residential distribution, and occupations of the Jews of Warsaw come from Haas, Ludwik. *The Political Attitudes of Warsaw's Residents as Reflected in the Results of Elections to Representative Bodies.* Warsaw: Panstwowc Wydawnictwo Nankowe, 1972, in Polish and Lestschinsky, Jacob. "The Professional and Social Status of Jews in Eastern and Central Europe." Jacob Lestschinsky. in *Writings on Economic and Statistics I,* edited by Jacob Lestschinsky. Berlin: YIVO, 1928, in Yiddish : 191-211. See also Block, Bronislaw. "Urban Ecology of the Jewish Population of Warsaw, 1897-1938." In *Papers in Jewish Demography,* edited by U. O. Schmelz, P. Glickson and S. Della Pergola. Jerusalem: Institute of Contemporary Jewry, The Hebrew University of Jerusalem, 1983, : 381-399; and Wynot, Edward D. Jr. *Warsaw Between the World Wars: Profile of a Capital City in a Developing Land, 1918-1939.* New York: Columbia University Press, 1983. Haas's 1972 data allow for the specification of the combined class and ethnic characteristics of each of the districts, e.g., the proportion of the population who were working-class Poles or Jewish independents, managers, and self-employed. Hence, it is possible to be more precise about the relationship among residential concentration, ethnicity, and occupation in Warsaw than in Vienna.

38. Mintzin, I. "School Enrollment of Russian and Polish Jews." In *Writings on Economic and Statistics I,* edited by Jacob Lestschinsky. Berlin: YIVO, in Yiddish, 1928 : 240-248.

39. Davies, Norman, *God's Playground: A History of Poland in Two Volumes*. New York: Columbia University Press, 1982 : II 418.

40. The data on voting patterns among the Jews and Poles of Warsaw have been taken from Haas 1972. Note that these data provide information on the class and ethnic backgrounds of residents in each of the city's districts, and so it is possible to specify the relationship between the class characteristics of the members of the ethnic groups and electoral results. The results of the analysis of the data described below are my own. In addition, I obtained information on the results of elections to the Jewish *kehilla*, of Warsaw from Danuta Dabrowska, of the Yad Vashem Institute, in Jerusalem. For a descriptive account of Jewish political movements during this period, see Shlomo Netzer. *The Struggle of Polish Jewry for Civil and National Minority Rights*. Tel-Aviv: Tel-Aviv University, 1980, in Hebrew.

41. Gancarska-Kadary, Bina. *The Role of Jews in the Development of Industry in Warsaw, 1816/20-1920* Tel Aviv: The Diaspora Research Institute, in Hebrew, 1985 : 112.

42. Marcus, Joseph. *The Social and Political History of the Jews in Poland, 1919-1939*. Berlin: Mouton, 1983 : 460.

43. See also Shapiro, Robert Moses. "The Polish Kehille Elections of 1936: A Revolution Re-examined." Paper presented to the Meetings of the Association for Jewish Studies, 1987.

10

Ethnic Definition, Social Mobility, and Residential Segregation in the United States

Michael J. White
Sharon Sassler

Introduction

Between 1871 and 1910, exactly 20,541,754 immigrants were admitted into the United States (INS, 1990). This mass movement of persons from many origins further diversified an already heterogeneous population composed of descendents of an indigenous population, the earlier European settlers, and a forced migration of labor from Africa. While immigration slowed during the middle of this century, the last few decades have witnessed an increase in absolute numbers. Immigrants as a fraction of the American population have grown in the past decade, even though their population share is still well below what it was at the turn of the century. The country's demographic diversity has made issues of ethnic identity, assimilation, and cultural pluralism particularly prominent in the United States.

Every wave of population migration that involves different ethnic groups (including both international migration and internal migration of minority groups) heightens concerns about the ability of groups to associate. The flood of immigrants from southern, eastern, and central Europe at the turn of the century led many scholars, historians, and statesmen in America to decry what they perceived as a dangerous weakening of the American character, due to the influx of "inferior" immigrants. Similar sentiments are expressed today about the most recent immigrants, who, like the immigrants at the turn of the century, are not from locations where the majority of the United States population claims ancestry.   Tensions over adherence to languages other than English; familiarity with urban industrial settings; and competition for jobs are some of the similarities between the debates that ensued at the turn of the century and those occurring today. These questions concerning ethnic minorities have made their way into the present-day arena of public discussion. Are these different groups able to assimilate into the majority culture (however defined)? Is the host society itself able to accommodate or adapt to these minorities?   Are either of these goals desirable?

In this paper we explore several issues related to ethnic identity in the United States. We employ demographic tools, including qualitative analysis of historical census schedules and statistical analysis of census and survey data from 1910 and 1980. Our purpose is to provide direct evidence on ethnic group competition and assimilation, and to call attention to how these issues of ethnic identification and assimilation are intertwined with the data collection mechanisms used by official agencies.

We first examine the issue of ethnic identity itself. It is common practice for social scientists and others to treat ethnicity (including race) as an immutable trait. Yet ethnic identity is partly a matter of self-identification; partly a matter of labeling by others in society, and partly a collective response to the particular array of groups present in the host society. Our window on the perception and measurement of ethnicity is provided by decennial census schedules. On the one hand, these census documents represent the "official" ethnic group identities recognized or imposed by the government. On the other hand, these categories frame the forms of analyses that can be conducted, and have a bearing on some of the results that can be developed.

For the purposes of this paper, our notion of ethnicity is a very inclusive one. Many definitions of ethnic group and racial group exist. We take ethnicity to represent a membership in a social subgroup whose basis for commonality arises out of cultural physiognomic, and linguistic traits passed on by birth. For our purposes here ethnicity will subsume national origin and race. Spanish origin and ancestry are also included for more recent decades; in the 1990 census the "ancestry" question used the term ethnicity.

We then turn to the issue of assimilation, and compare the status of groups in 1910 and in more recent times. While there are many areas of assimilation, we choose to focus on two that offer distinct insights into the adaptation of the group to the host society: employment and residence. First, we examine socioeconomic outcomes in 1910 and 1980, drawing a picture of relative position of the ethnic groups at each time point, and of changes in relative position over time. By examining and comparing both the "new" and "old" immigrant groups present at the turn of the century, we can assess whether assimilation, as measured by socioeconomic attainment, has occurred.   Second, we approach assimilation through the window of residence. Residential patterns represent the joint outcome of self segregation and discrimination. These patterns are of considerable importance. While the data and measures we use to examine segregation in 1910 and 1980 are not exactly comparable, knowledge of who lives near whom provides insight into the degree of a group's assimilation. We conclude the paper with a summary of our substantive findings, and we engage in a short discussion of the relationship between the measurement of ethnicity and the measurement of social science processes.

"Official" Ethnicity in the United States, 1790-1990

The definition of what constitutes "ethnicity" has changed dramatically over the history of the census. Some racial categories that were included in one census were omitted for a later census or dropped altogether; others hopscotched from one race to another. In some cases, an ethnic group was defined based on mother tongue rather than on country of origin. In the most recent censuses (1970-1990) respondents have been able to select their ethnic group or race themselves.   In addition, the U.S. Census Bureau has altered procedures for reclassification of individuals on the bases of reported information. The following survey of how ethnic groups were defined over the course of the census, and continue to be shaped in census history, reveals not only the continuing prominence of race and ethnicity, but also its fluidity.

The census was developed in response to issues of representation. Because of the original apportionment rules in the Constitution, whereby political representation in Congress and the Electoral College was distributed on the basis of enumerated population, issues of population growth and dispersion were transformed into political questions. Race emerged among the initial categories of the census because of blacks' and Indians' unique civil status (Anderson, 1988). The apportionment rule required the separate classification and enumeration of free white and black, slave, and Indian populations, thus building into the census a tradition of differentiating by color.1

In the late nineteenth and early twentieth centuries new population issues were added to the earlier concerns as rising immigration; rapid urban growth; the closing of the American frontier; a declining native white birth rate; and, in some areas of the country, rural depopulation occurred. Such new demographic trends automatically set in motion the apportionment mechanisms that were designed to redistribute political power to the growing areas. As in the 1850s, when the South faced decreasing power on the national scene, those identifying with old colonial-stock Americans worried over the increasing power of cities and immigrants. The large influx of foreigners from southern, central, and eastern Europe raised concern once again about representation, and shifted attention from race to national origin. This is reflected in additions and alterations in census questions. The debate over the meaning of ethnicity has continued into the last half of the twentieth century. Where questions are placed; how they are asked; which groups are to be included on the census; and the inclusiveness of the coverage demonstrate the increasingly political process of defining ethnicity.

Race in the Census

The first five censuses were mainly concerned with enumerating the numbers of free residents—both whites and coloreds—and slaves. (Figure 10.1). From 1790 through the census of 1840 the categories remained relatively uniform: free white males and females, all other free persons (which became free coloreds in the 1820 census), and slaves. The census of 1820 initiated the enumeration of foreigners who were not naturalized. Beginning in 1850 and continuing through the 1930 census, methods for classifying those of African heritage varied widely, as the pendulum of racial categorization swung erratically back and forth. Before the 1850 census, no instructions were given to enumerators for defining racial terms, and each enumerator was free to determine the race of people in his district. In 1850 enumerators were instructed to pay particular attention to color, and indicate whether the respondent was white, black, or mulatto.

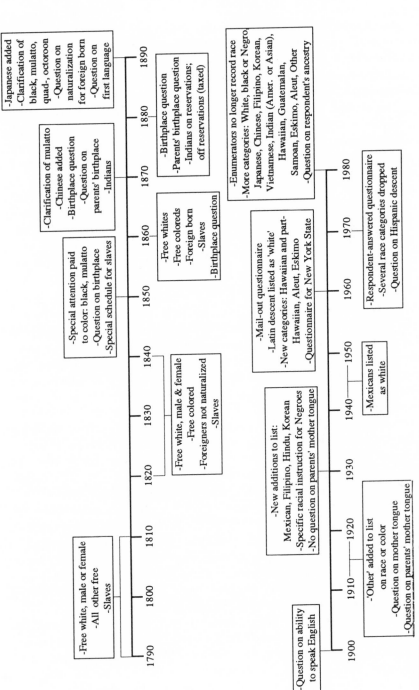

FIGURE 10.1 Race in the Census

1790 — 1800 — 1810 — 1820 — 1830 — 1840 — 1850 — 1860 — 1870 — 1880 — 1890

1900 — 1910 — 1920 — 1930 — 1940 — 1950 — 1960 — 1970 — 1980

-Free white, male or female
-All other free
-Slaves

-Free white, male & female
-Free colored
-Foreigners not naturalized
-Slaves

-Special attention paid to color: black, mulatto
-Question on birthplace
-Special schedule for slaves

-Free whites
-Free coloreds
-Foreign born
-Slaves
-Birthplace question

-Clarification of mulatto
-Chinese added
-Birthplace question
-Question on parents' birthplace
-Indians

-Birthplace question
-Parents' birthplace question
-Indians on reservations; off reservations (taxed)

-Japanese added
-Clarification of black, mulatto, quad., octoroon
-Question on naturalization for foreign born
-Question on first language

-Question on ability to speak English

-'Other' added to list on race or color
-Question on mother tongue
-Question on parents' mother tongue

-New additions to list: Mexican, Filipino, Hindu, Korean
-Specific racial instruction for Negroes
-No question on parents' mother tongue

-Mexicans listed as white

-Mail-out questionnaire
-Latin descent listed as 'white'
-New categories: Hawaiian and part-Hawaiian, Aleut, Eskimo
-Questionnaire for New York State

-Enumerators no longer record race
-More categories: White, black or Negro, Japanese, Chinese, Filipino, Korean, Vietnamese, Indian (Amer. or Asian), Hawaiian, Guatemalan, Samoan, Eskimo, Aleut, Other
-Question on respondent's ancestry

-Respondent-answered questionnaire
-Several race categories dropped
-Question on Hispanic descent

Racial definitions were further defined in instructions to enumerators in 1870: "Be particularly careful in reporting the class *mulatto*. The word here is generic, and includes quadroons, octoroons, and all persons having any perceptible trace of African blood" (U.S. Department of Commerce, 1989:18).

The period from 1890 through 1930 marks the time of greatest variability in defining blacks. By the 1890 census it was not enough to describe those of African descent as black or mulatto. Enumerators received detailed instructions on how to assign mixed-race blacks to a color gradient:

> The word "black" should be used to describe those persons who have three-fourths or more black blood; "mulatto" those persons who have from three-eights to five-eighths black blood; "quadroon" those persons who have one-fourth black blood; and "octoroon" those persons who have one-eighth or any trace of black blood.

Curiously, the 1900 census did not include a category for mulatto, although it appeared again in 1910. By 1930 the mulatto category had been dropped for good. Instead, detailed directions were given to classify respondents of mixed-race. Any mixture of white and some other race was to be reported according to the race of the parent who was not white. There was greater variation in classifying mixed descendants when white ancestry was not involved; mixed race respondents were to be listed according to the father's race, except for Negro-Indians. The social dimension of categorization emerged during attempts to define those of mixed black and Indian heritage; if Indian ancestry predominated, or the person was generally accepted as an Indian in the community, he was classified as Indian.

Other racial classifications gradually appear on the census form during this period. The census of 1870 contained a category for Chinese. The 1890 census appears to have been a highly color-conscious time; in addition to attempts to "scientifically" determine the gradation of black blood by counting quadroons and octaroons, the 1890 census was the first one to include Japanese on the list. "Other" was added as a color category in 1910, while the 1930 census added several new groups to the census paint box: Mexican, Filipino, Hindu, and Korean.

The difficulties of defining color or race continue to plague the Census Bureau (Alonso and Starr, 1987), as can be seen by the proliferation of categories in the 1980 and 1990 censuses. A total of 14 categories appeared on the census forms in each of the last two censuses. In addition to the multiplication of color categories, the way that descendents of mixed races are classified differs from that of the

1930 census. The mother's race is to serve as the racial assignment in 1980, rather than the earlier method of assigning mixed-race descendents to the father's race. Mixed-race descendents are lobbying for additional racial categories (Atkins, 1991; McKenney and Cresce, 1992), so that they will not be forced into one of the existing racial categories or the "other" classification.

Nationality and Linguistic Background

The importance of national origin in the census also arose due to issues of representation. While a question on citizenship status was asked first in 1820, not until the 1850 census were respondents asked about their place of birth. Information on birthplace became increasingly detailed in the last two decades of the nineteenth century as record numbers of foreigners arrived from southern, central, and eastern Europe, raising fears of the loss of traditional Anglo-American cultural dominance and the possibilities of assimilating populations seen by many as inferior and "unmeltable."

The inclusion of several questions on country of origin and mother tongue of respondent's parents enabled the census Bureau to produce tabulations relevant for the study of adaptation, not only of the first generation of immigrants, but of their American-born offspring as well. More detailed identification questions were added as the pace of immigration increased. For example, while the 1870 census had asked whether the respondent's parents were of foreign birth, the 1880 census required enumerators to detail which country the respondent's parents were from if they were foreign born, as was done for the respondent. Beginning in 1890, the census recorded the respondent's ability to speak English. The section on English-speaking ability was further refined in 1910. In addition to a question on whether the respondent could speak English, mother tongue was asked for foreign-born respondents and parents of respondents. English was regarded as the native language of all those born in the United States, including American Indians.[2]

Growing anti-immigrant sentiments, World War I, and economic depression resulted in a sharp curtailment by the mid-1920s of immigrants arriving in the United States. As a result, the issue of national origin assumed a less important place in American society. From 1930 on, census questions designed to elicit information on immigrants and their descendants remained substantially the same (although the question on mother tongue of parents was dropped in the

1930 census). Attention was increasingly focused on other population characteristics, such as employment and housing.

Spanish Origin and Ancestry

Two new factors further complicate the categorization of ethnicity from 1960 onwards. The first is the increasing representation of Hispanics, or those persons deriving from Spanish culture. The second important alteration in definitions of ethnic origin appeared in the 1980 census, with the substitution of a question on ancestry for one on parents' place of birth. Both of these developments represent a movement away from more objective classification methods to subjective measurements based to a large extent on self-identity.

In 1930, "Mexican" made its first appearance on the census form, under the category for racial identity, before being reclassified as white in the following census.[3] Various measures have been used to estimate the Hispanic population since 1950, including questions on birthplace, foreign parentage, mother tongue, home language, Spanish surname, and, in the most recent two censuses, Spanish origin or descent. Beginning in 1970, the census questionnaire asked a question on ancestry, limited to Hispanics. Respondents were to indicate if they were of Spanish-speaking origin or descent. This categorization differed from the origin question asked of descendents of European stock in that the label "Hispanic" included first-, second-, and third- or higher generation respondents.

The 1980 and 1990 censuses extended this approach to all ancestries, asking respondents an open-ended question about their ancestry rather than having respondents indicate parents' country of birth. Instructions for this question asked respondents to indicate the ancestry group with which they identified. In this fashion, those who had been in the country for three or more generations could be assigned to an ethnic group.

The ancestry question rectified one of the shortcomings of previous censuses, while it introduced a new weakness. Earlier censuses provided no way to determine ethnic groups beyond the second generation. While data were available for those of foreign birth and their descendents, ethnic groups disappeared statistically by the third generation. Because of the immigration restrictions of the 1920s and the aging of the population, the great majority of Americans in the last quarter of the twentieth century were third generation or higher, thereby rendering the country of origin question of rather limited value in studying differences among ethnic groups. However, data from the

1980 and 1990 censuses do not allow comparisons among those from different generations; there is no distinguishing of third-generation ethnics from second-generation ethnics. The elimination of the question on parents' place of birth reduces the number of items comparable over long periods of time. Data on parents' birthplace and respondent's birthplace are available for a period spanning 100 years, from 1870 and 1970, although the percentage of the population asked about parents' birthplace varied among censuses from 1950 through 1970.

While the administrative assimilation of white ethnic groups was a drawback of earlier censuses, a factor complicating ethnic identification in more recent censuses is the growing politicization of the categories determining race and origin (Choldin, 1986; Lieberson and Waters, 1988). Issues of political power deriving from population size, affirmative action, census undercount, and the distribution of federal dollars all have served to heighten tensions surrounding the measurement of ethnicity. Examples include the struggle over whether to ask Hispanic/Spanish origin on the short or long form in 1980; the proliferation of Asian racial categories; and even the institution of the ancestry question itself.

The Changing Meaning of Ethnicity

Ethnic categorization has changed in important ways over the 200 years of the census. "Ancestry," the term used in recent census questionnaires, is now largely a matter of self-identification, rather than something assigned by enumerators or determined by communal opinion. This has important consequences for the size of groups, as well as on the meaning of ethnicity. Census definitions of what constituted race or how ethnic groups were defined have shaped group size and composition, and have determined immigration restrictions.

Despite the possibility of racial mixing and "lightening," topics that were circuitously addressed in racial questions attempting to number the mulatto population (Miller, 1990), race has been considered immutable in American society. Non-whites remain separate forever, regardless of the number of generations in the country. The Census Bureau distinguishes those of European origin from racial groups by classifying them based upon different principles. Those of European origin have been specified as "foreign stock" if they, one, or both of their parents were born abroad. Therefore, white ethnics disappear statistically by the third generation, becoming part of the native-born of native-parentage group regardless of their ethnic background. Ethnicity among both whites and other races, however, may be socially constructed. Some ethnic groups developed an identity only upon arrival in the United States. For example, Neapolitans, Calabrians, Sicilians, and other immigrants from Italian provinces were perceived by Americans as Italian; their focus of identity therefore shifted from regional to national (Alba, 1985). Blacks, on the other hand, become identified as African-Americans regardless of their region of origin or ethnic identity within that region. Ethnic identification among whites is considerably more fluid than is the racial classification.

A new development on the ethnicity front is the growing proportions of those who identify themselves as American, or who alter their ancestral identification over time. A sizable proportion of the population either cannot or will not give an answer to the ancestry or ethnic identification question. About 6 percent of the United States population in 1980 selected "American" as their ancestry, making American a major ethnic group, the fifth most selected response (Lieberson and Waters, 1988). Others do not consistently report the same ancestry (Farley, 1991; Lieberson and Waters, 1988; Johnson, 1974). Despite heightened ethnic consciousness and advocacy of ethnic identification, this evidence indicates that a sizable proportion of Americans are unaware of their ethnic origins; do not choose to identify with their country of descent; are not fixed in their ethnic orientation but may instead identify with different countries at various times; or desire to identify themselves as Americans. Some argue that ethnic ancestry, therefore, is an unimportant dimension of self-identity for many third- and higher- generation whites; that it is waning in importance (Alba, 1985); and that whites of European descent are in an era of symbolic or imagined ethnicity (Farley, 1991; Gans, 1979). The ancestry question does not ascertain the meaning of ethnicity for those from different ethnic groups and generations.

Despite the obvious difficulty in defining ethnic groups, and the resulting lack of absolute comparability between groups measured in different time periods, what can we learn by looking at ethnic groups over time? Does ethnic membership continue to distinguish individuals in terms of their socioeconomic status or location of residence? Does ethnic membership have the same meaning at the end of the twentieth century that it did in earlier decades? We now turn to an examination of ethnic group placement on indices of economic attainment and residence, to determine what changes, if any, have occurred, and what these alterations might reveal about the nature of ethnic group membership.

Socioeconomic Status Mobility

We first turn to socioeconomic mobility as a measure of assimilation. Sociologists and social historians frequently examine the occupational positions of consecutive generations of men[4] to see if mobility occurs over time among various immigrant waves and ethnic groups. Studies of such diverse areas as Boston, Detroit, Cleveland, Pittsburgh, and New York City generally demonstrate that opportunities for upward social mobility existed for immigrants coming to America. The conventional assimilation model portrays occupational position as a continuum on a spectrum, or ladder. At the bottom of the ladder are the most recent immigrants. The arrival of new immigrants serves to elevate and improve the standing of those immigrants of longer duration in the country, and the highest positions are usually occupied by the native stock population. If the conventional assimilation framework holds, occupational attainment among various ethnic groups should gradually merge with increasing time in the country, so that after several generations there will no longer be marked occupational differences among immigrants from different waves.

This section uses the socioeconomic index to examine the occupational mobility of men and women from twelve ethnic groups. Originally developed by Duncan, using data from the 1950 census and the 1947 NORC prestige study, and later used by Featherman and Hauser, the socioeconomic index (SEI) appears to provide a better measure of the social distance between occupations (prestige) than traditional divisions of occupations into skill categories such as high or low white collar, skilled or unskilled work. The SEI score develops prestige rankings of various occupations, based on respondents' perceptions of their relative merits in terms of goodness, worth, status, and power. Socioeconomic scores have been revised several times over the last few decades to incorporate changes in occupational structure and to conform with adaptations to the census occupational classification schemes. The occupation and industry coding of the 1910 Public Use Sample was matched to 1980 codes; this enabled us to assign SEI scores for 1910 as well as 1980. Our data rely on the Socioeconomic Index as modified by Stevens and Cho (1985). An additional advantage of the 1980 SEI scores is that they are based on the total labor force, rather than being limited to the male workers, as were the 1970 and earlier versions of SEI scores. By using comparable 1910 to 1980 SEI scores we are able to calculate SEI scores for those women recorded as gainfully employed in the 1910 census, and can therefore expand our mobility study to women, in addition to examining the occupational progress over time of ethnic men.

If assimilation is occurring along socioeconomic lines, ethnic differences in average SEI scores should decrease over time. Those immigrants from ethnic groups newly arrived in America at the turn of the century should therefore demonstrate scores much more closely aligned with older immigrant groups by the end of the twentieth century. In order to test whether SEI scores at the beginning of the century hold predictive power for SEI standing at the century's close, we have calculated the socioeconomic index for twelve ethnic groups in two periods spanning the century, 1910 and 1980. Using national samples of populations living in urban areas, we examine twelve groups from various immigrant waves who were prominent in the United States in 1910 and whose ancestry is available in 1980.

Despite the passage of time and alterations in the way census information was obtained, the measures provide us with rough but comparable samples. The 1910 data provide us with information for the first two generations through inquiries about place of birth, parents' place of birth, and mother tongue. Group members of more than three generations are "administratively" assimilated, that is, they are subsequently recorded as native-white of native-parentage and therefore unavailable to us. The ancestry question on the 1980 census provides us with a different ethnic measure, capturing members of *all* generations who state their ethnic heritage, rather than limiting itself to the first two generations. Our use of the 1980 ancestry classifications excludes those of mixed parentage; that is, we use single ancestry reports.[5] The 1980 data do not enable us to distinguish second generation from those of third generation or higher. Despite some differences, the drawbacks inherent in using two different methods to measure ethnic group membership are outweighed by the new ability to examine the socioeconomic status for immigrants and their descendants at two widely spaced points in time.

The twelve ethnic groups selected for the comparison are: Irish, German, English, Scandinavian, other northern and western Europe, English Canadians, French Canadians, Italians, Poles, Jews,[6] other central and eastern Europeans, and blacks. Some of the groups represented, such as Irish and Germans, were among the immigrant groups who arrived in substantial numbers in the 1840s and 1850s. Immigration from these countries continued into the twentieth century and was supplemented by arrivals from England, Canada, and the Scandinavian countries (Norway, Sweden, and Finland), but a marked shift in origins had occurred by the closing decade of the nineteenth century. Arrivals from southern, eastern, and central Europe outnumbered the older immigrant groups after 1897. Poles, Italians, and Jews are often referred to as the "new" immigrants. Blacks, although of long standing in America, serve as a point of reference, being neither "old" nor "new" immigrants. Substantial evidence, however, attests to the fact that blacks' occupational opportunities were not even equivalent to those of the newest immigrants (Lieberson, 1980).

Findings

Males

We first take a look at the SEI scores for non-farm males ages 25 to 64 in 1910 (Table 10.1). The SEI scores of men in 1910 varied widely by ethnic group. The mean SEI score in 1910 for men from the twelve ethnic groups was 30.40, with a standard deviation of 17.41. Contrary to expectations, the hierarchy of men's SEI scores in 1910 does not fall neatly into the hypothesized scale. For example, English Canadian men have the second highest SEI score, followed by men from one of the new immigrant groups, Jews. The remaining groups, however, occupy predicted positions. Many of the men from the newest immigrant groups had SEI scores well below the mean. Men from the "old" immigrant groups, Germans, Irish, and other northern and western Europeans held middling positions, while those from the "new" immigrant waves, such as Italians, Poles, and others from eastern Europe assumed positions at the very bottom of the ladder. On the lowest rung stood blacks.

By 1980, the SEI scores of men from ten of these twelve ethnic groups are remarkably uniform. The mean score for non-farm men of European stock aged 25 to 64 was 40.51 in 1980, with a standard deviation of 20.79. Only two groups differ appreciably. Russian men, a group that is roughly equivalent to Jews in 1910, obtained the highest SEI score of 54.9. Blacks, on the other side of the scale, have a socioeconomic index of 28.50.

Examining the regression line for all twelve ethnic groups (Figure 10.2) suggests that the socioeconomic position of men in 1910 is in fact a modestly good predictor of their position in 1980. When all twelve groups are represented, the regression line has a statistically significant slope of .71, and the linear relation between SEI scores in 1910 and 1980 explains 36 percent of the variation around the regression line (significant at the .01 level).

TABLE 10.1 SEI Scores and Standard Deviations for 1910 and 1980 Non-Farm Men Ages 25 to 64

MEN	1910 Score	S.D.	1980 Score	S.D.
NWNP	34.57	18.80	NA	NA
English Canadian	34.35	18.89	40.51	18.89
Jewish	33.25	17.94	54.90*	20.98
English	32.28	17.81	43.18	20.73
German	30.46	16.60	41.00	20.44
Other NW Europe	30.16	16.64	42.21	20.91
Irish	29.61	15.99	40.88	20.36
Scandinavian	26.13	13.60	43.68	20.84
French Canadian	25.03	14.03	38.53	20.02
Other CE Europe	23.74	13.95	42.69	21.76
Mulatto	23.14	14.36	NA	NA
Italian	22.81	13.00	39.38	20.11
Polish	20.65	10.29	39.99	20.59
Black	20.06	9.78	28.50	16.64
Mean	30.40	17.41	40.51	20.79
New Groups				
Mexican			26.81	15.41
Puerto Rican			27.55	14.60
Cuban			36.49	20.78
Asian Indian			56.35	22.08
Chinese			42.61	24.62
Japanese			43.42	21.60
Korean			39.17	22.67
Total Mean			39.95	20.83

* Jewish estimates in 1980 rely on Russian as a proxy.

FIGURE 10.2 Socioeconomic Status for Men of Selected Ancestry Groups, 1910/1980

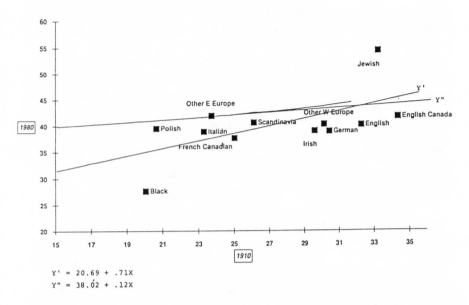

Y' = 20.69 + .71X
Y" = 38.02 + .12X

A cursory look at Figure 10.2, however, shows that most ethnic groups are clustered around a relatively horizontal line. Of the twelve ethnic groups, Blacks and Jews appear most distant from the regression line (Y'). In fact, removing blacks and Jews as outliers results in a flat regression line (Y"). The linear relationship between SEI scores among men in 1910 and 1980 is *not* a predictive one when these two groups are excluded. The slope of the regression line is a small and insignificant. While dispersion was distinctive in 1910, with groups spread out along the width of the X axis, by 1980 variation from the mean was minimal and insignificant, with all but two groups tightly concentrated around the 40 level on the Y axis.[7]

Females

Before examining the results for women, we must strongly qualify the extent to which information on women's occupational status is comparable between 1910 and 1980. For one thing, the majority of women employed in the labor force in 1910 were young single women under the age of 25 (Goldin, 1990; Oppenheimer, 1970). Our SEI scores are for non-farm women between the ages of 25 and 64. Since most married women were not recorded as being gainfully employed, despite the fact that many actually worked in the home by keeping boarders or taking in piecework, the samples of women in 1910 often are somewhat small. The consistency and accuracy of reporting also complicates comparisons across decades. Recording of women's employment has improved over the intervening decades; the undercount of women's gainful employment in 1980 is therefore far less that it was in 1910. Additionally, improvements in the ways of measuring employment enable us to include women working part-time or at home as gainfully employed. Statistics for women aged 25 to 64 will reflect those women who have completed their schooling. In recent times, increasing numbers of married women work outside the home, thereby providing a different and more numerous constituency of women who are also older and better educated than women in the past. It is not clear how these aspects of employment operate differently for women of various ethnic backgrounds, and might therefore bias our results.

Women's mean SEI scores in 1910 are a couple of points lower than their male counterparts (Table 10.2). In 1910 the mean SEI score for women from the twelve ethnic groups was 28.31, with a standard deviation of 17.09. Women demonstrate the expected pattern to a greater extent than did the men.

In 1910, English Canadians and the native-stock of native parentage women have the highest SEI scores, followed by the old immigrant groups such as Germans and Irish. While Jewish women place above other women from the "new" immigrant groups, such as Poles and Italians, their SEI score is still below average. Unlike Jewish men, Jewish women have scores that, while on the high end for "new" immigrants, do not surpass those of older immigrant waves. Again, black women occupy the lowest rung on the ladder.

By 1980 there is little variance among SEI scores among ethnic women. The mean SEI score for women from the twelve ethnic groups was 40.27, with a standard deviation of 17.71. Mirroring the standing of black men, women of African-American ancestry also have SEI scores well below the mean, at 33.33; their mean scores, however, are higher than the SEI scores of black men. Jewish women, on the other side of the SEI scale, have the highest mean SEI scores, at 49.45. As with men, women's SEI scores in 1910 do not seem to be good predictors of the positions women will hold in 1980. The linear relationship (correlation) between SEI scores in 1910 and 1980 is a weak and insignificant 0.38. Figure 10.3 depicts this relation. Again, the same two groups—Jews and blacks—differ appreciably from what is predicted by the line. While SEI scores in 1910 varied widely, ranging from about 19 to 35, by 1980 all but two groups of women were grouped between 36 and 42.

TABLE 10.2 SEI Scores and Standard Deviations for 1910 and 1980 Non-Farm Women Ages 25 to 64

WOMEN	1910 Score*	S.D.	1980 Score	S.D.
NWNP	34.06	18.79	NA	NA
English Canadian	34.70	19.84	43.03	19.90
Jewish	26.29	14.66	49.45*	17.33
English	30.45	18.16	42.09	17.19
German	27.84	15.72	40.86	17.36
Other NW Europe	27.65	16.70	41.57	17.74
Irish	27.42	16.88	40.67	17.10
Scandinavian	24.76	15.45	43.67	17.73
French Canadian	25.97	18.27	38.03	17.34
Other CE Europe	23.64	13.33	41.90	17.84
Mulatto	21.37	11.70	NA	NA
Italian	23.30	13.99	38.41	16.73
Polish	21.48	12.34	40.52	17.06
Black	18.92	7.21	33.33	18.06
Mean	28.31	17.09	40.27	17.71
New Groups**				
Mexican			28.78	15.78
Puerto Rican			31.84	17.18
Cuban			30.40	16.03
Asian Indian			42.78	23.41
Chinese			40.26	20.67
Japanese			38.47	19.23
Korean			27.08	15.11
Total Mean			399.75	17.83

* Jewish estimates in 1980 rely on Russian as a proxy.
** Small sample sizes for all the "new new" groups, except for Mexicans. Sample sizes are also small for almost all groups of women in 1910 (as our samples are for women age 25 and older, and most working women in 1910 were under age 25).

While SEI scores in 1910 varied widely, ranging from about 19 to 35, by 1980 all but two groups of women were grouped between 36 and 42.

FIGURE 10.3 Socioeconomic Status for Women of Selected Ancestry Groups, 1910/1980

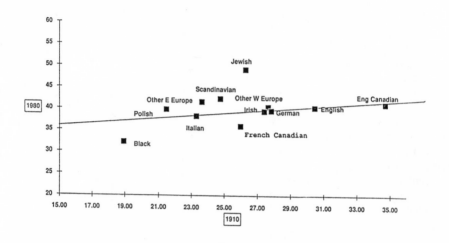

These findings suggest that with increasing duration of time in the country occupational differences among groups will disappear. Despite large differences in SEI levels in 1910 among immigrant groups, by 1980 these gaps for the most part had disappeared, among both men and women. While in 1910 most "new" immigrant groups did have SEI scores considerably lower than those ethnic groups who had resided in America for a longer period of time, by 1980 there were no discernable differences between immigrants from the "old" or "new" immigrant waves.

The two groups who are exceptions to this rule, for both men and women, are blacks and Jews. Blacks' continued deviance from the SEI mean for all other white ethnic groups demonstrates that they have not progressed as the "new" immigrant groups have. Although the SEI scores of blacks in 1910 were quite close to Italians and Poles, representatives of the "new" immigration, the Poles and Italians, had caught up to the other white ethnic groups by 1980, while blacks continued to lag behind. The assimilation framework clearly fails to depict the experience of those of African descent. This finding is not new (Lieberson, 1980; Thernstrom, 1973); while the gap between blacks and white ethnics along several dimensions has narrowed (Farley, 1984), it has not been eradicated. Jews also do not fall along the men have continued to maintain their relative occupational standing, now accompanied by Jewish women, so as to remain above the SEI scores attained by other ethnic groups.

The "New New" Immigrants: SEI Scores for Hispanics and Asians

The SEI scores of the "new" immigrants were not discernibly different from those of the "old" immigrants in 1980, despite wide differences in 1910. This indicates that the assimilation framework holds true, at least for European stock ethnics. Changes in immigration patterns, however, have once again raised the specter of the unmeltable ethnic. Since 1965, the majority of immigrants arriving in the United States are of either Spanish origin or are from Asian countries. Do these new arrivals appear similar to the recent immigrant groups in 1910?

Recalculating the mean SEI score for a sample including the twelve groups considered above, augmented by three Hispanic groups (Puerto Ricans, Mexicans, and Cubans) and four Asian groups (Asian Indian, Chinese, Japanese, and Korean) lowers the mean SEI score for men to 39.95. For women, the recalculated mean SEI score dips to 39.75. Not all of these new ethnic groups, have SEI scores below those of the older stock immigrants of the "old" and "new" immigrant waves. Looking at these seven "new new" groups highlights a radical split between the newest immigrants. The SEI scores for Hispanic men and women are below the mean, while those for the Asian groups are above the mean. In fact, Asian men, if ranked with the other twelve ethnic groups, would dominate the top positions, placing above both the "old" and the new" immigrant groups, with the exception of Jews. Most likely, the selective immigration from the various sending countries has contributed substantially to this differential but it may be that the opportunity structure is more open to some "new new" immigrants than to others. The arrival of new immigrants who do not assume positions on the lowest rung of the ladder may contribute to conflict between blacks and some of the most recent immigrants, such as Koreans.

Residential Assimilation

We next turn to segregation, using it as a window on assimilation of ethnic groups. As with socioeconomic mobility, we make comparisons from several sources over time. The number of groups, their definitions, and the sample of cities from which we draw shifts over the interval. Figure 10.4 presents the level of segregation exhibited by these groups from each study.

FIGURE 10.4 Ethnic Residential Segregation Selected Results, 1850-1980

	1850 Philadelphia	1910 10 Largest	1930 Philadelphia	1930 Cleveland
100				
95		Fr. Canadian (93)		
		& Mulatto (94)		
90		Polish (91)		
		& Jewish (92)		
85		Italian (86)		Nonwhite (86)
80		Black (80)		
75		SC Europe (75)		
70		& Scandinavian (69)		Yugoslavian (68)
				& Polish (68)
		Russian (71)		
65				Czech (64) & Italian (64)
				& Russian (66)
60			Black (61)	Lithuanian (60)
				& Hungarian (60)
55			Polish (55)	Greek (55)
			& Italian (58)	
50	Black (47)		Russian (53)	Rumanian (50)
45		Eng. Canadian (44)		
40		German (40)		Austrian (41)
35	German (33)			
30	Irish (30)	NW Europe (33)		German (33)
				& Irish Free (33)
25		Irish (25)	German (27)	
20	Foreign-born (21)		British (22)	British
			& Irish (21)	& N. Irish (19)
15				
10				
5		British (6)		
0				

FIGURE 10.4 (Continued)

	1930 Chicago	1950 Chicago	1980 21SMSAs
100			
95			
90			
85	Negro (85.2)		
80		Negro (79.7)	
75			Spanish (B) (78)
70			Black (NH) (70)
65			
60			
55	Lithuanian (57)		
50	Polish (50.8) & Czech (51.9)	Czech (48.8) & Lithuanian (51.5)	
45	Italian (48.3) & Russian (49.8)	Russian (44) & Polish (45.2)	
40		Italian (40.5)	Asian (40) & Indian (41)
35	Swedish (34)	Swedish (33.2)	Spanish (W) (37)
30	Irish Free (31.8)	Irish Free (31.8)	Polish (28)
25	Austrian (25) & German (26)	German (27.2)	Italian (26)
20	British (19.1)	British (18.9)	Other (White) (19)
15		Austrian (18.1)	German (14) & French (16)
10			Irish (12)
5			
0			English (0)

Our earliest reference period comes from the Philadelphia Social History Project, which drew on census manuscript data to carry out an in-depth analysis of social life in nineteenth-century Philadelphia (Hershberg, et al., 1981). Two immigrant groups from the waves arriving in the United States in the middle of the century, the Irish and Germans, accounted for the major European immigrant populations in Philadelphia. About one third of Irish and German individuals (according to the index of dissimilarity statistic, D) would have to change residence in order to be evenly mixed with the native white population. Black Americans in this antebellum time were even more segregated than the Irish or Germans. The foreign-born overall were less segregated than these three groups, presumably because immigration still contained substantial proportions of arrivals from previously established immigrant origins such as the United Kingdom and Scandinavia.

By 1910, different patterns can be observed. Our data for this time period draws on segregation measures calculated for fourteen distinct ethnic groups in the ten largest cities (White, et al., 1991). Here segregation is measured by the chance of having a neighbor (indicated by the "next" person in a geographically sorted data file) of the same ethnic group (Q). While not numerically comparable to the index of dissimilarity, Q gives the same general picture of relative segregation; a high value means that almost all of a persons neighbors are of the same ethnic group. As in the case of the Philadelphia study, above, and the socioeconomic results, comparisons of European origin groups are limited to the foreign "stock" (the first and second generations only). The British stock population exhibits very little segregation. Other "older" immigrant groups show very low levels of segregation. Those of English Canadian, German, Irish, and other Northwest European stock all fall in the 25 to 45 range. By contrast, "new" immigrant groups, mostly from southern and eastern Europe are on the order of twice as segregated. Blacks and mulattoes are also highly segregated at this time period. What is particularly striking about these results, however, is that some of these newly arriving groups are more segregated than blacks. For highly segregated households such as found among mulattoes and Jews,[8] almost all of their neighbors were from the same ethnic background.

For the years 1930 and 1950 we draw on the work of Lieberson (1963) and Duncan and Lieberson (1959) and the Philadelphia project. (These studies all rely on the index of dissimilarity, D.) They provide windows on segregation in Philadelphia, Cleveland, and Chicago. In this period we observe the increased segregation of the black population. From 1850 to 1930 the segregation of Philadelphia's blacks increased. In Chicago and Cleveland, persons of African descent are appreciably more segregated than many of the European heritage groups. The "new-old" distinction remains apparent in these data, but it is not as dramatic as that observed in 1910. Most of the "new" groups experience some decline in segregation, while, interestingly, segregation of the Irish, German, and British "old" groups changed very little over the decade.

The final time point for our data comes from 1980. We take our information from White (1987), who presents average levels of segregation for 21 metropolitan areas for each of twelve groups. These groups are identified through combining information on race, Spanish origin, and ancestry reported in the 1980 census. Segregation is measured by reference to the English stock population, who necessarily receive a value of zero here.

The 1980 results do not demonstrate the clear demarcations attributable to recency of immigration in the previous studies, but rather break down along racial lines. Americans of African descent, both Hispanic and non-Hispanic, are here much more segregated (from British ancestry persons) than any other group. More moderately segregated than African-Americans are some of the "new-new" immigrant groups, Asians and Hispanic whites, who are about as segregated as the American Indian population. The least segregated are European stock groups. Within the European stock population, however, earlier patterns of segregation remain visible. While less segregated than African Americans and the newest immigrant-ethnic groups, those of Italian and Polish ancestry still demonstrate a higher degree of segregation than do the Germans, French, Irish, and English. While this provides only one window on 1980 segregation by making reference to residence vis-a-vis the English ancestry population, related analysis (White 1987) buttresses the result that race (black vs. white) dominates in the determination of residential segregation. In 1980 the newest (non-black) immigrant groups, Asians and Hispanic whites, do not exhibit levels of segregation comparable to those experienced by blacks early after their mass migration North.

We have carried out one further analysis to try a get a sense of long-term assimilation among some of these groups. Table 10.3 shows comparative levels of ethnic residential segregation in 1910 and 1980; the 1910 listings parallels those groups for whom SEI scores were calculated.

Additionally, Figure 10.5 plots the level of segregation in 1910 and 1980 for seven groups for whom measurements were available in both 1910 and 1980. The simple regression line of the 1980 value vs. 1910 is also plotted. While group definitions are not strictly comparable (race and foreign stock in 1910; race and ancestry in 1980) and statistical measures are not identical (Q in 1910; D in 1980), the plot tells a useful story. We find that the higher the level of group segregation exhibited in 1910, the higher the predicted level for 1980.

TABLE 10.3 Comparative Levels of Ethnic Residential Segregation, 1910, 1980

1910 Isolation of Groups vs. All Others		1980 Segregation vs. "English" Ancestry	
100	Mulatto		100
90	French Canadian		90
	Jewish		
	Polish, Italian		
80	Black	Black	80
		Hispanic	
70	SC European, Russian	Black	70
	Scandianvian	Nonhispanic	
60			
50			
	(Native Born)		
	English Canadian		
40	German	Indian	40
		Asian	
		White Hispanic	
30		Polish	30
	NW European	Italian	
	Irish		
20		Other White	20
		French	
		German	
10		Irish	10
	British		
0		English (reference)	0

Source: Author's tabulations of 1980 and 1910 census data. Note: Scales differ but higher values on each indicate a greater degree of separation.

What is more, few groups differ appreciably from what is predicted by the line. Blacks, however, appear far above the line. The level of black segregation in 1980 is far above what would be predicted from levels observed on average in the ten largest cities in 1910. In fact, we have evidence of increasing segregation among blacks during the middle part of the twentieth century, as described above. On the other side of the segregation spectrum, the French ancestry population appears less segregated in 1980 than predicted. This may be due to more rapid residential intermingling, or perhaps the fact that the 1910 value for "French" includes only French Canadians, while the 1980 includes all persons who claim predominantly French ancestry.

FIGURE 10.5 Ethnic Residential Segregation, Selected Results, 1910/1980

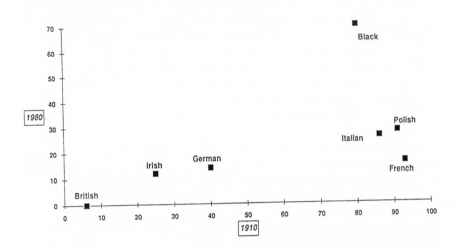

What is more, few groups differ appreciably from what is predicted by the line. Blacks, however, appear far above the line. The level of black segregation in 1980 is far above what would be predicted from levels observed on average in the ten largest cities in 1910. In fact, we have evidence of increasing segregation among blacks during the middle part of the twentieth century, as described above. On the other side of the segregation spectrum, the French ancestry population appears less segregated in 1980 than predicted. This may be due to more rapid residential intermingling, or perhaps the fact that the 1910 value for "French" includes only French Canadians, while the 1980 includes all persons who claim predominantly French ancestry.

Conclusion

In spite of the inevitable difficulties in making these sorts of comparisons across time, we can draw some conclusions, both about the pattern of immigrant adaptation and about the statistical system that gives rise to its measurement. In some sense, the key point is that the two are related. On the one hand, the adaptation of immigrants partly determines the way in which the statistical system measures ethnic groups. On the other hand, the statistical system fixes the categories of measurement for these very phenomena.

Our results lend limited support to the assimilation model, at least for those of European descent. In the case of occupational status attainment, differences across many of the groups were whittled away between 1910 and 1980. Consistent with a conventional model of assimilation, knowledge of a group's status in 1910 did little to help predict the level in 1980. In fact, most European stock groups exhibited modest variation about the mean in 1980 for both males and females.

Two very important exceptions to this evolution were observed, however. Blacks clearly received less gain to their (already low) position than would be predicted by the experience of other groups. Jews, by contrast, experienced greater than predicted gains over the seventy- year period. Interestingly, these are two groups that have experienced considerable discrimination from the wider society.

Results for residential segregation find several parallels with those of occupation. "New" groups are generally more segregated than old. In some comparisons, drawing on previous work in the literature, there are indications of decreasing segregation of European stock ethnic groups over time.

The residential assimilation model has also clearly failed for blacks through most of the twentieth century. Our finding here is not new, but echoes that of many others. We noted increases in black segregation in Philadelphia (for an expanded discussion of this point see Hershberg, et. al. 1981), and much higher levels of observed segregation in 1980 than would be predicted on the basis of 1910 values. Even within the European stock population there is reason to question the inevitability and quickness of residential intermingling. Although enough time has elapsed for a few generations to have resided in the United States "new" European groups remain slightly more segregated than "old."

Another important observation arises from these results. With regard to both socioeconomic status and residential segregation, the initial conditions (or at least those of 1910) were anything but equal across groups. Some first generation groups (e.g., English Canadians, Jews) clearly exhibited higher socioeconomic levels in 1910, probably reflecting higher levels upon arrival and maybe selective migration. Others (blacks, Poles) were observed to be much lower on the occupational status scale in 1910.

Although we did not investigate it formally, there is a broad consistency in these results with the notion that low socioeconomic status is associated with a high degree of segregation, particularly soon after arrival for immigrant groups. These conditions applied for blacks, Poles, and Italians in 1910 (note the contrast with Jews, however), and are maintained with respect to blacks in 1980.

Our results are, of course, prisoners to the measurement scheme. This creates several problems of data quality and comparability. In one census we identify groups by nativity and parentage, in another by "ancestry." For two groups (Jews, Poles) we resorted to language (mother tongue) to identify them in 1910; in 1980, Russian ancestral identification is used as a proxy for Jewish. While this creates weakness in the basic data analysis, it also serves to illuminate the wider process of ethnic group identification and change.

Such analytic strategies inform us about notions imbedded in the collection of the data. For instance European stock groups (who are almost all white in racial classification) are "administratively assimilated" as of the third generation in the 1910 (through 1970) census. Consider the consequences for the types of tabulations that Lieberson and Duncan were employing for mid-century residential segregation. The presence of third and higher order generations of a particular ancestry in the "ethnic" neighborhood would actually *reduce* apparent segregation because they were native of native parentage. Thus, the census's choice to classify some ethnic groups by generational heritage may suggest more ethnic residential intermingling than was actually the case. Of course no such administrative assimilation was allowed for racial groups, and yet by the 1980 census the introduction of the "ancestry" question allowed for individuals to record their origin, no matter how many generations intervened.

Still, assimilation of the European stock groups did proceed. Our results show this. Furthermore, even the shifting categories of measurement and tabulation reflect the trend. In 1980, substantial numbers of individuals in the white population reported multiple ancestries or could identify no specific ancestry. More recent work on the ancestry issues in the United States census (McKenney and Cresce, 1992) and in the Canadian census [see Pryor in this volume] indicate the relative permeability of some of these categories, and the degree to which they are very much a product of self-identification.

Interestingly, the process of assimilation and the tools we use to measure it (or the lack of it) are bound together. As the ethnic complexion of a population changes, the tools used to measure social change reflect both the demographic dynamics and prevailing assumptions about meaningful distinctions among groups and their assimilability. What we have attempted to do here is illustrate that point by drawing on our own analysis, using this information to help piece together part of the story of the long-term adaptation of ethnic groups in American society.

Notes

1. For the purpose of apportionment, slaves were counted as three-fifths of a free person, while Indians were included for apportionment only if they did not live on a reservation and paid taxes.

2. Mother tongue or native language was regarded as "the customary speech in the homes of the immigrants before immigration." Supplementing this working definition, enumerators were also warned that in some cases what was really reported was "ethnic stock" or "ancestral language" (Strong, Michael. 1989. *User's Guide: Public Use Sample of the 1910 United States Population.* The University of Pennsylvania Population Studies Center:59-60).

3. In the 1930 census, Mexicans were considered non-whites. Because many Spanish-origin people defined themselves as white by race and protested the 1930 categorization, the Census of 1940 did not include "Mexican" as a racial group.

4. Studies of generational occupational change among women are scarce. Women have been excluded from studies of intergenerational mobility "for both theoretical and practical reasons" (Thernstrom, 1973:6). Because women changed their names and moved in and out of the labor force for marriage, childbearing, and child rearing, female labor force participation is difficult to trace.

5. Those who report multiple ancestries in 1980, such as German-English or German-Irish-Italian, are not assigned to the respective ethnic group. Our measures therefore underestimate the total number of members identifying (in whatever way) with an ethnic group. In fact, this reduces our approximation of the oldest immigrant groups; some of the "new" immigrant groups arriving at the turn of the century, such as Italians, demonstrate a relatively lower rate of mixing and subsequent mixed-ancestry reporting, and also more consistently identify their ancestry. Among the ethnic groups of longer duration in the United States, such as the English and German stock, there is evidence of inconsistent reporting from year to year; that is, persons identifying as of English stock one year may select another ancestral group in a subsequent year (Johnson, 1974; Farley, 1991; Lieberson and Waters, 1990; McKenney and Cresce, 1992). The reliance on single-ancestry reporting in 1980 is also not strictly comparable to our 1910 measures, as ethnic members of mixed ancestry in 1910 were assigned to their fathers' ancestry.

6. Because the census has never asked a question on religious identification, determining the Jewish population is difficult. In 1910, language was used to estimate the Jewish population. All respondents whose mother tongue was Yiddish, or whose father's or mother's mother tongue was Yiddish were classified as Jewish. The major drawback to this approximation is that it is does not include non-Yiddish speaking Jews residing in America. This non-Yiddish speaking category includes both the population of Spanish and Dutch Jewish immigrants among the early settlers of America, as well as the German Jewish immigrants who began arriving in the 1840s, and a number of Jewish immigrants from countries other than eastern and central Europe who arrived during the major immigration period of 1880 to 1910. The actual numbers and

the proportion of these non-Yiddish speaking Jews are believed to be small. Between 1880 and 1899 approximately 95 percent of all immigrants from Russia were estimated to be Jewish (Rosenthal, 1975). While the total share of Jews among Russian immigrants declined somewhat in subsequent censuses (to 84 percent between 1899 and 1914), it is still widely accepted that in "the current composition of the American Jewish population the component of German Jews is very minor, indeed" (Rosenthal, 1975:280). The flood of eastern European Jewish immigrants that occurred in the late nineteenth century was so heavy that it reconstituted American Jewry.

Methods of estimating the Jewish population in the latter half of the twentieth century assume those of Russian stock or descent are Jewish, since most third or higher generation Jews do not indicate Yiddish as their mother tongue. Again, this method does not ascertain the number of Jews from other regions, such as Germany, Hungary, Poland, Iran, Morocco, or even Israel. The validity of utilizing Russian as a proxy for Jewish is under debate. In 1959, Duncan and Lieberson refer to the USSR foreign-born population as "predominantly Jewish" (1959:373). A rank correlation of the distribution of the Jewish population with that of the Russian-born population for 1930 for all 75 Community Areas (standardized neighborhoods) of the city of Chicago yielded a value of .798 (Rosenthal, 1975:276). However, the 1930s witnessed a large influx of German Jews, who did not speak Yiddish, while Israelis did not even exist until 1948. More recently, Lieberson and Waters have argued that the correspondence between Russian origin and Jewish has been overestimated. A majority of the Russian-origin population appears to be Jewish, but the majority of the Jewish population does not indicate a Russian ancestry. They therefore conclude that the relatively favorable socioeconomic position occupied by Jews is *underestimated* when the population reporting Russian origin is used as a surrogate for all Jews (Lieberson and Waters, 1990:11).

7. The correlation coefficient of 1910 and 1980 SEI scores for men of all twelve ethnic groups is 0.36, significant at the .01 level. The regression line is represented by $Y = 20.69 + .71X$. Excluding blacks and Jews from the equation, however, yields a weak and insignificant correlation coefficient of only 0.10, and the regression equation, $Y = 38.02 + .12X$, depicts the flatness of the line.

8. Here Jews are identified by language, as before.

References

Alba, Richard D. 1985. *Italian Americans: Into the Twilight of Ethnicity.* Englewood Cliffs: Prentice Hall, Inc.

Alonso, William and Paul Starr, eds. 1987. *The Politics of Numbers* New York: Russell Sage Foundation.

Anderson, Margo J. 1988. *The American Census: A Social History* New Haven: Yale University Press.

Atkins, Elizabeth. 1991. "When Life Isn't Simply Black or White," *The New York Times*, June 5 :C1+C7.

Bean, Frank D. and Marta Tienda. 1987. *The Hispanic Population of the United States* New York: Russell Sage Foundation.

Choldin, Harvey M. 1986. "Statistics and Politics: The "Hispanic Issue" in the 1980 Census," *Demography* 23 :403-418.

Duncan, Otis Dudley and Stanley Lieberson. 1959. "Ethnic Segregation and Assimilation," *American Journal of Sociology* 64:364-74.

Farley, Reynolds. 1990. "Blacks, Hispanics and White Ethnic Groups: Are Blacks Uniquely Disadvantaged?" *The American Economic Review* 80 :237-241.

_____. 1984. *Blacks and Whites: Narrowing the Gap?* Cambridge: Harvard University Press.

_____. 1991. "The New Census Question About Ancestry: What Did it Tell Us?" *Demography* 28 :411-430.

Gans, Herbert. 1979. "Symbolic Ethnicity: The Future of Ethnic Groups and Culture in America," *Ethnic and Racial Studies* 2 :1-20.

Goldin, Claudia. 1990. *Understanding the Gender Gap.* New York: Oxford University Press.

Hershberg, Theodore, ed. 1981. *Philadelphia: Work, Space, Family, and Groups Experience in the 19th Century.* New York: Oxford University Press.

Immigration and Naturalization Service. 1990. *1989 Statistical Yearbook.* Washington, DC: National Technical Information Service.

Johnson, Charles E., Jr. 1974. *Consistency of Reporting of Ethnic Origin in the Current Population Survey.* U.S. Department of Commerce, Bureau of the Census. Technical Paper 31, February.

Lieberson, Stanley. 1963. *Ethnic Patterns in American Cities.* The Free Press of Glencoe.

_____. 1980. *A Piece of the Pie: Black and White Immigrants Since 1880.* Berkeley: University of California Press.

Lieberson, Stanley and Mary Waters. 1988. *From Many Strands: Ethnic and Racial Groups in Contemporary America* New York: Russell Sage Foundation.

McKenney, Nampeo R. and Arthur R. Cresce. 1992. *Measurement of Ethnicity in the United States: Experiences of the U.S. Census Bureau.* Paper presented at the Joint Canada-United States Conference on the Measurement of Ethnicity, April 1-3, Ottawa, Canada.

Miller, Andrew T. 1991. "Measuring Mulattoes: The Changing U.S. Racial Regime in Census and Society." Presented at the Annual Meeting of the Population Association of America, Washington, D.C., March.

Oppenheimer, Valerie Kincade. 1970. *The Female Labor Force in the United States: Deomgraphic and Economic Factors Governing its Growth and Changing Composition*. Berkeley: Institute of International Studies.

Peterson, William, 1987. "Politics and the Measurement of Ethnicity." In *The Politics of Numbers*, William Alonso and Paul Starr, eds. New York: Russell Sage Foundation :187-233.

Rosenthal, Eric. 1975. "The Equivalence of United States Census Data for Persons of Russian Stock or Descent with American Jews: An Evaluation," *Demography* 12 :257-290.

Stevens, Gillian and Hoo Hyun Cho. 1985. "Socioeconomic Indexes and the New 1980 Census Occupational Classification Scheme." *Social Science Research* 14 :142-168.

Strong, Michael. 1989. *User's Guide: Public Use Sample of the 1910 United States Census of Population*. The University of Pennsylvania Population Studies Center.

Thernstrom, Stephan. 1973. *The Other Bostonians: Poverty and Progress in the American Metropolis, 1880-1970*. Cambridge: Harvard University Press.

U.S. Department of Commerce, Bureau of the Census. 1989. *200 Years of U.S. Census Taking: Population and Housing Questions, 1790-1990*.

White, Michael J. 1987. *American Neighborhoods and Residential Differentiation*. New York: Russell Sage.

White, Michael J., Robert Dymowski, and Shilian Wang. "Ethnic Neighborhoods and Ethnic Myths: Residential Segregation in 1910." In S. Watkins (ed.) *After Ellis Island*. New York: Russell Sage, Forthcoming.

White, Michael J., Ann R. Biddlecom, and Shenyang Guo. 1991. "Immigration, Naturalization, and Residential Assimilation Among Asian Americans." Population Studies and Training Center Working Paper 91-06, Brown University.

About the Contributors

Barbara A. Anderson is Professor of Sociology and former Director of the Population Studies Center at the University of Michigan.

Calvin Goldscheider is Professor of Sociology and Judaic Studies, and is Faculty Associate at the Population Studies and Training Center at Brown University. He formerly served as Chairman of the Department of Demography at the Hebrew University, Jerusalem.

Charles Hirschman is Professor of Sociology and Director of the Center for the Study of Population and Ecology at the University of Washington.

Philip E. Leis is Professor and Chairman of the Department of Anthropology at Brown University. He has engaged in field research projects in Nigeria and Cameroon, as well as in the United States, on topics related to questions of ethnic relations and political integration.

Rong Ma is Professor of Demography and Director of Population Studies at the Institute of Sociology at Beijing University, People's Republic of China. He recently completed a Post-Doctoral Fellowship in Sociology at Harvard University's Fairbanks Center.

Edward T. Pryor was Director General of the Census and Demographic Statistics Branch at Statistics Canada, Ottawa, and Adjunct Research Professor of Sociology and Anthropology at Carleton University, Ottawa.

Sharon Sassler completed her Ph.D. in Sociology at Brown University, and is currently a Post-Doctoral Fellow in Population at Johns Hopkins University.

Brian D. Silver is Professor of Political Science at Michigan State University.

Thomas E. Skidmore is Carlos Manuel de Céapedes Professor of History and Director of the Center for Latin American Studies at Brown University. In the fall of 1991, he was Hewlett Residential Fellow at the Helen Kellogg Institute for International Studies at the University of Notre Dame.

Michael J. White is Professor of Sociology at Brown University and affiliated with the Population Studies and Training Center.

Alan S. Zuckerman is Professor of Political Science and Judaic Studies, and formerly Director of the Social Science Data Center at Brown University. He has been a Fulbright Visiting Professor at Tel Aviv University and the Universtiy of Pisa, and a Visiting Research Fellow at the University of Essex.

About the Book

This volume focuses on the linkages between ethnicity and population processes in the context of nation-building. Using historical and contemporary illustrations in a variety of countries, parts of this complex puzzle are scrutinized through the prisms of sociology, history, political science, anthropology, and demography. Themes of ethnic group formation and transformation, persistence and assimilation, demographic transitions and convergences, and the processes of political mobilization and economic development are described and compared. Case studies from Southeast Asia, China, Africa, Brazil, Israel, the former Soviet Union, Canada, Europe, and the United States are presented by leading scholars. The examples illustrate the diversity of contexts that connect population, ethnicity, and nation-building, raising new questions and comparative problems. The importance of ethnic conflict for issues of inequality and group disadvantage in the emerging societies of Asia, Africa, and the Middle East; in the politics of race and immigration in western societies; and in European and American history emerges from the research. The multidisciplinary emphasis addresses core themes of ethnicity and nation-building in comparative perspectives.